T0192594

JDBC Metadata, MySQL, and Oracle Recipes

A Problem-Solution Approach

Mahmoud Parsian

Apress®

JDBC Metadata, MySQL, and Oracle Recipes: A Problem-Solution Approach

Copyright © 2006 by Mahmoud Parsian

ISBN-13: 978-1-4842-2095-5

ISBN-10: 1-59059-637-4

Printed and bound in the United States of America 9 8 7 6 5 4 3 2 1

Lead Editor: Steve Anglin

Technical Reviewer: Sumit Pal

Editorial Board: Steve Anglin, Dan Appleman, Ewan Buckingham, Gary Cornell, Jason Gilmore, Jonathan Hassell, James Huddleston, Chris Mills, Matthew Moodie, Dominic Shakeshaft, Jim Sumser, Matt Wade

Project Managers: Beckie Brand, Elizabeth Seymour

Copy Edit Manager: Nicole LeClerc

Copy Editor: Liz Welch

Assistant Production Director: Kari Brooks-Copony

Production Editor: Lori Bring

Compositor: Linda Weideman, Wolf Creek Press

Proofreader: Dan Shaw

Indexer: Lucie Haskins

Artist: Kinetic Publishing Services, LLC

Cover Designer: Kurt Krames

Manufacturing Director: Tom Debolski

Distributed to the book trade worldwide by Springer-Verlag New York, Inc., 233 Spring Street, 6th Floor, New York, NY 10013. Phone 1-800-SPRINGER, fax 201-348-4505, e-mail orders-ny@springer-sbm.com, or visit http://www.springeronline.com.

For information on translations, please contact Apress directly at 2560 Ninth Street, Suite 219, Berkeley, CA 94710. Phone 510-549-5930, fax 510-549-5939, e-mail info@apress.com, or visit http://www.apress.com.

The source code for this book is available to readers at http://www.apress.com in the Source Code section.

This book is dedicated to my dears

my beautiful wife, Behnaz;

my gozal daughter, Maral;

my gibldiz son, Yaseen, who taught me how to play Yu-Gi-Oh!

*my mother, Monireh, who taught me my mother
language and introduced me to the world of computer science;*

*memory of my father, Bagher,
who taught me honesty and hard work;*

my angel sister, Nayer Azam;

and my brother, Ahmad

Contents at a Glance

Contents

About the Author

 **MAHMOUD PARSIAN** is a Sun-certified Java programmer and a senior lead software engineer at Ask Jeeves (http://www.ask.com). Mahmoud earned his PhD in computer science from Iowa State University (Ames, Iowa) and has been working in the software industry for more than 22 years. His expertise is in Java technology, JDBC, database design/development, and server-side Java programming. Mahmoud's current project is MyJeeves (http://myjeeves.ask.com).

Mahmoud's honors include the following (partial list):

- Ask Jeeves Bright Star Award, Ask Jeeves; November 2004

- Octopus Award, Octopus.com; July 2001

- Cisco Systems Leadership Award, Cisco Systems; June 2000

- Individual Achievement Award, Cisco Systems; July 2000

- Winner of the Circle of Excellence Award; Digital Equipment Corporation, 1991

- Winner of the Best Quality (Alex Trotman, CEO) Award; Ford Motor Company, 1990

- Five-time winner of the Specialist of the Quarter Award; Digital Equipment Corporation, 1990–94

You can contact Mahmoud at admin@jdbccookbook.com.

About the Technical Reviewer

 **SUMIT PAL** is a Java and J2EE technical architect. He has more than 12 years of experience in software development and has worked for Microsoft and Oracle as a full-time employee. He has a master's degree in computer science.

Sumit loves to swim and play badminton and now loves to crawl with his little baby daughter.

Acknowledgments

I owe the biggest debt to my family. I'd like to thank my dear supportive wife Behnaz, my gozal daughter Maral, and my son Yaseen, who all had to put up with many lost family evenings and weekends. Without their love and support I could never have finished this book.

I thank my parents (Monireh and Bagher Parsian) for their unlimited support. Also, I thank my dear sister, Nayer Azam Parsian, and my dear brother, Dr. Ahmad Parsian, for their support and just being there for me.

I'd also like to thank my dear friend and teacher, Dr. Ramachandran Krishnaswamy. He taught me friendship, as well as the fundamentals of computer science, and showed me how to be a "good" teacher.

This book is a tremendous effort by a ton of people, and I'll try to mention most of them here. First, I'd like to thank a few special individuals at Apress:

- First, I owe a huge debt of gratitude to Steve Anglin, the lead editor of this book. Steve believed in my "metadata" project and provided tremendous support for writing this book. Thank you, Steve.

- I thank my technical reviewer, Sumit Pal, for doing a great job of reviewing the whole book. Sumit's critical questioning kept me on the right path. I value his input and objectivity. Sumit's attention to detail and JDBC coding skills are the reason this book is here today. I am grateful for that.

- I deeply thank Beckie Brand, the first project manager, for this book. Beckie's hard and outstanding work and caring attitude were always refreshing and rejuvenating. She was well organized and helped me tremendously in many ways. Also, I thank Elizabeth Seymour (who took over as project manager) for her great work and tremendous support.

- I thank Liz Welch, copy editor, for her outstanding editing and understanding of my language and JDBC code. She is very smart and understands a lot about "metadata." Her contributions have greatly improved the accuracy, readability, and value of this book.

- I thank Lori Bring, production editor, for supporting and helping me to produce this book.

- I'll also take this opportunity to thank many other fine people at Apress: Jim Sumser, Dan Appleman, Ewan Buckingham, Gary Cornell, Tony Davis, Jason Gilmore, Jonathan Hassell, Chris Mills, Dominic Shakeshaft, Nicole LeClerc, Kari Brooks-Copony, Kurt Krames, and Tom Debolski.

Introduction

This book focuses on database metadata (data about data) or annotation-based code recipes for JDBC API for use with Oracle and MySQL. The book provides complete and working solutions for performing database metadata tasks using JDBC. You can cut and paste solutions from this book to build your own database metadata applications. All the solutions have been compiled and tested against two leading databases: MySQL and Oracle. This book is ideal for anyone who knows some Java (can read/write basic Java programs) and some JDBC (can read/write basic queries using JDBC and SQL) and wants to learn more about database and result set metadata. Each section of this book is a complete recipe (including the database setup, the solution, and the solutions for both MySQL and Oracle), so you can use the code directly in your projects (although sometimes you may need to cut and paste only the sections you need). You may adopt my solutions to other databases (such as Microsoft SQLServer, DB2, PostgreSQL) by just changing the database parameters (such as the driver, database URL, or database username/password).

What Is in This Book?

This book provides solid solutions and guidelines for using JDBC metadata to solve tough problems, such as how to write customized metadata for RowSet(s) and how to retrieve your tables/views names from the database as a URL. Most of the solutions presented in this book have been used and tested in real-world database applications. In fact, I have designed and developed all the JDBC code for MyJeeves (http://myjeeves.ask.com) using the same philosophies you'll find in this book. You can cut and paste the provided solutions and tailor them to your own JDBC metadata applications. For production environments, you should replace my getConnection() method with a production-quality connection pool management product (such as Apache's DBCP or Excalibur).

What Is the Focus of This Book?

The main focus of this book is to show how to use database metadata (DatabaseMetaData) and result set metadata (ResultSetMetaData) by JDBC API. All of the JDBC's metadata is discussed, and I have provided lots of examples for MySQL and Oracle databases. You may use all of these metadata recipes freely (no copyrights attached to these recipes!). This book focuses on the JDBC metadata API for database application writers. Also, you may use my recipes for reverse-engineering the whole database, for developing GUI-based database applications, and for developing SQL adapters and connectors.

What This Book Is Not

This book is not designed to teach the Java programming language, JDBC, and the basics of object-oriented programming. I assume you already know the basics of Java, JDBC, SQL, and object-oriented programming.

What Is the Structure of This Book?

This book is filled with database metadata recipes: it asks real metadata questions and provides real, compiled working answers. You can use Java/JDBC to access many kinds of database metadata (such as database table types and tables/columns names) for relational database management systems (including Oracle, MySQL, DB2, SQL Server, and Access, to mention a few).

The goal of this book is to provide step-by-step instructions for using JDBC metadata with two popular relational databases: Oracle and MySQL. I selected these two databases for the following reasons:

- Oracle is the de facto standard in the commercial database applications of major companies.

- MySQL is a high-speed, open-source relational database (you can even use a debugger to debug your JDBC method calls).

For every metadata problem raised, you'll see two solutions: one expressed using the Oracle database and the other one in MySQL.

What Does JDBC Metadata Do?

In a nutshell, JDBC is a Java API for executing SQL statements (such as querying a database, inserting new records, creating a table, and so on). JDBC makes it possible to perform three tasks:

- Establish a connection with a relational database.

- Using the established database connection, send SQL statements (such as a select, insert, update, metadata request, and so on) and result sets.

- Process the result sets (retrieved from the database).

JDBC allows Java programs (applets and applications) to communicate with relational databases (so-called SQL databases) easily and efficiently. JDBC consists of classes in the package java.sql and some JDBC extensions in the package javax.sql. Both of these packages are included in the Java 2 Standard Edition (J2SE) version 1.5 (which covers JDBC 3.0).

On the other hand, JDBC metadata (data about data) deals with database metadata and result set metadata. Using JDBC's metadata API, you should be able to answer the following questions:

- What are the column names/types for a SQL query?

- What are table types for a database?

- What are table/view/stored procedure names?

- What is the signature of a stored procedure?

- What is a `RowSet`'s and `ResultSet`'s metadata?

- Is a given database read only?

- What are table/column privileges?

I have answered all of these questions, plus much, much more.

Who Is This Book For?

This book is for software engineers and database application developers who know the basics of Java and JDBC. I also assume you know the basics of the Java programming language (writing a class, defining a new class from an existing class, using basic control structures such as `while-loop`, `if-then-else`, and so on). Also, I assume you have a basic understanding of relational databases concepts and SQL. Like in any Apress recipe book, you are encouraged to tweak the solutions presented to fit your own database metadata applications and discover new database metadata solutions using Java/JDBC technology. You can also customize these solutions/recipes as you apply them to a particular metadata problem.

What Software Is Used in This Book?

When developing solutions and examples for this book, I used the following software and programming environments:

- Relational databases:

    - Oracle 9*i* Enterprise Edition Release 9.2.0.1.0 (from `http://www.oracle.com`)

    - Oracle 10*g* Release 10.1.0.2.0 (from `http://www.oracle.com`)

    - MySQL 4.1.7 (from `http://www.mysql.com`)

    - MySQL 5.0.0 (from `http://www.mysql.com`)

- Programming languages:

    - Java programming language, J2SE 1.4.2 (from `http://java.sun.com`)

    - Java programming language, J2SE 5.0 (from `http://java.sun.com`)

- Operating systems:

    - Linux Enterprise Edition (from `http://www.redhat.com`)

    - Windows XP Professional (from `http://www.microsoft.com`)

- Web servers

    - Tomcat (`http://jakarta.apache.org/tomcat/`)

All programs in this book were tested with J2SE 1.4.2 and J2SE 5.0 (from http://java.sun.com/). Examples are given in mixed operating system environments (Linux and Windows XP Professional). For all examples and solutions, I developed them using basic text editors (such as Notepad from Microsoft, TextPad from http://www.textpad.com, and vi in Linux) and compiled them using the Java command-line compiler (javac).

Comments and Questions for This Book?

I am always interested in your feedback and comments regarding the problems and solutions described in this book. Please e-mail comments and questions for this book to admin@jdbccookbook.com. You can also find me at http://www.jdbccookbook.com.

CHAPTER 1

■■■

What Is JDBC Programming?

It is the theory that decides what we can observe.

Albert Einstein

This chapter explains JDBC programming by using a set of questions and answers. Java and JDBC are trademarks or registered trademarks of Sun Microsystems, Inc. in the United States and other countries. According to Sun Microsystems, JDBC is not an acronym and does not stand for Java Database Connectivity (but the fact of the matter is that most Java engineers believe that JDBC stands for **J**ava **D**ata**B**ase **C**onnectivity).

JDBC is a platform-independent interface between relational databases and Java. In today's Java world, JDBC is a standard API for accessing enterprise data in relational databases (such as Oracle, MySQL, Sybase, PostgreSQL, and DB2) using SQL (Structured Query Language). In this chapter, we will examine the basic aspects of JDBC, and save the details about JDBC metadata for upcoming chapters. Data and metadata (data about data/information) are at the heart of most business applications, and JDBC deals with data and metadata stored and manipulated in relational database systems (RDBMSs). Note that each RDBMS has a lot of metadata, and JDBC maps some of those metadata in a uniform and consistent fashion by its API.

Note In using the word *metadata*, we must use the exact term when it is a Java API (since Java is a case-sensitive language)—for example, `DatabaseMetaData`, `RowSetMetaData`, and `ResultSetMetaData`—but in our discussion and descriptions, we will use *metadata* (and not *MetaData*).

This book takes an examples-based approach to describing the metadata features available in JDBC (such as getting a list of tables or views, or getting a signature of a stored procedure). Whether you are a new or an experienced database or JDBC developer, you should find the examples and accompanying text a valuable and accessible knowledge base for creating your own database solutions. Using JDBC's database metadata, you can generate GUI/web-based applications (for example, see `http://dev2dev.bea.com/lpt/a/257`). Also, you can develop web entry forms based on metadata (for example, see `http://www.elet.polimi.it/conferences/wq04/final/paper03.pdf`).

In this book, we use some basic Java/JDBC utility classes (such as the `DatabaseUtil` class), which are available for download from the Source Code section of the Apress website. The `DatabaseUtil` class provides methods for closing JDBC objects (such as `Connection`, `ResultSet`,

Statement, and PreparedStatement). The reason for using the DatabaseUtil class is to make the code compact and more readable (for example, closing a ResultSet object by DatabaseUtil takes one line of code versus a couple of lines without using DatabaseUtil).

VeryBasicConnectionManager is a very simple class that provides Connection objects for Oracle and MySQL by using getConnection(dbVendor). In real production applications, the VeryBasicConnectionManager class is not an acceptable solution and should be replaced by a connection pool manager (such as the Excalibur from http://excalibur.apache.org/ and the commons-dbcp package from http://jakarta.apache.org/commons/dbcp/). We use these classes to demonstrate JDBC concepts for different vendors such as Oracle and MySQL. Connection pooling is a technique used for reusing and sharing Connection objects among requesting clients.

The remaining chapters in this book will deal with JDBC metadata and nothing but JDBC metadata.

1.1. What Is JDBC?

JDBC is a set of programming APIs that allows easy connection to a wide range of databases (especially relational databases) through Java programs. In this book, we will be using JDBC 2.0 and 3.0 versions (JDBC 4.0 is just a specification and has not been implemented extensively yet.) In Java 2 Platform Standard Edition (J2SE) 5.0 (which supports JDBC 3.0), the JDBC API is defined by two packages:

- java.sql provides the API for accessing and processing data stored in a data source (usually a relational database) using the Java programming language. This package provides the foundation and most commonly used objects (such as Connection, ResultSet, Statement, and PreparedStatement). Also, this package provides classes and interfaces to get both database and result set metadata from the database server. This package has a set of classes and interfaces (such as DatabaseMetaData and ResultSetMetaData) that deal with database metadata, which will be one of the focuses of this book.

- javax.sql provides the API for server-side data source access. According to the Java Development Kit (JDK) documentation, "This package supplements the java.sql package and, as of the version 1.4 release, is included in the JDK. It remains an essential part of the Java 2 SDK, Enterprise Edition (J2EE)." This package provides services for J2EE (such as DataSource and RowSets). Also, the package has a set of classes and interfaces (such as RowSetMetaData) that deal with row set metadata. In this book we focus on the metadata components of this package.

In a nutshell, JDBC is a database-independent API for accessing a relational database. You pass SQL to Java methods in the JDBC classes (the packages java.sql and javax.sql) and get back JDBC objects (such as ResultSet, DatabaseMetaData, and ResultSetMetaData) that represent the results of your query. JDBC is designed so simply that most database programmers need learn only a few methods to accomplish most of what they need to do.

Figure 1-1 shows how a database application (such as a Java application/applet/servlet) uses JDBC to interact with one or more databases.

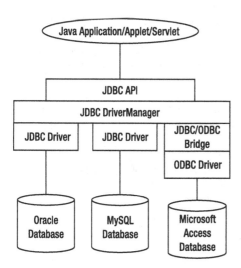

Figure 1-1. *Java database application using JDBC*

Figure 1-1 presents the basic outline of the JDBC architecture. JDBC's DriverManager class provides the basic service for managing a set of JDBC drivers. The DriverManager loads JDBC drivers in memory, and can also be used to create java.sql.Connection objects to data sources (such as Oracle and MySQL). For more details, refer to *JDBC Recipes: A Problem-Solution Approach* (Apress, 2005) and Sun's official site on JDBC: http://java.sun.com/products/jdbc/index.jsp.

Note that you can have more than one driver and therefore more than one database. Figure 1-2 illustrates how a Java application uses JDBC to interact with one or more relational databases (such as Oracle and MySQL) without knowing about the underlying JDBC driver implementations. Figure 1-2 illustrates the core JDBC classes and interfaces that interact with Java and JDBC applications. This figure also shows the basic relationships of the DatabaseMetaData and ResultSetMetaData interfaces with other JDBC objects.

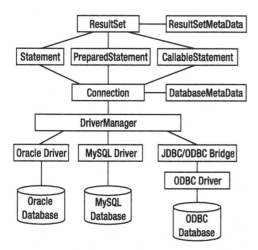

Figure 1-2. *Using JDBC database metadata*

The following are core JDBC classes, interfaces, and exceptions in the java.sql package:

- DriverManager: This class loads JDBC drivers in memory. It is a "factory" class and can also be used to create java.sql.Connection objects to data sources (such as Oracle, MySQL, etc.).

- Connection: This interface represents a connection with a data source. The Connection object is used for creating Statement, PreparedStatement, and CallableStatement objects.

- DatabaseMetaData: This interface provides detailed information about the database as a whole. The Connection object is used for creating DatabaseMetaData objects.

- Statement: This interface represents a static SQL statement. It can be used to retrieve ResultSet objects.

- PreparedStatement: This interface extends Statement and represents a precompiled SQL statement. It can be used to retrieve ResultSet objects.

- CallableStatement: This interface represents a database stored procedure. It can execute stored procedures in a database server.

- ResultSet: This interface represents a database result set generated by using SQL's SELECT statement. Statement, PreparedStatement, CallableStatement, and other JDBC objects can create ResultSet objects.

- ResultSetMetaData: This interface provides information about the types and properties of the columns in a ResultSet object.

- SQLException: This class is an exception class that provides information on a database access error or other errors.

1.2. What Is JDBC Programming?

JDBC programming can be explained in the following simple steps:

- Importing required packages

- Registering the JDBC drivers

- Opening a connection to a database

- Creating a Statement/PreparedStatement/CallableStatement object

- Executing a SQL query and returning a ResultSet object

- Processing the ResultSet object

- Closing the ResultSet and Statement objects

- Closing the connection

The first hands-on experience with JDBC in this book involves a basic and complete example to illustrate the overall concepts related to creating and accessing data in a database. Here, we assume that a database (MySQL or Oracle) is created and available for use. Database creation is DBMS-specific. This means that each vendor has a specific set of commands for creating a database. For this obvious reason, database creation commands are not portable (this is the main reason why JDBC has stayed away from database creation commands).

Step 1: Import the Required Packages

Before you can use the JDBC driver to get and use a database connection, you must import the following packages: java.sql and javax.sql.

```
import java.sql.*;
import javax.sql.*;
```

To import classes and interfaces properly, refer to the Java Language Specification (http://java.sun.com/docs/books/jls/).

Step 2: Register the JDBC Drivers

A JDBC driver is a set of database-specific implementations for the interfaces defined by JDBC. These driver classes come into being through a bootstrap process. This is best shown by stepping through the process of using JDBC to connect to a database,

Let's use Oracle's type 4 JDBC driver as an example. First, the main driver class must be loaded into the Java virtual machine (VM):

```
Class.forName("oracle.jdbc.driver.OracleDriver");
```

The specified driver (i.e., the oracle.jdbc.driver.OracleDriver class) must implement the java.sql.Driver interface. A class initializer (a static code block) within the oracle.jdbc. driver.OracleDriver class registers the driver with the java.sql.DriverManager.

Now let's use MySQL's JDBC driver as an example. First, the main driver class must be loaded into the Java VM:

```
Class.forName("com.mysql.jdbc.Driver");
```

The specified driver (i.e., the com.mysql.jdbc.Driver class) must implement the java.sql.Driver interface. A class initializer (a static code block) within the com.mysql.jdbc.Driver class registers the driver with the java.sql.DriverManager. Note that when loading a JDBC driver, you must make sure that the database-specific driver API (usually a JAR file) is in your CLASSPATH environment variable. Each database vendor has its own specific implementation of the JDBC driver.

Step 3: Opening a Connection to a Database

Next, we need to obtain a connection to the database. To get a connection object to a database, you need at least three pieces of information: the database URL, the database username, and the database user's password.

```
import java.sql.Connection;
import java.sql. DriverManager;
...
String dbURL = "jdbc:oracle:thin:@localhost:1521:kitty";
String dbUsername = "scott";
String dbPassword = "tiger";
Connection conn = DriverManager.getConnection(dbURL, dbUsername, dbPassword);
```

DriverManager determines which registered driver to use by invoking the acceptsURL(String url) method of each driver, passing each the JDBC URL. The first driver to return true in response will be used for this connection. In this example, OracleDriver will return true, so DriverManager then invokes the connect() method of OracleDriver to obtain an instance of OracleConnection. It is this database-specific connection instance implementing the java.sql.Connection interface that is passed back from the java.sql.DriverManager.getConnection() call.

There is an alternate method for creating a database connection: first get a JDBC driver, then use that driver to get a connection:

```
import java.sql.Connection;
import java.sql. Driver;
import java.sql. DriverManager;
import java.util.Properties;
...
String dbURL = "jdbc:oracle:thin:@localhost:1521:kitty";
String dbUsername = "scott";
String dbPassword = "tiger";
Properties dbProps = new Properties();
String driverName = "oracle.jdbc.driver.OracleDriver";
Driver jdbcDriver = (Driver) Class.forName(driverName).newInstance();
dbProps.put("user", dbUsername);
dbProps.put("password", dbPassword);
Connection conn = jdbcDriver.connect(databaseURL, dbProps);
```

Step 4: Creating a Statement/PreparedStatement/CallableStatement Object

Once you have a valid java.sql.Connection object, you can create statement objects (such as Statement, PreparedStatement, and CallableStatement). The bootstrap process continues when you create a statement:

```
Connection conn = <get-a-valid-Connection-object>;
Statement stmt = conn.createStatement();
```

In order to do something useful with a database, we create the following table:

```
create table MyEmployees (
    id INT PRIMARY KEY,
    firstName VARCHAR(20),
    lastName VARCHAR(20),
    title VARCHAR(20),
    salary INT
);
```

Then we insert two records:

```
insert into MyEmployees(id, firstName, lastName, title, salary)
    values(60,  'Bill',  'Russel',  'CTO',     980000);

insert into MyEmployees(id, firstName, lastName, title, salary)
    values(70, 'Alex',  'Baldwin',  'Software Engineer', 88000);
```

The connection reference points to an instance of OracleConnection. This database-specific implementation of Connection returns a database-specific implementation of Statement, namely OracleStatement.

Step 5: Executing a Query and Returning a ResultSet Object

Invoking the execute() method of this statement object will execute the database-specific code necessary to issue a SQL statement against the Oracle database and retrieve the results (as a table):

```
String query = "SELECT id, lastName FROM MyEmployees";
ResultSet result = stmt.executeQuery(query);
```

The result is a table (as a ResultSet object) returned by executing the SELECT statement. Again, what is actually returned is an instance of OracleResultSet, which is an Oracle-specific implementation of the java.sql.ResultSet interface. By iterating the result, we can get all of the selected records.

So the purpose of a JDBC driver is to provide these implementations that hide all the database-specific details behind standard Java interfaces.

Step 6: Processing the ResultSet Object

ResultSet.next() returns a boolean: true if there is a next row or record and false if not (meaning the end of the data or set has been reached). Conceptually, a pointer or cursor is positioned just before the first row when the ResultSet is obtained. Invoking the next() method moves to the first row, then the second, and so on.

Once positioned at a row, the application can get the data on a column-by-column basis using the appropriate ResultSet.getXXX() method. Here are the methods used in the example to collect the data:

```
if (rs.next()) {
    String firstName = rs.getString(1);
    String lastName = rs.getString(2);
    String title = rs.getString(3);
    int salary = rs.getInt(4);
}
```

or we may use the column names (instead of column positions):

```
if (rs.next()) {
    String firstName = rs.getString("firstName");
    String lastName = rs.getString("lastName");
    String title = rs.getString("title");
    int salary = rs.getInt("salary");
}
```

The order of the getString(columnNumber) should be the same as the order of columns selected in the SQL SELECT statement; otherwise, we could run into an error.

Step 7: Closing JDBC Objects

Releasing or closing JDBC resources (such as ResultSet, Statement, PreparedStatement, and Connection objects) immediately instead of waiting for it to happen on its own can improve the overall performance of your application. From a good software engineering point of view, you should put close() statements in a finally clause, because it guarantees that the statements in the finally clause will be executed as the last step regardless of whether an exception has occurred.

Closing ResultSet

ResultSet has a close() method that releases the ResultSet object's database and JDBC resources immediately instead of waiting for that to happen when it is automatically closed. Another major reason to close the ResultSet objects immediately after they are done is that we increase concurrency; as long as the ResultSet object is open, the DBMS internally holds a lock.

Here is some sample code for closing a ResultSet object. It is always a good idea to have utility classes to close these JDBC resources, and the following method can do the job:

```java
/**
 * Close the ResultSet object.  Releases the
 * ResultSet object's database and JDBC resources
 * immediately instead of waiting for them to be
 * automatically released.
 * @param rs a ResultSet object.
 */
public static  void close(java.sql.ResultSet rs) {
   if (rs == null) {
      return;
   }

   try {
      rs.close();
      // result set is closed now
   }
   catch(Exception ignore) {
      // ignore the exception
      // could not close the result set
      // cannot do much here
   }
}
```

Closing Statement

Statement has a close() method, which releases this Statement object's database and JDBC resources immediately instead of waiting for this to happen when it is automatically closed. Here is some sample code for closing a Statement object. It is always a good idea to have utility classes to close these JDBC resources, and the following method can do the job:

```java
/**
 * Close the Statement object.  Releases the Statement
 * object's database and JDBC resources immediately instead
 * of waiting for them to be automatically released.
 * @param stmt a Statement object.
 */
public static  void close(java.sql.Statement stmt) {
    if (stmt == null) {
        return;
    }

    try {
        stmt.close();
        // result set is closed now
    }
    catch(Exception ignore) {
        // ignore the exception
        // could not close the statement
        // can not do much here
    }
}
```

Closing PreparedStatement

PreparedStatement does not have a direct close() method, but since PreparedStatement extends Statement, then you may use the Statement.close() method for PreparedStatement objects. It is always a good idea to have utility classes to close these JDBC resources, and the following method can do the job:

```java
/**
 * Close the PreparedStatement object.  Releases the
 * PreparedStatement object's database and JDBC
 * resources immediately instead of waiting for them
 * to be automatically released.
 * @param pstmt a PreparedStatement object.
 */
public static  void close(java.sql.PreparedStatement pstmt) {
    if (pstmt == null) {
        return;
    }

    try {
        pstmt.close();
        // PreparedStatement object is closed now
    }
```

```
    catch(Exception ignore) {
       // ignore the exception
       // could not close the PreparedStatement
       // can not do much here
    }
  }
```

Closing Connection

If you are using a connection pool manager to manage a set of database connection objects, then you need to release the Connection object to the connection pool manager (this is called a "soft" close). Alternatively, you can use the close() method, which releases the Connection object's database and JDBC resources immediately instead of waiting for them to be automatically released. Here is some sample code for closing a Connection object. It is always a good idea to have utility classes to close these JDBC resources, and the following method can do the job:

```
/**
 * Close the Connection object.  Releases the Connection
 * object's database and JDBC resources immediately instead
 * of waiting for them to be automatically released.
 * @param conn a Connection object.
 */
public static  void close(java.sql.Connection conn) {
   if (conn == null) {
      return;
   }

   try {
      if (!conn.isClosed()) {
         // close the connection-object
         conn.close();
      }
      // connection object is closed now
   }
   catch(Exception ignore) {
      // ignore the exception
      // could not close the connection-object
      // can not do much here
   }
}
```

1.3. How Do You Handle JDBC Errors/Exceptions?

In JDBC, errors and exceptions are identified by the java.sql.SQLException class (which extends the java.lang.Exception class). SQLException is a *checked* exception. There are two types of exceptions in Java: checked and unchecked, or runtime, exceptions. A checked exception is a subclass of java.lang.Throwable (the Throwable class is the superclass of all errors and exceptions in the Java language) but not of RunTimeException (RuntimeException is the super-class of those exceptions that can be thrown during the normal operation of the Java VM). Checked exceptions have to be caught (and handled properly) or appear in a method that specifies in its signature that it throws that kind of exception.

When a JDBC object (such as Connection, Statement, or ResultSet) encounters a serious error, it throws a SQLException. For example, an invalid database URL, an invalid database user-name or password, database connection errors, malformed SQL statements, an attempt to access a nonexistent table or view, and insufficient database privileges all throw SQLException objects.

The client (the database application program) accessing a database server needs to be aware of any errors returned from the server. JDBC give access to such information by provid-ing several levels of error conditions:

- SQLException: SQLExceptions are Java exceptions that, if not handled, will terminate the client application. SQLException is an exception that provides information on a database access error or other errors.

- SQLWarning: SQLWarnings are subclasses of SQLException, but they represent nonfatal errors or unexpected conditions, and as such, can be ignored. SQLWarning is an excep-tion that provides information on database access warnings. Warnings are silently chained to the object whose method caused it to be reported.

- BatchUpdateException: BatchUpdateException is an exception thrown when an error occurs during a batch update operation. In addition to the information provided by SQLException, a BatchUpdateException provides the update counts for all commands that were executed successfully during the batch update, that is, all commands that were executed before the error occurred. The order of elements in an array of update counts corresponds to the order in which commands were added to the batch.

- DataTruncation: DataTruncation is an exception that reports a DataTruncation warning (on reads) or throws a DataTruncation exception (on writes) when JDBC unexpectedly truncates a data value.

The SQLException class extends the java.lang.Exception class and defines an additional method called getNextException(). This allows JDBC classes to chain a series of SQLException objects together. In addition, the SQLException class defines the getMessage(), getSQLState(), and getErrorCode() methods to provide additional information about an error or exception. In general, a JDBC client application might have a catch block that looks something like this:

```
String dbURL = ...;
String dbUser = ...;
String dbPassword = ...;
Connection conn = null;
try {
   conn = DriverManager.getConnection(dbURL, dbUser, dbPassword);
   //
   // when you are here, it means that an exception has not
   // happened and you can use the connection object
   // (i.e., conn) to do something useful with the database
   ...
}
```

```
catch (SQLException e) {
    // something went wrong: maybe dbUser/dbPassword is not defined
    // maybe te dbURL is malformed, and other possible reasons.
    // now handle the exception, maybe print the error code
    // and maybe log the error, ...
    while(e != null) {
        System.out.println("SQL Exception/Error:");
        System.out.println("error message=" + e.getMessage());
        System.out.println("SQL State= " + e.getSQLState());
        System.out.println("Vendor Error Code= " + e.getErrorCode());
        // it is possible to chain the errors and find the most
        // detailed errors about the exception
        e = e.getNextException(  );
    }
}
catch (Exception e2) {
    // handle non-SQL exception ...
}
```

To understand transaction management, you need to understand the Connection.setAutoCommit() method. Its signature is

```
void setAutoCommit(boolean autoCommit) throws SQLException
```

According to J2SE 1.5, setAutoCommit() sets this connection's autocommit mode to the given state. If a connection is in autocommit mode, then all its SQL statements will be executed and committed as individual transactions. Otherwise, its SQL statements are grouped into transactions that are terminated by a call to either the commit() or the rollback() method. By default, new connections are in autocommit mode.

The following example shows how to handle commit() and rollback() when an exception happens:

```
String dbURL = ...;
String dbUser = ...;
String dbPassword = ...;
Connection conn = null;
try {
    conn = DriverManager.getConnection(dbURL, dbUser, dbPassword);
    conn.setAutoCommit(false);  // begin transaction
    stmt.executeUpdate("CREATE TABLE cats_tricks(" +
        "name VARCHAR(30), trick VARHAR(30))") ;
    stmt.executeUpdate("INSERT INTO cats_tricks(name, trick) " +
        "VALUES('mono', 'rollover')") ;
    conn.commit() ;  // commit/end transaction
    conn.setAutoCommit(true) ;
}
```

```
catch(SQLException e) {
    // print some useful error messages
    System.out.println("SQL Exception/Error:");
    System.out.println("error message=" + e.getMessage());
    System.out.println("SQL State= " + e.getSQLState());
    System.out.println("Vendor Error Code= " + e.getErrorCode());
    // rollback the transaction
    // note that this rollback will not undo the creation of
    // DDL statements (such as CREATE TABLE statement)
    conn.rollback();
    // optionally, you may set the auto commit to "true"
    conn.setAutoCommit(true) ;
}
```

In the following example we force the exception to happen: instead of VARCHAR (when creating the cats_tricks table), we type VARZCHAR (the database server will not understand VARZCHAR and therefore it will throw an exception):

```
String dbURL = ...;
String dbUser = ...;
String dbPassword = ...;
Connection conn = null;
try {
    conn = DriverManager.getConnection(dbURL, dbUser, dbPassword);
    conn.setAutoCommit(false);
    stmt.executeUpdate("CREATE TABLE cats_tricks("+
        "name VARZCHAR(30), trick VARHAR(30))") ;
    stmt.executeUpdate("INSERT INTO cats_tricks(name, trick) "+
        "VALUES('mono', 'rollover')") ;
    conn.commit() ;
    conn.setAutoCommit(true) ;
}
catch(SQLException e) {
    // print some useful error messages
    System.out.println("SQL Exception/Error:");
    System.out.println("error message=" + e.getMessage());
    System.out.println("SQL State= " + e.getSQLState());
    System.out.println("Vendor Error Code= " + e.getErrorCode());
    // rollback the transaction
    conn.rollback();
    // optionally, you may set the auto commit to "true"
    conn.setAutoCommit(true) ;
}
```

1.4. What Is JDBC Metadata Programming?

JDBC metadata programming is very similar to JDBC programming with one exception: you deal with metadata instead of data. For example, in JDBC programming you are interested in getting employee data and then processing it, but in JDBC metadata programming, you are not interested in getting actual data, but you want to get metadata (data about data, such as the table names in a database).

In JDBC metadata programming, we're interested in database metadata and result set metadata. For example, for metadata, we want answers to such questions as

- What is the list of tables or views available in the database?

- What are the names and types of the columns in tables or views?

- What is the signature of a specific stored procedure?

In JDBC, several key interfaces comprise the metadata portion:

- DatabaseMetaData: Provides information about the database as a whole.

- ResultSetMetaData: Used to identify the types and properties of the columns in a ResultSet object.

- RowSetMetaData: An object that contains information about the columns in a RowSet object. This interface is an extension of the ResultSetMetaData interface with methods for setting the values in a RowSetMetaData object.

- ParameterMetaData: An object that can be used to get information about the types and properties of the parameters in a PreparedStatement object.

- DriverPropertyInfo: Driver properties for making a connection. The DriverPropertyInfo class is of interest only to advanced programmers who need to interact with a Driver via the method getDriverProperties() to discover and supply properties for connections.

The remaining chapters will dissect these metadata classes and interfaces and will provide detailed information about using them. Figure 1-3 shows the creation of metadata interfaces and classes.

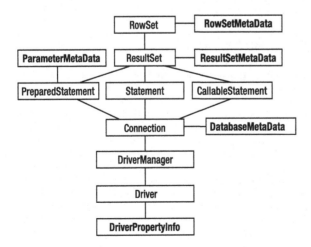

Figure 1-3. *JDBC's metadata classes and interfaces*

Database metadata is most often used by tools or developers who write programs that use advanced, nonstandard database features and by programs that dynamically discover database objects such as schemas, catalogs, tables, views, and stored procedures.

Some of the DatabaseMetaData methods return results in the form of a ResultSet object. The question is how should we handle ResultSet objects as return values? Metadata is retrieved from these ResultSet objects using the normal ResultSet.getXXX() methods, such as getString() and getInt(). To make the metadata useful for any kind of clients, I have mapped these ResultSet objects into XML.

1.5. What Is an Example of JDBC Metadata Programming?

Suppose you want to get the major and minor JDBC version number for the driver you are using. You can use the following methods from DatabaseMetaData:

```
int getDriverMajorVersion()
// Retrieves this JDBC driver's major version number.

int getDriverMinorVersion()
// Retrieves this JDBC driver's minor version number.
```

As you can see, these methods do not return the employee or inventory data, but they return metadata.

Our solution combines these into a single method and returns the result as an XML String object, which any client can use. The result has the following syntax:

```
<?xml version='1.0'>
<DatabaseInformation>
    <majorVersion>database-major-version</majorVersion>
    <minorVersion>database-minor-version</minorVersion>
    <productName>database-product-name</productName>
    <productVersion>database-product-version</productVersion>
</DatabaseInformation>
```

The Solution

The solution is generic and can support MySQL, Oracle, and other relational databases. If Connection.getMetaData() returns null, then it means that vendor's driver does not support/implement thejava.sql.DatabaseMetaData interface. Note that the getDatabaseMajorVersion() method (implemented by the oracle.jdbc.OracleDatabaseMetaData class) is an unsupported feature; therefore, we have to use a try-catch block. If the method returns a SQLException, we return the message "unsupported feature" in the XML result:

```
import java.sql.Connection;
import java.sql.DatabaseMetaData;
...
/**
 * Get database product name and version information.
 * This method calls 4 methods (getDatabaseMajorVersion(),
 * getDatabaseMinorVersion(), getDatabaseProductName(),
 * getDatabaseProductVersion()) to get the required information
 * and it represents the information as an XML.
```

```
     *
     * @param conn the Connection object
     * @return database product name and version information
     * as an XML document (represented as a String object).
     */
public static String getDatabaseInformation(Connection conn)
    throws Exception {
        DatabaseMetaData meta = conn.getMetaData();
        if (meta == null) {
            return null;
        }

        StringBuffer sb = new StringBuffer("<?xml version='1.0'>");
        sb.append("<DatabaseInformation>");

        // Oracle (and some other vendors) do not
        // support some of the following methods
        // (such as getDatabaseMajorVersion() and
        // getDatabaseMajorVersion()); therefore,
        // we need to use try-catch block.
        try {
            int majorVersion = meta.getDatabaseMajorVersion();
            appendXMLTag(sb, "majorVersion", majorVersion);
        }
        catch(Exception e) {
            appendXMLTag(sb, "majorVersion", "unsupported feature");
        }

        try {
            int minorVersion = meta.getDatabaseMinorVersion();
            appendXMLTag(sb, "minorVersion", minorVersion);
        }
        catch(Exception e) {
            appendXMLTag(sb, "minorVersion", "unsupported feature");
        }

        String productName = meta.getDatabaseProductName();
        String productVersion = meta.getDatabaseProductVersion();
        appendXMLTag(sb, "productName", productName);
        appendXMLTag(sb, "productVersion", productVersion);
        sb.append("</DatabaseInformation>");
        return sb.toString();
    }
}
```

Client: Program for Getting Database Information

```java
import java.util.*;
import java.io.*;
import java.sql.*;

import jcb.util.DatabaseUtil;
import jcb.meta.DatabaseMetaDataTool;
import jcb.db.VeryBasicConnectionManager;

public class TestDatabaseMetaDataTool_DatabaseInformation {

    public static void main(String[] args) {
        String dbVendor = args[0];  // { "mysql", "oracle" }
        Connection conn = null;
        try {
            conn = VeryBasicConnectionManager.getConnection(dbVendor);
            System.out.println("-------- getDatabaseformation -------------");
            System.out.println("conn="+conn);
            String dbInfo = DatabaseMetaDataTool.getDatabaseInformation(conn);
            System.out.println(dbInfo);
            System.out.println("-----------------------------------");
        }
        catch(Exception e){
            e.printStackTrace();
            System.exit(1);
        }
        finally {
            DatabaseUtil.close(conn);
        }
    }
}
```

Running the Solution for a MySQL Database

```
$ javac TestDatabaseMetaDataTool_DatabaseInformation.java
$ java TestDatabaseMetaDataTool_DatabaseInformation mysql
```

```
-------- getDatabaseformation -------------
conn=com.mysql.jdbc.Connection@1837697
<?xml version='1.0'>
<DatabaseInformation>
    <majorVersion>4</majorVersion>
    <minorVersion>0</minorVersion>
    <productName>MySQL</productName>
    <productVersion>4.0.4-beta-max-nt</productVersion>
</DatabaseInformation>
-----------------------------------
```

Running the Solution for an Oracle Database

The following output is formatted to fit the page:

```
$ javac TestDatabaseMetaDataTool_DatabaseInformation.java
$ java TestDatabaseMetaDataTool_DatabaseInformation oracle
```

```
-------- getDatabaseInformation -------------
conn= oracle.jdbc.driver.OracleConnection@169ca65
<?xml version='1.0'>
<DatabaseInformation>
    <majorVersion>unsupported feature</majorVersion>
    <minorVersion>unsupported feature</minorVersion>
    <productName>Oracle</productName>
    <productVersion>
        Oracle9i Enterprise Edition Release 9.2.0.1.0 - Production
        With the Partitioning, OLAP and Oracle Data Mining options
        JServer Release 9.2.0.1.0 - Production
    </productVersion>
</DatabaseInformation>
------------------------------------
```

CHAPTER 2

■ ■ ■

Database Metadata, Part 1

Example isn't another way to teach, it is the only way to teach.

Albert Einstein

The goal of this chapter (and the next) is to show you how to use JDBC's database metadata API, which you can use to get information about tables, views, column names, column types, stored procedures, result sets, and databases. It will be of most interest to those who need to write applications that adapt themselves to the specific capabilities of several database systems or to the content of any database. If you write programs—such as graphical user interface (GUI) database applications using database adapters—that use advanced database features or programs that discover database stored procedures and tables or views at runtime (i.e., dynamically), you will have to use metadata. You can use database metadata to

- Discover database schema and catalog information.

- Discover database users, tables, views, and stored procedures.

- Understand and analyze the result sets returned by SQL queries.

- Find out the table, view, or column privileges.

- Determine the signature of a specific stored procedure in the database.

- Identify the primary/foreign keys for a given table.

As you will discover, metadata not only helps you to effectively manage resources, it also helps you find the data you need and determine how best to use it. In addition, metadata provides a structured description of database information resources and services. Some JDBC methods, such as getProcedureColumns() and getProcedures(), return the result as a ResultSet object. Unfortunately, this is not very useful to the client; because the ResultSet object cannot be passed to some client programs, these programs cannot analyze and understand the content of the ResultSet object. For this reason, you need to return the results in XML (and possibly an XML object serialized as a String object), which is suitable for all clients. To be efficient, you generate XML expressed as a String object, which can be easily converted to an XML document (using the org.w3c.dom.Document interface). The Source Code section of the Apress website provides utilities for converting Strings to org.w3.dom.Document and org.w3.dom.Document objects to Strings.

When you write JDBC applications, you should strive for good performance. But what is "good" performance? Should it be subjective or objective? This depends on the requirements of your application. In other words, if you write "slow" code, the JDBC driver does not throw an exception, but you get a performance hit (which might translate to losing clients). "Good" performance means that you are satisfying your project's performance requirements, which should be defined precisely in requirements and design documents. To get acceptable performance from JDBC drivers, avoid passing null parameters to most of the methods; for example, passing a null value to the schema parameter might result in a search of all database schemas— so if you know the name of your desired schema, then pass the actual schema value.

In general, developing performance-oriented JDBC applications is not easy. In every step of the solution, you must make sure that your application will not choke under heavy requirements. For performance reasons, you should avoid excessive metadata calls, because database metadata methods that generate ResultSet objects are relatively slow. JDBC applications may cache information returned from result sets that generate database metadata methods so that multiple executions are not needed. For this purpose you may use Java Caching System (JCS) from the Apache Software Foundation. JCS is a distributed caching system written in Java for server-side Java applications; for more information, see http://jakarta.apache.org/turbine/jcs/.

A Java class called DatabaseMetaDataTool (which is defined in the jcb.meta package) will be available for download from the Source Code section of the Apress website. It provides ready-to-use methods for answering the database metadata questions. For questions about database metadata, I list portions of these classes in some sections of this book, but you'll find the complete class definitions (including JavaDoc-style comments) at the Apress website.

All of the methods in this chapter are static, and each method is written to be as independent as possible. This is so you can cut and paste solutions from this book whenever possible. The methods will return the result as XML (serialized as a String object, which can be easily converted to an XML document such as org.w3c.dom.Document or org.jdom.Document). Also, I provide a utility class, DocumentManager, which can

- Convert org.w3c.dom.Document to XML as a serialized String object

- Convert org.jdom.Document to XML as a serialized String object

- Convert XML as a serialized String object into org.w3c.dom.Document

- Convert XML as a serialized String object into org.jdom.Document

In general, it is efficient to create XML as a serialized String object. The Java and JDBC solutions are grouped in a Java package called jcb (JDBC CookBook). Table 2-1 shows the structure of the package. All of the code will be available from the Source Code section of the Apress website.

Table 2-1. *JCB Package Structure*

Component	Description
jcb	Package name for **JDBC CookBook**
jcb.meta	Database and ResultSet metadata-related interfaces and classes
jcb.db	Database-related interfaces and classes
jcb.util	Utility classes
servlets	Java servlets
client	All client and test programs using the jcb package

When using the DatabaseMetaData object, you should observe two key facts:

- The MySQL database does not understand "schema"; you have to use "catalog."

- The Oracle database does not understand "catalog"; you have to use "schema."

2.1. What Is Metadata?

Metadata is data about data (or information about information), which provides structured, descriptive information about other data. According to Wikipedia (http://en.wikipedia.org/wiki/Metadata):

> *Metadata (Greek: meta-+ Latin: data "information"), literally "data about data", is information that describes another set of data. A common example is a library catalog card, which contains data about the contents and location of a book: It is data about the data in the book referred to by the card. Other common contents of metadata include the source or author of the described dataset, how it should be accessed, and its limitations.*

The following quote from the NOAA Coastal Services Center, or CSC (http://www.csc.noaa.gov/metadata/text/whatismet.htm), illustrates the importance of the concept of metadata:

> *Imagine trying to find a book in a library without the help of a card catalog or computerized search interface. Could you do it? Perhaps, but it would be difficult at best. The information contained in such a system is essentially metadata about the books that are housed at that library or at other libraries. It provides you with vital information to help you find a particular book and aids you in making a decision as to whether that book might fit your needs. Metadata serves a similar purpose for geospatial data.*

The NOAA CSC further adds that "metadata is a component of data which describes the data. It is 'data about data.'" Metadata describes the content, quality, condition, and other characteristics of data. Metadata describes the who, what, when, where, why, and how of a data set. Without proper documentation, a data set is incomplete.

KTWEB (http://www.ktweb.org/rgloss.cfm) defines metadata as "data about data, or information about information; in practice, metadata comprises a structured set of descriptive elements to describe an information resource or, more generally, any definable entity."

Relational databases (such as MySQL and Oracle) use tables and other means (such as operating system file systems) to store their own data and metadata. Each relational database has its own proprietary methods for storing metadata. Examples of relational database metadata include

- A list of all the tables in the database, including their names, sizes, and the number of rows

- A list of the columns in each database, and what tables they are used in, as well as the type of data stored in each column

For example, the Oracle database keeps metadata in several tables (I have listed two here):

- ALL_TABLES: A list of all tables in the current database

- ALL_TAB_COLS: A list of all columns in the database

Imagine, at runtime, trying to execute a SQL query in a relational database without knowing the name of tables, columns, or views. Could you do it? Of course not. Metadata helps you to find out what is available in the database and then, with the help of that information (called metadata), you can build proper SQL queries at runtime. Also, having access to structured database metadata relieves a JDBC programmer of having to know the characteristics of relational databases in advance.

Metadata describes the data but is not the actual data itself. For example, the records in a card catalog in a local library give brief details about the actual book. The card catalog—as metadata—provides enough information to tell you what the book is called, its unique identification number, and how and where you can find it. These details are metadata—in this case, bibliographic elements such as author, title, abstract, publisher, and published date.

In a nutshell, database metadata enables *dynamic database access*. Typically, most JDBC programmers know their target database's schema definitions: the names of tables, views, columns, and their associated types. In this case, the JDBC programmer can use the strongly typed JDBC interfaces. However, there is another important class of database access where an application (or an application builder) dynamically (in other words, at runtime) discovers the database schema information and uses that information to perform appropriate dynamic data access. This chapter describes the JDBC support for dynamic access. A dynamic database access application may include building dynamic queries, dynamic browsers, and GUI database adapters, just to mention a few.

For further research on metadata, refer to the following websites:

- "Metadata: An Overview": http://www.nla.gov.au/nla/staffpaper/cathro3.html

- "Introduction to Metadata": http://www.getty.edu/research/conducting_research/standards/intrometadata/index.html

- USGS CMG "Formal Metadata" Definition: http://walrus.wr.usgs.gov/infobank/programs/html/definition/fmeta.html

2.2. What Is Database Metadata?

The database has emerged as a major business tool across all enterprises, and the concept of *database metadata* has become a crucial topic. Metadata, which can be broadly defined as "data about data," refers to the searchable definitions used to locate information. On the other hand, *database* metadata, which can be broadly defined as "data about database data," refers to the searchable definitions used to locate database metadata (such as a list of all the tables for a specific schema). For example, you may use database metadata to generate web-based applications (see http://dev2dev.bea.com/pub/a/2004/06/GenApps_hussey.html). Or, you may use database metadata to reverse-engineer the whole database and dynamically build your desired SQL queries.

JDBC allows clients to discover a large amount of metadata information about a database (including tables, views, columns, stored procedures, and so on) and any given ResultSet via metadata classes.

Most of JDBC's metadata consists of information about one of two things:

- `java.sql.DatabaseMetaData` (database metadata information)

- `java.sql.ResultSetMetaData` (metadata information about a `ResultSet` object)

You should use `DatabaseMetaData` to find information about your database, such as its capabilities and structure, and use `ResultSetMetaData` to find information about the results of a SQL query, such as size and types of columns.

JDBC provides the following important interfaces that deal with database and result set metadata:

- `java.sql.DatabaseMetaData`: Provides comprehensive information about the database as a whole: table names, table indexes, database product name and version, and actions the database supports. Most of the solutions in this chapter are extracted from our solution class `DatabaseMetaDataTool` (you can download this class from the Source Code section of the Apress website). The `DatabaseMetaData` interface includes a number of methods that can be used to determine which SQL features are supported by a particular database. According to the JDBC specification, "The `java.sql.DatabaseMetaData` interface provides methods for retrieving various metadata associated with a database. This includes enumerating the stored procedures in the database, the tables in the database, the schemas in the database, the valid table types, the valid catalogs, finding information on the columns in tables, access rights on columns, access rights on tables, minimal row identification, and so on." Therefore, `DatabaseMetaData` methods can be categorized as

    - The schemas, catalogs, tables, views, columns, and column types

    - The database, users, drivers, stored procedures, and functions

    - The database limits (upper and lower bounds, minimums and maximums)

    - The features supported (and those not supported) by the database

- `java.sql.ResultSetMetaData`: Gets information about the types and properties of the columns in a `ResultSet` object. This interface is discussed in Chapter 4.

- `java.sql.ParameterMetaData`: Gets information about the types and properties of the parameters in a `PreparedStatement` object. `ParameterMetaData`, introduced in JDBC 3.0, retrieves information such as the number of parameters in the `PreparedStatement`, the type of data that can be assigned to the parameter, and whether or not the parameter value can be set to `null`. This interface is discussed in Chapter 5.

- `javax.sql.RowSetMetaData`: Extends the `ResultSetMetaData`, an object that contains information about the columns in a `RowSet` object. This interface is an extension of the `ResultSetMetaData` interface and has methods for setting the values in a `RowSetMetaData` object. When a `RowSetReader` object reads data into a `RowSet` object, it creates a `RowSetMetaData` object and initializes it using the methods in the `RowSetMetaData` interface. Then the reader passes the `RowSetMetaData` object to the rowset. The methods in this interface are invoked internally when an application calls the method `RowSet.execute()`; an application programmer would not use them directly.

2.3. How Do You Discover Database Metadata?

To discover metadata information about a database, you must create a DatabaseMetaData object. Note that some database vendors might not implement the DatabaseMetaData interface. Once a client program has obtained a valid database connection, the following code can get a database metadata object:

```
import java.sql.Connection;
import java.sql.DatabaseMetaData;
import jcb.util.DatabaseUtil;
...
Connection conn = null;
DatabaseMetaData dbMetaData = null;
try {
    // Get a valid database connection
    conn = getConnection();
    // Create a database metadata object as DatabaseMetaData
    dbMetaData = conn.getMetaData();
    if (dbMetaData == null) {
        // Database metadata is not supported
        // therefore, you cannot get metadata at runtime
    }
    else {
        // Then we are in business and can invoke
        // over 100 methods defined in DatabaseMetaData

        // Check to see if transactions are supported
        if (dbMetaData.supportsTransactions()) {
            // Transactions are supported
        }
        else {
            // Transactions are not supported
        }
    }
}
catch(SQLException e) {
    // deal and handle the exception
    e.printStackTrace();

    // other things to handle the exception
}
finally {
    // close resources
    DatabaseUtil.close(conn);
}
```

You can use a dbMetaData object to invoke over 100 methods that are defined in the DatabaseMetaData interface. Therefore, to do something useful with DatabaseMetaData, you must get a valid Connection object of type java.sql.Connection. The DatabaseMetaData object provides information about the entire database, such as the names of database tables or the names of a table's columns. Since various databases support different variants of SQL, there are also a large number of methods querying the database about what SQL methods it supports. Table 2-2 offers a partial listing of these methods.

Table 2-2. *Some DatabaseMetaData Methods*

Method Name	Description
getCatalogs()	Returns a list of catalogs of information (as a ResultSet object) in that database. With the JDBC-ODBC bridge driver, you get a list of databases registered with ODBC. According to JDBC, a database may have a set of catalogs, and each catalog may have a set of schemas. The terms *catalog* and *schema* can have different meanings depending on the database vendor. In general, the DBMS maintains a set of tables containing information about most of the objects in the database. These tables and views are collectively known as the *catalog*. The catalog tables contain metadata about objects such as tables, views, indexes, stored procedures, triggers, and constraints. To do anything (read, write, update) with these catalog tables and views, you need a special privilege. It is the DBMS's responsibility to ensure that the catalog contains accurate descriptions of the metadata objects in the database at all times. Oracle treats *schema* as a database name, while MySQL treats *catalog* as a database name. So, to get the name of databases from Oracle, you must use getSchemas(); to get the name of databases from MySQL, you must use getCatalogs().
getSchemas()	Retrieves the schema names (as a ResultSet object) available in this database. Typically, a schema is a set of named objects. Schemas provide a logical classification of database objects (tables, views, aliases, stored procedures, user-defined types, and triggers) in an RDBMS.
getTables(catalog, schema, tableNames, columnNames)	Returns table names for all tables matching tableNames and all columns matching columnNames.
getColumns(catalog, schema, tableNames, columnNames)	Returns table column names for all tables matching tableNames and all columns matching columnNames.
getURL()	Gets the name of the URL you are connected to.
getPrimaryKeys(catalog, schema, tableName)	Retrieves a description of the given table's primary key columns.
getDriverName()	Gets the name of the database driver you are connected to.

2.4. What Is JDBC's Answer to Database Metadata?

JDBC provides a low-level interface called DatabaseMetaData. This chapter explains how to dissect the DatabaseMetaData object in order to find out the table names, column names or types, stored procedures names and signatures, and other useful information. Before delving into the solution, let's take a look at the relationships (see Figure 2-1) between important low-level interfaces and classes. There are several ways that you can create a Connection object. Once you have a valid Connection object, then you can create a DatabaseMetaData object.

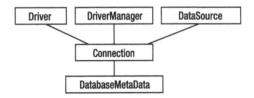

Figure 2-1. *Relationships between important interfaces and classes*

According to JDK 1.5, the DatabaseMetaData allows you to obtain information about the database and has over one hundred methods. You can find a description of DatabaseMetaData at http://java.sun.com/j2se/1.5.0/docs/api/java/sql/DatabaseMetaData.html.

To obtain a DatabaseMetaData object, use these general steps:

1. Connect to a database by using an instance of the Connection object.

2. To find out the names of the database schema, tables, and columns, get an instance of the DatabaseMetaData object from the Connection.

3. Perform the actual query by issuing a SQL query string. Then use the Connection to create a Statement class to represent your query.

4. The query returns a ResultSet. To find out the names of the column rows in that ResultSet, obtain an instance of the ResultSetMetaData class.

To get a DatabaseMetaData, use the following snippet:

```
Connection conn = null;
DatabaseMetaData dbMetaData = null;
try {
   // Get a valid database connection
   conn = getConnection();        // Get an instance of a DatabaseMetaData object
   dbMetaData = conn.getMetaData();
   if (dbMetaData == null) {
      // Database metadata is NOT supported
   }
   else {
      // Database metadata is supported and you can invoke
      // over 100 methods defined in DatabaseMetaData

      // Now that we have a valid database metadata (DatabaseMetaData) object
      // it can be used to do something useful:

      // Retrieves whether this database supports using columns not included in
      // the SELECT statement in a GROUP BY clause provided that all of the
      // columns in the SELECT statement are included in the GROUP BY clause.
      System.out.println(dbMetaData.supportsGroupByBeyondSelect());
```

```
        // Retrieves whether this database supports using a column that is not in
        // the SELECT statement in a GROUP BY clause.
        System.out.println(dbMetaData.supportsGroupByUnrelated());
        ...
    }
}
catch(SQLException e) {
    // deal and handle the SQLException
    ...
}
catch(Exception e2) {
    // deal with other exceptions
    ...
}
```

2.5. What Is the Vendor Name Factor in Database Metadata?

Sometimes, for a given problem, there are different solutions based on the database vendor. For example, the code that gets the table names for an Oracle database is different from the code that gets the tables names for a MySQL database. When you develop an application or framework for a relational database, be sure that your connection pool manager takes the vendor name as a parameter. Depending on the vendor name, you might be calling different methods, or you might be issuing a different set of SQL queries. For example, when you're using the BLOB data type, the vendor name makes a difference in reading or writing BLOB data. For instance, Oracle requires an empty_blob() function use for setting empty BLOBs, but MySQL does not (empty BLOBs are denoted by NULL in MySQL).

The vendor name also plays an important role in connection pool management and database metadata. Suppose you have a pool of connections that you use in a production environment. If for some reason the database server goes down, then all of the connections in the pool will be obsolete or defunct—that is, they become dead connections. Using a dead connection will throw an exception. One of the important tasks a pool manager must do is that, before handing a connection to the client, it must make sure that the connection is valid. For this reason, a pool manager must issue a *minimal SQL query* against that database to make sure that the connection is valid. If it is valid, then it can be given to a client; otherwise, you need to obtain another available connection or throw an exception. This minimal SQL query is called a validity check statement, which can differ from vendor to vendor. A validity check statement is a SQL statement that will return at least one row. For Oracle, this validity check statement is "select 1 from dual" and for MySQL and Sybase Adaptive Server, it is "select 1". Without knowing the vendor parameter, it is impossible to check for the validity of database connections. Also, note that without a valid database connection, you cannot get a DatabaseMetaData object. Therefore, you have to make sure that you have a valid database connection before attempting to create a DatabaseMetaData object.

Some JDBC metadata methods require knowledge of the database vendor. For example, getting the name of database tables is not the same in every case. For an Oracle database, you need to select the names from Oracle's user_objects table, while for other databases, the DatabaseMetaData.getTables() method will be sufficient.

Therefore, when you write a Java or JDBC application program or framework, you have to keep in mind that the same program will run against many relational databases (MySQL, Oracle, Sybase, and others). For example, if your application or framework runs on Oracle, you should be able to run the same program, with minimal changes to parameters and configurations, using MySQL. This means that you need to create database-dependent parameters (such as vendor code—specifying the vendor of the database) for your database URLs, SQL queries, and connection properties; avoid hard-coding any values that depend on a specific database vendor.

Here is an example of a vendor name in a configuration file. Based on the `<db-name>.vendor` key, you will be able to make smart decisions.

```
db.list=db1,db2,db3

db1.vendor=mysql
db1.url=jdbc:mysql://localhost/octopus
db1.driver=org.gjt.mm.mysql.Driver
db1.username=root
db1.password=mysql
db1.<…>=…

db2.vendor=oracle
db2.url=jdbc:oracle:thin:@localhost:1521:kitty
db2.driver=oracle.jdbc.driver.OracleDriver
db2.username=scott
db2.password=tiger
db2.<…>=…

db3.vendor=hsql
db3.url=jdbc:hsqldb:/members/alex/vrc/vrcdb
db3.driver=org.hsqldb.jdbcDriver
db3.username=alexis
db3.password=mypassword
db3.<…>=…
```

Here is another example of a vendor name in an XML document. In this example, the `<db-name>.vendor` key helps you make smart decisions.

```
<?xml version='1.0'>
<databases>
    <database id="db1">
        <vendor>mysql</vendor>
        <url>jdbc:mysql://localhost/octopus</url>
        <driver>org.gjt.mm.mysql.Driver</driver>
        <username>root</username>
        <password>mysql</password>

        ...
    </database>
```

```
<database id="db2">
  <vendor>oracle</vendor>
  <url>jdbc:oracle:thin:@localhost:1521:kitty</url>
  <driver>oracle.jdbc.driver.OracleDriver</driver>
  <username>scott</username>
  <password>tiger</password>
  ...
</database>
<database id="db3">
  <vendor>hsql</vendor>
  <url>jdbc:hsqldb:/members/alex/vrc/vrcdb</url>
  <driver>org.hsqldb.jdbcDriver</driver>
  <username>alexis</username>
  <password>mypassword</password>
  ...
</database>
</databases>
```

Now, using this configuration file, depending on the name of the vendor, you may select the appropriate database connection's validity check statement. Also, based on the name of the vendor, you might issue different JDBC methods for getting the database's table or view names.

2.6. How Do You Find JDBC's Driver Information?

To find out a database's vendor name and version information, you can invoke the following four methods from the `DatabaseMetaData` interface:

- `int getDatabaseMajorVersion()`: Retrieves the major version number of the underlying database. (Note that in `oracle.jdbc.OracleDatabaseMetaData`, this method is not supported. Therefore, use a `try-catch` block in code. If the method returns a `SQLException`, we return the message "unsupported feature" in the XML result.)

- `int getDatabaseMinorVersion()`: Retrieves the minor version number of the underlying database.

- `String getDatabaseProductName()`: Retrieves the name of this database product.

- `String getDatabaseProductVersion()`: Retrieves the version number of this database product.

Our solution combines these methods into a single method and returns the result as an XML `String` object, which any client can use. The result has the following syntax:

```
<?xml version='1.0'>
<DatabaseInformation>
    <majorVersion>database-major-version</majorVersion>
    <minorVersion>database-minor-version</minorVersion>
    <productName>database-product-name</productName>
    <productVersion>database-product-version</productVersion>
</DatabaseInformation>
```

The Solution

The solution is generic and can support MySQL, Oracle, and other relational databases. Note that the getDatabaseMajorVersion() method (implemented by the oracle.jdbc.Oracle⟶ DatabaseMetaData class) is an unsupported feature; therefore, we have to use a try-catch block. If the method returns a SQLException, we return the message "unsupported feature" in the XML result.

```java
import java.sql.Connection;
import java.sql.DatabaseMetaData;
...
/**
 * Get database product name and version information.
 * This method calls 4 methods (getDatabaseMajorVersion(),
 * getDatabaseMinorVersion(), getDatabaseProductName(),
 * getDatabaseProductVersion()) to get the required information
 * and it represents the information as XML.
 *
 * @param conn the Connection object
 * @return database product name and version information
 * as an XML document (represented as a String object).
 */
public static String getDatabaseInformation(Connection conn)
    throws Exception {
    try {
        DatabaseMetaData meta = conn.getMetaData();
        if (meta == null) {
            return null;
        }

        StringBuffer sb = new StringBuffer("<?xml version='1.0'>");
        sb.append("<DatabaseInformation>");

        // Oracle (and some other vendors) do not
        // support some of the following methods
        // (such as getDatabaseMajorVersion() and
        // getDatabaseMajorVersion()); therefore,
        // we need to use a try-catch block.
        try {
            int majorVersion = meta.getDatabaseMajorVersion();
            appendXMLTag(sb, "majorVersion", majorVersion);
        }
        catch(Exception e) {
            appendXMLTag(sb, "majorVersion", "unsupported feature");
        }
```

```
        try {
            int minorVersion = meta.getDatabaseMinorVersion();
            appendXMLTag(sb, "minorVersion", minorVersion);
        }
        catch(Exception e) {
            appendXMLTag(sb, "minorVersion", "unsupported feature");
        }

        String productName = meta.getDatabaseProductName();
        String productVersion = meta.getDatabaseProductVersion();
        appendXMLTag(sb, "productName", productName);
        appendXMLTag(sb, "productVersion", productVersion);
        sb.append("</DatabaseInformation>");
        return sb.toString();
    }
    catch(Exception e) {
        e.printStackTrace();
        throw new Exception("could not get the database information:"+
                            e.toString());
    }
}
```

Client: Program for Getting Database Information

```
import java.util.*;
import java.io.*;
import java.sql.*;

import jcb.util.DatabaseUtil;
import jcb.meta.DatabaseMetaDataTool;
import jcb.db.VeryBasicConnectionManager;

public class TestDatabaseMetaDataTool_DatabaseInformation {

    public static void main(String[] args) {
        String dbVendor = args[0];  // { "mysql", "oracle" }
        Connection conn = null;
        try {
            conn = VeryBasicConnectionManager.getConnection(dbVendor);
            System.out.println("--- getDatabaseInformation ---");
            System.out.println("conn="+conn);
            String dbInfo = DatabaseMetaDataTool.getDatabaseInformation(conn);
            System.out.println(dbInfo);
            System.out.println("-----------------------------------");
        }
```

```
        catch(Exception e){
            e.printStackTrace();
            System.exit(1);
        }
        finally {
            DatabaseUtil.close(conn);
        }
    }
}
```

Running the Solution for a MySQL Database

```
$ javac TestDatabaseMetaDataTool_DatabaseInformation.java
$ java TestDatabaseMetaDataTool_DatabaseInformation mysql
--- getDatabaseInformation ---
conn=com.mysql.jdbc.Connection@1837697
<?xml version='1.0'>
<DatabaseInformation>
    <majorVersion>4</majorVersion>
    <minorVersion>0</minorVersion>
    <productName>MySQL</productName>
    <productVersion>4.0.4-beta-max-nt</productVersion>
</DatabaseInformation>
------------------------------------
```

Running the Solution for an Oracle Database

The following output is formatted to fit the page:

```
$ javac TestDatabaseMetaDataTool_DatabaseInformation.java
$ java TestDatabaseMetaDataTool_DatabaseInformation oracle
--- getDatabaseInformation ---
conn= oracle.jdbc.driver.OracleConnection@169ca65
<?xml version='1.0'>
<DatabaseInformation>
    <majorVersion>unsupported feature</majorVersion>
    <minorVersion>unsupported feature</minorVersion>
    <productName>Oracle</productName>
    <productVersion>
        Oracle9i Enterprise Edition Release 9.2.0.1.0 - Production
        With the Partitioning, OLAP and Oracle Data Mining options
        JServer Release 9.2.0.1.0 - Production
    </productVersion>
</DatabaseInformation>
------------------------------------
```

2.7. What Are a Database's SQL Keywords?

In GUI database applications, if you are forming a SQL query at runtime, then you might need the database's SQL keywords. DatabaseMetaData provides the getSQLKeywords() method for getting the database's SQL keywords. This method retrieves a comma-separated list of all of the database's SQL keywords but excludes SQL-92 keywords. The return type of this method is not very useful, because once the client receives the result as a String, it has to be tokenized to find the actual keywords. Our solution returns this as a java.util.List, where each element will be a keyword. You can try the following two solutions for this problem. The first solution returns the list of SQL keywords as a java.util.List object, where each element is a SQL keyword (as a String object). The second solution returns the result as XML.

Solution 1: Returns the SQL Keywords as a List

```java
import java.util.List;
import java.util.ArrayList;
import java.sql.*;

/**
 * Get the SQL keywords for a database.
 * @param conn the java.sql.Connection object.
 * @return the list of SQL keywords for a database.
 * Each element in the list is a SQL keyword.
 * @exception Failed to get the SQL keywords for a database.
 */
public static List getSQLKeywords(Connection conn)
    throws Exception {
    DatabaseMetaData meta = conn.getMetaData();
    if (meta == null) {
        return null;
    }

    String sqlKeywords = meta.getSQLKeywords();
    if ((sqlKeywords == null) || (sqlKeywords.length() == 0)) {
        return null;
    }

    List list = new ArrayList();
    // SQL keywords are separated by ","
    StringTokenizer st = new StringTokenizer(sqlKeywords, ",");
    while(st.hasMoreTokens()) {
        list.add(st.nextToken().trim());
    }
    return list;
}
```

MySQL Client Code Using getSQLKeywords()

This code is the same for the Oracle client:

```
//
// Get list of SQL Keywords as a java.util.List
// print the list of SQL Keywords
//
List list = DatabaseMetaDataTool.getSQLKeywords(conn);
System.out.println("--- Got results: list of SQL Keywords ---");
for (int i=0; i < list.size(); i++) {
    String sqlKeyword = (String) list.get(i);
    System.out.println("sqlKeyword= " + sqlKeyword);
}
```

Output: MySQL Database

```
--- Got results: list of SQL Keywords ---
sqlKeyword= AUTO_INCREMENT
sqlKeyword= BINARY
sqlKeyword= BLOB
sqlKeyword= ENUM
sqlKeyword= INFILE
sqlKeyword= LOAD
sqlKeyword= MEDIUMINT
sqlKeyword= OPTION
sqlKeyword= OUTFILE
sqlKeyword= REPLACE
sqlKeyword= SET
sqlKeyword= TEXT
sqlKeyword= UNSIGNED
sqlKeyword= ZEROFILL
```

Output: Oracle Database

```
--- Got results: list of SQL Keywords ---
sqlKeyword= ACCESS
sqlKeyword= ADD
sqlKeyword= ALTER
sqlKeyword= AUDIT
sqlKeyword= CLUSTER
sqlKeyword= COLUMN
sqlKeyword= COMMENT
sqlKeyword= COMPRESS
sqlKeyword= CONNECT
sqlKeyword= DATE
sqlKeyword= DROP
sqlKeyword= EXCLUSIVE
```

```
sqlKeyword= FILE
sqlKeyword= IDENTIFIED
sqlKeyword= IMMEDIATE
sqlKeyword= INCREMENT
sqlKeyword= INDEX
sqlKeyword= INITIAL
sqlKeyword= INTERSECT
sqlKeyword= LEVEL
sqlKeyword= LOCK
sqlKeyword= LONG
sqlKeyword= MAXEXTENTS
sqlKeyword= MINUS
sqlKeyword= MODE
sqlKeyword= NOAUDIT
sqlKeyword= NOCOMPRESS
sqlKeyword= NOWAIT
sqlKeyword= NUMBER
sqlKeyword= OFFLINE
sqlKeyword= ONLINE
sqlKeyword= PCTFREE
sqlKeyword= PRIOR
sqlKeyword= all_PL_SQL_reserved_ words
```

Solution 2: Returns the SQL Keywords as XML

```java
import java.sql.*;
import java.util.*;

/**
 * Get the SQL Keywords for a database.
 * @param conn the Connection object.
 * @return the list of SQL keywords for a database as XML.
 * @exception Failed to get the SQL keywords for a database.
 */
public static String getSQLKeywordsAsXML(Connection conn)
    throws Exception {
    DatabaseMetaData meta = conn.getMetaData();
    if (meta == null) {
        return null;
    }

    String sqlKeywords = meta.getSQLKeywords();
    if ((sqlKeywords == null) || (sqlKeywords.length() == 0)) {
        return null;
    }
```

```
        StringBuffer sb = new StringBuffer("<?xml version='1.0'>");
        sb.append("<sql_keywords>");

        // SQL keywords are separated by ","
        StringTokenizer st = new StringTokenizer(sqlKeywords, ",");
        while(st.hasMoreTokens()) {
            sb.append("<keyword>");
            sb.append(st.nextToken().trim());
            sb.append("</keyword>");
        }
        sb.append("</sql_keywords>");
        return sb.toString();
    }
```

Client Code: MySQL Database

This code is the same for the Oracle client:

```
//
// Get list of SQL keywords as XML
// print the list of SQL keywords
//
String listOfSQLKeywords = DatabaseMetaDataTool.getSQLKeywordsAsXML(conn);
System.out.println("--- Got results: list of SQL Keywords ---");
System.out.println("listOfSQLKeywords= " + listOfSQLKeywords);
```

Output: MySQL Database

```
<?xml version='1.0'>
<sql_keywords>
    <keyword>AUTO_INCREMENT</keyword>
    <keyword>BINARY</keyword>
    <keyword>BLOB</keyword>
    <keyword>ENUM</keyword>
    <keyword>INFILE</keyword>
    <keyword>LOAD</keyword>
    <keyword>MEDIUMINT</keyword>
    <keyword>OPTION</keyword>
    <keyword>OUTFILE</keyword>
    <keyword>REPLACE</keyword>
    <keyword>SET</keyword>
    <keyword>TEXT</keyword>
    <keyword>UNSIGNED</keyword>
    <keyword>ZEROFILL</keyword>
</sql_keywords>
```

Output: Oracle Database

```
<?xml version='1.0'>
<sql_keywords>
    <keyword>ACCESS</keyword>
    <keyword>ADD</keyword>
    <keyword>ALTER</keyword>
    <keyword>AUDIT</keyword>
    <keyword>CLUSTER</keyword>
    <keyword>COLUMN</keyword>
    <keyword>COMMENT</keyword>
    <keyword>COMPRESS</keyword>
    <keyword>CONNECT</keyword>
    <keyword>DATE</keyword>
    <keyword>DROP</keyword>
    <keyword>EXCLUSIVE</keyword>
    <keyword>FILE</keyword>
    <keyword>IDENTIFIED</keyword>
    <keyword>IMMEDIATE</keyword>
    <keyword>INCREMENT</keyword>
    <keyword>INDEX</keyword>
    <keyword>INITIAL</keyword>
    <keyword>INTERSECT</keyword>
    <keyword>LEVEL</keyword>
    <keyword>LOCK</keyword>
    <keyword>LONG</keyword>
    <keyword>MAXEXTENTS</keyword>
    <keyword>MINUS</keyword>
    <keyword>MODE</keyword>
    <keyword>NOAUDIT</keyword>
    <keyword>NOCOMPRESS</keyword>
    <keyword>NOWAIT</keyword>
    <keyword>NUMBER</keyword>
    <keyword>OFFLINE</keyword>
    <keyword>ONLINE</keyword>
    <keyword>PCTFREE</keyword>
    <keyword>PRIOR</keyword>
    <keyword>all_PL_SQL_reserved_ words</keyword>
<sql_keywords>
```

2.8. What Are the Available SQL Data Types?

If you want to provide table-creation services from GUI database applications, then you may need to provide available SQL data types for databases. The DatabaseMetaData interface contains methods that list the available SQL types used by a database. The method getAvailableSqlTypes() retrieves the SQL data types supported by a database and driver. How do you get the name of a JDBC type? The following method implements a convenient way to convert a java.sql.Types integer value into a printable name. This method, which is useful for debugging purposes, uses reflection to get all the field names from java.sql.Types. It then retrieves their values and creates a map of values to names.

```java
import java.sql.Connection;
import java.sql.DatabaseMetaData;

...
/**
 * Listing of available SQL types used by a database. This method
 * retrieves the SQL data types supported by a database and driver.
 *
 *
 * @param conn the Connection object
 * @return an XML (as a String object).
 * @exception Failed to get the available SQL types used by a database.
 */
public static String getAvailableSqlTypes(Connection conn)
    throws Exception {
    ResultSet rs = null;
    try {
        // Get database metadata
        DatabaseMetaData meta = conn.getMetaData();
        if (meta == null) {
            return null;
        }

        // Get type infornmation
        rs = meta.getTypeInfo();

        // Retrieve type info from the result set
        StringBuffer sb = new StringBuffer();
        sb.append("<sqlTypes>");
        while (rs.next()) {
            // Get the database-specific type name
            String typeName = rs.getString("TYPE_NAME");

            // Get the java.sql.Types type to which this
            // database-specific type is mapped
            short dataType = rs.getShort("DATA_TYPE");

            // Get the name of the java.sql.Types value.
            String jdbcTypeName = getJdbcTypeName(dataType);
```

```
            sb.append("<typeName>");
            sb.append(typeName);
            sb.append("</typeName>");
            sb.append("<dataType>");
            sb.append(dataType);
            sb.append("</dataType>");
            sb.append("<jdbcTypeName>");
            sb.append(jdbcTypeName);
            sb.append("</jdbcTypeName>");
        }
        sb.append("</sqlTypes>");
        return sb.toString();
    }
    finally {
        DatabaseUtil.close(rs);
    }
}


/**
 * Get the name of a JDBC type. This method implements a
 * convenient method for converting a java.sql.Types integer
 * value into a printable name. This method is useful for debugging.
 * The method uses reflection to get all the field names from
 * java.sql.Types. It then retrieves their values and creates a
 * map of values to names.
 * This method returns the name of a JDBC type.
 * Returns null if jdbcType is not recognized.
 *
 * @param jdbcType the JDBC type as an interger
 * @return the equivalent JDBC type name
 */
public static String getJdbcTypeName(int jdbcType) {
    // Return the JDBC type name
    return (String) JDBC_TYPE_NAME_MAP.get(new Integer(jdbcType));
}
```

The JDBC_TYPE_NAME_MAP table is defined as follows:

```
static final Map JDBC_TYPE_NAME_MAP = new HashMap();
static {
    // Get all fields in java.sql.Types
    Field[] fields = java.sql.Types.class.getFields();
    for (int i=0; i<fields.length; i++) {
        try {
            // Get field name
            String name = fields[i].getName();
```

```
            // Get field value
            Integer value = (Integer)fields[i].get(null);

            // Add to map
            JDBC_TYPE_NAME_MAP.put(value, name);
        }
        catch (IllegalAccessException e) {
            // ignore
        }
    }
}
```

Testing getAvailableSqlTypes(): Using a MySQL Database

```
//
// getAvailableSqlTypes
//
String  availableSqlTypes = DatabaseMetaDataTool.getAvailableSqlTypes(conn);
System.out.println("-------- MySQL availableSqlTypes -------------");
System.out.println(availableSqlTypes);
System.out.println("---------------------------------------");

-------- MySQL availableSqlTypes -------------
<sqlTypes>
    <type name="TINYINT" dataType="-6" jdbcTypeName="TINYINT"/>
    <type name="BIGINT" dataType="-5" jdbcTypeName="BIGINT"/>
    <type name="MEDIUMBLOB" dataType="-4" jdbcTypeName="LONGVARBINARY"/>
    <type name="LONGBLOB" dataType="-4" jdbcTypeName="LONGVARBINARY"/>
    <type name="BLOB" dataType="-4" jdbcTypeName="LONGVARBINARY"/>
    <type name="TINYBLOB" dataType="-3" jdbcTypeName="VARBINARY"/>
    <type name="CHAR" dataType="1" jdbcTypeName="CHAR"/>
    <type name="NUMERIC" dataType="2" jdbcTypeName="NUMERIC"/>
    <type name="DECIMAL" dataType="3" jdbcTypeName="DECIMAL"/>
    <type name="INT" dataType="4" jdbcTypeName="INTEGER"/>
    <type name="MEDIUMINT" dataType="4" jdbcTypeName="INTEGER"/>
    <type name="SMALLINT" dataType="5" jdbcTypeName="SMALLINT"/>
    <type name="FLOAT" dataType="6" jdbcTypeName="FLOAT"/>
    <type name="DOUBLE" dataType="8" jdbcTypeName="DOUBLE"/>
    <type name="DOUBLE PRECISION" dataType="8" jdbcTypeName="DOUBLE"/>
    <type name="REAL" dataType="8" jdbcTypeName="DOUBLE"/>
    <type name="VARCHAR" dataType="12" jdbcTypeName="VARCHAR"/>
    <type name="DATE" dataType="91" jdbcTypeName="DATE"/>
    <type name="TIME" dataType="92" jdbcTypeName="TIME"/>
    <type name="DATETIME" dataType="93" jdbcTypeName="TIMESTAMP"/>
    <type name="TIMESTAMP" dataType="93" jdbcTypeName="TIMESTAMP"/>
</sqlTypes>
---------------------------------------
```

Testing getAvailableSqlTypes(): Using an Oracle Database

```
//
// getAvailableSqlTypes
//
String  availableSqlTypes = DatabaseMetaDataTool.getAvailableSqlTypes(conn);
System.out.println("-------- Oracle availableSqlTypes -------------");
System.out.println(availableSqlTypes);
System.out.println("----------------------------------------");
Output:

-------- Oracle availableSqlTypes -------------
<sqlTypes>
    <type name="INTERVALDS" dataType="-104" jdbcTypeName="null"/>
    <type name="INTERVALYM" dataType="-103" jdbcTypeName="null"/>
    <type name="TIMESTAMP WITH LOCAL TIME ZONE" dataType="-102" jdbcTypeName="null"/>
    <type name="TIMESTAMP WITH TIME ZONE" dataType="-101" jdbcTypeName="null"/>
    <type name="NUMBER" dataType="-7" jdbcTypeName="BIT"/>
    <type name="NUMBER" dataType="-6" jdbcTypeName="TINYINT"/>
    <type name="NUMBER" dataType="-5" jdbcTypeName="BIGINT"/>
    <type name="LONG RAW" dataType="-4" jdbcTypeName="LONGVARBINARY"/>
    <type name="RAW" dataType="-3" jdbcTypeName="VARBINARY"/>
    <type name="LONG" dataType="-1" jdbcTypeName="LONGVARCHAR"/>
    <type name="CHAR" dataType="1" jdbcTypeName="CHAR"/>
    <type name="NUMBER" dataType="2" jdbcTypeName="NUMERIC"/>
    <type name="NUMBER" dataType="4" jdbcTypeName="INTEGER"/>
    <type name="NUMBER" dataType="5" jdbcTypeName="SMALLINT"/>
    <type name="FLOAT" dataType="6" jdbcTypeName="FLOAT"/>
    <type name="REAL" dataType="7" jdbcTypeName="REAL"/>
    <type name="VARCHAR2" dataType="12" jdbcTypeName="VARCHAR"/>
    <type name="DATE" dataType="91" jdbcTypeName="DATE"/>
    <type name="DATE" dataType="92" jdbcTypeName="TIME"/>
    <type name="TIMESTAMP" dataType="93" jdbcTypeName="TIMESTAMP"/>
    <type name="STRUCT" dataType="2002" jdbcTypeName="STRUCT"/>
    <type name="ARRAY" dataType="2003" jdbcTypeName="ARRAY"/>
    <type name="BLOB" dataType="2004" jdbcTypeName="BLOB"/>
    <type name="CLOB" dataType="2005" jdbcTypeName="CLOB"/>
    <type name="REF" dataType="2006" jdbcTypeName="REF"/>
</sqlTypes>
----------------------------------------
```

2.9. What Are Catalogs and Schemas?

If you want to provide catalog and schema services to database applications, then you might need to provide catalog and schema values to client applications. The words *catalog* and *schema* have different meanings, depending on the database vendor. Again, the vendor parameter is very important in understanding the semantics of catalogs and schemas. Oracle treats "schema" as a database name, while MySQL treats "catalog" as a database name. So, in order to get the name of databases from Oracle, you must use getSchemas(); to get the name of databases from MySQL, you must use getCatalogs(). If you use getCatalogs() for an Oracle database, or getSchemas() for MySQL, it returns nothing (as null objects). In the JDBC API, getSchemas() claims that it returns a set of two columns ("table schema" and "table catalog"), but in reality it just returns "table schema" as a first column of the result set. Once again, this proves at least two points:

- You have to test your code against different databases; that is, databases can have different semantics by using the same JDBC API.

- When you define connections, make sure that the vendor parameter is defined. When you know the database vendor, you can invoke the correct methods.

getSchemas() Used for an Oracle Database

```
/**
 * Get Schemas(): Retrieves the schema names available
 * in this database. The results are ordered by schema name.
 *
 *
 * @param conn the Connection object.
 * @return an XML.
 * @exception Failed to get the Get Schemas.
 */
public static String getSchemas(java.sql.Connection conn)
    throws Exception {
    ResultSet schemas = null;
    StringBuffer sb = new StringBuffer();
    try {
        DatabaseMetaData meta = conn.getMetaData();
        if (meta == null) {
            return null;
        }

        schemas = meta.getSchemas();
        sb.append("<schemas>");
        while (schemas.next()) {
            String tableSchema = schemas.getString(1);    // "TABLE_SCHEM"
            //String tableCatalog = schemas.getString(2); // "TABLE_CATALOG"
            sb.append("<tableSchema>");
            sb.append(tableSchema);
            sb.append("</tableSchema>");
        }
        sb.append("</schemas>");
        return sb.toString();
    }
    catch(Exception e) {
        throw new Exception("Error: could not get schemas: "+e.toString());
    }
```

```
        finally {
            DatabaseUtil.close(schemas);
        }
}
```

getCatalogs() Used for a MySQL Database

```java
/**
 * Get Catalogs: Retrieves the catalog names available in
 * this database.  The results are ordered by catalog name.
 *
 * @param conn the Connection object
 * @return an XML.
 * @exception Failed to get the Get Catalogs.
 */
public static String getCatalogs(java.sql.Connection conn)
    throws Exception {
    ResultSet catalogs = null;
    StringBuffer sb = new StringBuffer();
    try {
        DatabaseMetaData meta = conn.getMetaData();
        if (meta == null) {
            return null;
        }

        catalogs = meta.getCatalogs();
        sb.append("<catalogs>");
        while (catalogs.next()) {
            String catalog = catalogs.getString(1);  // "TABLE_CATALOG"
            sb.append("<catalog>");
            sb.append(catalog);
            sb.append("</catalog>");
        }
        sb.append("</catalogs>");
        return sb.toString();
    }
    catch(Exception e) {
        throw new Exception("Error: could not get catalogs: "+e.toString());
    }
    finally {
        DatabaseUtil.close(catalogs);
    }
}
```

2.10. What Are the Table Names for a Database?

If you are providing dynamic SQL queries for a GUI database application, then you might need the names of the user tables. In building database adapters and GUI database applications, the GUI developers often need the name of the tables. The following program provides such a solution. The solution can vary depending on the database vendor. For a complete solution, refer to the DatabaseMetaDataTool class, described under the jcb.meta package (you can download the entire package from the Source Code section of the Apress website). Here, I'll just list the portions of the programs that are most relevant to this topic.

The DatabaseMetaData.getTables() method returns the table names for a given database connection object. The getTables() method works well for MySQL, but it does not work well for Oracle databases (in addition to user's tables, it returns system tables, which are not needed by most of the client programs). To get a list of user-defined tables and views, I use the Oracle's metadata table called user_objects, which keeps track of objects (tables, views, ...) owned by the user. To get a list of user's tables for an Oracle database, you may use the following SQL query:

```
select object_name from user_objects
  where object_type = 'TABLE';
```

The DatabaseMetaData.getTables() has the following signature:

```
ResultSet getTables(String catalog,
                    String schemaPattern,
                    String tableNamePattern,
                    String[] types)  throws SQLException
```

This method retrieves a description of the tables available in the given catalog. Only table descriptions matching the catalog, schema, table name and type criteria are returned. The returned ResultSet object has 10 columns (for details, see JDK 1.5 documentation), which are ordered by TABLE_TYPE, TABLE_SCHEM and TABLE_NAME (column names for the returned Result-Set object). Here, for MySQL solution, I use the getTables() method. For better performance of this method and other metadata methods, it is highly recommended not to pass null/empty values as an actual parameters to these methods. Try to pass non-null and non-empty values to these metadata methods.

MySQL Solution

```
import java.util.*;
import java.io.*;
import java.sql.*;

/**
 * This class provides class-level methods for getting database
 * metadata.  This class provides wrapper methods for most of
 * the useful methods in DatabaseMetaData and whenever possible
 * it returns the result as an XML (serialized as a String object
 * -- for efficiency purposes) rather than a ResultSet object.
 * The reason for returning the result as XML is so it can be used
 * by all types of clients.
```

```
 *
 * The wrapper methods in this class are generic and have been
 * tested with MySQL 4.0 and Oracle 9.2. These methods should run
 * with other relational databases such as DB2, Sybase,
 * and MS SQL Server 2000.
 *
 */
public class DatabaseMetaDataTool {

    private static final String[] DB_TABLE_TYPES = { "TABLE" };
    private static final String[] DB_VIEW_TYPES = { "VIEW" };
    private static final String[] DB_MIXED_TYPES = { "TABLE", "VIEW" };

    private static final String COLUMN_NAME_TABLE_NAME = "TABLE_NAME";
    private static final String COLUMN_NAME_COLUMN_NAME = "COLUMN_NAME";
    private static final String COLUMN_NAME_DATA_TYPE = "DATA_TYPE";
    private static final String COLUMN_NAME_VIEW_NAME = "VIEW_NAME";
    private static final String COLUMN_NAME_TYPE_NAME = "TYPE_NAME";


    /**
     * Get the table names for a given connection object.
     * @param conn the Connection object
     * @return the list of table names as a List.
     * @exception Failed to get the table names from the database.
     */
    public static List getTableNames(Connection conn)
        throws Exception {
        ResultSet rs = null;
        try {
            DatabaseMetaData meta = conn.getMetaData();
            if (meta == null) {
                return null;
            }

            rs = meta.getTables(null, null, null, DB_TABLE_TYPES);
            if (rs == null) {
                return null;
            }

            List list = new ArrayList();
            while (rs.next()) {
                String tableName =
                    DatabaseUtil.getTrimmedString(rs, COLUMN_NAME_TABLE_NAME);
                System.out.println("getTableNames(): tableName="+tableName);
                if (tableName != null) {
                    list.add(tableName);
                }
            }
```

```
            return list;
        }
        catch(Exception e) {
            e.printStackTrace();
            throw e;
        }
        finally {
            DatabaseUtil.close(rs);
        }
    }

    // other methods ...
}
```

Testing the MySQL Solution: Client Program

```
    //
    // Print the list of tables
    //
    java.util.List tables = DatabaseMetaDataTool.getTableNames(conn);
    System.out.println("--- Got results: list of tables ---");
    for (int i=0; i < tables.size(); i++) {
        // process results one element at a time
        String tableName = (String) tables.get(i);
        System.out.println("table name = " + tableName);
    }
```

Testing the MySQL Solution: Output of the Client Program

```
--- Got results: list of tables ---
table name = artist
table name = artist_exhibit
...
table name = zdepts
table name = zemps
table name = zperson
table name = zz
table name = zzz
```

Oracle Solution

For Oracle databases, DatabaseMetaData.getTables() method does not work well (in addition to the user's tables, it returns system-level tables). To get user's tables, I use the following query:

```
    select object_name from user_objects
      where object_type = 'TABLE';
```

Oracle's user_object's table keeps track of user objects (tables, views, and other useful objects). As you can observe, again, the database vendor name plays an important role in fetching metadata (based on vendor name, you may apply different methods for solving a specific metadata problem).

```java
import java.util.*;
import java.io.*;
import java.sql.*;

/**
 * This class provides class-level methods
 * for getting database metadata.
 *
 */
public class DatabaseMetaDataTool {

    private static final String[] DB_TABLE_TYPES = { "TABLE" };
    private static final String[] DB_VIEW_TYPES = { "VIEW" };
    private static final String[] DB_MIXED_TYPES = { "TABLE", "VIEW" };

    private static final String COLUMN_NAME_TABLE_NAME = "TABLE_NAME";
    private static final String COLUMN_NAME_COLUMN_NAME = "COLUMN_NAME";
    private static final String COLUMN_NAME_DATA_TYPE = "DATA_TYPE";
    private static final String COLUMN_NAME_VIEW_NAME = "VIEW_NAME";
    private static final String COLUMN_NAME_TYPE_NAME = "TYPE_NAME";

    private static final String  ORACLE_VIEWS =
        "select object_name from user_objects where object_type = 'VIEW'";
    private static final String  ORACLE_TABLES =
        "select object_name from user_objects where object_type = 'TABLE'";
    private static final String  ORACLE_TABLES_AND_VIEWS =
        "select object_name from user_objects where object_type = 'TABLE' "+
        "or object_type = 'VIEW'";


    /**
     * Get the Oracle table names for a given connection object.
     * If you use getTableNames() for an Oracle database, you
     * will get lots of auxiliary tables, which belong to the user,
     * but the user is not interested in seeing them.
     *
     * @param conn the Connection object
     * @return the list of table names as a List.
     * @exception Failed to get the table names from the database.
     */
```

```
public static java.util.List getOracleTableNames(java.sql.Connection conn)
    throws Exception {
    Statement stmt = null;
    ResultSet rs = null;
    try {
        stmt = conn.createStatement();
        rs = stmt.executeQuery(ORACLE_TABLES);

        if (rs == null) {
            return null;
        }

        java.util.List list = new java.util.ArrayList();
        while (rs.next()) {
            String tableName = DatabaseUtil.getTrimmedString(rs, 1);
            System.out.println("tableName="+tableName);
            if (tableName != null) {
                list.add(tableName);
            }
        }

        return list;
    }
    catch (Exception e ) {
        e.printStackTrace();
        throw e;
    }
    finally {
        DatabaseUtil.close(rs);
        DatabaseUtil.close(stmt);
    }
}

// other methods ...
}
```

Testing the Oracle Solution: Client Program

```
//
// Print the list of tables
//
java.util.List tables = DatabaseMetaDataTool.getOracleTableNames(conn);
System.out.println("Got results: list of tables --------------");
for (int i=0; i < tables.size(); i++) {
    // process results one element at a time
    String tableName = (String) tables.get(i);
    System.out.println("table name = " + tableName);
}
```

Output of the Client Program

```
Got results: list of tables --------------
table name = ALL_TYPES
table name = AUTHENTICATION_TYPES
table name = COMPANIES
...
table name = LOGS
table name = MYPAYROLLTABLE
table name = VIEW_CATEGORY_MEMBERS
table name = VIEW_CATEGORY_PERMISSIONS
table name = VIEW_DEFINITIONS
table name = ZDEPTS
table name = ZEMPS
```

To simplify this for clients (so that you don't have to call different methods to get the table names), we can introduce a wrapper object, which includes a Connection object and a vendor name:

```
public class ConnectionWrapper {

    private Connection conn = null;
    private String vendorName = null;

    public ConnectionWrapper() {
    }

    public ConnectionWrapper(Connection conn, String vendorName) {
        this.conn = conn;
        this.vendorName = vendorName;
    }

    public Connection getConnection() {
        return this.conn;
    }

    public void setConnection(Connection conn) {
        this.conn = conn;
    }

    public String getVendorName() {
        return this.vendorName;
    }

    public void setVendorName(String vendorName) {
        this.vendorName = vendorName;
    }
}
```

Now, we can get the table names from the following method:

```
/**
 * Get the table names for a given connection wrapper object.
 *
 * @param connWrapper the ConnectionWrapper object
 * @return the list of table names as a List.
 * @exception Failed to get the table names from the database.
 */
public static java.util.List getTableNames(ConnectionWrapper connWrapper)
    throws Exception {
    if (connWrapper == null) {
        return null;
    }

    if (connWrapper.getVendorName().equals("oracle")) {
        return getOracleTableNames(connWrapper.getConnection());
    }
    else {
        return getTableNames(connWrapper.getConnection());
    }
}
```

2.11. What Are the View Names for a Database?

A *view* is an alternative representation of data from one or more tables or views. A view can include all or some of the columns contained in one or more tables on which it is defined. A view is effectively a SQL query stored in the database catalog. Some database vendors, including Oracle, support the concept of views, while others, such as MySQL, do not at the present time (however, MySQL will support views starting with version 5.0). Therefore, a view is a virtual table and can be defined by SQL statements, but it may be vendor dependent. In general, views can be used for security purposes, such as hiding a salary field, or for the convenience of programmers or database administrators. Views enable the user to see only the information he or she needs at the moment, and provides security for the database managers.

Using DatabaseMetaData.getTables(catalog, schemaPattern, tableNamePattern, types) method, and by passing {"VIEW"} to the types parameter, you can get a list of views belonging to a database user. For Oracle databases, this method returns user-defined and system views. To get only user-created views, I use Oracle's metadata table, user_objects, which includes user-created tables and views. To get the views, use the following query:

```
select object_name from user_objects
  where object_type = 'VIEW';
```

To get the tables and views together, you can issue:

```
select object_name from user_objects
    where object_type = 'TABLE' or object_type = 'VIEW';
```

Consider the following table, which lists names of employees and their salaries:

```
create table MyPayrollTable(
    id varchar(9) not null primary key,
    name varchar(30) not null,
    salary int not null
);
```

If you want the employee names available but not their salaries, you can define the following view:

```
create view EmployeeNamesView (id, name)
    as select id, name from MyPayrollTable;
```

Here is how the EmployeeNamesView is created in the Oracle 9i SQL*Plus program:

```
$ sqlplus octopus/octopus
SQL*Plus: Release 9.2.0.1.0 - Production on Mon Dec 2 14:08:29 2002
Oracle9i Enterprise Edition Release 9.2.0.1.0 - Production

SQL> create table MyPayrollTable(
  2     id varchar(9) not null primary key,
  3     name varchar(30) not null,
  4     salary int not null
  5  );
Table created.
SQL> create view MyView2 (id, name)
  2     as select id, name from MyPayrollTable;
View created.
SQL> describe MyView2;
 Name                     Null?     Type
 --------------------     --------  ------------
 ID                       NOT NULL  VARCHAR2(9)
 NAME                     NOT NULL  VARCHAR2(30)
SQL> select object_name from user_objects where object_type='VIEW';
OBJECT_NAME
-----------
MYVIEW2
```

Oracle Solution: getOracleViewNames()

Next, let's look at the JDBC solution for finding the views for a given database. Here is the solution for Oracle:

```
/**
 * Get the Oracle view names for a given connection object.
 * If you use the getViewNames() for an Oracle database, you
 * will get lots of auxiliary views, which belong to the user,
 * but the user is not interested in seeing them.
 *
```

```
 * @param conn the Connection object
 * @return the list of view names as a List.
 * @exception Failed to get the view names from the database.
 */
public static java.util.List getOracleViewNames(java.sql.Connection conn)
    throws Exception {

    Statement stmt = null;
    ResultSet rs = null;
    try {
        stmt = conn.createStatement();
        // private static final String  ORACLE_VIEWS =
        // "select object_name from user_objects where object_type = 'VIEW'";
        rs = stmt.executeQuery(ORACLE_VIEWS);

        if (rs == null) {
            return null;
        }

        java.util.List list = new java.util.ArrayList();
        while (rs.next()) {
            String viewName = DatabaseUtil.getTrimmedString(rs, 1);
            System.out.println("viewName="+viewName);
            if (viewName != null) {
                list.add(viewName);
            }
        }

        return list;
    }
    finally {
        DatabaseUtil.close(rs);
        DatabaseUtil.close(stmt);
    }
}
```

Testing getOracleViewNames()

```
//
// print the list of views
//
java.util.List views = DatabaseMetaDataTool.getOracleViewNames(conn);
System.out.println("Got results: list of views -----------");
if (views != null) {
    for (int i=0; i < views.size(); i++) {
        // process results one element at a time
        String viewName = (String) views.get(i);
        System.out.println("view name = " + viewName);
    }
}
```

Output

```
view name = MYVIEW2
```

2.12. Does a Table Exist in a Database?

How do you test whether a given table name exists in a database? For the sake of our discussion, let's say that the table name is TABLE_NAME. At least four possible solutions exist:

- **Solution 1**: Use the getTableNames() method as described earlier and then check to see if the list contains your desired table (e.g., TABLE_NAME).

- **Solution 2**: Execute the following SQL statement; if execution is successful (meaning there was no SQLException) then the table exists; otherwise the table does not exist:

    ```
    select * from TABLE_NAME where 1=0;
    ```

    This solution is preferable to others. Because the boolean expression 1=0 evaluates to false, no rows will be selected. This expression only checks whether or not the table exists (in other words, if the table exists, then it returns no records and no exception is raised; otherwise it will throw a SQLException).

- **Solution 3**: Execute the following SQL statement; if execution is successful (meaning there was no SQLException) then the table exists; otherwise the table does not exist:

    ```
    select count(*) from TABLE_NAME;
    ```

    This solution might require a full table scan (to obtain the number of rows or records), and therefore using this solution might be more expensive than the others.

- **Solution 4**: You may use a database vendor's catalog to find out if a given table exists (this will be a proprietary solution). Using an Oracle database, for example, you may execute the following SQL query:

    ```
    select object_name from user_objects
        where object_type = 'TABLE' and
              object_name = 'YOUR-TABLE-NAME';
    ```

    If this query returns any rows, then the table does exist; otherwise it does not. This solution is an optimal one for Oracle databases (but it's not portable to other databases).

Solution 1: Use getTableNames()

```
/**
 * Table Exist: Solution 1
 * Check whether a given table (identified by a tableName
 * parameter) exists for a given connection object.
 * @param conn the Connection object
 * @param tableName the table name (to check to see if it exists)
 * @return true if table exists, otherwise return false.
 */
```

```java
public static boolean tableExist1(java.sql.Connection conn,
                                  String tableName) {

    if ((tableName == null) || (tableName.length() == 0)) {
        return false;
    }

    try {
        java.util.List allTables = getTableNames(conn);
        for (int i = 0; i < allTables.size(); i++) {
            String dbTable = (String) allTables.get(i);
            if (dbTable != null) {
                if (dbTable.equalsIgnoreCase(tableName)) {
                    return true;
                }
            }
        }

        // table does not exist
        return false;
    }
    catch(Exception e) {
        //e.printStackTrace();
        // table does not exist or some other problem
        return false;
    }
}
```

Testing Solution 1

```java
//
// does table TestTable77 exist
//
boolean exist77 = DatabaseMetaDataTool.tableExist1(conn, "TestTable77");
System.out.println("-------- does table TestTable77 exist -------");
System.out.println(exist77);
System.out.println("---------------------------------------------");


//
// does table TestTable88 exist
//
boolean exist88 = DatabaseMetaDataTool.tableExist1(conn, "TestTable88");
System.out.println("-------- does table TestTable88 exist -------");
System.out.println(exist88);
System.out.println("---------------------------------------------");
```

Output for Testing Solution 1

```
-------- does table TestTable77 exist -------
true
-------------------------------------------
-------- does table TestTable88 exist -------
false
-------------------------------------------
```

Solution 2: Execute select * from TABLE_NAME where 1=0;

```java
/**
 * Table Exist: Solution 2
 * Check whether a given table (identified by a tableName
 * parameter) exists for a given connection object.
 * @param conn the Connection object
 * @param tableName the table name (to check to see if it exists)
 * @return true if table exists, otherwise return false.
 */
public static boolean tableExist2(java.sql.Connection conn,
                                  String tableName) {

    if ((tableName == null) || (tableName.length() == 0)) {
        return false;
    }

    String query = "select * from " + tableName + " where 1=0";
    Statement stmt = null;
    ResultSet rs = null;
    try {
        stmt = conn.createStatement();
        rs = stmt.executeQuery(query);
        return true;
    }
    catch (Exception e ) {
        // table does not exist or some other problem
        //e.printStackTrace();
        return false;
    }
    finally {
        DatabaseUtil.close(rs);
        DatabaseUtil.close(stmt);
    }
}
```

Testing Solution 2

```
//
// does table TestTable77 exist
//
boolean exist77 = DatabaseMetaDataTool.tableExist2(conn, "TestTable77");
System.out.println("-------- does table TestTable77 exist -------");
System.out.println(exist77);
System.out.println("--------------------------------------------");

//
// does table TestTable88 exist
//
boolean exist88 = DatabaseMetaDataTool.tableExist2(conn, "TestTable88");
System.out.println("-------- does table TestTable88 exist -------");
System.out.println(exist88);
System.out.println("--------------------------------------------");
```

Output for Testing Solution 2

```
-------- does table TestTable77 exist -------
true
--------------------------------------------
-------- does table TestTable88 exist -------
false
--------------------------------------------
```

Solution 3: Execute select count(*) from TABLE_NAME;

This solution will work for both MySQL and Oracle databases:

```
/**
 * Table Exist: Solution 3
 * Check whether a given table (identified by a tableName
 * parameter) exists for a given connection object.
 * @param conn the Connection object
 * @param tableName the table name (to check to see if it exists)
 * @return true if table exists, otherwise return false.
 */
public static boolean tableExist3(java.sql.Connection conn,
                                  String tableName) {

    if ((tableName == null) || (tableName.length() == 0)) {
        return false;
    }
```

```
        String query = "select count(*) from " + tableName;
        Statement stmt = null;
        ResultSet rs = null;
        try {
            stmt = conn.createStatement();
            rs = stmt.executeQuery(query);
            return true;
        }
        catch (Exception e ) {
            // table does not exist or some other problem
            //e.printStackTrace();
            return false;
        }
        finally {
            DatabaseUtil.close(rs);
            DatabaseUtil.close(stmt);
        }
    }
}
```

Testing Solution 3

```
        //
        // does table TestTable77 exist
        //
        boolean exist77 = DatabaseMetaDataTool.tableExist3(conn, "TestTable77");
        System.out.println("-------- does table TestTable77 exist -------");
        System.out.println(exist77);
        System.out.println("--------------------------------------------");

        //
        // does table TestTable88 exist
        //
        boolean exist88 = DatabaseMetaDataTool.tableExist3(conn, "TestTable88");
        System.out.println("-------- does table TestTable88 exist -------");
        System.out.println(exist88);
        System.out.println("--------------------------------------------");
```

Output for Testing Solution 3

```
        -------- does table TestTable77 exist -------
        true
        --------------------------------------------
        -------- does table TestTable88 exist -------
        false
        --------------------------------------------
```

2.13. What Are a Table's Column Names?

When you're building SQL adapters and database GUI applications, keep in mind that clients might be interested in viewing and selecting columns (and their associated data types). Before you insert new records into a table, you might want to check the table columns' associated types. Doing so can prevent redundant network traffic.

You can use DatabaseMetaData.getColumns() to get list of columns for a table or view. In production environments, try to minimize passing null/empty parameter values to this method. Passing non-null and non-empty parameter values to JDBC metadata methods can improve the overall performance of your applications.

getColumnNames()

```java
/**
 * Get column names and their associated types. The result
 * is returned as a Hashtable, where key is "column name"
 * and value is "column type". If table name is null/empty
 * it returns null.
 *
 * @param conn the Connection object
 * @param tableName name of a table in the database.
 * @return an Hashtable, where key is "column name"
 * and value is "column type".
 * @exception Failed to get the column names for a given table.
 */
public static java.util.Hashtable getColumnNames(java.sql.Connection conn,
                                                 String tableName)
    throws Exception {
    ResultSet rsColumns = null;
    try {
        if ((tableName == null) || (tableName.length() == 0)) {
            return null;
        }

        DatabaseMetaData meta = conn.getMetaData();
        if (meta == null) {
            return null;
        }

        // Oracle requires table names to in uppercase characters
        // MySQL is case-insensitive to table names
        rsColumns = meta.getColumns(null, null, tableName.toUpperCase(), null);
        Hashtable columns = new Hashtable();
        while (rsColumns.next()) {
            // private static final String COLUMN_NAME_COLUMN_NAME = "COLUMN_NAME";
            // private static final String COLUMN_NAME_TYPE_NAME = "TYPE_NAME";
            String columnType = rsColumns.getString(COLUMN_NAME_TYPE_NAME);
```

```
                    String columnName = rsColumns.getString(COLUMN_NAME_COLUMN_NAME);
                    if (columnName != null) {
                        columns.put(columnName, columnType);
                    }
                }
            return columns;
        }
        catch(Exception e) {
            throw new Exception("Error: could not get column names: "+e.toString());
        }
        finally {
            DatabaseUtil.close(rsColumns);
        }
    }
}
```

Test Program

The following test program prints a listing of the column names for the table MyPayrollTable:

```
//
// print the list of column names for table MyPayrollTable
//
java.util.Hashtable result =
    DatabaseMetaDataTool.getColumnNames(conn, "MyPayrollTable");
System.out.println("Got results: list of column names -------------");
java.util.Enumeration columns = result.keys();
while (columns.hasMoreElements()) {
    Object columnKey = columns.nextElement();
    String columnName = (String) columnKey;
    String columnType = (String) result.get(columnKey);
    System.out.println("column name = " + columnName);
    System.out.println("column type = " + columnType);
}
```

Output of the Test Program

```
Got results: list of column names -------------
column name = ID
column type = VARCHAR2
column name = SALARY
column type = NUMBER
column name = NAME
column type = VARCHAR2
```

The name and type combination provides information about the table schema, but it is not enough. You need to get other useful information, such as the size of the column and whether the column is nullable. (*Nullable* means that the column accepts the NULL value; note that NULL in SQL is not a zero or an empty value but instead indicates that the value is missing.) So, you can modify the program to provide more detailed information for each column. Since you are returning four distinct pieces of information for each column, you will return the result as an XML String object. For each column, the following information will be returned:

```
<column name="NameOfColumn">
    <type>TypeOfColumn</type>
    <size>SizeOfColumn</size>
    <nullable>true|false</nullable>
</column>
```

Testing getColumnDetails()

```
//
// print the detail of columns for table TestTable77
//
String columnDetails = DatabaseMetaDataTool.getColumnDetails(conn, "TestTable77");
System.out.println("-------- columnDetails -------------");
System.out.println(columnDetails);
System.out.println("----------------------------------");
```

Output of Testing getColumnDetails()

```
<columns>
    <column name="id">
        <type>varchar</type>
        <size>10</size>
        <nullable>false</nullable>
        <position>1</position>
    </column>
    <column name="name">
        <type>varchar</type>
        <size>20</size>
        <nullable>false</nullable>
        <position>2</position>
    </column>
    <column name="age">
        <type>int</type>
        <size>11</size>
        <nullable>true</nullable>
        <position>3</position>
    </column>
    <column name="address">
        <type>varchar</type>
        <size>100</size>
        <nullable>true</nullable>
        <position>4</position>
    </column>
</columns>
```

getColumnDetails() Method

```java
/**
 * Get column names and their associated attributes (type,
 * size, nullable, ordinal position). The result is returned
 * as XML (as a string object);  if table name is null/empty
 * it returns null.
 *
 * @param conn the Connection object
 * @param tableName name of a table in the database.
 * @return XML (column names and their associated attributes:
 * type, size, nullable, ordinal position).
 * @exception Failed to get the column details for a given table.
 */
public static String getColumnDetails(java.sql.Connection conn,
                                      String tableName)
    throws Exception {

    ResultSet rsColumns = null;
    StringBuilder sb = new StringBuilder();
    try {
        if ((tableName == null) || (tableName.length() == 0)) {
            return null;
        }

        DatabaseMetaData meta = conn.getMetaData();
        if (meta == null) {
            return null;
        }

        rsColumns = meta.getColumns(null, null, tableName.toUpperCase(), null);
        sb.append("<columns>");
        while (rsColumns.next()) {

            String columnType = rsColumns.getString(COLUMN_NAME_TYPE_NAME);
            String columnName = rsColumns.getString(COLUMN_NAME_COLUMN_NAME);
            int size = rsColumns.getInt(COLUMN_NAME_COLUMN_SIZE);
            int nullable = rsColumns.getInt(COLUMN_NAME_NULLABLE);
            int position = rsColumns.getInt(COLUMN_NAME_ORDINAL_POSITION);

            sb.append("<column name=\"");
            sb.append(columnName);
            sb.append("\"><type>");
            sb.append(columnType);
            sb.append("</type><size>");
            sb.append(size);
            sb.append("</size><nullable>");
            if (nullable == DatabaseMetaData.columnNullable) {
                sb.append("true");
            }
```

```
                else {
                    sb.append("false");
                }
                sb.append("</nullable><position>");
                sb.append(position);
                sb.append("</position></column>");
            }
            sb.append("</columns>");
            return sb.toString();
        }
        catch(Exception e) {
            throw new Exception("Error: could not get column names: "+e.toString());
        }
        finally {
            DatabaseUtil.close(rsColumns);
        }
    }
}
```

getColumnDetails() Method: Selecting Type, Size, Nullable, Position

The following method selects the specific metadata that you are interested in by passing a boolean flag for each metadata:

```
/**
 * Get column names and their associated attributes (type,
 * size, nullable). The result is returned as an XML (as
 * a string object);  if table name is null/empty
 * it returns null.
 *
 * @param conn the Connection object
 * @param tableName name of a table in the database.
 * @param includeType if true, then include type information.
 * @param includeSize if true, then include size information.
 * @param includeNullable if true, then include nullable information.
 * @param includePosition if true, then include ordinal position information.
 * @return an XML: column names and their associated attributes: type,
 * size, nullable.
 * @exception Failed to get the column details for a given table.
 */
public static String getColumnDetails(java.sql.Connection conn,
                                      String tableName,
                                      boolean includeType,
                                      boolean includeSize,
                                      boolean includeNullable,
                                      boolean includePosition)
```

```
throws Exception {
ResultSet rsColumns = null;
StringBuffer sb = new StringBuffer();
try {
    if ((tableName == null) || (tableName.length() == 0)) {
        return null;
    }

    DatabaseMetaData meta = conn.getMetaData();
    if (meta == null) {
        return null;
    }

    rsColumns = meta.getColumns(null, null, tableName.toUpperCase(), null);
    sb.append("<columns>");
    while (rsColumns.next()) {
        String columnName = rsColumns.getString(COLUMN_NAME_COLUMN_NAME);
        sb.append("<column name=\"");
        sb.append(columnName);
        sb.append("\">");
        if (includeType) {
            String columnType = rsColumns.getString(COLUMN_NAME_TYPE_NAME);
            sb.append("<type>");
            sb.append(columnType);
            sb.append("</type>");
        }

        if (includeSize) {
            int size = rsColumns.getInt(COLUMN_NAME_COLUMN_SIZE);
            sb.append("<size>");
            sb.append(size);
            sb.append("</size>");
        }

        if (includeNullable) {
            int nullable = rsColumns.getInt(COLUMN_NAME_NULLABLE);
            sb.append("<nullable>");
            if (nullable == DatabaseMetaData.columnNullable) {
                sb.append("true");
            }
            else {
                sb.append("false");
            }
            sb.append("</nullable>");
        }
```

```
            if (includePosition) {
                int position = rsColumns.getInt(COLUMN_NAME_ORDINAL_POSITION);
                sb.append("<position>");
                sb.append(position);
                sb.append("</position>");
            }
            sb.append("</column>");
        }
        sb.append("</columns>");
        return sb.toString();
    }
    catch(Exception e) {
        throw new Exception("Error: could not get column names: "+e.toString());
    }
    finally {
        DatabaseUtil.close(rsColumns);
    }
}
```

2.14. What Are the Table Types Used in a Database?

Using RDBMS, we store data and metadata in logical tables (which are stored in operating system files). Typically, each database vendor has different types of logical storage types (such as TABLE, VIEW, SYSTEM TABLE, etc.) for storing data and metadata. For example, Oracle does support most of the table types, but some databases (such as MySQL) do not support "views" (MySQL 5.0 does support views, however). In GUI database applications, you might want to distinguish different table types. The getTableTypes() method, defined in the DatabaseMetaData interface, retrieves the table types available in this database. The results are ordered by table type. The result is returned as a ResultSet object in which each row has a single String column that is a table type. A single column is named as TABLE_TYPE.

The table type is

- "TABLE"

- "VIEW"

- "SYSTEM TABLE"

- "GLOBAL TEMPORARY"

- "LOCAL TEMPORARY"

- "ALIAS"

- "SYNONYM"

The Solution: getTableTypes()

```java
/**
 * Get the table types for a database.
 * @param conn the Connection object.
 * @return the list of table types as a List.
 * @exception Failed to get the table types from the database.
 */
public static java.util.List getTableTypes(java.sql.Connection conn)
    throws Exception {
    ResultSet rs = null;
    try {
        DatabaseMetaData meta = conn.getMetaData();
        if (meta == null) {
            return null;
        }

        rs = meta.getTableTypes();
        if (rs == null) {
            return null;
        }

        java.util.List list = new java.util.ArrayList();
        //System.out.println("getTableTypes(): --------------");
        while (rs.next()) {
            String tableType = DatabaseUtil.getTrimmedString(rs, 1);
            //System.out.println("tableType="+tableType);
            if (tableType != null) {
                list.add(tableType);
            }
        }
        //System.out.println("--------------");
        return list;
    }
    catch(Exception e) {
        e.printStackTrace();
        throw e;
    }
    finally {
        DatabaseUtil.close(rs);
    }
}
```

Oracle Client Program

```
//
// print the list of table types
//
java.util.List tableTypes = DatabaseMetaDataTool.getTableTypes(conn);
System.out.println("Got results: list of table types --------------");
for (int i=0; i < tableTypes.size(); i++) {
    // process results one element at a time
    String tableType = (String) tableTypes.get(i);
    System.out.println("table type = " + tableType);
}
```

Oracle Client Program Output

```
Got results: list of table types --------------
table type = SYNONYM
table type = TABLE
table type = VIEW
```

MySQL Client Program

```
//
// print the list of table types
//
java.util.List tableTypes = DatabaseMetaDataTool.getTableTypes(conn);
System.out.println("Got results: list of table types --------------");
for (int i=0; i < tableTypes.size(); i++) {
    // process results one element at a time
    String tableType = (String) tableTypes.get(i);
    System.out.println("table type = " + tableType);
}
```

MySQL Client Program Output

```
Got results: list of table types --------------
table type = TABLE
table type = LOCAL TEMPORARY
```

2.15. What Are the Primary Keys for a Table?

The primary key (PK) of a relational table uniquely identifies each row (or record) in the table. DatabaseMetaData provides the getPrimaryKeys() method, which retrieves a description of the given table's primary key columns:

```
ResultSet getPrimaryKeys(String catalog, String schema, String table)
```

When invoking the DatabaseMetaData.getPrimaryKeys() method, be sure to pass catalog and schema values (if they are known); if you pass null values for the first two parameters, then it might take too long to return the result. Database applications that involve the dynamic insertion of records need to know which columns form the primary key. In this way, the application can control the values sent for the insertion of new records. Again, this can be useful when you build database adapters. The solution is as follows:

```java
import java.util.*;
import java.io.*;
import java.sql.*;

/**
 * This class provides class-level methods for getting database metadata.
 *
 */
public class DatabaseMetaDataTool {

    /**
     * Retrieves a description of the given table's primary key columns.
     * @param conn the Connection object
     * @param tableName name of a table in the database.
     * @return the list of column names (which form the Primary Key) as a List.
     * @exception Failed to get the PrimaryKeys for a given table.
     */
    public static java.util.List getPrimaryKeys(java.sql.Connection conn,
                                                String tableName)
        throws Exception {
        ResultSet rs = null;
        try {
            if ((tableName == null) || (tableName.length() == 0)) {
                return null;
            }

            DatabaseMetaData meta = conn.getMetaData();
            if (meta == null) {
                return null;
            }

            //
            // The Oracle database stores its table names as uppercase,
            // if you pass a table name in lowercase characters, it will not work.
            // MySQL database does not care if table name is uppercase/lowercase.
            // if you know catalog and schema, then pass them explicitly
            // rather than passing null values (you might pay a performance
            // penalty for passing null values)
            rs = meta.getPrimaryKeys(null, null, tableName.toUpperCase());
            if (rs == null) {
                return null;
            }
```

```
            java.util.List list = new java.util.ArrayList();
            while (rs.next()) {
                String columnName =
                  DatabaseUtil.getTrimmedString(rs, COLUMN_NAME_COLUMN_NAME);
                System.out.println("getPrimaryKeys(): columnName="+columnName);
                if (columnName != null) {
                    list.add(columnName);
                }
            }
            return list;
        }
        catch(Exception e) {
            e.printStackTrace();
            throw e;
        }
        finally {
            DatabaseUtil.close(rs);
        }
    }

    // other methods and constants ...
}
```

Consider the following table in a MySQL database:

```
mysql> describe TestTable77;
```

```
+---------+--------------+------+-----+---------+-------+
| Field   | Type         | Null | Key | Default | Extra |
+---------+--------------+------+-----+---------+-------+
| id      | varchar(10)  |      | PRI |         |       |
| name    | varchar(20)  |      | PRI |         |       |
| age     | int(11)      | YES  |     | NULL    |       |
| address | varchar(100) | YES  |     | NULL    |       |
+---------+--------------+------+-----+---------+-------+
4 rows in set (0.02 sec)
```

In order to find the Primary Key column names for the TestTable77 table, we need to write the following code segment:

```
//
// print the list of PKs
//
java.util.List pks = DatabaseMetaDataTool.getPrimaryKeys(conn, "TestTable77");
System.out.println("Got results: list of PKs -------------");
for (int i=0; i < pks.size(); i++) {
  // process results one element at a time
  String columnName = (String) pks.get(i);
  System.out.println("column name = " + columnName);
}
```

The output will be:

```
getPrimaryKeys(): columnName=id
getPrimaryKeys(): columnName=name
Got results: list of PKs ------------
column name = id
column name = name
```

2.16. What Are a Table's Privileges?

A database table's *privileges* refer to finding a description of the access rights for each table available in a catalog or schema. DatabaseMetaData provides a method, getTablePrivileges(), to do just that. This method returns the result as a ResultSet where each row is a table privilege description. In production applications, returning the result as a ResultSet is not quite useful. It is better to return the result as an XML object so that the client can extract the required information and display it in a desired format. It would be wrong to assume that this privilege applies to all columns; while this may be true for some systems, it is not true for all.

getTablePrivileges() returns only privileges that match the schema and table name criteria. They are ordered by TABLE_SCHEM, TABLE_NAME, and PRIVILEGE. Each privilege description has the columns shown in Table 2-3.

Table 2-3. *Columns for Result of getTablePrivileges()*

Column's Position	Column's Name	Description
1	TABLE_CAT	Table catalog (may be null)
2	TABLE_SCHEM	Table schema (may be null)
3	TABLE_NAME	Table name (as a String)
4	GRANTOR	Grantor of access (may be null)
5	GRANTEE	Grantee of access
6	PRIVILEGE	Name of access (SELECT, INSERT, UPDATE, REFERENCES, etc.)
7	IS_GRANTABLE	YES if grantee is permitted to grant to others; NO if not; null if unknown

The getTablePrivileges() method has the following signature:

```
public java.sql.ResultSet getTablePrivileges(String catalog,
                                             String schemaPattern,
                                             String tableNamePattern)
            throws java.sql.SQLException
```

where

- catalog: A catalog name; "" retrieves those without a catalog.

- schemaPattern: A schema name pattern; "" retrieves those without a schema.

- tableNamePattern: A table name pattern.

The Solution: Get Table Privileges

```
/**
 * Get Table Privileges: retrieves a description of the access
 * rights for each table available in a catalog. Note that a
 * table privilege applies to one or more columns in the table.
 * It would be wrong to assume that this privilege applies to
 * all columns (this may be true for some systems but is not
 * true for all.)  The result is returned as XML (as a string
 * object);  if table name is null/empty it returns null.
 *
 * In JDBC, Each privilege description has the following columns:
 *
 * TABLE_CAT String => table catalog (may be null)
 * TABLE_SCHEM String => table schema (may be null)
 * TABLE_NAME String => table name
 * GRANTOR => grantor of access (may be null)
 * GRANTEE String => grantee of access
 * PRIVILEGE String => name of access (SELECT, INSERT,
 *     UPDATE, REFERENCES, ...)
 * IS_GRANTABLE String => "YES" if grantee is permitted to grant
 *     to others; "NO" if not; null if unknown
 *
 *
 * @param conn the Connection object
 * @param catalogPattern a catalog pattern.
 * @param schemaPattern a schema pattern.
 * @param tableNamePattern a table name pattern; must match
 *   the table name as it is stored in the database .
 * @return an XML.
 * @exception Failed to get the Get Table Privileges.
 */
public static String getTablePrivileges(java.sql.Connection conn,
                                        String catalogPattern,
                                        String schemaPattern,
                                        String tableNamePattern)
    throws Exception {

    ResultSet privileges = null;
    StringBuffer sb = new StringBuffer();
    try {
        if ((tableNamePattern == null) ||
            (tableNamePattern.length() == 0)) {
            return null;
        }

        DatabaseMetaData meta = conn.getMetaData();
        if (meta == null) {
            return null;
        }
```

```java
        // The '_' character represents any single character.
        // The '%' character represents any sequence of zero
        // or more characters.
        privileges = meta.getTablePrivileges(catalogPattern,
                                             schemaPattern,
                                             tableNamePattern);
    sb.append("<privileges>");
    while (privileges.next()) {

        String catalog = privileges.getString(COLUMN_NAME_TABLE_CATALOG);
        String schema = privileges.getString(COLUMN_NAME_TABLE_SCHEMA);
        String tableName = privileges.getString(COLUMN_NAME_TABLE_NAME);
        String privilege = privileges.getString(COLUMN_NAME_PRIVILEGE);
        String grantor = privileges.getString(COLUMN_NAME_GRANTOR);
        String grantee = privileges.getString(COLUMN_NAME_GRANTEE);
        String isGrantable = privileges.getString(COLUMN_NAME_IS_GRANTABLE);

        sb.append("<table name=\"");
        sb.append(tableName);
        sb.append("\"><catalog>");
        sb.append(catalog);
        sb.append("</catalog><schema>");
        sb.append(schema);
        sb.append("</schema><privilege>");
        sb.append(privilege);
        sb.append("</privilege><grantor>");
        sb.append(grantor);
        sb.append("</grantor><isGrantable>");
        sb.append(isGrantable);
        sb.append("</isGrantable><grantee>");
        sb.append(grantee);
        sb.append("</grantee></table>");
    }
    sb.append("</privileges>");
    return sb.toString();
}
catch(Exception e) {
    throw new Exception("Error: could not get table privileges:"+
        e.toString());
}
finally {
    DatabaseUtil.close(privileges);
}
}
```

Oracle: Client Call: Get Table Privileges

```
String tablePrivileges = DatabaseMetaDataTool.getTablePrivileges
    (conn,                  // connection
     conn.getCatalog(),    // catalog
     "%",                   // schema
     "EMP%");               // table name pattern
System.out.println("-------- TablePrivileges -------------");
System.out.println(tablePrivileges);
System.out.println("----------------------------------");
```

And here's the output:

```
-------- TablePrivileges -------------
<privileges>
    <table name="EMPLOYEE_PHOTOS">
        <catalog>null</catalog>
        <schema>SYS</schema>
        <privilege>READ</privilege>
        <grantor>SYS</grantor>
        <isGrantable>YES</isGrantable>
        <grantee>OCTOPUS</grantee>
    </table>
    <table name="EMPLOYEE_PHOTOS">
        <catalog>null</catalog>
        <schema>SYS</schema>
        <privilege>WRITE</privilege>
        <grantor>SYS</grantor>
        <isGrantable>YES</isGrantable>
        <grantee>OCTOPUS</grantee>
    </table>
</privileges>
----------------------------------
```

MySQL: Client Call: Get Table Privileges

The MySQL database stores table privileges in the tables_priv table. Here is the description of that table (note that the MySQL database uses the mysql database to manage users and privileges):

```
mysql> use mysql;
mysql> desc tables_priv;
+-------------+------------------+------+-----+-------------------+-------+
| Field       | Type             | Null | Key | Default           | Extra |
+-------------+------------------+------+-----+-------------------+-------+
| Host        | char(60)         |      | PRI |                   |       |
| Db          | char(64)         |      | PRI |                   |       |
| User        | char(16)         |      | PRI |                   |       |
| Table_name  | char(64)         |      | PRI |                   |       |
| Grantor     | char(77)         |      | MUL |                   |       |
| Timestamp   | timestamp        | YES  |     | CURRENT_TIMESTAMP |       |
| Table_priv  | set('Select',    |      |     |                   |       |
|             |         'Insert', |      |     |                   |       |
|             |         'Update', |      |     |                   |       |
|             |         'Delete', |      |     |                   |       |
|             |         'Create', |      |     |                   |       |
|             |         'Drop',   |      |     |                   |       |
|             |         'Grant',  |      |     |                   |       |
|             |         'References'|    |     |                   |       |
|             |         ,'Index', |      |     |                   |       |
|             |          'Alter') |      |     |                   |       |
| Column_priv | set('Select',    |      |     |                   |       |
|             |         'Insert', |      |     |                   |       |
|             |         'Update', |      |     |                   |       |
|             |         'References' |   |     |                   |       |
+-------------+------------------+------+-----+-------------------+-------+
8 rows in set (0.00 sec)
```

Client Call

```java
String tablePrivileges = DatabaseMetaDataTool.getTablePrivileges
    (conn, // connection
     conn.getCatalog(), // catalog
     null, //"%", // schema
     "%");
System.out.println("-------- TablePrivileges -------------");
System.out.println(tablePrivileges);
System.out.println("----------------------------------");
```

Output

```
-------- TablePrivileges -------------
<privileges>

<table name="artist">
<catalog>octopus</catalog>
<schema>null</schema>
<privilege>SELECT</privilege>
```

```
<grantor>root@127.0.0.1</grantor>
<isGrantable>null</isGrantable>
<grantee>%@%</grantee>
</table>

<table name="artist_exhibit">
<catalog>octopus</catalog>
<schema>null</schema>
<privilege>SELECT</privilege>
<grantor>root@127.0.0.1</grantor>
<isGrantable>null</isGrantable>
<grantee>%@%</grantee>
</table>

<table name="artist_exhibit">
<catalog>octopus</catalog>
<schema>null</schema>
<privilege>INSERT</privilege>
<grantor>root@127.0.0.1</grantor>
<isGrantable>null</isGrantable>
<grantee>%@%</grantee>
</table>

<table name="artist_exhibit">
<catalog>octopus</catalog>
<schema>null</schema>
<privilege>DROP</privilege>
<grantor>root@127.0.0.1</grantor>
<isGrantable>null</isGrantable>
<grantee>%@%</grantee>
</table>

</privileges>
-----------------------------------
```

2.17. What Are a Table Column's Privileges?

To retrieve a description of a given table column's privileges—that is, its access rights—you can use the DatabaseMetaData interface's getColumnPrivileges() method. This method returns a list of columns and associated privileges for the specified table. The getColumnPrivileges() method returns the result as a ResultSet, where each row is a column privilege description. In production applications, returning the result as a ResultSet is not that useful. It is better to return the result as XML so that the client application can extract the required information and display it in a desired fashion. Note that this privilege does not apply to all columns this may be true for some systems, but it is not true for all.

The getColumnPrivileges() method retrieves a description of the access rights for a table's columns. Only privileges matching the column name criteria are returned. They are ordered by COLUMN_NAME and PRIVILEGE.

Each privilege description has the columns shown in Table 2-4.

Table 2-4. *Columns for Result of getColumnPrivileges()*

Column's Position	Column's Name	Description
1	TABLE_CAT	Table catalog (may be null)
2	TABLE_SCHEM	Table schema (may be null)
3	TABLE_NAME	Table name (as a String)
4	COLUMN_NAME	Column name (as a String)
5	GRANTOR	Grantor of access (may be null)
6	GRANTEE	Grantee of access
7	PRIVILEGE	Name of access (SELECT, INSERT, UPDATE, REFERENCES, etc.)
8	IS_GRANTABLE	YES if grantee is permitted to grant to others; NO if not; null if unknown

getColumnPrivileges

```
public ResultSet getColumnPrivileges(String catalog,
                                     String schema,
                                     String table,
                                     String pattern)
                        throws SQLException
```

Here are the parameters for the getColumnPrivileges() method:

- catalog: A catalog name; it must match the catalog name as it is stored in the database. "" retrieves those without a catalog; null means that the catalog name should not be used to narrow the search.

- schema: A schema name; it must match the schema name as it is stored in the database. "" retrieves those without a schema; null means that the schema name should not be used to narrow the search.

- table: A table name; it must match the table name as it is stored in the database.

- pattern: A column name pattern; it must match the column name as it is stored in the database.

getColumnPrivileges returns a ResultSet, where each row is a column privilege description. It throws a SQLException if a database access error occurs.

The Solution: Get Table Column Privileges

```java
/**
 * Get Table Column Privileges: retrieves a description
 * of the access rights for a table's columns available in
 * a catalog.  The result is returned as XML (as a string
 * object);  if table name is null/empty it returns null.
 *
 * In JDBC, each privilege description has the following columns:
 *
 * TABLE_CAT String => table catalog (may be null)
 * TABLE_SCHEM String => table schema (may be null)
 * TABLE_NAME String => table name
 * COLUMN_NAME String => column name
 * GRANTOR => grantor of access (may be null)
 * GRANTEE String => grantee of access
 * PRIVILEGE String => name of access (SELECT, INSERT, UPDATE, REFERENCES, ...)
 * IS_GRANTABLE String => "YES" if grantee is permitted to grant
 *      to others; "NO" if not; null if unknown
 *
 * @param conn the Connection object
 * @param catalog a catalog.
 * @param schema a schema.
 * @param tableName a table name; must match
 *   the table name as it is stored in the database .
 * @param columnNamePattern a column name pattern.
 * @return an XML.
 * @exception Failed to get the Get Table Column Privileges.
 */
public static String getColumnPrivileges(java.sql.Connection conn,
                                    String catalog,
                                    String schema,
                                    String tableName,
                                    String columnNamePattern)
    throws Exception {
    ResultSet privileges = null;
    StringBuffer sb = new StringBuffer();
    try {
        if ((tableName == null) ||
            (tableName.length() == 0)) {
            return null;
        }

        DatabaseMetaData meta = conn.getMetaData();
        if (meta == null) {
            return null;
        }
```

```
            // The '_' character represents any single character.
            // The '%' character represents any sequence of zero
            // or more characters.
            // NOTE: if you pass a null to schema/tableName, then you might get
            // an exception or you might get an empty ResultSet object
            privileges = meta.getColumnPrivileges(catalog,
                                                  schema,
                                                  tableName,
                                                  columnNamePattern);
        sb.append("<privileges>");
        while (privileges.next()) {
            String dbCatalog = privileges.getString(COLUMN_NAME_TABLE_CATALOG);
            String dbSchema = privileges.getString(COLUMN_NAME_TABLE_SCHEMA);
            String dbTable = privileges.getString(COLUMN_NAME_TABLE_NAME);
            String dbColumn = privileges.getString(COLUMN_NAME_COLUMN_NAME);
            String dbPrivilege = privileges.getString(COLUMN_NAME_PRIVILEGE);
            String dbGrantor = privileges.getString(COLUMN_NAME_GRANTOR);
            String dbGrantee = privileges.getString(COLUMN_NAME_GRANTEE);
            String dbIsGrantable = privileges.getString(COLUMN_NAME_IS_GRANTABLE);

            sb.append("<column name=\"");
            sb.append(dbColumn);
            sb.append("\" table=\"");
            sb.append(tableName);
            sb.append("\"><catalog>");
            sb.append(dbCatalog);
            sb.append("</catalog><schema>");
            sb.append(dbSchema);
            sb.append("</schema><privilege>");
            sb.append(dbPrivilege);
            sb.append("</privilege><grantor>");
            sb.append(dbGrantor);
            sb.append("</grantor><isGrantable>");
            sb.append(dbIsGrantable);
            sb.append("</isGrantable><grantee>");
            sb.append(dbGrantee);
            sb.append("</grantee></column>");
        }
        sb.append("</privileges>");
        return sb.toString();
    }
    catch(Exception e) {
        throw new Exception("Error: could not get table column privileges: "+
                            e.toString());
    }
    finally {
        DatabaseUtil.close(privileges);
    }
}
```

Oracle: Test the Solution: Get Table Column Privileges

I tested getColumnPrivileges() for several Oracle tables, but I could not get any results (it seems that the Oracle driver does not support this feature at all).

The client call looks like this:

```
String columnPrivileges = DatabaseMetaDataTool.getColumnPrivileges
    (conn,                 // connection
     conn.getCatalog(),    // catalog
     "SYSTEM",             // schema
     "HELP",               // the help table
     "%");
System.out.println("---- Table's Columns Privileges ----");
System.out.println(columnPrivileges);
System.out.println("------------------------------------");
```

The output is

```
---- Table Column Privileges ----
<privileges>
</privileges>
------------------------------------
```

MySQL: Test the Solution: Get Table Column Privileges

The client call looks like this:

```
String columnPrivileges = DatabaseMetaDataTool.getColumnPrivileges
    (conn,                 // connection
     conn.getCatalog(),    // catalog
     null,                 // schema
     "artist",
     "%");
System.out.println("---- Table Column Privileges ----");
System.out.println(columnPrivileges);
System.out.println("------------------------------------");
```

The output is

```
---- Table Column Privileges ----
<privileges>
    <column name="ARTIST_ID" table="artist">
        <catalog>octopus</catalog>
        <schema>null</schema>
        <privilege>SELECT</privilege>
        <grantor>root@127.0.0.1</grantor>
        <isGrantable>null</isGrantable>
        <grantee>%@%</grantee>
    </column>
```

```
        <column name="ARTIST_NAME" table="artist">
            <catalog>octopus</catalog>
            <schema>null</schema>
            <privilege>SELECT</privilege>
            <grantor>root@127.0.0.1</grantor>
            <isGrantable>null</isGrantable>
            <grantee>%@%</grantee>
        </column>
    </privileges>
    -----------------------------------
```

2.18. How Do You Find the Number of Rows Affected by a SQL Query?

Suppose you execute a query to delete some rows and you want to know how many rows were deleted. In general, the JDBC API provides two methods (available in the java.sql.Statement interface) to find the number of rows affected by a SQL query: execute() and executeUpdate().

Get the Number of Rows Affected Using the executeUpdate() Method

Using the executeUpdate() method, we can get the number of rows affected:

```
Connection conn = ... get a java.sql.Connection object ...
String sqlQuery = "delete from employees where employee_status = 'inactive'";
Statement stmt = conn.createStatement();
int rowsAffected = stmt.executeUpdate(sqlQuery);
System.out.println("number of rows affected = "+ rowsAffected);
```

Also, we may write this as a method:

```
/**
 * Get the number of rows affected for a given SQL query.
 * @param conn the connection object.
 * @param sqlQuery the SQL query to be executed.
 * @return the number of rows affected by the execution of the SQL query.
 * @exception Failed to execute the SQL query.
 *
 */
public static int getNumberOfRowsAffected(Connection conn,
                                          String sqlQuery)
    throws Exception {
    Statement stmt = null;
    try {
        stmt = conn.createStatement();
        int rowsAffected = stmt.executeUpdate(sqlQuery);
        System.out.println("number of rows affected = "+ rowsAffected);
        return rowsAffected;
    }
```

```
        catch(Exception e) {
            throw new Exception(e.toString+
                        "could not get the number of rows affected");
        }
        finally {
            DatabaseUtil.close(stmt);
        }
    }
```

Get the Number of Rows Affected Using the execute() Method

The execute() method executes the given SQL query, which may return multiple results. This method returns a boolean (true/false). The execute() method returns true if the first result is a ResultSet object; it returns false if it is an update count or there are no results.

```
Connection conn = ... get a java.sql.Connection object ...
String sqlQuery = "delete from employees where employeeStatus = 'inactive'";
Statement stmt = conn.createStatement();
if (!stmt.execute(sqlQuery)) {
    //
    // then there is no result set
    // get the number of rows affected
    //
    int rowsAffected = stmt.getUpdateCount();
    System.out.println("number of rows affected = "+ rowsAffected);
}
```

Also, we may write this as a method:

```
/**
 * Get the number of rows affected for a given SQL query.
 * @param conn the connection object.
 * @param sqlQuery the SQL query to be executed.
 * @return the number of rows affected by the execution of the SQL query.
 * @exception Failed to execute the SQL query.
 *
 */
public static int getNumberOfRowsAffected(Connection conn,
                                          String sqlQuery)
    throws Exception {
    Statement stmt = null;
    try {
        stmt = conn.createStatement();
        if (!stmt.execute(sqlQuery)) {
            //
            // then there is no result set
            // get the number of rows affected
            //
            int rowsAffected = stmt.getUpdateCount();
```

```
            System.out.println("number of rows affected = "+ rowsAffected);
            return rowsAffected;
        }
        else {
            return 0;
        }
    }
    catch(Exception e) {
        throw new Exception(e.toString+
                "could not get the number of rows affected");
    }
    finally {
        DatabaseUtil.close(stmt);
    }
}
```

2.19. What Is a Table's Optimal Set of Columns That Uniquely Identify a Row?

To return a table's optimal set of columns that uniquely identify a row, you can use the DatabaseMetaData interface's getBestRowIdentifier() method. This method returns the result as a ResultSet object, which is not very useful to clients. You can provide a wrapper method, getBestRowIdentifier(), which is defined in the DatabaseMetaDataTool class. It returns the result in XML, and hence can be used by any type of client.

DatabaseMetaData.getBestRowIdentifier() Declaration

```
public ResultSet getBestRowIdentifier(String catalog,
                                      String schema,
                                      String table,
                                      int scope,
                                      boolean nullable)      throws SQLException
```

This method retrieves a description of a table's optimal set of columns that uniquely identifies a row. They are ordered by SCOPE. Table 2-5 describes the columns of a ResultSet object returned by getBestRowIdentifier().

Table 2-5. *Columns of ResultSet Returned by getBestRowIdentifier()*

Column Name	Column Type	Description
SCOPE	short	Actual scope of result: DatabaseMetaData.bestRowTemporary: Very temporary; only valid while using row DatabaseMetaData.bestRowTransaction: Valid for remainder of current transaction DatabaseMetaData.bestRowSession: Valid for remainder of current session
COLUMN_NAME	String	Column name.

Continued

Table 2-5. *Continued*

Column Name	Column Type	Description
DATA_TYPE	int	SQL data type from java.sql.Types.
TYPE_NAME	String	Data source–dependent type name; for a UDT the type name is fully qualified.
COLUMN_SIZE	int	Precision.
BUFFER_LENGTH	int	Not used.
DECIMAL_DIGITS	short	Scale.
PSEUDO_COLUMN	short	A pseudocolumn like an Oracle ROWID DatabaseMetaData.bestRowUnknown: May or may not be pseudocolumn DatabaseMetaData.bestRowNotPseudo: Is *not* a pseudocolumn DatabaseMetaData.bestRowPseudo: Is a pseudocolumn

Here are the getBestRowIdentifier() parameters:

- catalog: A catalog name; it must match the catalog name as it is stored in the database. "" retrieves those without a catalog; null means that the catalog name should not be used to narrow the search.

- schema: A schema name; it must match the schema name as it is stored in the database. "" retrieves those without a schema; null means that the schema name should not be used to narrow the search.

- table: A table name; it must match the table name as it is stored in the database.

- scope: The scope of interest; it uses the same values as SCOPE (defined earlier).

- nullable: Include columns that are nullable.

XML Syntax for Output

To be as complete as possible, I've expressed the output in XML syntax. This can help clients find the best row identifiers as easily as possible.

```xml
<?xml version='1.0'>
<BestRowIdentifier>
    <RowIdentifier tableName="database-table-name">
        <scope>actual-scope-of-result</scope>
        <columnName>column-name</columnName>
        <dataType>data-type</dataType>
        <typeName>type-name</typeName>
        <columnSize>size-of-column</columnSize>
        <decimalDigits>scale-for-numeric-columns</decimalDigits>
        <pseudoColumn>pseudo-column</pseudoColumn>
    </RowIdentifier>
    <RowIdentifier tableName="...">
    </RowIdentifier>
```

```
    ...
    <RowIdentifier tableName="...">
    </RowIdentifier>
</BestRowIdentifier>
```

The Solution: getBestRowIdentifier()

The solution is generic enough and can support MySQL, Oracle, and other relational databases.

```
/**
 * Retrieves a description of a table's optimal set of columns that
 * uniquely identifies a row. They are ordered by SCOPE  The result
 * is returned as an XML (as a serialized string object);  if table
 * name is null/empty it returns null.
 *
 * @param conn the Connection object
 * @param catalog  a catalog name; must match the catalog name
 *       as it is stored in the database; "" retrieves those without
 *       a catalog; null means that the catalog name should not be
 *       used to narrow the search
 * @param schema a schema name; must match the schema name as it
 *       is stored in the database; "" retrieves those without a
 *       schema; null means that the schema name should not be
 *       used to narrow the search
 * @param table  a table name; must match the table name as it
 *       is stored in the database
 * @param scope  the scope of interest; possible values are:
 *
 *       bestRowTemporary - very temporary, while using row
 *       bestRowTransaction - valid for remainder of current transaction
 *       bestRowSession - valid for remainder of current session
 *
 * @param nullable  include columns that are nullable.
 * @return the result is returned as an XML (serialized as a String object)
 * @exception Failed to get the Index Information.
 */
public static String getBestRowIdentifier(java.sql.Connection conn,
                                          String catalog,
                                          String schema,
                                          String table,
                                          int scope,
                                          boolean nullable)
    throws Exception {
    ResultSet rs = null;
    try {
        if ((table == null) || (table.length() == 0)) {
            return null;
        }
```

```java
        DatabaseMetaData meta = conn.getMetaData();
        if (meta == null) {
            return null;
        }

        // The '_' character represents any single character.
        // The '%' character represents any sequence of zero
        // or more characters.
        rs = meta.getBestRowIdentifier(catalog,
                                       schema,
                                       table,
                                       scope,
                                       nullable);
        StringBuilder sb = new StringBuilder("<?xml version='1.0'>");
        sb.append("<BestRowIdentifier>");
        while (rs.next()) {

            short actualScope = rs.getShort(COLUMN_NAME_SCOPE);
            String columnName = rs.getString(COLUMN_NAME_COLUMN_NAME);
            int dataType = rs.getInt(COLUMN_NAME_DATA_TYPE);
            String typeName = rs.getString(COLUMN_NAME_TYPE_NAME);
            int columnSize = rs.getInt(COLUMN_NAME_COLUMN_SIZE);
            short decimalDigits = rs.getShort(COLUMN_NAME_DECIMAL_DIGITS);
            short pseudoColumn = rs.getShort(COLUMN_NAME_PSEUDO_COLUMN);

            sb.append("<RowIdentifier tableName=\"");
            sb.append(table);
            sb.append("\">");
            appendXMLTag(sb, "scope", actualScope);
            appendXMLTag(sb, "columnName", columnName);
            appendXMLTag(sb, "dataType", dataType);
            appendXMLTag(sb, "typeName", typeName);
            appendXMLTag(sb, "columnSize", columnSize);
            appendXMLTag(sb, "decimalDigits", decimalDigits);
            appendXMLTag(sb, "pseudoColumn", pseudoColumn);
            sb.append("</RowIdentifier>");
        }
        sb.append("</BestRowIdentifier>");
        return sb.toString();
    }
    catch(Exception e) {
        throw new Exception("Error: could not get table's "+
            "Best Row Identifier: "+e.toString());
    }
    finally {
        DatabaseUtil.close(rs);
    }
}
```

Discussion of Schema and Catalog

- The MySQL database does not understand "schema"; you have to use "catalog."

- The Oracle database does not understand "catalog"; you have to use "schema."

- For databases, check their JDBC documentation.

Client Using MySQL

```java
import java.util.*;
import java.io.*;
import java.sql.*;

import jcb.db.*;
import jcb.meta.*;

public class TestMySqlDatabaseMetaDataTool_BestRowIdentifier {

    public static Connection getConnection() throws Exception {
        String driver = "org.gjt.mm.mysql.Driver";
        String url = "jdbc:mysql://localhost/octopus";
        String username = "root";
        String password = "root";
        Class.forName(driver);  // load MySQL driver
        return DriverManager.getConnection(url, username, password);
    }

    public static void main(String[] args) {
        Connection conn = null;
        try {
            conn = getConnection();
            System.out.println("-------- getBestRowIdentifier ------");
            System.out.println("conn="+conn);
            String bestRowIdentifier =
                DatabaseMetaDataTool.getBestRowIdentifier
                    (conn,
                    "",                  // schema
                    conn.getCatalog(), // catalog
                    "MYPICTURES",  // table name
                    DatabaseMetaData.bestRowTemporary, // scope
                    false);     // nullable
            System.out.println(bestRowIdentifier);
            System.out.println("----------------------------------");
        }
        catch(Exception e){
            e.printStackTrace();
            System.exit(1);
        }
```

```
        finally {
            DatabaseUtil.close(conn);
        }
    }
}
```

Output Using MySQL

```
-------- getBestRowIdentifier ------
conn=com.mysql.jdbc.Connection@1837697
<?xml version='1.0'>
<BestRowIdentifier>
    <RowIdentifier tableName="MYPICTURES">
        <scope>2</scope>
        <columnName>id</columnName>
        <dataType>0</dataType>
        <typeName>(11)</typeName>
        <columnSize>11</columnSize>
        <decimalDigits>0</decimalDigits>
        <pseudoColumn>1</pseudoColumn>
    </RowIdentifier>
</BestRowIdentifier>
------------------------------------
```

Oracle Database Setup

```
$ sqlplus octopus/octopus
SQL*Plus: Release 9.2.0.1.0 - Production on Thu Feb 20 17:02:51 2003
SQL> describe employees;
 Name              Null?    Type
 ----------------- -------- ----------------------------
 BADGENUMBER       NOT NULL NUMBER(38)
 NAME                       VARCHAR2(60)
 EMPLOYEETYPE               VARCHAR2(30)
 PHOTO                      BINARY FILE LOB
```

Client Using an Oracle Database

```
import java.util.*;
import java.io.*;
import java.sql.*;

import jcb.db.*;
import jcb.meta.*;

public class TestOracleDatabaseMetaDataTool_BestRowIdentifier {
```

```java
public static Connection getConnection() throws Exception {
    String driver = "oracle.jdbc.driver.OracleDriver";
    String url = "jdbc:oracle:thin:@localhost:1521:maui";
    String username = "octopus";
    String password = "octopus";
    Class.forName(driver);  // load Oracle driver
    return DriverManager.getConnection(url, username, password);
}

public static void main(String[] args) {
    Connection conn = null;
    try {
        conn = getConnection();
        System.out.println("-------- getBestRowIdentifier -------------");
        System.out.println("conn="+conn);
        String bestRowIdentifier =
            DatabaseMetaDataTool.getBestRowIdentifier
                (conn,
                 "",              // schema
                 "OCTOPUS",       // user
                 "EMPLOYEES",     // table name
                 DatabaseMetaData.bestRowTransaction,   // scope
                 false);     // nullable
        System.out.println(bestRowIdentifier);
        System.out.println("-----------------------------------");
    }
    catch(Exception e){
        e.printStackTrace();
        System.exit(1);
    }
    finally {
        DatabaseUtil.close(conn);
    }
}

}
```

Running the Solution for an Oracle Database

The following output is formatted to fit the page:

```
-------- getBestRowIdentifier -------------
conn=oracle.jdbc.driver.OracleConnection@169ca65
<?xml version='1.0'>
<BestRowIdentifier>
    <RowIdentifier tableName="EMPLOYEES">
        <scope>1</scope>
```

```
            <columnName>ROWID</columnName>
            <dataType>-8</dataType>
            <typeName>ROWID</typeName>
            <columnSize>0</columnSize>
            <decimalDigits>0</decimalDigits>
            <pseudoColumn>2</pseudoColumn>
        </RowIdentifier>
        <RowIdentifier tableName="EMPLOYEES">
            <scope>2</scope>
            <columnName>BADGENUMBER</columnName>
            <dataType>3</dataType>
            <typeName>NUMBER</typeName>
            <columnSize>22</columnSize>
            <decimalDigits>0</decimalDigits>
            <pseudoColumn>1</pseudoColumn>
        </RowIdentifier>
    </BestRowIdentifier>
    -----------------------------------
```

CHAPTER 3

∎∎∎

Database Metadata, Part 2

Those who are enamored of practice without theory are like a pilot who goes into a ship without rudder or compass and never has any certainty where he is going.

Leonardo da Vinci

This chapter continues where Chapter 2 left off and shows you how to use JDBC's database metadata API. This API lets you obtain information about tables, views, column names, column types, indexes, table and column privileges, stored procedures, result sets, and databases.

3.1. What Are a Table's Indexes?

According to Wikipedia, "an index is a feature in a database that allows quick access to the rows in a table. The index is created using one or more columns of the table." You can use the `DatabaseMetaData` interface's `getIndexInfo()` method to find the indexes for a specified table. This section illustrates how you'd use `getIndexInfo()`; we define a couple of indexes and then run our solution against a sample table called `ACCOUNT`. The signature of `getIndexInfo()` is

```
public ResultSet getIndexInfo(String catalog,
                              String schema,
                              String table,
                              boolean unique,
                              boolean approximate)
        throws SQLException;
```

The method's parameters are

- `catalog`: A catalog name. It must match the catalog name as it is stored in this database. `""` retrieves those without a catalog; `null` means that the catalog name should not be used to narrow the search.

- `schema`: A schema name. It must match the schema name as it is stored in this database. `""` retrieves those without a schema; `null` means that the schema name should not be used to narrow the search.

- `table`: A table name; must match the table name as it is stored in this database.

- `unique`: When `true`, returns only indexes for unique values; when `false`, returns indexes regardless of whether or not values are unique.

- approximate: When true, the result is allowed to reflect approximate or out-of-date values; when false, the results are requested to be accurate (all table statistics are exact). Some drivers (such as the MiniSoft JDBC Driver) ignore this parameter and ensure that all table statistics are exact.

This method retrieves a ResultSet object containing information about the indexes or keys for the table. The returned ResultSet is ordered by NON_UNIQUE, TYPE, INDEX_NAME, and ORDINAL_POSITION. Each index column description has the columns shown in Table 3-1 (each row has 13 columns).

Table 3-1. *Result Columns for Invoking getIndexInfo()*

Field Name	Type	Description
TABLE_CAT	String	Table catalog (may be null).
TABLE_SCHEM	String	Table schema (may be null).
TABLE_NAME	String	Table name.
NON_UNIQUE	boolean	Indicates whether index values can be non-unique. false when TYPE is tableIndexStatistic.
INDEX_QUALIFIER	String	Index catalog (may be null); null when TYPE is tableIndexStatistic.
INDEX_NAME	String	Index name; null when TYPE is tableIndexStatistic.
TYPE	short	Index type: tableIndexStatistic: Identifies table statistics that are returned in conjunction with a table's index descriptions tableIndexClustered: Is a clustered index tableIndexHashed: Is a hashed index tableIndexOther: Is some other style of index
ORDINAL_POSITION	short	Column sequence number within the index; zero when TYPE is tableIndexStatistic.
COLUMN_NAME	String	Column name; null when TYPE is tableIndexStatistic.
ASC_OR_DESC	String	Column sort sequence. A means ascending; D means descending; may be null if sort sequence is not supported; null when TYPE is tableIndexStatistic.
CARDINALITY	int	When TYPE is tableIndexStatistic, then this is the number of rows in the table; otherwise, it is the number of unique values in the index.
PAGES	int	When TYPE is tableIndexStatistic, then this is the number of pages used for the table, otherwise it is the number of pages used for the current index.
FILTER_CONDITION	String	Filter condition, if any (may be null).

This method returns ResultSet, in which each row is an index column description. If a database access error occurs, it throws SQLException.

As you can see from the returned ResultSet, it contains a lot of information. The best way to represent that information is XML, which may be used by any type of client.

The Solution: getIndexInformation()

The index information can be useful in sending proper SQL queries to the database. During runtime, for better response from the database, in formulating SQL's SELECT statement you can use the index columns in the WHERE clauses (otherwise, the database tables will be scanned sequentially). In passing actual parameters to the DatabaseMetaData.getIndexInfo() method, try to minimize passing null and empty values (passing null values might slow down your metadata retrieval).

```
/**
 * Retrieves a description of the given table's indexes and
 * statistics.  The result is returned as XML (as a string
 * object);  if table name is null/empty it returns null.
 *
 *
 * @param conn the Connection object
 * @param catalog a catalog.
 * @param schema a schema.
 * @param tableName a table name; must match
 *  the table name as it is stored in the database.
 * @param unique when true, return only indexes for unique values;
 * when false, return indexes regardless of whether unique or not
 * @param approximate when true, result is allowed to reflect
 * approximate or out of data values; when false, results are
 * requested to be accurate
 * @return an XML.
 * @exception Failed to get the Index Information.
 */
public static String getIndexInformation(java.sql.Connection conn,
                                         String catalog,
                                         String schema,
                                         String tableName,
                                         boolean unique,
                                         boolean approximate)
    throws Exception {
    ResultSet rs = null;
    try {
        if ((tableName == null) ||
            (tableName.length() == 0)) {
            return null;
        }

        DatabaseMetaData meta = conn.getMetaData();
        if (meta == null) {
            return null;
        }
```

```
                // The '_' character represents any single character.
                // The '%' character represents any sequence of zero
                // or more characters.
                rs = meta.getIndexInfo(catalog, schema, tableName,
                                       unique, approximate);
                StringBuffer sb = new StringBuffer("<?xml version='1.0'>");
                sb.append("<indexInformation>");
                while (indexInformation.next()) {
                   String dbCatalog = rs.getString(COLUMN_NAME_TABLE_CATALOG);
                   String dbSchema = rs.getString(COLUMN_NAME_TABLE_SCHEMA);
                   String dbTableName = rs.getString(COLUMN_NAME_TABLE_NAME);
                   boolean dbNoneUnique =rs.getBoolean(COLUMN_NAME_NON_UNIQUE);
                   String dbIndexQualifier = rs.getString(COLUMN_NAME_INDEX_QUALIFIER);
                   String dbIndexName = rs.getString(COLUMN_NAME_INDEX_NAME);
                   short dbType = rs.getShort(COLUMN_NAME_TYPE);
                   short dbOrdinalPosition = rs.getShort(COLUMN_NAME_ORDINAL_POSITION);
                   String dbColumnName = rs.getString(COLUMN_NAME_COLUMN_NAME);
                   String dbAscOrDesc = rs.getString(COLUMN_NAME_ASC_OR_DESC);
                   int dbCardinality = rs.getInt(COLUMN_NAME_CARDINALITY);
                   int dbPages = rs.getInt(COLUMN_NAME_PAGES);
                   String dbFilterCondition = rs.getString(COLUMN_NAME_FILTER_CONDITION);
                   sb.append("<index name=\"");
                   sb.append(dbIndexName);
                   sb.append("\" table=\"");
                   sb.append(dbTableName);
                   sb.append("\" column=\"");
                   sb.append(dbColumnName);
                   sb.append("\">");
                   appendXMLTag(sb, "catalog", dbCatalog);
                   appendXMLTag(sb, "schema", dbSchema);
                   appendXMLTag(sb, "nonUnique", dbNoneUnique);
                   appendXMLTag(sb, "indexQualifier", dbIndexQualifier);
                   appendXMLTag(sb, "type", dbType);
                   appendXMLTag(sb, "ordinalPosition", dbOrdinalPosition);
                   appendXMLTag(sb, "ascendingOrDescending", dbAscOrDesc);
                   appendXMLTag(sb, "cardinality", dbCardinality);
                   appendXMLTag(sb, "pages", dbPages);
                   appendXMLTag(sb, "filterCondition", dbFilterCondition);
                   sb.append("</index>");
                }
                sb.append("</indexInformation>");
                    return sb.toString();
                }
                catch(Exception e) {
                    throw new Exception("could not get table's Index Info: "+e.toString());
                }
                finally {
                    DatabaseUtil.close(rs);
                }
            }
```

Oracle Database Setup

For testing, let's create an ACCOUNT table and a couple of indexes:

```
$ sqlplus octopus/octopus
SQL*Plus: Release 9.2.0.1.0 - Production on Sat Feb 15 18:07:05 2003

SQL> create table ACCOUNT(
  2     id   varchar(20) not null primary key,
  3     owner varchar(60) not null,
  4     balance number,
  5     status  varchar(10));

Table created.

SQL> describe ACCOUNT;
 Name              Null?    Type
 ----------------  -------- ------------
 ID                NOT NULL VARCHAR2(20)
 OWNER             NOT NULL VARCHAR2(60)
 BALANCE                    NUMBER
 STATUS                     VARCHAR2(10)
```

Next, let's create some indexes on the ACCOUNT table using the Oracle database. Since id is a primary key, Oracle will automatically create a unique index for this column; we define three additional indexes.

```
SQL> create index ID_OWNER_INDEX on ACCOUNT(id, owner);
SQL> create index ID_STATUS_INDEX on ACCOUNT(id, status);
SQL> create unique index OWNER_INDEX on ACCOUNT(owner);
SQL> commit;
Commit complete.
```

Client 1: Oracle

```
System.out.println("-------- getIndexInformation -------------");
String indexInformation = DatabaseMetaDataTool.getIndexInformation
                (conn,
                "",
                "OCTOPUS",      // user
                "ACCOUNT",      // table name
                true,           // unique indexes?
                true);
System.out.println("-------- getIndexInformation -------------");
System.out.println(indexInformation);
System.out.println("----------------------------------");
```

Output 1: Oracle

Note that when the index type is tableIndexStatistic, the index name will be null. When the schema does not assign a proper index name (for example, for primary keys), the database server will assign a generated name.

```xml
<?xml version='1.0'>
<indexInformation>
    <index name="null" table="ACCOUNT" column="null">
        <catalog>null</catalog>
        <schema>OCTOPUS</schema>
        <nonUnique>false</nonUnique>
        <indexQualifier>null</indexQualifier>
        <type>tableIndexStatistic</type>
        <ordinalPosition>0</ordinalPosition>
        <ascendingOrDescending>null</ascendingOrDescending>
        <cardinality>0</cardinality>
        <pages>0</pages>
        <filterCondition>null</filterCondition>
    </index>
    <index name="OWNER_INDEX" table="ACCOUNT" column="OWNER">
        <catalog>null</catalog>
        <schema>OCTOPUS</schema>
        <nonUnique>false</nonUnique>
        <indexQualifier>null</indexQualifier>
        <type>tableIndexClustered</type>
        <ordinalPosition>1</ordinalPosition>
        <ascendingOrDescending>null</ascendingOrDescending>
        <cardinality>0</cardinality>
        <pages>0</pages>
        <filterCondition>null</filterCondition>
    </index>
    <index name="SYS_C003011" table="ACCOUNT" column="ID">
        <catalog>null</catalog>
        <schema>OCTOPUS</schema>
        <nonUnique>false</nonUnique>
        <indexQualifier>null</indexQualifier>
        <type>tableIndexClustered</type>
        <ordinalPosition>1</ordinalPosition>
        <ascendingOrDescending>null</ascendingOrDescending>
        <cardinality>0</cardinality>
        <pages>0</pages>
        <filterCondition>null</filterCondition>
    </index>
</indexInformation>
```

Client 2: Oracle

```
System.out.println("-------- getIndexInformation -------------");
String indexInformation = DatabaseMetaDataTool.getIndexInformation
                    (conn,
                    "",
                    "OCTOPUS",      // user
                    "ACCOUNT",      // table name
                    false,          // unique indexes?
                    true);
System.out.println("-------- getIndexInformation -------------");
System.out.println(indexInformation);
System.out.println("----------------------------------");
```

Output 2: Oracle

```
<?xml version='1.0'>
<indexInformation>
    <index name="null" table="ACCOUNT" column="null">
        <catalog>null</catalog>
        <schema>OCTOPUS</schema>
        <nonUnique>false</nonUnique>
        <indexQualifier>null</indexQualifier>
        <type>tableIndexStatistic</type>
        <ordinalPosition>0</ordinalPosition>
        <ascendingOrDescending>null</ascendingOrDescending>
        <cardinality>0</cardinality>
        <pages>0</pages>
        <filterCondition>null</filterCondition>
    </index>
    <index name="OWNER_INDEX" table="ACCOUNT" column="OWNER">
        <catalog>null</catalog>
        <schema>OCTOPUS</schema>
        <nonUnique>false</nonUnique>
        <indexQualifier>null</indexQualifier>
        <type>tableIndexClustered</type>
        <ordinalPosition>1</ordinalPosition>
        <ascendingOrDescending>null</ascendingOrDescending>
        <cardinality>0</cardinality>
        <pages>0</pages>
        <filterCondition>null</filterCondition>
        </index>
    <index name="SYS_C003011" table="ACCOUNT" column="ID">
        <catalog>null</catalog>
        <schema>OCTOPUS</schema>
        <nonUnique>false</nonUnique>
        <indexQualifier>null</indexQualifier>
        <type>tableIndexClustered</type>
```

```
    <ordinalPosition>1</ordinalPosition>
    <ascendingOrDescending>null</ascendingOrDescending>
    <cardinality>0</cardinality>
    <pages>0</pages>
    <filterCondition>null</filterCondition>
</index>
<index name="ID_OWNER_INDEX" table="ACCOUNT" column="ID">
    <catalog>null</catalog>
    <schema>OCTOPUS</schema>
    <nonUnique>true</nonUnique>
    <indexQualifier>null</indexQualifier>
    <type>tableIndexClustered</type>
    <ordinalPosition>1</ordinalPosition>
    <ascendingOrDescending>null</ascendingOrDescending>
    <cardinality>0</cardinality>
    <pages>0</pages>
    <filterCondition>null</filterCondition>
</index>
<index name="ID_OWNER_INDEX" table="ACCOUNT" column="OWNER">
    <catalog>null</catalog>
    <schema>OCTOPUS</schema>
    <nonUnique>true</nonUnique>
    <indexQualifier>null</indexQualifier>
    <type>tableIndexClustered</type>
    <ordinalPosition>2</ordinalPosition>
    <ascendingOrDescending>null</ascendingOrDescending>
    <cardinality>0</cardinality>
    <pages>0</pages>
    <filterCondition>null</filterCondition>
</index>
<index name="ID_STATUS_INDEX" table="ACCOUNT" column="ID">
    <catalog>null</catalog>
    <schema>OCTOPUS</schema>
    <nonUnique>true</nonUnique>
    <indexQualifier>null</indexQualifier>
    <type>tableIndexClustered</type>
    <ordinalPosition>1</ordinalPosition>
    <ascendingOrDescending>null</ascendingOrDescending>
    <cardinality>0</cardinality>
    <pages>0</pages>
    <filterCondition>null</filterCondition>
</index>
<index name="ID_STATUS_INDEX" table="ACCOUNT" column="STATUS">
    <catalog>null</catalog>
    <schema>OCTOPUS</schema>
    <nonUnique>true</nonUnique>
    <indexQualifier>null</indexQualifier>
```

```
        <type>tableIndexClustered</type>
        <ordinalPosition>2</ordinalPosition>
        <ascendingOrDescending>null</ascendingOrDescending>
        <cardinality>0</cardinality>
        <pages>0</pages>
        <filterCondition>null</filterCondition>
    </index>
</indexInformation>
```

MySQL Database Setup

For testing, let's create an ACCOUNT table and a couple of indexes:

```
mysql> create table ACCOUNT( id  varchar(20) not null primary key,
    -> owner varchar(60) not null,
    -> balance integer, status  varchar(10));
Query OK, 0 rows affected (0.10 sec)
mysql> describe ACCOUNT;
+---------+-------------+------+-----+---------+-------+
| Field   | Type        | Null | Key | Default | Extra |
+---------+-------------+------+-----+---------+-------+
| id      | varchar(20) |      | PRI |         |       |
| owner   | varchar(60) |      |     |         |       |
| balance | int(11)     | YES  |     | NULL    |       |
| status  | varchar(10) | YES  |     | NULL    |       |
+---------+-------------+------+-----+---------+-------+
4 rows in set (0.05 sec)
```

Next, let's create some indexes on the ACCOUNT table using the MySQL database. Because id is a primary key, MySQL will automatically create a unique index for this column; we define three additional indexes.

```
mysql> create index ID_OWNER_INDEX on ACCOUNT(id, owner);
Query OK, 0 rows affected (0.29 sec)
Records: 0  Duplicates: 0  Warnings: 0
mysql>  create index ID_STATUS_INDEX on ACCOUNT(id, status);
Query OK, 0 rows affected (0.29 sec)
Records: 0  Duplicates: 0  Warnings: 0
mysql> create unique index OWNER_INDEX on ACCOUNT(owner);
Query OK, 0 rows affected (0.26 sec)
Records: 0  Duplicates: 0  Warnings: 0
mysql> commit;
Query OK, 0 rows affected (0.00 sec)
mysql>  describe ACCOUNT;
```

```
+---------+-------------+------+-----+---------+-------+
| Field   | Type        | Null | Key | Default | Extra |
+---------+-------------+------+-----+---------+-------+
| id      | varchar(20) |      | PRI |         |       |
| owner   | varchar(60) |      | UNI |         |       |
| balance | int(11)     | YES  |     | NULL    |       |
| status  | varchar(10) | YES  |     | NULL    |       |
+---------+-------------+------+-----+---------+-------+
4 rows in set (0.02 sec)
```

Client 1: MySQL

```java
System.out.println("-------- getIndexInformation -------------");
String indexInformation = DatabaseMetaDataTool.getIndexInformation
                    (conn,
                    conn.getCatalog(),
                    null,          // MySQL has no schema
                    "ACCOUNT",      // table name
                    true,          // unique indexes?
                    true);
System.out.println("-------- getIndexInformation -------------");
System.out.println(indexInformation);
System.out.println("----------------------------------");
```

Output 1: MySQL

```xml
<?xml version='1.0'>
<indexInformation>
    <index name="PRIMARY" table="ACCOUNT" column="id">
        <catalog>tiger</catalog>
        <schema>null</schema>
        <nonUnique>false</nonUnique>
        <indexQualifier></indexQualifier>
        <type>tableIndexOther</type>
        <ordinalPosition>1</ordinalPosition>
        <ascendingOrDescending>A</ascendingOrDescending>
        <cardinality>0</cardinality>
        <pages>0</pages>
        <filterCondition>null</filterCondition>
    </index>
    <index name="OWNER_INDEX" table="ACCOUNT" column="owner">
        <catalog>tiger</catalog>
        <schema>null</schema>
        <nonUnique>false</nonUnique>
        <indexQualifier></indexQualifier>
        <type>tableIndexOther</type>
        <ordinalPosition>1</ordinalPosition>
```

```
        <ascendingOrDescending>A</ascendingOrDescending>
        <cardinality>0</cardinality>
        <pages>0</pages>
        <filterCondition>null</filterCondition>
    </index>
    <index name="ID_OWNER_INDEX" table="ACCOUNT" column="id">
        <catalog>tiger</catalog>
        <schema>null</schema>
        <nonUnique>true</nonUnique>
        <indexQualifier></indexQualifier>
        <type>tableIndexOther</type>
        <ordinalPosition>1</ordinalPosition>
        <ascendingOrDescending>A</ascendingOrDescending>
        <cardinality>0</cardinality>
        <pages>0</pages>
        <filterCondition>null</filterCondition>
    </index>
    <index name="ID_OWNER_INDEX" table="ACCOUNT" column="owner">
        <catalog>tiger</catalog>
        <schema>null</schema>
        <nonUnique>true</nonUnique>
        <indexQualifier></indexQualifier>
        <type>tableIndexOther</type>
        <ordinalPosition>2</ordinalPosition>
        <ascendingOrDescending>A</ascendingOrDescending>
        <cardinality>0</cardinality>
        <pages>0</pages>
        <filterCondition>null</filterCondition>
    </index>
    <index name="ID_STATUS_INDEX" table="ACCOUNT" column="id">
        <catalog>tiger</catalog>
        <schema>null</schema>
        <nonUnique>true</nonUnique>
        <indexQualifier></indexQualifier>
        <type>tableIndexOther</type>
        <ordinalPosition>1</ordinalPosition>
        <ascendingOrDescending>A</ascendingOrDescending>
        <cardinality>0</cardinality>
        <pages>0</pages>
        <filterCondition>null</filterCondition>
    </index>
    <index name="ID_STATUS_INDEX" table="ACCOUNT" column="status">
        <catalog>tiger</catalog>
        <schema>null</schema>
        <nonUnique>true</nonUnique>
        <indexQualifier></indexQualifier>
        <type>tableIndexOther</type>
```

```
        <ordinalPosition>2</ordinalPosition>
        <ascendingOrDescending>A</ascendingOrDescending>
        <cardinality>0</cardinality>
        <pages>0</pages>
        <filterCondition>null</filterCondition>
    </index>
</indexInformation>
```

Client 2: MySQL

```
    System.out.println("-------- getIndexInformation -------------");
    String indexInformation = DatabaseMetaDataTool.getIndexInformation
                    (conn,
                     conn.getCatalog(),
                     null,          // MySQL has no schema
                     "ACCOUNT",     // table name
                     false,         // unique indexes?
                     true);
    System.out.println("-------- getIndexInformation -------------");
    System.out.println(indexInformation);
    System.out.println("----------------------------------");
```

Output 2: MySQL

```
<?xml version='1.0'>
<indexInformation>
    <index name="PRIMARY" table="ACCOUNT" column="id">
        <catalog>tiger</catalog>
        <schema>null</schema>
        <nonUnique>false</nonUnique>
        <indexQualifier></indexQualifier>
        <type>tableIndexOther</type>
        <ordinalPosition>1</ordinalPosition>
        <ascendingOrDescending>A</ascendingOrDescending>
        <cardinality>0</cardinality>
        <pages>0</pages>
        <filterCondition>null</filterCondition>
    </index>
    <index name="OWNER_INDEX" table="ACCOUNT" column="owner">
        <catalog>tiger</catalog>
        <schema>null</schema>
        <nonUnique>false</nonUnique>
        <indexQualifier></indexQualifier>
        <type>tableIndexOther</type>
        <ordinalPosition>1</ordinalPosition>
        <ascendingOrDescending>A</ascendingOrDescending>
```

```
        <cardinality>0</cardinality>
        <pages>0</pages>
        <filterCondition>null</filterCondition>
    </index>
    <index name="ID_OWNER_INDEX" table="ACCOUNT" column="id">
        <catalog>tiger</catalog>
        <schema>null</schema>
        <nonUnique>true</nonUnique>
        <indexQualifier></indexQualifier>
        <type>tableIndexOther</type>
        <ordinalPosition>1</ordinalPosition>
        <ascendingOrDescending>A</ascendingOrDescending>
        <cardinality>0</cardinality>
        <pages>0</pages>
        <filterCondition>null</filterCondition>
    </index>
    <index name="ID_OWNER_INDEX" table="ACCOUNT" column="owner">
        <catalog>tiger</catalog>
        <schema>null</schema>
        <nonUnique>true</nonUnique>
        <indexQualifier></indexQualifier>
        <type>tableIndexOther</type>
        <ordinalPosition>2</ordinalPosition>
        <ascendingOrDescending>A</ascendingOrDescending>
        <cardinality>0</cardinality>
        <pages>0</pages>
        <filterCondition>null</filterCondition>
    </index>
    <index name="ID_STATUS_INDEX" table="ACCOUNT" column="id">
        <catalog>tiger</catalog>
        <schema>null</schema>
        <nonUnique>true</nonUnique>
        <indexQualifier></indexQualifier>
        <type>tableIndexOther</type>
        <ordinalPosition>1</ordinalPosition>
        <ascendingOrDescending>A</ascendingOrDescending>
        <cardinality>0</cardinality>
        <pages>0</pages>
        <filterCondition>null</filterCondition>
    </index>
    <index name="ID_STATUS_INDEX" table="ACCOUNT" column="status">
        <catalog>tiger</catalog>
        <schema>null</schema>
        <nonUnique>true</nonUnique>
        <indexQualifier></indexQualifier>
        <type>tableIndexOther</type>
        <ordinalPosition>2</ordinalPosition>
```

```
            <ascendingOrDescending>A</ascendingOrDescending>
            <cardinality>0</cardinality>
            <pages>0</pages>
            <filterCondition>null</filterCondition>
        </index>
</indexInformation>
```

3.2. Does an Index Exist for a Specific Table?

Given a table, such as the ACCOUNT table created in the previous section, you can find out
whether a particular index exists. There is no such explicit method in the JDBC API, but you
can use the DatabaseMetaData.getIndexInfo() method in the solution to solve the problem.

The Solution: indexExists()

```
public static boolean indexExists(java.sql.Connection conn,
                                  String catalog,
                                  String schema,
                                  String tableName,
                                  String indexName)
    throws Exception {
    if ((tableName == null) || (tableName.length() == 0) ||
        (indexName == null) || (indexName.length() == 0)) {
        return false;
    }

    DatabaseMetaData dbMetaData = conn.getMetaData();
    if (dbMetaData == null) {
        return false;
    }

    ResultSet rs = dbMetaData.getIndexInfo(catalog,
                schema, tableName, false, true);
    while (rs.next()) {
        String dbIndexName = rs.getString(COLUMN_NAME_INDEX_NAME);
        if (indexName.equalsIgnoreCase(dbIndexName)) {
            return true;
        }
    }
    return false;
}
```

A Client: MySQL

```
System.out.println("-------- Does index exist? -------------");
System.out.println("conn="+conn);
boolean indexExist = DatabaseMetaDataTool.indexExists
            (conn,
             conn.getCatalog(),     // catalog
             null,                  // schema
             "ACCOUNT",             // table name
             "ID_STATUS_INDEX");    // index name
System.out.println("Index name: ID_STATUS_INDEX");
System.out.println("Table name: ACCOUNT");
System.out.println("Index Exist?: " + indexExist);

System.out.println("-------- Does index exist? -------------");
boolean indexExist22 = DatabaseMetaDataTool.indexExists
            (conn,
             conn.getCatalog(),     // catalog
             null,                  // schema
             "ACCOUNT",             // table name
             "ID_STATUS_INDEX22");  // index name
System.out.println("Index name: ID_STATUS_INDEX22");
System.out.println("Table name: ACCOUNT");
System.out.println("Index Exist?: " + indexExist22);
```

Output: MySQL

```
-------- Does index exist? -------------
conn=com.mysql.jdbc.Connection@337d0f
Index name: ID_STATUS_INDEX
Table name: ACCOUNT
Index Exist?: true
-------- Does index exist? -------------
Index name: ID_STATUS_INDEX22
Table name: ACCOUNT
Index Exist?: false
```

A Client: Oracle

```
System.out.println("-------- Does index exist? -------------");
System.out.println("conn="+conn);
boolean indexExist = DatabaseMetaDataTool.indexExists
            (conn,
             conn.getCatalog(),     // catalog
             null,                  // schema
             "ACCOUNT",             // table name
             "ID_STATUS_INDEX");    // index name
```

```
System.out.println("Index name: ID_STATUS_INDEX");
System.out.println("Table name: ACCOUNT");
System.out.println("Index Exist?: " + indexExist);

System.out.println("-------- Does index exist? -------------");
boolean indexExist22 = DatabaseMetaDataTool.indexExists
            (conn,
             conn.getCatalog(),      // catalog
             null,                   // schema
             "ACCOUNT",           // table name
             "ID_STATUS_INDEX22");   // index name
System.out.println("Index name: ID_STATUS_INDEX22");
System.out.println("Table name: ACCOUNT");
System.out.println("Index Exist?: " + indexExist22);
```

Output: Oracle

```
-------- Does index exist? -------------
conn=oracle.jdbc.driver.OracleConnection@d0a5d9
Index name: ID_STATUS_INDEX
Table name: ACCOUNT
Index Exist?: true
-------- Does index exist? -------------
Index name: ID_STATUS_INDEX22
Table name: ACCOUNT
Index Exist?: false
```

3.3. What Are the Names of a Database's Stored Procedures?

In a relational database management system such as Oracle, a *stored procedure* is a precompiled set of SQL statements and queries that can be shared by a number of programs. It is stored under a name as an executable unit. A *stored function* is similar to a function (like in Java and C/C++); it accepts zero, one, or more parameters and returns a single result.

Stored procedures and functions are helpful in the following ways:

- **Controlling access to data**: They can restrict client programs to data accessible only through the stored procedure.

- **Preserving data integrity**: They ensure that information is entered in a consistent manner.

- **Improving productivity**: You need to write a stored procedure only once.

Oracle, Microsoft SQL Server 2000, and Sybase Adaptive Server support stored procedures, but MySQL does not (stored procedures and views will be supported in MySQL 5.0.1, however). In general, you can use stored procedures to maximize security and increase data access efficiency. Because stored procedures execute in the database server, they minimize the network traffic between applications and the database, increasing application and system performance. Most of the time, stored procedures run faster than SQL. They also allow you to isolate your SQL code from your application.

Using Oracle9i database, consider the following table:

```
SQL> describe zemps;
```

Name	Null?	Type
ID	NOT NULL	NUMBER(38)
FIRSTNAME	NOT NULL	VARCHAR2(32)
LASTNAME	NOT NULL	VARCHAR2(32)
DEPT	NOT NULL	VARCHAR2(32)
TITLE		VARCHAR2(32)
SALARY		NUMBER(38)
EMAIL		VARCHAR2(64)
COUNTRY		VARCHAR2(32)

Next, try a basic query of the zemps table:

```
SQL> select id, firstName, lastName from zemps;
       ID  FIRSTNAME          LASTNAME
---------- ----------         -----------
     4401  Donald             Knuth
     4402  Charles            Barkeley
     4403  Alex               Badame
     4404  Jeff               Torrango
     4405  Mary               Smith
     4406  Alex               Sitraka
     4408  Jessica            Clinton
     4409  Betty              Dillon
     5501  Troy               Briggs
     5502  Barb               Tayloy
     6601  Pedro              Hayward
     6602  Chris              Appleseed
     6603  Tao                Yang
     6604  Kelvin             Liu

14 rows selected.
```

The following stored procedure, getEmpCount, returns the number of records in the zemps table:

```
SQL> CREATE OR REPLACE function getEmpCount return int is
  2      empCount int;
  3  BEGIN
  4      SELECT count(*) INTO empCount FROM zEmps;
  5      RETURN empCount;
  6  END getEmpCount;
  7
  8
  9  /
```

```
Function created.
```

In order to make sure that getEmpCount is created correctly, you can execute it as follows, without passing any parameters:

```
SQL> var empCount number;
SQL> exec :empCount := getEmpCount;
PL/SQL procedure successfully completed.
SQL> print empCount;
   EMPCOUNT
----------
        14
```

The output proves that the getEmpCount performed correctly because it returned 14, which is the total number of records in the zemps table.

Overloading Stored Procedures

Oracle's PL/SQL allows two or more packaged subprograms to have the same name. A *package* is a set of logically related functions and procedures, also known as a stored procedure. When stored procedures have the same name but different parameters, this is called *overloading*. This option is useful when you want a subprogram or function to accept parameters that have different data types. Be very cautious when you call overloaded subprogram or functions. You must make sure that you are passing the expected number of arguments and data types. For example, in Oracle 9i, the following package defines two functions named empPackage.

Oracle's package specification is as follows:

```
CREATE or REPLACE PACKAGE empPackage AS
    FUNCTION getEmployeeID(eFirstName VARCHAR2) return INT;
    FUNCTION getEmployeeID(eFirstName VARCHAR2, eLastName VARCHAR2) return INT;
END empPackage;
```

Oracle's package implementation is as follows:

```
CREATE or REPLACE PACKAGE BODY empPackage AS
    FUNCTION getEmployeeID (eFirstName VARCHAR2) return INT is
       cmpID INT;
    BEGIN
       SELECT id INTO empID FROM zEmps where firstName = eFirstName;
       RETURN empID;
    END getEmployeeID;
```

```
    FUNCTION getEmployeeID (eFirstName VARCHAR2, eLastName VARCHAR2) return INT is
        empID INT;
    BEGIN
        SELECT id INTO empID FROM zEmps
                where firstName = eFirstName and lastName = eLastName;
        RETURN empID;
    END getEmployeeID;
END empPackage;
```

Here's the `empPackage` description from the database:

```
SQL> describe empPackage;
FUNCTION GETEMPLOYEEID RETURNS NUMBER(38)
 Argument Name                  Type                    In/Out Default?
 ------------------------------ ----------------------- ------ --------
 EFIRSTNAME                     VARCHAR2                IN
FUNCTION GETEMPLOYEEID RETURNS NUMBER(38)
 Argument Name                  Type                    In/Out Default?
 ------------------------------ ----------------------- ------ --------
 EFIRSTNAME                     VARCHAR2                IN
 ELASTNAME                      VARCHAR2                IN
```

Now execute these two functions:

```
SQL> var id1 NUMBER;
SQL> exec :id1:= empPackage.getEmployeeID('Donald');
PL/SQL procedure successfully completed.
SQL> print id1;
     ID1
----------
     4401
SQL> var id2 NUMBER;
SQL> exec :id2:= empPackage.getEmployeeID('Betty', 'Dillon');
PL/SQL procedure successfully completed.
SQL> print id2;
     ID2
----------
     4409
```

■ **Note** You may be wondering what this discussion has to do with getting the names of the stored procedures. This is because stored procedure names can be overloaded, and so you must be very careful in selecting the stored procedure names and their associated input parameter types.

How Can You Find the Package Code in Oracle?

The following SQL statement provides a way to see the Oracle package code:

```
select LINE, TEXT
    from USER_SOURCE
        where NAME ='&PKG' and TYPE = '&PACKAGE_TYPE'
```

where:

- PKG refers to the package name.

- PACKAGE_TYPE is the PACKAGE for the package specification.

- PACKAGE BODY displays the body.

What Is the user_source Table?

The user_source table, which is a property of Oracle's SYS user, is as follows. The output has been modified to include a description column.

```
SQL> describe user_source;
 Name   Type           Description
 ----   -------------- ----------------------------
 NAME   VARCHAR2(30)   Name of the object
 TYPE   VARCHAR2(12)   Type of the object: "TYPE", "TYPE BODY",
                       "PROCEDURE", "FUNCTION", "PACKAGE",
                       "PACKAGE BODY" or "JAVA SOURCE"'
 LINE   NUMBER         Line number of this line of source
 TEXT   VARCHAR2(4000) Source text

SQL> select name, type, line from user_source;

NAME                            TYPE            LINE
------------------------------- ------------- ----------
EMPPACKAGE                      PACKAGE            1
EMPPACKAGE                      PACKAGE            2
EMPPACKAGE                      PACKAGE            3
EMPPACKAGE                      PACKAGE            4
EMPPACKAGE                      PACKAGE BODY       1
EMPPACKAGE                      PACKAGE BODY       2
EMPPACKAGE                      PACKAGE BODY       3
EMPPACKAGE                      PACKAGE BODY       4
EMPPACKAGE                      PACKAGE BODY       5
EMPPACKAGE                      PACKAGE BODY       6
EMPPACKAGE                      PACKAGE BODY       7
EMPPACKAGE                      PACKAGE BODY       8
EMPPACKAGE                      PACKAGE BODY       9
EMPPACKAGE                      PACKAGE BODY      10
EMPPACKAGE                      PACKAGE BODY      11
```

EMPPACKAGE	PACKAGE BODY	12
EMPPACKAGE	PACKAGE BODY	13
EMPPACKAGE	PACKAGE BODY	14
EMPPACKAGE	PACKAGE BODY	15
GETEMPCOUNT	FUNCTION	1
GETEMPCOUNT	FUNCTION	2
GETEMPCOUNT	FUNCTION	3
GETEMPCOUNT	FUNCTION	4
GETEMPCOUNT	FUNCTION	5
GETEMPCOUNT	FUNCTION	6
GETEMPCOUNT	FUNCTION	7

```
26 rows selected.
```

What Are the Names of a Database's Stored Procedures?

In the JDBC API, you can use the DatabaseMetaData.getProcedures() method to get the names of a database's stored procedures and functions. However, this is not sufficient for very large databases. For example, in an Oracle database, DatabaseMetadata.getProcedures() can return hundreds of stored procedures; most are system stored procedures, which most likely you do not need to retrieve. When you call this method, be as specific as possible when you provide names and patterns.

JDBC Solution: getProcedures()

Using JDBC, you can use DatabaseMetaData.getProcedures() to retrieve stored procedure names: To have a better performance, try to pass as much as information you can and avoid passing empty and null values to the DatabaseMetaData.getProcedures() method. Passing empty and null values might have a poor performance, and this is due to the fact that it might search all database catalogs and schemas. Therefore, it is best to pass as much as information (actual parameter values) to the DatabaseMetaData.getProcedures() method.

```
/**
 * Get the stored procedures names.
 * @param conn the Connection object
 * @return a table of stored procedures names
 * as an XML document (represented as a String object).
 * Each element of XML document will have the name and
 * type of a stored procedure.
 *
 */
public static String getStoredProcedureNames
    (java.sql.Connection conn,
     String catalog,
     String schemaPattern,
     String procedureNamePattern) throws Exception {
    ResultSet rs = null;
```

```
    try {
        DatabaseMetaData meta = conn.getMetaData();
        if (meta == null) {
            return null;
        }

        rs = meta.getProcedures(catalog, schemaPattern, procedureNamePattern);
        StringBuffer sb = new StringBuffer();
        sb.append("<storedProcedures>");

        while (rs.next()) {
            String spName = rs.getString("PROCEDURE_NAME");
            String spType = getStoredProcedureType(rs.getInt("PROCEDURE_TYPE"));
            sb.append("<storedProcedure name=\"");
            sb.append(spName);
            sb.append("\" type=\"");
            sb.append(spType);
            sb.append("\"/>");
        }
        sb.append("</storedProcedures>");
        return sb.toString();
    }
    finally {
        DatabaseUtil.close(rs);
    }
}

private static String getStoredProcedureType(int spType) {
    if (spType == DatabaseMetaData.procedureReturnsResult) {
        return STORED_PROCEDURE_RETURNS_RESULT;
    }
    else if (spType == DatabaseMetaData.procedureNoResult) {
        return STORED_PROCEDURE_NO_RESULT;
    }
    else {
        return STORED_PROCEDURE_RESULT_UNKNOWN;
    }
}
```

A Client Program

Before invoking a client program, let's add another stored function: the getEmployeeCount stored function returns the number of employees for a specific department.

```
SQL> create FUNCTION getEmployeeCount(dept INTEGER) RETURN INTEGER IS
  2     empCount INTEGER;
  3  BEGIN
  4     SELECT count(*) INTO empCount FROM EMPLOYEE
  5            WHERE deptNumber = dept;
  6     RETURN empCount;
  7  END getEmployeeCount;
  8  /

Function created.

SQL> describe getEmployeeCount;
FUNCTION getEmployeeCount RETURNS NUMBER(38)
 Argument Name             Type                 In/Out Default?
 ------------------------- -------------------- ------ --------
 DEPT                      NUMBER(38)           IN

SQL> var empCount number;
SQL> exec :empCount := getEmployeeCount(23)

PL/SQL procedure successfully completed.

SQL> print empCount;

  EMPCOUNT
----------
         3
```

A Client Program

```
String spNames = DatabaseMetaDataTool.getStoredProcedureNames
                    (conn,
                     "",
                     "OCTOPUS",
                     "%");
System.out.println("-------- getStoredProcedureNames -------------");
System.out.println(spNames);
System.out.println("-----------------------------------");
```

Output of the Client Program

```
<storedProcedures>
    <storedProcedure name="GETEMPLOYEECOUNT" type="procedureReturnsResult"/>
    <storedProcedure name="RAISESALARY" type="procedureNoResult"/>
    <storedProcedure name="SHOWUSERS" type="procedureNoResult"/>
</storedProcedures>
```

3.4. What Is the Signature of a Stored Procedure?

How can a client investigate the parameters to send into and receive from a database stored procedure? Understanding the signature of a stored procedure is important for SQL adapter development in order to obtain the signature information at runtime. A signature is the name of the procedure and the name and type of its arguments. The DatabaseMetaData interface provides a method, getProcedureColumns(), which returns detailed metadata information on arguments (columns) of stored procedures. This section provides a few tables and stored procedures that will help you understand how best to use the getProcedureColumns() method.

The MySQL database does not support stored procedures yet, but it will in future releases (starting with MySQL 5.0.1). We'll focus here on the Oracle database. We'll define a table, called EMPLOYEE, and a stored procedure, raiseSalary, to retrieve the salary of a specific department as a percentage.

Oracle Database Setup

```
SQL> create table EMPLOYEE (
  2     badgeNumber number(4) not null,
  3     empName varchar2(40) not null,
  4     jobTitle varchar2(30),
  5     manager number(4),
  6     hireDate date,
  7     salary number(7,2),
  8     deptNumber number(2)
  9  );

Table created.

SQL> describe employee;
 Name               Null?     Type
 ----------------   --------  -------------
 BADGENUMBER        NOT NULL  NUMBER(4)
 EMPNAME            NOT NULL  VARCHAR2(40)
 JOBTITLE                     VARCHAR2(30)
 MANAGER                      NUMBER(4)
 HIREDATE                     DATE
 SALARY                       NUMBER(7,2)
 DEPTNUMBER                   NUMBER(2)
```

Next, let's insert some records into an EMPLOYEE table:

```
SQL> insert into EMPLOYEE(badgeNumber , empName, jobTitle, hireDate,
  2  salary, deptNumber)
  3  values(1111, 'Alex Smith', 'Manager', '12-JAN-1981', 78000.00, 23);

SQL> insert into EMPLOYEE(badgeNumber , empName, jobTitle, manager,
  2  hireDate, salary, deptNumber)
  3  values(2222, 'Jane Taylor', 'Engineer', 1111, '12-DEC-1988', 65000.00, 23);
```

```
SQL> insert into EMPLOYEE(badgeNumber , empName, jobTitle, manager,
  2 hireDate, salary, deptNumber)
  3 values(3333, 'Art Karpov', 'Engineer', 1111, '12-DEC-1978', 80000.00, 23);

SQL> insert into EMPLOYEE(badgeNumber , empName, jobTitle, manager,
  2 hireDate, salary, deptNumber)
  3 values(4444, 'Bob Price', 'Engineer', 1111, '12-DEC-1979', 70000.00, 55);

SQL> commit;
Commit complete.

SQL> select badgeNumber, empName, salary, deptNumber  from employee;

BADGENUMBER EMPNAME              SALARY DEPTNUMBER
----------- ---------------- ---------- ----------
       1111 Alex Smith         78000         23
       2222 Jane Taylor        65000         23
       3333 Art Karpov         80000         23
       4444 Bob Price          70000         55
```

Next, let's create a stored procedure called raiseSalary:

```
SQL> create procedure raiseSalary(deptNumber_Param number,
  2                               percentage_Param number DEFAULT 0.20) is
  3     cursor empCursor (dept_number number) is
  4            select salary from EMPLOYEE where deptNumber = dept_number
  5                    for update of salary;
  6
  7     empsal number(8);
  8  begin
  9     open empCursor(deptNumber_Param);
 10     loop
 11            fetch empCursor into empsal;
 12            exit when empCursor%NOTFOUND;
 13            update EMPLOYEE set salary = empsal * ((100 + percentage_Param)/100)
 14                    where current of empCursor;
 15     end loop;
 16     close empCursor;
 17     commit;
 18  end raisesalary;
 19  /

Procedure created.
```

```
SQL> describe raiseSalary;
PROCEDURE raiseSalary
 Argument Name                    Type                    In/Out Default?
 ------------------------------   ----------------------- ------ --------
 DEPTNUMBER_PARAM                 NUMBER                  IN
 PERCENTAGE_PARAM                 NUMBER                  IN     DEFAULT
```

Invoking/Executing raiseSalary As a Stored Procedure

In order to raise the salary of all employees in department number 23, run raiseSalary as follows:

```
SQL> execute raiseSalary(23, 10);
PL/SQL procedure successfully completed.


SQL> select badgeNumber, empName, salary, deptNumber  from employee;

BADGENUMBER EMPNAME             SALARY DEPTNUMBER
----------- ---------------- ---------- ----------
       1111 Alex Smith          85800         23
       2222 Jane Taylor         71500         23
       3333 Art Karpov          88000         23
       4444 Bob Price           70000         55
```

The Solution: getStoredProcedureSignature()

The getStoredProcedureSignature() method retrieves the signature of a stored procedure and returns the metadata as an XML object, serialized as a String object for efficiency purposes. Here is the signature of getStoredProcedureSignature():

```
/**
 * Retrieves a description of the given catalog's stored
 * procedure parameter and result columns. This method
 * calls getProcedureColumns() to get the signature
 * and then transforms the result set into XML.
 *
 * @param conn the Connection object
 * @param catalog a catalog.
 * @param schemaPattern a schema pattern.
 * @param procedureNamePattern name of a stored procedure
 * @param columnNamePattern a column name pattern.
 * @return an XML.
 * @throws Exception Failed to get the stored procedure's signature.
 */
```

```
public static String getStoredProcedureSignature(
        java.sql.Connection conn,
        String catalog,
        String schemaPattern,
        String procedureNamePattern,
        String columnNamePattern)

    throws Exception {...}
```

Oracle9i Considerations for the getProcedureColumns() Method

Inside our solution, getStoredProcedureSignature(), we call getProcedureColumns(), to which we have to give special consideration. According to Oracle, the methods getProcedures() and getProcedureColumns() (defined in the DatabaseMetaData interface) treat the catalog, schemaPattern, columnNamePattern, and procedureNamePattern parameters in the same way. In the Oracle definition of these methods, the parameters are treated differently. Table 3-2 is taken from the Oracle 9i documentation.

Table 3-2. *The getProcedureColumns() Method According to Oracle*

Field Name	Description
catalog	Oracle does not have multiple catalogs, but it does have packages. Consequently, the catalog parameter is treated as the package name. This applies both on input (the catalog parameter) and output (the catalog column in the returned ResultSet). On input, the construct "" (the empty string) retrieves procedures and arguments without a package, that is, standalone objects. A null value means to drop from the selection criteria, that is, return information about both standalone and packaged objects (same as passing in "%"). Otherwise, the catalog parameter should be a package name pattern (with SQL wildcards, if desired).
schemaPattern	All objects within Oracle must have a schema, so it does not make sense to return information for those objects without one. Thus, the construct "" (the empty string) is interpreted on input to mean the objects in the current schema (that is, the one to which you are currently connected). To be consistent with the behavior of the catalog parameter, null is interpreted to drop the schema from the selection criteria (same as passing in "%"). It can also be used as a pattern with SQL wildcards.
procedureNamePattern	The empty string ("") does not make sense for either parameter, because all procedures and arguments must have names. Thus, the construct "" will raise an exception. To be consistent with the behavior of other parameters, null has the same effect as passing in "%".
columnNamePattern	The empty string ("") does not make sense for either parameter, because all procedures and arguments must have names. Thus, the construct "" will raise an exception. To be consistent with the behavior of other parameters, null has the same effect as passing in "%".

A Weakness for the JDBC Metadata

Before we delve into the signature of this method, let's look at a weakness of the getProcedureColumns() method: inside getStoredProcedureSignature(), we use the method getProcedureColumns() in the interface DatabaseMetaData to obtain a stored procedure's metadata. The exact usage is described in the code that follows. You should note that this method (getProcedureColumns()) can only discover *parameter* values. Some databases (such as Sybase and Microsoft's SQL Server 2000) can return multiple result sets without using any arguments. For databases where a returning ResultSet is created simply by executing a SQL SELECT statement within a stored procedure (thus not sending the return ResultSet to the client application via a declared parameter), the real return value of the stored procedure cannot be detected. This is a weakness for the JDBC metadata.

Signature of getProcedureColumns()

The getProcedureColumns() method's signature is defined in JDK1.4.2 as follows:

```
public ResultSet getProcedureColumns
   (String catalog,
    String schemaPattern,
    String procedureNamePattern, // in Oracle it must be uppercase
    String columnNamePattern)
throws SQLException
```

This method retrieves a description of the given catalog's stored procedure parameter and result columns. Only descriptions matching the schema, procedure, and parameter name criteria are returned. They are ordered by PROCEDURE_SCHEM and PROCEDURE_NAME. Within this, the return value, if any, is first. Next are the parameter descriptions in call order. The column descriptions follow in column number order.

Each row in the ResultSet is a parameter or column description with the fields shown in Table 3-3.

Table 3-3. *Parameter or Column Description Fields*

Field Name	Type	Description
PROCEDURE_CAT	String	The procedure catalog (may be null).
PROCEDURE_SCHEM	String	The procedure schema (may be null).
PROCEDURE_NAME	String	The procedure name.
COLUMN_NAME	String	The column/parameter name.
COLUMN_TYPE	Short	The kind of column or parameter: procedureColumnUnknown: Unknown procedureColumnIn: The IN parameter procedureColumnInOut: The INOUT parameter procedureColumnOut: The OUT parameter procedureColumnReturn: The procedure's return value procedureColumnResult: The result column in ResultSet
DATA_TYPE	int	SQL type from java.sql.Types
TYPE_NAME	String	SQL type name; for a UDT type, the type name is fully qualified.
PRECISION	int	Precision.
LENGTH	int	The length in bytes of data.
SCALE	short	The scale.
RADIX	short	The radix.

Field Name	Type	Description
NULLABLE	short	Specifies whether it can contain NULL: procedureNoNulls: Does not allow NULL values procedureNullable: Allows NULL values procedureNullableUnknown: Nullability unknown
REMARKS	String	A comment describing the parameter or column.

Note Some databases may not return the column descriptions for a procedure. Additional columns beyond REMARKS can be defined by the database.

The parameters for this method are as follows:

- catalog: A catalog name; it must match the catalog name as it is stored in the database. "" retrieves those without a catalog; null means that the catalog name should not be used to narrow the search.

- schemaPattern: A schema name pattern; it must match the schema name as it is stored in the database. "" retrieves those without a schema; null means that the schema name should not be used to narrow the search.

- procedureNamePattern: A procedure name pattern; it must match the procedure name as it is stored in the database.

- columnNamePattern: A column name pattern; it must match the column name as it is stored in the database.

This method returns a ResultSet in which each row describes a stored procedure parameter or column. If a database access error occurs, it throws a SQLException.

The Complete Solution: getStoredProcedureSignature()

You need to be careful in invoking the DatabaseMetaData.getProcedureColumns() method. First, make sure that you pass actual parameter values for catalogs and schemas rather than passing empty and null values (this will speed up your method call). Second, be aware of overloaded stored procedures (each database vendor might handle overloaded stored procedures differently—refer to the vendor's database documentation).

```
/**
    * Retrieves a description of the given catalog's stored
    * procedure parameter and result columns.
    *
    * @param conn the Connection object
    * @param catalog a catalog.
    * @param schemaPattern a schema pattern.
    * @param procedureNamePattern name of a stored procedure
```

```
 * @param columnNamePattern a column name pattern.
 * @return XML.
 * @throws Exception Failed to get the stored procedure's signature.
 */
public static String getStoredProcedureSignature(
        java.sql.Connection conn,
        String catalog,
        String schemaPattern,
        String procedureNamePattern,
        String columnNamePattern) throws Exception {

    // Get DatabaseMetaData
    DatabaseMetaData dbMetaData = conn.getMetaData();
    if (dbMetaData == null) {
        return null;
    }
    ResultSet rs = dbMetaData.getProcedureColumns(catalog,
                                      schemaPattern,
                                      procedureNamePattern,
                                      columnNamePattern);

    StringBuffer sb = new StringBuffer("<?xml version='1.0'>");
    sb.append("<stored_procedures_signature>");
    while(rs.next()) {
        // get stored procedure metadata
        String procedureCatalog    = rs.getString(1);
        String procedureSchema     = rs.getString(2);
        String procedureName       = rs.getString(3);
        String columnName          = rs.getString(4);
        short  columnReturn        = rs.getShort(5);
        int    columnDataType      = rs.getInt(6);
        String columnReturnTypeName = rs.getString(7);
        int    columnPrecision     = rs.getInt(8);
        int    columnByteLength    = rs.getInt(9);
        short  columnScale         = rs.getShort(10);
        short  columnRadix         = rs.getShort(11);
        short  columnNullable      = rs.getShort(12);
        String columnRemarks       = rs.getString(13);

        sb.append("<storedProcedure name=\"");
        sb.append(procedureName);
        sb.append("\">");
        appendXMLTag(sb, "catalog", procedureCatalog);
        appendXMLTag(sb, "schema", procedureSchema);
        appendXMLTag(sb, "columnName", columnName);
        appendXMLTag(sb, "columnReturn", getColumnReturn(columnReturn));
        appendXMLTag(sb, "columnDataType", columnDataType);
```

```
            appendXMLTag(sb, "columnReturnTypeName", columnReturnTypeName);
            appendXMLTag(sb, "columnPrecision", columnPrecision);
            appendXMLTag(sb, "columnByteLength", columnByteLength);
            appendXMLTag(sb, "columnScale", columnScale);
            appendXMLTag(sb, "columnRadix", columnRadix);
            appendXMLTag(sb, "columnNullable", columnNullable);
            appendXMLTag(sb, "columnRemarks", columnRemarks);
            sb.append("</storedProcedure>");
        }
        sb.append("</stored_procedures_signature>");

        // Close database resources
        rs.close();
        //conn.close();
        return sb.toString();
    }
```

getColumnReturn():

```
    private static String getColumnReturn(short columnReturn) {
        switch(columnReturn) {
            case DatabaseMetaData.procedureColumnIn:
                return "In";
            case DatabaseMetaData.procedureColumnOut:
                return "Out";
            case DatabaseMetaData.procedureColumnInOut:
                return "In/Out";
            case DatabaseMetaData.procedureColumnReturn:
                return "return value";
            case DatabaseMetaData.procedureColumnResult:
                return "return ResultSet";
            default:
              return "unknown";
        }
    }
```

appendXMLTag():

```
    private static void appendXMLTag(StringBuffer buffer,
                                     String tagName,
                                     int value) {
        buffer.append("<");
        buffer.append(tagName);
        buffer.append(">");
        buffer.append(value);
        buffer.append("</");
        buffer.append(tagName);
        buffer.append(">");
    }
```

```
    private static void appendXMLTag(StringBuffer buffer,
                                     String tagName,
                                     String value) {
        buffer.append("<");
        buffer.append(tagName);
        buffer.append(">");
        buffer.append(value);
        buffer.append("</");
        buffer.append(tagName);
        buffer.append(">");
    }
}
```

Client Program 1

```
    String signature = DatabaseMetaDataTool.getStoredProcedureSignature
                        (conn,
                         "",
                         "OCTOPUS",       // user
                         "RAISESALARY",   // stored procedure name
                         "%");            // all columns
    System.out.println(signature);
```

Output of Client Program 1

```
<?xml version='1.0'>
<stored_procedures_signature>

    <storedProcedure name="RAISESALARY">
        <catalog>null</catalog>
        <schema>OCTOPUS</schema>
        <columnName>DEPTNUMBERPARAM</columnName>
        <columnReturn>In</columnReturn>
        <columnDataType>3</columnDataType>
        <columnReturnTypeName>NUMBER</columnReturnTypeName>
        <columnPrecision>22</columnPrecision>
        <columnByteLength>22</columnByteLength>
        <columnScale>0</columnScale>
        <columnRadix>10</columnRadix>
        <columnNullable>1</columnNullable>
        <columnRemarks>null</columnRemarks>
    </storedProcedure>

    <storedProcedure name="RAISESALARY">
        <catalog>null</catalog>
        <schema>OCTOPUS</schema>
        <columnName>PERCENTAGE</columnName>
        <columnReturn>In</columnReturn>
```

```
            <columnDataType>3</columnDataType>
            <columnReturnTypeName>NUMBER</columnReturnTypeName>
            <columnPrecision>22</columnPrecision>
            <columnByteLength>22</columnByteLength>
            <columnScale>0</columnScale>
            <columnRadix>10</columnRadix>
            <columnNullable>1</columnNullable>
            <columnRemarks>null</columnRemarks>
        </storedProcedure>

</stored_procedures_signature>
```

Client Program 2

For this client program, let's define another stored procedure (call it showUsers, which lists all of the users) that does not have any arguments. Note that the all_users table holds all of the users in the Oracle database.

```
SQL> describe all_users;
 Name                                     Null?    Type
 ---------------------------------------- -------- ------------------
 USERNAME                                 NOT NULL VARCHAR2(30)
 USER_ID                                  NOT NULL NUMBER
 CREATED                                  NOT NULL DATE
SQL>
SQL> CREATE OR REPLACE PROCEDURE showUsers AS
  2  BEGIN
  3    for A_USER  in ( SELECT *  from all_users ) LOOP
  4  --       do something
  5            DBMS_OUTPUT.PUT_LINE('UserName: '|| A_USER.UserName);
  6    end loop;
  7  END showUsers;
  8  /
Procedure created.
SQL> describe showusers;
PROCEDURE showusers

SQL> set serveroutput on
SQL> exec showUsers;
UserName: SYS
UserName: SYSTEM
UserName: OUTLN
UserName: DBSNMP
...
```

```
UserName: QS_CBADM
UserName: QS_CB
UserName: QS_CS
UserName: SCOTT
UserName: OCTOPUS

PL/SQL procedure successfully completed.
    String signature = DatabaseMetaDataTool.getStoredProcedureSignature
                          (conn,
                          "",
                          "OCTOPUS",      // user
                          "SHOWUSERS",    // stored procedure name
                          "%");           // all columns
        System.out.println(signature);
```

Output of Client Program 2

As you can observe, there are no signature definitions for the showUsers stored procedure because showUsers has no arguments whatsoever.

```
<?xml version='1.0'>
<stored_procedures_signature>
</stored_procedures_signature>
```

3.5. What Is the Username of the Database Connection?

You can use DatabaseMetaData to get the name of the database user used in creating a connection object. The following snippet shows how:

```
import java.sql.Connection;
import java.sql.DatabaseMetaData;
...
Connection conn = null;
try {
    conn = getConnection(); // returns a Connection
    DatabaseMetaData dbMetaData = conn.getMetaData();
    if (dbMetaData == null) {
        System.out.prinln("database does not support metadata.");
        System.exit(0);
    }

    // retrieve the user name as known to this database.
    String user = dbMetaData.getUserName();
    System.out.prinln("database user="+user);
}
catch(Exception e) {
    // handle the exception
    e.printStackTrace();
}
```

3.6. Is the Database Connection Read-Only?

In GUI database applications, before letting the user insert or update records, you need to make sure that the given Connection object is updatable (which means that records can be inserted or updated). To check for this, you can use the DatabaseMetaData.isReadOnly() method. This method returns true if the associated database is in read-only mode (which means that inserts or updates are not allowed). The following snippet shows how to use this method:

```
import java.sql.Connection;
import java.sql.DatabaseMetaData;
...
Connection conn = null;
DatabaseMetaData dbMetaData = null;
try {
  conn = getConnection();   // get a valid database connection
  dbMetaData = conn.getMetaData();
  if (dbMetaData == null) {
    // database metadata is NOT supported
  }
  else {
    // database metadata is supported and you can invoke
    // over 100 methods defined in DatabaseMetaData

    // check to see if the database is read-only
    boolean readOnly = dbMetaData.isReadOnly();
    if (readOnly) {
      // insert/updates are not allowed
    }
    else {
      // insert/updates are allowed
    }
    ...
  }
}
catch(SQLException e) {
  // deal and handle the exception
  ...
}
finally {
  // close resources
}
```

3.7. What Is the JDBC's Driver Information?

DatabaseMetaData has four driver-related methods, which are discussed in this section. We will combine all of them into a single method called getDriverInformation() and return the result as XML (serialized as a String object).

DatabaseMetaData Methods Supporting Driver Information

```
int getJDBCMajorVersion()
    // Retrieves the major JDBC version number for this driver.
int getJDBCMinorVersion()
    // Retrieves the minor JDBC version number for this driver.
String getDriverName()
    // Retrieves the name of this JDBC driver.
String getDriverVersion()
    // Retrieves the version number of this JDBC driver as a String.
```

XML Syntax for Output (Driver Information)

```
<?xml version='1.0'>
<DriverInformation>
    <driverName>driver name</driverName>
    <driverVersion>driver version</driverVersion>
    <jdbcMajorVersion>JDBC major version</jdbcMajorVersion>
    <jdbcMinorVersion>JDBC minor version</jdbcMinorVersion>
</DriverInformation>
```

The Solution

The solution is generic enough and can support MySQL, Oracle, and other relational databases.

```
/**
 * Get driver name and version information.
 * This method calls 4 methods (getDriverName(),
 * getDriverVersion(), getJDBCMajorVersion(),
 * getJDBCMinorVersion()) to get the required information
 * and it returns the information as XML.
 *
 * @param conn the Connection object
 * @return driver name and version information
 * as an XML document (represented as a String object).
 *
 */
public static String getDriverInformation(java.sql.Connection conn)
    throws Exception {
    try {
        DatabaseMetaData meta = conn.getMetaData();
        if (meta == null) {
            return null;
        }

        StringBuffer sb = new StringBuffer("<?xml version='1.0'>");
        sb.append("<DriverInformation>");
```

```
            // Oracle (and some other vendors) do not support
            // some the following methods; therefore, we need
            // to use a try-catch block.
            try {
                int jdbcMajorVersion = meta.getJDBCMajorVersion();
                appendXMLTag(sb, "jdbcMajorVersion", jdbcMajorVersion);
            }
            catch(Exception e) {
                appendXMLTag(sb, "jdbcMajorVersion", "unsupported feature");
            }

            try {
                int jdbcMinorVersion = meta.getJDBCMinorVersion();
                appendXMLTag(sb, "jdbcMinorVersion", jdbcMinorVersion);
            }
            catch(Exception e) {
                appendXMLTag(sb, "jdbcMinorVersion", "unsupported feature");
            }

            String driverName = meta.getDriverName();
            String driverVersion = meta.getDriverVersion();
            appendXMLTag(sb, "driverName", driverName);
            appendXMLTag(sb, "driverVersion", driverVersion);
            sb.append("</DriverInformation>");

            return sb.toString();
        }
        catch(Exception e) {
            // handle exception
            e.printStackTrace();
            throw new Exception("could not get the database information:"+
                e.toString());
        }
    }
}
```

Discussion

To get the driver information (such as the name and version), we call the methods (listed earlier) and the result is returned as XML. The advantage of our solution is that you get the required information with a single call and the result (as XML) can be used by any kind of client. Note that oracle.jdbc.OracleDatabaseMetaData.getJDBCMajorVersion() and oracle.jdbc.OracleDatabaseMetaData.getJDBCMinorVersion() are unsupported features; therefore, we have to use a try-catch block. If the method returns a SQLException, we return the message "unsupported feature" in the XML result. The driver information does not change frequently and therefore it can be cached in the server-side.

Client Using MySQL

```java
import java.util.*;
import java.io.*;
import java.sql.*;

import jcb.db.*;
import jcb.meta.*;

public class TestMySqlDatabaseMetaDataTool_DriverInformation {

    public static Connection getConnection() throws Exception {
        String driver = "org.gjt.mm.mysql.Driver";
        String url = "jdbc:mysql://localhost/octopus";
        String username = "root";
        String password = "root";
        Class.forName(driver);  // load MySQL driver
        Return DriverManager.getConnection(url, username, password);
    }

    public static void main(String[] args) {
        Connection conn = null;
        try {
            conn = getConnection();
            System.out.println("-------- getDriverInformation -------------");
            System.out.println("conn="+conn);
            String driverInfo = DatabaseMetaDataTool.getDriverInformation(conn);
            System.out.println(driverInfo);
            System.out.println("-----------------------------------");
        }
        catch(Exception e){
            e.printStackTrace();
            System.exit(1);
        }
        finally {
            DatabaseUtil.close(conn);
        }
    }
}
```

Output Using MySQL

```
-------- getDriverInformation ------
conn=com.mysql.jdbc.Connection@1837697
<?xml version='1.0'>
<DriverInformation>
   <jdbcMajorVersion>3</jdbcMajorVersion>
   <jdbcMinorVersion>0</jdbcMinorVersion>
```

```
   <driverName>MySQL-AB JDBC Driver</driverName>
   <driverVersion>3.0.5-gamma</driverVersion>
</DriverInformation>
------------------------------------
```

Client Using Oracle

```java
import java.util.*;
import java.io.*;
import java.sql.*;

import jcb.db.*;
import jcb.meta.*;

public class TestOracleDatabaseMetaDataTool_DriverInformation {
   public static Connection getConnection() throws Exception {
      String driver = "oracle.jdbc.driver.OracleDriver";
      String url = "jdbc:oracle:thin:@localhost:1521:maui";
      String username = "octopus";
      String password = "octopus";
      Class.forName(driver);    // load Oracle driver
      return DriverManager.getConnection(url, username, password);
   }

   public static void main(String[] args) {
      Connection conn = null;
      try {
         conn = getConnection();
         System.out.println("-------- getDriverInformation ------------");
         System.out.println("conn="+conn);
         String driverInfo = DatabaseMetaDataTool.getDriverInformation(conn);
         System.out.println(driverInfo);
         System.out.println("-----------------------------------");
      }
      catch (Exception e){
         e.printStackTrace();
         System.exit(1);
      }
      finally {
         DatabaseUtil.close(conn);
      }
   }
}
```

Output Using Oracle

The following output is formatted to fit the page:

```
-------- getDriverInformation ------
conn=oracle.jdbc.driver.OracleConnection@169ca65
<?xml version='1.0'>
<DriverInformation>
   <jdbcMajorVersion>unsupported feature</jdbcMajorVersion>
   <jdbcMinorVersion>unsupported feature</jdbcMinorVersion>
   <driverName>Oracle JDBC driver</driverName>
   <driverVersion>9.2.0.1.0</driverVersion>
   </DriverInformation>
------------------------------------
```

3.8. How Can You Determine Where a Given Table Is Referenced via Foreign Keys?

DatabaseMetaData.getExportedKeys() returns a ResultSet object, which relates to other tables that reference the given table as a foreign key container. In other words, it tells us which tables have foreign keys that reference this table. A *primary key (PK)* is a column or set of columns that uniquely identifies a row or record in a table. A *foreign key (FK)* is one or more columns in one table that are used as a primary key in another table. First, we'll look at these concepts in a simple example, and then we'll develop a JDBC solution and a test client program to show these relationships using DatabaseMetaData.getExportedKeys().

Oracle Database Setup

First, let's create two tables (dept_table and emp_table) and define the PK and FK for these tables. Figure 3-1 illustrates the relationship of these tables.

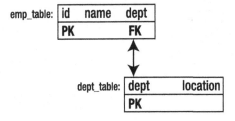

Figure 3-1. *Relationship of tables*

Keep in mind that if you violate the PK and FK rules, the SQL INSERT operation will fail:

```
$ sqlplus scott/tiger
SQL*Plus: Release 10.1.0.2.0 - Production on Tue Aug 24 14:17:06 2004
Copyright (c) 1982, 2004, Oracle.  All rights reserved.
```

```
SQL> create table dept_table (
  2     dept varchar2(2) not null primary key,
  3     location varchar2(8)
  4  );
Table created.
SQL> desc dept_table;
 Name                                      Null?    Type
 ----------------------------------------- -------- -----------
 DEPT                                      NOT NULL VARCHAR2(2)
 LOCATION                                           VARCHAR2(8)
SQL> create table emp_table (
  2     id varchar2(5) not null primary key,
  3     name varchar2(10),
  4     dept varchar2(2) not null references dept_table(dept)
  5  );
Table created.
SQL> desc emp_table;
 Name                                      Null?    Type
 ----------------------------------------- -------- ------------
 ID                                        NOT NULL VARCHAR2(5)
 NAME                                               VARCHAR2(10)
 DEPT                                      NOT NULL VARCHAR2(2)
SQL> insert into dept_table(dept, location) values('11', 'Boston');
SQL> insert into dept_table(dept, location) values('22', 'Detroit');
SQL> insert into emp_table(id, name, dept) values('55555', 'Alex', '11');
SQL> insert into emp_table(id, name, dept) values('66666', 'Mary', '22');
SQL> select * from dept_table;
DEPT LOCATION
---- --------
11   Boston
22   Detroit
SQL> select * from emp_table;
ID    NAME       DEPT
----- ---------- ----
55555 Alex       11
66666 Mary       22
SQL> insert into emp_table(id, name, dept) values('77777', 'Bob', '33');
insert into emp_table(id, name, dept) values('77777', 'Bob', '33')
*
ERROR at line 1:
ORA-02291: integrity constraint (SCOTT.SYS_C005465) violated - parent key not
Found
```

Note Since dept 33 is not defined in dept_table, Oracle issues an error.

```
SQL> select * from emp_table;
ID     NAME        DEPT
-----  ----------  ----
55555  Alex          11
66666  Mary          22
SQL> commit;
```

DatabaseMetaData.getExportedKeys() According to J2SE

```
public ResultSet getExportedKeys(String catalog,
                                 String schema,
                                 String table)
    throws SQLException
```

This method retrieves a description of the foreign key columns that reference the given table's primary key columns (the foreign keys exported by a table). They are ordered by FKTABLE_CAT, FKTABLE_SCHEM, FKTABLE_NAME, and KEY_SEQ. Each foreign key column description has columns shown in Table 3-4.

Table 3-4. *ResultSet Object's Columns for Invoking getExportedKeys()*

Field Name	Type	Description
PKTABLE_CAT	String	The primary key table catalog (may be null)
PKTABLE_SCHEM	String	The primary key table schema (may be null)
PKTABLE_NAME	String	The primary key table name
PKCOLUMN_NAME	String	The primary key column name
FKTABLE_CAT	String	The foreign key table catalog (may be null) that is being exported (may be null)
FKTABLE_SCHEM	String	The foreign key table schema (may be null) that being exported (may be null)
FKTABLE_NAME	String	The foreign key table name that is being exported
FKCOLUMN_NAME	String	The foreign key column name that is being exported
KEY_SEQ	short	The sequence number within the foreign key
UPDATE_RULE	short	Indicates what happens to the foreign key when the primary key is updated: importedNoAction: Do not allow the update of the primary key if it has been imported importedKeyCascade: Change the imported key to agree with the primary key update importedKeySetNull: Change the imported key to NULL if its primary key has been updated importedKeySetDefault: Change the imported key to the default values if its primary key has been updated importedKeyRestrict: The same as importedKeyNoAction (for ODBC 2.*x* compatibility)
DELETE_RULE	short	Indicates what happens to the foreign key when the primary key is deleted: importedKeyNoAction: Do not allow the delete of the primary key if it has been imported importedKeyCascade: Delete rows that import a deleted key importedKeySetNull: Change the imported key to NULL if its primary key has been deleted importedKeyRestrict: The same as importedKeyNoAction (for ODBC 2.*x* compatibility) importedKeySetDefault: Change the imported key to the default if its primary key has been deleted

Field Name	Type	Description
FK_NAME	String	The foreign key name (may be null)
PK_NAME	String	The primary key name (may be null)
DEFERRABILITY	short	Indicates whether the evaluation of foreign key constraints can be deferred until commit: importedKeyInitiallyDeferred: See SQL-92 for definition importedKeyInitiallyImmediate: See SQL-92 for definition importedKeyNotDeferrable: See SQL-92 for definition

The method's parameters are as follows:

- catalog: A catalog name; it must match the catalog name as it is stored in this database. "" retrieves those without a catalog; null means that the catalog name should not be used to narrow the search.

- schema: A schema name; it must match the schema name as it is stored in the database. "" retrieves those without a schema; null means that the schema name should not be used to narrow the search.

- table: A table name; it must match the table name as it is stored in this database.

This method returns a ResultSet object in which each row is a foreign key column description. If a database access error occurs, it throws a SQLException.

The Solution: Using DatabaseMetaData.getExportedKeys()

In using the DatabaseMetaData.getExportedKeys() method, try to pass all required parameters with non-null and non-empty values. Passing null/empty values might slow down getting the results from this method. If your database is not changing often, you may cache the returned values on the server side.

```
/**
 * class name: jcb.meta.DatabaseMetaDataTool
 *
 * Retrieves a description of the foreign key columns that
 * reference the given table's primary key columns (the foreign
 * keys exported by a table). They are ordered by FKTABLE_CAT,
 * FKTABLE_SCHEM, FKTABLE_NAME, and KEY_SEQ.
 *
 * @param conn the Connection object
 * @param catalog database catalog.
 * @param schema database schema.
 * @param tableName name of a table in the database.
 * @return the list (as an XML string) of the foreign key columns
 * that reference the given table's primary key columns
 *
 * @exception Failed to get the ExportedKeys for a given table.
 */
```

```java
public static String getExportedKeys(java.sql.Connection conn,
                                     String catalog,
                                     String schema,
                                     String tableName)
    throws Exception {
ResultSet rs = null;
try {
    if ((tableName == null) || (tableName.length() == 0)) {
        return null;
    }

    DatabaseMetaData meta = conn.getMetaData();
    if (meta == null) {
        return null;
    }

    // The Oracle database stores its table names as uppercase,
    // if you pass a table name in lowercase characters, it will not work.
    // MySQL database does not care if table name is uppercase/lowercase.
    rs = meta.getExportedKeys(catalog, schema, tableName.toUpperCase());
    if (rs == null) {
        return null;
    }

    StringBuffer buffer = new StringBuffer();
    buffer.append("<exportedKeys>");
    while (rs.next()) {
        String fkTableName =
            DatabaseUtil.getTrimmedString(rs, "FKTABLE_NAME");
        String fkColumnName =
            DatabaseUtil.getTrimmedString(rs, "FKCOLUMN_NAME");
        int fkSequence = rs.getInt("KEY_SEQ");
        buffer.append("<exportedKey>");
        buffer.append("<catalog>");
        buffer.append(catalog);
        buffer.append("</catalog>");
        buffer.append("<schema>");
        buffer.append(schema);
        buffer.append("</schema>");
        buffer.append("<tableName>");
        buffer.append(tableName);
        buffer.append("</tableName>");
        buffer.append("<fkTableName>");
        buffer.append(fkTableName);
        buffer.append("</fkTableName>");
        buffer.append("<fkColumnName>");
        buffer.append(fkColumnName);
```

```
                    buffer.append("</fkColumnName>");
                    buffer.append("<fkSequence>");
                    buffer.append(fkSequence);
                    buffer.append("</fkSequence>");
                    buffer.append("</exportedKey>");
                }
                buffer.append("</exportedKeys>");
                return buffer.toString();
            }
            finally {
                DatabaseUtil.close(rs);
            }
        }
    }
```

The Oracle Client Test Program

```java
import java.util.*;
import java.io.*;
import java.sql.*;

import jcb.db.*;
import jcb.meta.*;

public class DemoGetExportedKeys_Oracle {

    public static Connection getConnection() throws Exception {
        String driver = "oracle.jdbc.driver.OracleDriver";
        String url = "jdbc:oracle:thin:@localhost:1521:caspian";
        String username = "scott";
        String password = "tiger";
        Class.forName(driver);  // load Oracle driver
        return DriverManager.getConnection(url, username, password);
    }

    public static void main(String[] args) {
        Connection conn = null;
        Statement stmt = null;
        ResultSet rs = null;
        try {
            System.out.println("------DemoGetExportedKeys_Oracle begin---------");
            conn = getConnection();
            System.out.println("DemoGetExportedKeys_Oracle: conn="+conn);
            String exportedKeysAsXML = DatabaseMetaDataTool.getExportedKeys(
                                    conn, null, "SCOTT", "DEPT_TABLE");
            System.out.println("exportedKeysAsXML=" + exportedKeysAsXML);
            System.out.println("------DemoGetExportedKeys_Oracle end---------");
        }
```

```
        catch(Exception e){
            e.printStackTrace();
            System.exit(1);
        }
        finally {
            // release database resources
            DatabaseUtil.close(conn);
        }
    }
}
```

Running the Client Test Program

```
$ javac DemoGetExportedKeys_Oracle.java
$ java DemoGetExportedKeys_Oracle
```

```
------DemoGetExportedKeys_Oracle begin---------
DemoGetExportedKeys_Oracle: conn=oracle.jdbc.driver.OracleConnection@1c6f579
exportedKeysAsXML=
<exportedKeys>
    <exportedKey>
        <catalog>null</catalog>
        <schema>SCOTT</schema>
        <tableName>DEPT_TABLE</tableName>
        <fkTableName>EMP_TABLE</fkTableName>
        <fkColumnName>DEPT</fkColumnName>
        <fkSequence>1</fkSequence>
    </exportedKey>
</exportedKeys>
------DemoGetExportedKeys_Oracle end---------
```

The MySQL Database Setup

In the current version of MySQL (version 4.0.8), only InnoDB table types support the foreign key concept. According to MySQL, starting with MySQL 5.1, foreign keys will be supported for all table types, not just InnoDB. Let's create two tables (dept_table and emp_table) and define the PK and FK. Keep in mind that if you violate the PK and FK rules, the SQL INSERT operation will fail.

```
$ mysql --user=root --password=root
Welcome to the MySQL monitor.  Commands end with ; or \g.
Your MySQL connection id is 130 to server version: 4.0.18-nt
mysql> use octopus;
Database changed
```

```
mysql> create table dept_table (
    -> dept char(2) not null,
    -> location varchar(8),
    -> PRIMARY KEY(dept)
    -> ) TYPE=InnoDB;
Query OK, 0 rows affected (0.15 sec)
mysql> create table emp_table (
    -> dept char(2) not null,
    -> id varchar(5) not null,
    -> name varchar(10),
    -> PRIMARY KEY(id),
    -> INDEX dept_index (dept),
    -> CONSTRAINT fk_dept FOREIGN KEY(dept) REFERENCES dept_table(dept)
    -> ) TYPE=InnoDB;
Query OK, 0 rows affected (0.11 sec)
mysql> insert into dept_table(dept, location) values('11', 'Boston');
mysql> insert into dept_table(dept, location) values('22', 'Detroit');
mysql> insert into emp_table(id, name, dept) values('55555', 'Alex', '11');
mysql> insert into emp_table(id, name, dept) values('66666', 'Mary', '22');
mysql> insert into emp_table(id, name, dept) values('77777', 'Bob', '33');
ERROR 1216: Cannot add or update a child row: a foreign key constraint fails
mysql> select * from emp_table;
+------+-------+------+
| dept | id    | name |
+------+-------+------+
| 11   | 55555 | Alex |
| 22   | 66666 | Mary |
+------+-------+------+
2 rows in set (0.00 sec)
mysql> select * from dept_table;
+------+----------+
| dept | location |
+------+----------+
| 11   | Boston   |
| 22   | Detroit  |
+------+----------+
2 rows in set (0.00 sec)
```

The MySQL Client Test Program

```java
import java.util.*;
import java.io.*;
import java.sql.*;

import jcb.db.*;
import jcb.meta.*;

public class DemoGetExportedKeys_MySQL {
```

```
    public static Connection getConnection() throws Exception {
        String driver = "org.gjt.mm.mysql.Driver";
        String url = "jdbc:mysql://localhost/octopus";
        String username = "root";
        String password = "root";
        Class.forName(driver);   // load MySQL driver
        return DriverManager.getConnection(url, username, password);
    }

    public static void main(String[] args) {
        Connection conn = null;
        Statement stmt = null;
        ResultSet rs = null;
        try {
            System.out.println("------DemoGetExportedKeys_MySQL begin---------");
            conn = getConnection();
            System.out.println("DemoGetExportedKeys_MySQL: conn="+conn);

            String exportedKeysAsXML = DatabaseMetaDataTool.getExportedKeys(
                                conn, "octopus", null, "DEPT_TABLE");
            System.out.println("exportedKeysAsXML=" + exportedKeysAsXML);
            System.out.println("------DemoGetExportedKeys_MySQL end---------");
        }
        catch(Exception e){
            e.printStackTrace();
            System.exit(1);
        }
        finally {
            // release database resources
            DatabaseUtil.close(conn);
        }
    }
}
```

Running the Client Test Program

```
$ javac  DemoGetExportedKeys_MySQL.java
$ java DemoGetExportedKeys_MySQL
```

```
------DemoGetExportedKeys_MySQL begin---------
DemoGetExportedKeys_MySQL: conn=com.mysql.jdbc.Connection@a1807c
exportedKeysAsXML=
<exportedKeys>
    <exportedKey>
        <catalog>octopus</catalog>
        <schema>null</schema>
        <tableName>DEPT_TABLE</tableName>
```

```
        <fkTableName>emp_table</fkTableName>
        <fkColumnName>dept</fkColumnName>
        <fkSequence>1</fkSequence>
    </exportedKey>
</exportedKeys>
------DemoGetExportedKeys_MySQL end---------
```

3.9. What Foreign Keys Are Used in a Table?

DatabaseMetaData.getImportedKeys() returns a ResultSet object with data about foreign key columns, tables, sequence, and update and delete rules. DatabaseMetaData's getImportedKeys() returns a ResultSet that retrieves a description of the primary key columns referenced by a table's foreign key columns (the primary keys imported by a table). The ResultSet object's records are ordered by the column names PKTABLE_CAT, PKTABLE_SCHEM, PKTABLE_NAME, and KEY_SEQ.

A *primary key (PK)* is a column or set of columns that uniquely identifies a row or record in a table. A *foreign key (FK)* is one or more columns in one table that are used as a primary key in another table. First, we'll look at these concepts in a simple example, and then we'll develop a JDBC solution and a test client program to show these relationships using DatabaseMetaData.getImportedKeys().

Oracle Database Setup

Let's create three tables (roles_table, emps_table, and emps_roles) and define the PK and FK. Figure 3-2 illustrates the relationships of these tables.

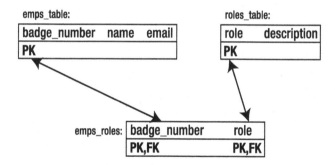

Figure 3-2. *Relationships of three database tables*

Keep in mind that if you violate the PK and FK rules, the SQL INSERT operation will fail.

```
create table emps_table (
    badge_number varchar(5) not null,
    name varchar(20) not null,
    email varchar(20) not null,
    primary key (badge_number)
);
```

```
create table roles_table (
    role varchar(5) not null,
    description varchar(25) not null,
    primary key (role)
);


create table emps_roles (
    badge_number varchar(5) not null,
    role varchar(5) not null,

    primary key (badge_number, role),
    foreign key (badge_number) references emps_table(badge_number),
    foreign key (role) references roles_table(role)
);

insert into roles_table(role, description) values('dba', 'database administrator');
insert into roles_table(role, description) values('mgr', 'database manager');
insert into roles_table(role, description) values('dev', 'database developer');

insert into emps_table(badge_number, name, email)
    values('11111', 'Alex', 'alex@yahoo.com');

insert into emps_table(badge_number, name, email)
    values('22222', 'Mary', 'mary@yahoo.com');

insert into emps_roles(badge_number, role)
    values('11111', 'mgr');
insert into emps_roles(badge_number, role)
    values('11111', 'dev');
insert into emps_roles(badge_number, role)
    values('22222', 'dba');


SQL> select * from roles_table;

ROLE  DESCRIPTION
----- ----------------------
dba   database administrator
mgr   database manager
dev   database developer
SQL> select * from emps_table;
```

```
BADGE   NAME   EMAIL
-----   ----   --------------
11111   Alex   alex@yahoo.com
22222   Mary   mary@yahoo.com
SQL> select * from emps_roles;
BADGE   ROLE
-----   -----
11111   dev
11111   mgr
22222   dba
```

DatabaseMetaData.getImportedKeys() Signature

```
public ResultSet getImportedKeys(String catalog,
                                 String schema,
                                 String table)
   throws SQLException
```

This method retrieves a description of the primary key columns that are referenced by a table's foreign key columns (the primary keys imported by a table). They are ordered by PKTABLE_CAT, PKTABLE_SCHEM, PKTABLE_NAME, and KEY_SEQ.

Each primary key column description has the columns shown in Table 3-5.

Table 3-5. *ResultSet Object's Columns for Invoking getImportedKeys()*

Field Name	Type	Description
PKTABLE_CAT	String	The primary key table catalog being imported (may be null)
PKTABLE_SCHEM	String	The primary key table schema being imported (may be null)
PKTABLE_NAME	String	The primary key table name being imported
PKCOLUMN_NAME	String	The primary key column name being imported
FKTABLE_CAT	String	The foreign key table catalog (may be null)
FKTABLE_SCHEM	String	The foreign key table schema (may be null)
FKTABLE_NAME	String	The foreign key table name
FKCOLUMN_NAME	String	The foreign key column name
KEY_SEQ	short	The sequence number within a foreign key
UPDATE_RULE	short	Indicates what happens to a foreign key when the primary key is updated: importedNoAction: Do not allow the update of the primary key if it has been imported importedKeyCascade: Change the imported key to agree with the primary key update importedKeySetNull: Change the imported key to NULL if its primary key has been updated importedKeySetDefault: Change the imported key to the default values if its primary key has been updated importedKeyRestrict: The same as importedKeyNoAction (for ODBC 2.x compatibility)

Continued

Table 3-5. *Continued*

Field Name	Type	Description
DELETE_RULE	short	Indicates what happens to the foreign key when the primary key is deleted: importedKeyNoAction: Do not allow the delete of the primary key if it has been imported importedKeyCascade: Delete rows that import a deleted key importedKeySetNull: Change the imported key to NULL if its primary key has been deleted importedKeyRestrict: The same as importedKeyNoAction (for ODBC 2.*x* compatibility) importedKeySetDefault: Change the imported key to the default if its primary key has been deleted
FK_NAME	String	The foreign key name (may be null)
PK_NAME	String	The primary key name (may be null)
DEFERRABILITY	short	Specifies whether the evaluation of foreign key constraints can be deferred until commit: importedKeyInitiallyDeferred: See SQL-92 for definition importedKeyInitiallyImmediate: See SQL-92 for definition importedKeyNotDeferrable: See SQL-92 for definition

This method's parameters are as follows:

- catalog: A catalog name; it must match the catalog name as it is stored in the database. "" retrieves those without a catalog; null means that the catalog name should not be used to narrow the search.

- schema: A schema name; it must match the schema name as it is stored in the database. "" retrieves those without a schema; null means that the schema name should not be used to narrow the search.

- table: A table name; it must match the table name as it is stored in the database.

This method returns a ResultSet in which each row is a primary key column description. If a database access error occurs, it throws a SQLException.

The Solution: Using DatabaseMetaData.getImportedKeys()

When using the DatabaseMetaData.getImportedKeys() method, try to pass all required parameters with non-null and non-empty values. Passing null/empty values might slow down getting the results from this method. If your database is not changing often, you may cache the returned values on the server side. This method will give you a good idea about the dependency of your database tables.

```
/**
 * class name: jcb.meta.DatabaseMetaDataTool
 *
 * Retrieves a description of the primary key columns that are
 * referenced by a table's foreign key columns (the primary keys
 * imported by a table). They are ordered by PKTABLE_CAT,
 * PKTABLE_SCHEM, PKTABLE_NAME, and KEY_SEQ.
 *
```

```
* @param conn the Connection object
* @param catalog database catalog.
* @param schema database schema.
* @param tableName name of a table in the database.
* @return the list (as an XML string) of the primary key columns
* that are referenced by a table's foreign key columns
*
* @exception Failed to get the ExportedKeys for a given table.
*/
public static String getImportedKeys(java.sql.Connection conn,
                                     String catalog,
                                     String schema,
                                     String tableName)
    throws Exception {
    ResultSet rs = null;
    try {
        if ((tableName == null) || (tableName.length() == 0)) {
            return null;
        }

        DatabaseMetaData meta = conn.getMetaData();
        if (meta == null) {
            return null;
        }

        //
        // The Oracle database stores its table names as uppercase,
        // if you pass a table name in lowercase characters, it will not work.
        // MySQL database does not care if table name is uppercase/lowercase.
        //
        rs = meta.getImportedKeys(catalog, schema, tableName.toUpperCase());
        if (rs == null) {
            return null;
        }

        StringBuffer buffer = new StringBuffer();
        buffer.append("<importedKeys>");
        while (rs.next()) {

            String pkTableName =
                DatabaseUtil.getTrimmedString(rs, "PKTABLE_NAME");
            String pkColumnName =
                DatabaseUtil.getTrimmedString(rs, "PKCOLUMN_NAME");
            String fkTableName =
                DatabaseUtil.getTrimmedString(rs, "FKTABLE_NAME");
            String fkColumnName =
                DatabaseUtil.getTrimmedString(rs, "FKCOLUMN_NAME");
            int fkSequence = rs.getInt("KEY_SEQ");
```

```
                        buffer.append("<importedKey>");
                        buffer.append("<catalog>");
                        buffer.append(catalog);
                        buffer.append("</catalog>");
                        buffer.append("<schema>");
                        buffer.append(schema);
                        buffer.append("</schema>");
                        buffer.append("<tableName>");
                        buffer.append(tableName);
                        buffer.append("</tableName>");
                        buffer.append("<pkTableName>");
                        buffer.append(pkTableName);
                        buffer.append("</pkTableName>");
                        buffer.append("<pkColumnName>");
                        buffer.append(pkColumnName);
                        buffer.append("</pkColumnName>");
                        buffer.append("<fkTableName>");
                        buffer.append(fkTableName);
                        buffer.append("</fkTableName>");
                        buffer.append("<fkColumnName>");
                        buffer.append(fkColumnName);
                        buffer.append("</fkColumnName>");
                        buffer.append("<fkSequence>");
                        buffer.append(fkSequence);
                        buffer.append("</fkSequence>");
                        buffer.append("</importedKey>");
                    }
                    buffer.append("</importedKeys>");
                    return buffer.toString();
                }
                finally {
                    DatabaseUtil.close(rs);
                }
        }
```

Oracle Client Test Program

```
import java.util.*;
import java.io.*;
import java.sql.*;

import jcb.db.*;
import jcb.meta.*;

public class DemoGetImportedKeys_Oracle {
```

```java
    public static Connection getConnection() throws Exception {
        String driver = "oracle.jdbc.driver.OracleDriver";
        String url = "jdbc:oracle:thin:@localhost:1521:caspian";
        String username = "scott";
        String password = "tiger";
        Class.forName(driver);  // load Oracle driver
        return DriverManager.getConnection(url, username, password);
    }

    public static void main(String[] args) {
        Connection conn = null;
        Statement stmt = null;
        ResultSet rs = null;
        try {
            System.out.println("------DemoGetImportedKeys_Oracle begin---------");
            conn = getConnection();
            System.out.println("DemoGetImportedKeys_Oracle: conn="+conn);
            String tableName = args[0];
            System.out.println("tableName=" + tableName);
            String importedKeysAsXML =
                DatabaseMetaDataTool.getImportedKeys(conn, null, "SCOTT", tableName);
            System.out.println("importedKeysAsXML=" + importedKeysAsXML);
            System.out.println("------DemoGetImportedKeys_Oracle end---------");
        }
        catch(Exception e){
            e.printStackTrace();
            System.exit(1);
        }
        finally {
            // release database resources
            DatabaseUtil.close(conn);
        }
    }
}
```

Running the Client Test Program

```
$ javac DemoGetImportedKeys_Oracle.java
$ java DemoGetImportedKeys_Oracle roles_table
------DemoGetImportedKeys_Oracle begin---------
DemoGetImportedKeys_Oracle: conn=oracle.jdbc.driver.OracleConnection@1c6f579
tableName=roles_table
importedKeysAsXML=
<importedKeys>
</importedKeys>
```

```
------DemoGetImportedKeys_Oracle end---------
$ java DemoGetImportedKeys_Oracle emps_table
------DemoGetImportedKeys_Oracle begin---------
DemoGetImportedKeys_Oracle: conn=oracle.jdbc.driver.OracleConnection@1c6f579
tableName=emps_table
importedKeysAsXML=
<importedKeys>
</importedKeys>

------DemoGetImportedKeys_Oracle end---------
$ java DemoGetImportedKeys_Oracle emps_roles
------DemoGetImportedKeys_Oracle begin---------
DemoGetImportedKeys_Oracle: conn=oracle.jdbc.driver.OracleConnection@1c6f579
tableName=emps_roles
importedKeysAsXML=
<importedKeys>
    <importedKey>
        <catalog>null</catalog>
        <schema>SCOTT</schema>
        <tableName>emps_roles</tableName>
        <pkTableName>EMPS_TABLE</pkTableName>
        <pkColumnName>BADGE_NUMBER</pkColumnName>
        <fkTableName>EMPS_ROLES</fkTableName>
        <fkColumnName>BADGE_NUMBER</fkColumnName>
        <fkSequence>1</fkSequence>
    </importedKey>
    <importedKey>
        <catalog>null</catalog>
        <schema>SCOTT</schema>
        <tableName>emps_roles</tableName>
        <pkTableName>ROLES_TABLE</pkTableName>
        <pkColumnName>ROLE</pkColumnName>
        <fkTableName>EMPS_ROLES</fkTableName>
        <fkColumnName>ROLE</fkColumnName>
        <fkSequence>1</fkSequence>
    </importedKey>
</importedKeys>
------DemoGetImportedKeys_Oracle end---------
```

MySQL Database Setup

In the current version of MySQL (version 4.0.8), only InnoDB table types support the foreign key concept. According to MySQL, starting with MySQL 5.1, foreign keys will be supported for all table types, not just InnoDB. Let's create two tables (dept_table and emp_table) and define the PK and FK. Keep in mind that if you violate the PK and FK rules, the SQL INSERT operation will fail.

```
$ mysql --user=root --password=root
Welcome to the MySQL monitor.  Commands end with ; or \g.
Your MySQL connection id is 1 to server version: 4.0.18-nt
mysql> use octopus;
Database changed
mysql> create table emps_table (
    ->      badge_number varchar(5) not null,
    ->      name varchar(20) not null,
    ->      email varchar(20) not null,
    ->
    ->      primary key (badge_number)
    -> ) TYPE=InnoDB;
Query OK, 0 rows affected (0.24 sec)
mysql> create table roles_table (
    ->      role varchar(5) not null,
    ->      description varchar(25) not null,
    ->
    ->      primary key (role)
    -> ) TYPE=InnoDB;
Query OK, 0 rows affected (0.13 sec)
mysql> create table emps_roles (
    ->      badge_number varchar(5) not null,
    ->      role varchar(5) not null,
    ->
    ->      primary key (badge_number, role),
    ->      INDEX badge_number_index (badge_number),
    ->      foreign key (badge_number) references emps_table(badge_number),
    ->      INDEX role_index (role),
    ->      foreign key (role) references roles_table(role)
    -> ) TYPE=InnoDB;
Query OK, 0 rows affected (0.24 sec)
mysql> insert into roles_table(role, description)
       values('dba', 'database administrator');

mysql> insert into roles_table(role, description)
       values('mgr', 'database manager');

mysql> insert into roles_table(role, description)
       values('dev', 'database developer');

mysql> insert into emps_table(badge_number, name, email)
       values('11111', 'Alex', 'alex@yahoo.com');

mysql> insert into emps_table(badge_number, name, email)
       values('22222', 'Mary', 'mary@yahoo.com');
```

```
mysql> insert into emps_roles(badge_number, role)
       values('11111', 'mgr');

mysql> insert into emps_roles(badge_number, role)
       values('11111', 'dev');

mysql> insert into emps_roles(badge_number, role)
       values('22222', 'dba');

mysql> insert into emps_roles(badge_number, role) values('22222', 'a');
ERROR 1216: Cannot add or update a child row: a foreign key constraint fails
mysql> insert into emps_roles(badge_number, role) values('2222', 'a');
ERROR 1216: Cannot add or update a child row: a foreign key constraint fails
mysql> select * from emps_table;
+--------------+------+-----------------+
| badge_number | name | email           |
+--------------+------+-----------------+
| 11111        | Alex | alex@yahoo.com  |
| 22222        | Mary | mary@yahoo.com  |
+--------------+------+-----------------+
2 rows in set (0.02 sec)
mysql> select * from roles_table;
+------+------------------------+
| role | description            |
+------+------------------------+
| dba  | database administrator |
| dev  | database developer     |
| mgr  | database manager       |
+------+------------------------+
3 rows in set (0.00 sec)
mysql> select * from emps_roles;
+--------------+------+
| badge_number | role |
+--------------+------+
| 11111        | dev  |
| 11111        | mgr  |
| 22222        | dba  |
+--------------+------+
3 rows in set (0.00 sec)
```

The MySQL Client Test Program

```java
import java.util.*;
import java.io.*;
import java.sql.*;

import jcb.db.*;
import jcb.meta.*;
```

```java
public class DemoGetImportedKeys_MySQL {

    public static Connection getConnection() throws Exception {
        String driver = "org.gjt.mm.mysql.Driver";
        String url = "jdbc:mysql://localhost/octopus";
        String username = "root";
        String password = "root";
        Class.forName(driver);  // load MySQL driver
        return DriverManager.getConnection(url, username, password);
    }

    public static void main(String[] args) {
        Connection conn = null;
        Statement stmt = null;
        ResultSet rs = null;
        try {
            System.out.println("------DemoGetImportedKeys_MySQL begin---------");
            conn = getConnection();
            System.out.println("DemoGetImportedKeys_MySQL: conn="+conn);
            String tableName = args[0];
            System.out.println("tableName=" + tableName);
            String importedKeysAsXML = DatabaseMetaDataTool.getImportedKeys(
                                        conn, "octopus", null, tableName);
            System.out.println("importedKeysAsXML=" + importedKeysAsXML);
            System.out.println("------DemoGetImportedKeys_MySQL end---------");
        }
        catch(Exception e){
            e.printStackTrace();
            System.exit(1);
        }
        finally {
            // release database resources
            DatabaseUtil.close(conn);
        }
    }
}
```

Running the Client Test Program

```
$ javac DemoGetImportedKeys_MySQL.java
$ java DemoGetImportedKeys_MySQL emps_table
```

```
------DemoGetImportedKeys_MySQL begin---------
DemoGetImportedKeys_MySQL: conn=com.mysql.jdbc.Connection@a1807c
tableName=emps_table
importedKeysAsXML= <importedKeys></importedKeys>
------DemoGetImportedKeys_MySQL end---------
```

```
$ java DemoGetImportedKeys_MySQL roles_table
```

```
------DemoGetImportedKeys_MySQL begin---------
DemoGetImportedKeys_MySQL: conn=com.mysql.jdbc.Connection@a1807c
tableName=roles_table
importedKeysAsXML= <importedKeys></importedKeys>
------DemoGetImportedKeys_MySQL end---------
```

```
$ java DemoGetImportedKeys_MySQL emps_roles
```

```
------DemoGetImportedKeys_MySQL begin---------
DemoGetImportedKeys_MySQL: conn=com.mysql.jdbc.Connection@a1807c
tableName=emps_roles
importedKeysAsXML=
<importedKeys>
    <importedKey>
        <catalog>octopus</catalog>
        <schema>null</schema>
        <tableName>emps_roles</tableName>
        <pkTableName>emps_table</pkTableName>
        <pkColumnName>badge_number</pkColumnName>
        <fkTableName>EMPS_ROLES</fkTableName>
        <fkColumnName>badge_number</fkColumnName>
        <fkSequence>1</fkSequence>
    </importedKey>
    <importedKey>
        <catalog>octopus</catalog>
        <schema>null</schema>
        <tableName>emps_roles</tableName>
        <pkTableName>roles_table</pkTableName>
        <pkColumnName>role</pkColumnName>
        <fkTableName>EMPS_ROLES</fkTableName>
        <fkColumnName>role</fkColumnName>
        <fkSequence>1</fkSequence>
    </importedKey>
</importedKeys>
------DemoGetImportedKeys_MySQL end---------
```

3.10. What Is the JDBC View of a Database's Internal Structure?

The JDBC views a database in terms of catalog, schema, table, view, column, triggers, indexes, and stored procedures. The JDBC view of a database's internal structure appears in Figure 3-3.

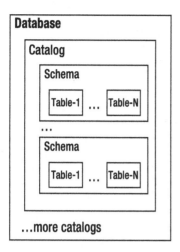

Figure 3-3. *Internal structure of a database*

From the JDBC view of a database:

- A database server has several catalogs (such as database partitions and databases).

- A catalog has several schemas (these are user-specific namespaces).

- A schema has several database objects (tables, views, triggers, indexes, stored procedures, etc.).

The java.sql.DatabaseMetaData interface has methods for discovering all the catalogs, schemas, tables, views, indexes, and stored procedures in the database server. These methods return a ResultSet, which can be traversed for getting the desired information.

```
public static ·void main(String[] args) throws Exception {
    // Load the database driver - in this case, we
    // use the Jdbc/Odbc bridge driver.
    Connection conn = null;
    try {
        Class.forName("sun.jdbc.odbc.JdbcOdbcDriver");

        // Open a connection to the database
        conn = DriverManager.getConnection(
            "[jdbcURL]", "[login]", "[passwd]");

        // Get DatabaseMetaData
        DatabaseMetaData dbmd = conn.getMetaData();

        // Get all Catalogs
        System.out.println("\nCatalogs are called '" + dbmd.getCatalogTerm()
            + "' in this RDBMS.");
        processResultSet(dbmd.getCatalogTerm(), dbmd.getCatalogs());
```

```
            // Get all Schemas
            System.out.println("\nSchemas are called '" + dbmd.getSchemaTerm()
                + "' in this RDBMS.");
            processResultSet(dbmd.getSchemaTerm(), dbmd.getSchemas());

            // Get all Table-like types
            System.out.println("\nAll table types supported in this RDBMS:");
            processResultSet("Table type", dbmd.getTableTypes());
        }
        finally {
          // Close the Connection object
        }
    }

    public static void processResultSet(String preamble, ResultSet rs)
          throws SQLException {
      // Printout table data
      while(rs.next()) {
          // Printout
          System.out.println(preamble + ": " + rs.getString(1));
      }

      // Close database resources
      rs.close();
    }
```

3.11. Does a Database Support Batching?

With batch updating, a set of SQL statements is assembled and then sent to the database for execution. Batch updating can improve performance if you send lots of update statements to the database. According to Sun's JDBC Tutorial (http://java.sun.com/docs/books/tutorial/jdbc/jdbc2dot0/batchupdates.html), "A batch update is a set of multiple update statements that is submitted to the database for processing as a batch. Sending multiple update statements to the database together as a unit can, in some situations, be much more efficient than sending each update statement separately. This ability to send updates as a unit, referred to as the batch update facility, is one of the features provided with the JDBC 2.0 API."

Determine Whether a Database Supports Batching

```
/**
 * Check to see if database supports batching.
 * @param conn connection object to the desired database
 * @return true if database supports batching.
 */
public static boolean supportsBatching(java.sql.Connection conn) {
    if (conn == null) {
        return false;
    }
```

```
    try {
        DatabaseMetaData dbmd = conn.getMetaData();
        if (dbmd == null) {
            // database metadata not supported
            return false;
        }

        if (dbmd.supportsBatchUpdates()) {
            // batching is supported
            return true;
        }
        else {
            // batching is not supported
            return false;
        }
    }
    catch (Exception e) {
        // handle the exception
        return false;
    }
}
```

Making Batch Updates

Next I'll provide an example that will perform batch updates. This example will be accomplished in several steps:

Step 1: Setting up the database

Step 2: Developing a sample program for batch updating

Step 3: Running the sample program

Step 4: Verifying the database results

Step 5: Discussing the solution

Step 1: Setting up the Database

Let's create a simple table, which will perform batch updates.

```
$ mysql --user=root --password=root
Welcome to the MySQL monitor.  Commands end with ; or \g.
Your MySQL connection id is 4240 to server version: 4.0.18-nt
mysql> use octopus;
Database changed
mysql> create table batch_table(
    -> id varchar(5) not null,
    -> name varchar(10) not null,
    -> primary key(id)
    -> );
```

```
Query OK, 0 rows affected (0.05 sec)
mysql> describe batch_table;
+-------+-------------+------+-----+---------+-------+
| Field | Type        | Null | Key | Default | Extra |
+-------+-------------+------+-----+---------+-------+
| id    | varchar(5)  |      | PRI |         |       |
| name  | varchar(10) |      |     |         |       |
+-------+-------------+------+-----+---------+-------+
2 rows in set (0.01 sec)
```

Step 2: Developing a Sample Program for Batch Updating

Here is the solution for batch updates. For discussion purposes, I have added line numbers.

```
1   import java.sql.Connection;
2   import java.sql.Statement;
3   import java.sql.ResultSet;
4   import java.sql.SQLException;
5   import java.sql.BatchUpdateException;
6   import jcb.util.DatabaseUtil;
7
8   public class TestBatchUpdate {
9
10      public static Connection getConnection() throws Exception {
11          String driver = "org.gjt.mm.mysql.Driver";
12          String url = "jdbc:mysql://localhost/octopus";
13          String username = "root";
14          String password = "root";
15          Class.forName(driver);  // load MySQL driver
16          return DriverManager.getConnection(url, username, password);
17      }
18
19      public static void main(String args[]) {
20          ResultSet rs = null;
21          Statement stmt = null;
22          Connection conn = null;
23          try {
24              conn = getConnection();
25              stmt = conn.createStatement(ResultSet.TYPE_SCROLL_SENSITIVE,
26                                          ResultSet.CONCUR_UPDATABLE);
27              conn.setAutoCommit(false);
28              stmt.addBatch("INSERT INTO batch_table(id, name) "+
29                              "VALUES('11', 'Alex')");
30              stmt.addBatch("INSERT INTO batch_table(id, name) "+
31                              "VALUES('22', 'Mary')");
32              stmt.addBatch("INSERT INTO batch_table(id, name) "+
33                              "VALUES('33', 'Bob')");
```

```
34                int[] updateCounts = stmt.executeBatch();
35                conn.commit();
36                rs = stmt.executeQuery("SELECT * FROM batch_table");
37                System.out.println("-- Table batch_table after insertion --");
38
39                while (rs.next()) {
40                    String id = rs.getString("id");
41                    String name = rs.getString("name");
42                    System.out.println("id="+id +"   name="+name);
43                }
44            }
45        catch(BatchUpdateException b) {
46            System.err.println("SQLException: " + b.getMessage());
47            System.err.println("SQLState: " + b.getSQLState());
48            System.err.println("Message: " + b.getMessage());
49            System.err.println("Vendor error code: " + b.getErrorCode());
50            System.err.print("Update counts: ");
51            int [] updateCounts = b.getUpdateCounts();
52            for (int i = 0; i < updateCounts.length; i++) {
53                System.err.print(updateCounts[i] + " ");
54            }
55        }
56        catch(SQLException ex) {
57            System.err.println("SQLException: " + ex.getMessage());
58            System.err.println("SQLState: " + ex.getSQLState());
59            System.err.println("Message: " + ex.getMessage());
60            System.err.println("Vendor error code: " + ex.getErrorCode());
61        }
62        catch(Exception e) {
63            e.printStackTrace();
64            System.err.println("Exception: " + e.getMessage());
65        }
66        finally {
67            DatabaseUtil.close(rs);
68            DatabaseUtil.close(stmt);
69            DatabaseUtil.close(conn);
70        }
71    }
72 }
```

Step 3: Running the Sample Program

```
$ javac TestBatchUpdate.java
$ java TestBatchUpdate
-- Table batch_table after insertion --
id=11   name=Alex
id=22   name=Mary
id=33   name=Bob
```

Step 4: Verifying the Database Results

```
$ mysql --user=root --password=root
Welcome to the MySQL monitor.  Commands end with ; or \g.
Your MySQL connection id is 3 to server version: 4.0.18-nt
mysql> use octopus;
Database changed
mysql> select * from batch_table;
+----+------+
| id | name |
+----+------+
| 11 | Alex |
| 22 | Mary |
| 33 | Bob  |
+----+------+
3 rows in set (0.00 sec)
```

Step 5: Discussing the Solution

Let's look at this solution in detail:

Lines 1–6: Import required classes and interfaces from the java.sql package.

Lines 10–17: The getConnection() method loads the JDBC driver, and then creates and returns a new database Connection object.

Lines 24–35: With the JDBC 2.0 API, Statement, PreparedStatement, and CallableStatement objects have the ability to maintain a list of SQL commands that can be submitted together as a batch. They are created with an associated list, which is initially empty. You can add SQL commands to this list with the method addBatch(), and you can empty the list with the method clearBatch(). You send all of the commands in the list to the database with the method executeBatch(). In lines 32–33, the stmt object sends the three SQL commands that were added to its list of commands off to the database to be executed as a batch. Note that stmt uses the method executeBatch() to send the batch of insertions, not the method executeUpdate(), which sends only one command and returns a single update count. The database server will execute the SQL commands in the order in which they were added to the list of commands.

Lines 36–43: The ResultSet object is used to retrieve all records from the batch_table. The ResultSet object is iterated to get information from all of the rows.

Lines 45–61: There are two exceptions that can be thrown during a batch update operation: SQLException and BatchUpdateException. If a batch update fails, then BatchUpdateException will be thrown by the JDBC driver. If there are other database problems, then SQLException will be thrown.

Lines 62–65: Finally, if there is any other exception, java.lang.Exception will be thrown.

Lines 66–70: This code closes all database resources. It releases the database and JDBC resources immediately instead of waiting for them to be automatically released.

CHAPTER 4

■■■

ResultSet Metadata

The most important motive for work in school and in life is pleasure in work, pleasure in its result, and the knowledge of the value of the result to the community.

Albert Einstein

The main purpose of this chapter is to introduce you to the use of JDBC's result set metadata (the `java.sql.ResultSetMetaData` interface). `ResultSetMetaData` provides metadata for the `ResultSet` object. `ResultSetMetaData` enables us to get information about the types and properties of the columns in a `ResultSet` object. Typically, IDEs and GUI tools often use the JDBC `ResultSetMetaData` class to get information about data in a particular table. In order to help you understand this interface, I will list some important questions about metadata for `ResultSet` objects and then answer each one in detail. Before delving into `ResultSetMetaData`, we will look at the meaning of *metadata*. Note that `ResultSetMetaData` is an important interface in JDBC since RowSetMetaData extends this interface.

To answer questions about result set metadata, I'll provide a Java class called `jcb.meta.ResultSetMetaDataTool`. This class gives you ready-to-use `public static` methods for answering the questions listed in this chapter. For answering questions about result set metadata, I list portions of these classes at some sections, but the complete class definitions (including JavaDoc-style comments) is given in the Source Code section of the Apress website. All of the methods in this chapter are `static`, and each method is written to be as independent as possible. Whenever possible, the methods will return the result as XML (serialized as a `String` object, which can be easily converted to an XML document—`org.w3c.dom.Document`). Also, I'll provide a utility class, `DocumentManager`, which can

- Convert `org.w3c.dom.Document` to XML as a serialized `String` object

- Convert XML as a serialized `String` object into an XML document—`org.w3c.dom.Document`

In general, it is efficient to create XML as a serialized `String` object. The Java/JDBC solutions are grouped in a Java package called `jcb` (**J**DBC **C**ook **B**ook). The `jcb` package and all its associated classes will be available from the Apress website as well.

For some questions in this chapter, I will combine all of our answers into a single XML output. This can save lots of time and enables a client to get all of the required information regarding result set metadata with a single call (this way, you can improve performance of your database applications for metadata access).

4.1. What Is ResultSet Metadata?

What is *metadata*? Metadata is *data about data*, which provides structured descriptive information about other data. Result set metadata relieves the user of having to obtain full knowledge of the characteristics of relational databases in advance. Therefore, we conclude that metadata describes the data and its properties, but is not the actual data itself. For example, the records in a card catalog in a local library give brief details about the actual book. A record provides enough information to know what the book is called, its unique identification number, and how and where to find it. These details are metadata—in this case, bibliographic elements such as author, title, abstract, publisher, and published date.

In a nutshell, result set metadata enables dynamic discovery of a ResultSet object's structure. Typically, most JDBC programmers will be programming with knowledge of their target database's schema definitions (the names of tables, views, columns, and their associated types). In this case, programmers can use the strongly typed JDBC interfaces. However, there is also another important class of database access where an application (or an application builder) dynamically generates the result sets from ad hoc queries (submitted by different clients). This chapter describes the JDBC support for dynamic access.

ResultSet metadata has many applications. It can be used to

- Discover the number of columns, column names, types, and length

- Find out the table names for all columns in the result set

- Determine whether a given column is readable/writable

- Determine whether a given column is searchable (indicates whether the designated column can be used in a SQL WHERE clause or in SQL SELECT, UPDATE, and DELETE queries)

As we observe, metadata not only enables us to do effective management of resources, but also helps us to use metadata to find the data we need and determine how best to use it. Also, metadata provides structured descriptions of database information resources and services.

4.2. What Is a ResultSetMetaData Object?

JDBC's result set metadata, expressed as the java.sql.ResultSetMetaData interface, is a set of structured data that can be used to get information about the types and properties of the columns in a ResultSet object.

It is very easy to create a ResultSetMetaData object. The following code fragment creates a ResultSet object rs, and then uses rs to create a ResultSetMetaData object rsMetadata, and finally uses rsMetadata to find out how many columns rs has:

```
ResultSet rs = null;
Statement stmt = null;
Connection conn = null;
ResultSetMetaData rsmd = null;
String query = "SELECT id, name, photo FROM  employees";
```

```
try {
  conn = getConnection();
  stmt = conn.createStatement();
  rs = stmt.executeQuery(query);
  rsMetaData = rs.getMetaData();
  if (rsMetaData == null) {
      // ResultSetMetaData is not supported by db vendor
      // or there was a problem in getting the ResultSetMetaData.
      // In general, it is a good idea to check if ResultSetMetaData
      // is null or not.
      ...
  }
  else {
      // ResultSetMetaData is supported by db vendor
      int numberOfColumns = rsMetaData.getColumnCount();
  }
  …
}
catch(SQLException e) {
  // handle exception
}
finally {
  // close resources such as ResultSet, Statement, and Connection
}
```

If you do not know exactly the table structure (the schema) of the ResultSet, you can obtain it via a ResultSetMetaData object. The ResultSetMetaData interface answers the following questions:

- How many columns are in a result set (ResultSet object)?

- What is the name of a given column?

- What is the name of a table for a given column?

- Are the column names case sensitive?

- What is the data type of a specific column?

- What is the maximum character size of a column?

- Can you search on a given column?

- Is a given column readable/writable?

4.3. How Do You Create a ResultSetMetaData Object?

ResultSetMetaData is a Java class, which provides information about the ResultSet and implements the java.sql.ResultSetMetaData interface. The column name, column type, and so forth are provided by the ResultSetMetaData object. Database vendors provide different classes for implementing the ResultSetMetaData interface.

To learn about a given result set from a database (expressed as a ResultSet object), you must obtain (or create) a ResultSetMetaData object. Once a client program has obtained a valid ResultSet, the following code gets a metadata object:

```
ResultSet rs = null;
...
try {
   ...
   rs = <get a result set>;
   ResultSetMetaData rsMetaData = rs.getMetaData();
   if (rsMetaData == null) {
      // there is no metadata for a given result set

      ...
   }
   else {
      // once you are here, then you can execute methods
      // given in the ResultSetMetaData.

      // get the number of columns for a given result set
      int numberOfColumns = rsMetaData.getColumnCount();
   }
   ...
}
catch(SQLException e) {
   // handle the exception
}
finally {
   // close the rs (result set object)
}
```

The ResultSetMetaData interface has over two dozen methods. Using ResultSetMetaData, an application can discover the number of columns returned, as well as an individual column's suggested display size, column names, column types, and so on. Note that a given JDBC driver may not provide information for all of the methods, so you need to check returned objects for nulls or empty strings.

A ResultSet object provides a table of data representing a database result set, which is usually generated by executing a statement that queries the database. The ResultSet object is one of the most important objects in the JDBC API. ResultSet is basically an abstraction of a table of general width and unknown length. Most of the methods and queries return result data as a ResultSet. A ResultSet contains any number of named columns that you can ask for by name. It also consists of one or more rows, which you can move through sequentially from top to bottom, one at a time. Before you can use a ResultSet, you need to inspect the number of columns it contains. This information is stored in the ResultSetMetaData object.

```
//get the number of columns from the "ResultSet metadata"
Connection conn = null;
Statement stmt = null;
ResultSet rs = null;
...
try {
    // get a result set
    conn = ... get a java.sql.Connection object ...
    stmt = conn.createStatement();
    rs = stmt.executeQuery("SELECT id, name FROM employees");
    ResultSetMetaData rsmd = rs.getMetaData();
    if (rsmd == null) {
        // no result set metadata

        ...
    }
    else {
        int numberOfColumns = rsmd.getColumnCount();
        if (numberOfColumns != 2) {
          // error
        }
    }
}
catch(SQLException e) {
  // handle the exception
}
finally {
    // close the rs (result set object)
    // close the stmt (Statement object)
    // close the conn (connection object)
}
```

When you obtain a ResultSet, it points just before the first row. To iterate all of the rows, you can use the next() method to obtain each additional row, and the method returns false when no more rows remain. Since fetching data from a database can result in errors, you must always enclose your result set manipulations in a try/catch block.

Here's an example:

```
import java.sql.*;
import jcb.util.DatabaseUtil;
...
public static Connection getConnection()
   throws Exception {
   // return a valid database connection object
}

...
```

```
ResultSet rs = null;
Statement stmt = null;
Connection conn = null;
try {
    conn = getConnection();
    stmt = conn.createStatement();
    rs = stmt.executeQuery("SELECT id, name FROM employees");
    ResultSetMetaData rsmd = rs.getMetaData();
    if (rsmd == null) {
        // ResultSetMetaData is not supported
    }
    else {
        int numberOfColumns = rsmd.getColumnCount();
        while(rs.next()) {
            for (i = 1; i <= numberOfColumns; i++) {
                System.out.println(rs.getString(i)+"       ");
            }
            System.out.println("------");
        }
    }
}
catch(Exception e) {
    // handle and deal with the exception
    System.out.println(e.getMessage());
}
finally {
    // close database resources
    DatabaseUtil.close(rs);
    DatabaseUtil.close(stmt);
    DatabaseUtil.close(conn);
}
```

4.4. How Does JDBC Define ResultSetMetaData?

In this section, I provide ResultSetMetaData's definition, field summary, and method summary
(the output is slightly modified). The J2SE 5.0 documentation defines ResultSetMetaData as
"an object that can be used to get information about the types and properties of the columns
in a ResultSet object." The ResultSetMetaData is an interface defined in the java.sql package:

```
package java.sql;
public interface ResultSetMetaData {
}
```

The following code fragment creates the ResultSet object rs, then creates the
ResultSetMetaData object rsmd and uses rsmd to find out how many columns rs has and
whether the first column in rs can be used in a WHERE clause:

```
ResultSet rs = null;
Statement stmt = null;
Connection conn = null;
ResultSetMetaData rsmd = null;
try {
   conn = getConnection(); // get a valid Connection object
   stmt = conn.createStatement();
   rs = stmt.executeQuery("SELECT column1, column2 FROM MY_TABLE");
   rsmd = rs.getMetaData();
   if (rsmd == null) {
      // ResultSetMetaData is not supported
      ...
   }
   else {
      // ResultSetMetaData is supported
      int numberOfColumns = rsmd.getColumnCount();
      boolean b = rsmd.isSearchable(1);
   }
}
catch(SQLException se) {
   // handle database exceptions
}
catch(Exception e) {
   // handle other exceptions
}
finally {
   // close ResultSet, Statement, Connection objects
}
```

Therefore, the ResultSetMetaData interface provides

- Information about the types and properties of the DDL properties of a ResultSet object

- Various methods for finding out information about the structure of a ResultSet object

ResultSetMetaData Field Summary

Table 4-1 shows the ResultSetMetaData field summary.

Table 4-1. ResultSetMetaData Field Summary

Type	Field	Summary
static int	columnNoNulls	The constant indicating that a column does not allow NULL values
static int	columnNullable	The constant indicating that a column allows NULL values
static int	columnNullableUnknown	The constant indicating that the nullability of a column's values is unknown

ResultSetMetaData Method Summary

Table 4-2 shows the ResultSetMetaData method summary.

Table 4-2. *ResultSetMetaData Method Summary*

Method Signature	Summary
String getCatalogName(int column)	Gets the designated column's table's catalog name
String getColumnClassName(int column)	Returns the fully qualified name of the Java class whose instances are manufactured if the method ResultSet.getObject is called to retrieve a value from the column
int getColumnCount()	Returns the number of columns in this ResultSet object
int getColumnDisplaySize(int column)	Indicates the designated column's normal maximum width in characters
String getColumnLabel(int column)	Gets the designated column's suggested title for use in printouts and displays
String getColumnName(int column)	Gets the designated column's name
int getColumnType(int column)	Retrieves the designated column's SQL type
String getColumnTypeName(int column)	Retrieves the designated column's database-specific type name
int getPrecision(int column)	Gets the designated column's number of decimal digits
int getScale(int column)	Gets the designated column's number of digits to right of the decimal point
String getSchemaName(int column)	Gets the designated column's table's schema
String getTableName(int column)	Gets the designated column's table name
boolean isAutoIncrement(int column)	Indicates whether the designated column is automatically numbered, thus read-only
boolean isCaseSensitive(int column)	Indicates whether a column's case matters
boolean isCurrency(int column)	Indicates whether the designated column is a cash value
boolean isDefinitelyWritable(int column)	Indicates whether a write on the designated column will definitely succeed
int isNullable(int column)	Indicates the nullability of values in the designated column
boolean isReadOnly(int column)	Indicates whether the designated column is definitely not writable
boolean isSearchable(int column)	Indicates whether the designated column can be used in a SQL WHERE clause
boolean isSigned(int column)	Indicates whether values in the designated column are signed numbers
boolean isWritable(int column)	Indicates whether it is possible for a write on the designated column to succeed

4.5. What Is the Weakness of the ResultSetMetaData Interface?

In distributed client-server applications, ResultSetMetaData might provide a minor performance problem. That is, for every bit of information, you have to call a specific method. There is no single method call to get most of the metadata from a ResultSet object. In order to eliminate this minor problem, server-side code should return the metadata result as an XML object (which represents ResultSetMetaData information in a structured fashion) rather than returning an instance of ResultSetMetaData. This way, the client can invoke a single method and get the desired answer from an XML document.

4.6. What Is the Relationship of ResultSetMetaData to Other Objects?

Before delving into the solution, let's take a look at the relationships (Figure 4-1) between important low-level interfaces and classes.

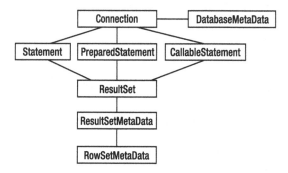

Figure 4-1. *Relationships between important low-level interfaces and classes*

To connect to a database, you use an instance of the Connection class. Then, to find out the names of the database tables and fields, you need to get an instance of the DatabaseMetaData class from the Connection. Next, to issue a query, you compose the SQL query string and use the Connection to create a Statement class. By executing the statement, you obtain a ResultSet class, and to find out the names of the column rows in that ResultSet, you must obtain an instance of the ResultsetMetaData object.

To obtain the ResultSet metadata, follow these steps:

1. To connect to a database, you use an instance of the Connection object.

2. To find out the names of the database schemas/tables/columns, you get an instance of the DatabaseMetaData object from the Connection.

3. To issue a query, you compose the SQL query string and use the Connection to create a Statement.

4. By executing the statement, you obtain a ResultSet object.

5. Finally, to find out the names of the column rows in that ResultSet, you obtain an instance of the ResultsetMetaData object.

What does ResultSetMetaData provide? ResultSetMetaData objects can be used to get information about the types and properties of the columns in a ResultSet object. ResultSetMetaData encapsulates the column's information—such as the number of columns, their names, and the column data type and its precision—contained in a ResultSet. ResultSetMetaData provides many methods to deal with the column's information; for example, the getColumnName() method of the ResultSetMetaData object returns the column's name in the ResultSet.

4.7. How Do You Express ResultSetMetaData in XML?

What follows is a single method, ResultSetMetaDataTool.getResultSetMetaData(), which creates an XML document for a ResultSetMetaData from a given ResultSet. The method getResultSetMetaData() can be used by any type of client (based on XML tags, clients may extract their needed information). The generated XML will have the following syntax:

```
<?xml version="1.0"?>
<resultSetMetaData columnCount="number-of-columns">
    <columnMetaData column="column-number"
                    columnDisplaySize="column-display-size"
                    columnLabel="column-label"
                    columnName="column-name"
                    columnType="column-type"
                    columnTypeName="column-type-name"
                    columnClassName="column-class-name"
                    tableName="table-name"
                    precision="precision-of-column"
                    scale="scale-of-column"
                    isAutoIncrement="true/false"
                    isCurrency="true/false"
                    isWritable="true/false"
                    isDefinitelyWritable="true/false"
                    isNullable="0/1"
                    isReadOnly="true/false"
                    isCaseSensitive="true/false"
                    isSearchable="true/false"
                    isSigned="true/false"
                    catalog="catalog-name"
                    schema="schema-name" />
    <columnMetaData ... />
    ...
    <columnMetaData ... />
</resultSetMetaData>
```

getResultSetMetaData()

The getResultSetMetaData() method accepts an instance of ResultSet and outputs its meta-data as XML (expressed as a serialized String object):

```
/**
 * Gets column names and their associated attributes (type,
 * size, nullable). The result is returned as XML (as
 * a String object);  if table name is null/empty
 * it returns null.
 *
 * @param rs the result set (ResultSet) object.
 * @return result set's metadata as XML as String object;
 * this metadata includes column names and their associated
 * attributes: type, size, nullable.
 * @exception Failed to get the result set's metadata as XML.
 */
public static String getResultSetMetaData(ResultSet rs)
    throws Exception {

    if (rs == null ) {
        return null;
    }

    // Retrieves the number, types and properties
    // of this ResultSet object's columns.
    ResultSetMetaData rsMetaData = rs.getMetaData();
    if (rsMetaData == null ) {
        return null;
    }

    StringBuffer sb = new StringBuffer();
    sb.append("<resultSetMetaData columnCount=\"");
    int numberOfColumns = rsMetaData.getColumnCount();
    sb.append(numberOfColumns);
    sb.append("\">");

    for (int i=1; i<=numberOfColumns; i++) {
        sb.append(getColumnMetaData(rsMetaData, i));
    }

    sb.append("</resultSetMetaData>");
    return sb.toString();

}
```

getColumnMetaData() method:

```
/**
 * Gets specific column's associated attributes
 * (type, size, nullable). The result is returned
 * as XML (represented as a String object).
 * XML attributes (as constants) are prefixed
 * with the "XML_METADATA_TAG_".
 *
 * @param rsMetaData the result set metadata object.
 * @param columnNumber the column number.
 * @return result set's metadata as XML as
 *  String object; this metadata includes
 *  column names and their associated attributes:
 *  type, size, nullable.
 * @exception Failed to get the result set's
 *  meta data as an XML.
 */
private static String getColumnMetaData
        (ResultSetMetaData rsMetaData,
         int columnNumber)
    throws Exception {
    StringBuffer sb = new StringBuffer();
    sb.append("<columnMetaData ");
    append(sb, XML_METADATA_TAG_COLUMN, columnNumber);

    // Indicates the designated column's normal
    // maximum width in characters
    append(sb, XML_METADATA_TAG_COLUMN_DISPLAY_SIZE,
        rsMetaData.getColumnDisplaySize(columnNumber));

    // Gets the designated column's suggested title
    // for use in printouts and displays.
    append(sb, XML_METADATA_TAG_COLUMN_LABEL,
        rsMetaData.getColumnLabel(columnNumber));

    // Gets the designated column's name.
    append(sb, XML_METADATA_TAG_COLUMN_NAME,
        rsMetaData.getColumnName(columnNumber));

    // Gets the designated column's SQL type.
    append(sb, XML_METADATA_TAG_COLUMN_TYPE,
        rsMetaData.getColumnType(columnNumber));

    // Gets the designated column's SQL type name.
    append(sb, XML_METADATA_TAG_COLUMN_TYPE_NAME,
        rsMetaData.getColumnTypeName(columnNumber));
```

```
// Gets the designated column's class name.
append(sb, XML_METADATA_TAG_COLUMN_CLASS_NAME,
    rsMetaData.getColumnClassName(columnNumber));

// Gets the designated column's table name.
append(sb, XML_METADATA_TAG_TABLE_NAME,
    rsMetaData.getTableName(columnNumber));

// Gets the designated column's number of decimal digits.
append(sb, XML_METADATA_TAG_PRECISION,
    rsMetaData.getPrecision(columnNumber));

// Gets the designated column's number of
// digits to right of the decimal point.
append(sb, XML_METADATA_TAG_SCALE,
    rsMetaData.getScale(columnNumber));

// Indicates whether the designated column is
// automatically numbered, thus read-only.
append(sb, XML_METADATA_TAG_IS_AUTO_INCREMENT,
    rsMetaData.isAutoIncrement(columnNumber));

// Indicates whether the designated column is a cash value.
append(sb, XML_METADATA_TAG_IS_CURRENCY,
    rsMetaData.isCurrency(columnNumber));

// Indicates whether a write on the designated
// column will succeed.
append(sb, XML_METADATA_TAG_IS_WRITABLE,
    rsMetaData.isWritable(columnNumber));

// Indicates whether a write on the designated
// column will definitely succeed.
append(sb, XML_METADATA_TAG_IS_DEFINITELY_WRITABLE,
    rsMetaData.isDefinitelyWritable(columnNumber));

// Indicates the nullability of values
// in the designated column.
append(sb, XML_METADATA_TAG_IS_NULLABLE,
    rsMetaData.isNullable(columnNumber));

// Indicates whether the designated column
// is definitely not writable.
append(sb, XML_METADATA_TAG_IS_READ_ONLY,
    rsMetaData.isReadOnly(columnNumber));
```

```
            // Indicates whether a column's case matters
            // in the designated column.
            append(sb, XML_METADATA_TAG_IS_CASE_SENSITIVE,
                rsMetaData.isCaseSensitive(columnNumber));

            // Indicates whether a column's case matters
            // in the designated column.
            append(sb, XML_METADATA_TAG_IS_SEARCHABLE,
                rsMetaData.isSearchable(columnNumber));

            // Indicates whether values in the designated
            // column are signed numbers.
            append(sb, XML_METADATA_TAG_IS_SIGNED,
                rsMetaData.isSigned(columnNumber));

            // Gets the designated column's table's catalog name.
            append(sb, XML_METADATA_TAG_CATALOG_NAME,
                rsMetaData.getCatalogName(columnNumber));

            // Gets the designated column's table's schema name.
            append(sb, XML_METADATA_TAG_SCHEMA_NAME,
                rsMetaData.getSchemaName(columnNumber));

            sb.append("/>");
            return sb.toString();

    }
```

Support methods are provided here:

```
/**
 * Append attribute=value to the string buffer denoted by sb.
 * @param sb the string buffer.
 * @param attribute the attribute name.
 * @param value the value of the attribute.
 */
private static void append(StringBuffer sb,
                           String attribute,
                           String value) {
    sb.append(attribute);
    sb.append("=\"");
    sb.append(value);
    sb.append("\" ");
}
```

```
/**
 * Append attribute=value to the string buffer denoted by sb.
 * @param sb the string buffer.
 * @param attribute the attribute name.
 * @param value the value of the attribute.
 */
private static void append(StringBuffer sb,
                           String attribute,
                           int value) {
    sb.append(attribute);
    sb.append("=\"");
    sb.append(value);
    sb.append("\" ");
}

/**
 * Append attribute=value to the string buffer denoted by sb.
 * @param sb the string buffer.
 * @param attribute the attribute name.
 * @param value the value of the attribute.
 */
private static void append(StringBuffer sb,
                           String attribute,
                           boolean value) {
    sb.append(attribute);
    sb.append("=\"");
    sb.append(value);
    sb.append("\" ");
}
```

Oracle Database Setup

The client using Oracle database will use the employees table described here:

```
$ sqlplus octopus/octopus
SQL*Plus: Release 9.2.0.1.0 - Production on Tue Feb 25 08:13:46 2003
Connected to: Oracle9i Enterprise Edition Release 9.2.0.1.0 - Production
SQL> describe employees;
 Name              Null?    Type
 ----------------- -------- ----------------
 BADGENUMBER       NOT NULL NUMBER(38)
 NAME                       VARCHAR2(60)
 EMPLOYEETYPE               VARCHAR2(30)
 PHOTO                      BINARY FILE LOB
```

Client Using Oracle

```java
import java.util.*;
import java.io.*;
import java.sql.*;

import jcb.db.*;
import jcb.meta.*;

public class TestOracleResultSetMetaDataTool {

    public static Connection getConnection() throws Exception {
        String driver = "oracle.jdbc.driver.OracleDriver";
        String url = "jdbc:oracle:thin:@localhost:1521:maui";
        String username = "octopus";
        String password = "octopus";
        Class.forName(driver);  // load Oracle driver
        return DriverManager.getConnection(url, username, password);
    }

    public static void main(String[] args) {
        Connection conn = null;
        Statement stmt = null;
        ResultSet rs = null;
        try {
            conn = getConnection();
            // Create a result set
            stmt = conn.createStatement();
            rs = stmt.executeQuery("SELECT * FROM employees");

            System.out.println("-------- getResultSetMetaData -------------");
            System.out.println("conn="+conn);
            String rsMetaData = ResultSetMetaDataTool.getResultSetMetaData(rs);
            System.out.println(rsMetaData);
            System.out.println("----------------------------------");
        }
        catch(Exception e){
            e.printStackTrace();
            System.exit(1);
        }
        finally {
            DatabaseUtil.close(stmt);
            DatabaseUtil.close(rs);
            DatabaseUtil.close(conn);
        }
    }
}
```

Client Output Using Oracle

```
-------- getResultSetMetaData -------------
conn=oracle.jdbc.driver.OracleConnection@66e815
<?xml version='1.0'>
<resultSetMetaData columnCount="4">
    <columnMetaData column="1"
                columnDisplaySize="22" columnLabel="BADGENUMBER"
                columnName="BADGENUMBER" columnType="2"
                columnTypeName="NUMBER" columnClassName="java.math.BigDecimal"
                tableName=""  precision="38" scale="0"
                isAutoIncrement="false" isCurrency="true"
                isWritable="true" isDefinitelyWritable="false"
                isNullable="0" isReadOnly="false"
                isCaseSensitive="false" isSearchable="true" isSigned="true"
                catalog="" schema="" />
    <columnMetaData column="2"
                columnDisplaySize="60" columnLabel="NAME"
                columnName="NAME" columnType="12"
                columnTypeName="VARCHAR2" columnClassName="java.lang.String"
                tableName="" precision="60" scale="0"
                isAutoIncrement="false" isCurrency="false"
                isWritable="true" isDefinitelyWritable="false"
                isNullable="1" isReadOnly="false"
                isCaseSensitive="true" isSearchable="true" isSigned="true"
                catalog="" schema="" />
    <columnMetaData column="3"
                columnDisplaySize="30" columnLabel="EMPLOYEETYPE"
                columnName="EMPLOYEETYPE" columnType="12"
                columnTypeName="VARCHAR2" columnClassName="java.lang.String"
                tableName="" precision="30" scale="0"
                isAutoIncrement="false" isCurrency="false"
                isWritable="true" isDefinitelyWritable="false"
                isNullable="1" isReadOnly="false"
                isCaseSensitive="true" isSearchable="true" isSigned="true"
                catalog="" schema="" />
    <columnMetaData column="4"
                columnDisplaySize="530" columnLabel="PHOTO"
                columnName="PHOTO" columnType="-13"
                columnTypeName="BFILE" columnClassName="oracle.sql.BFILE"
                tableName="" precision="0" scale="0"
                isAutoIncrement="false" isCurrency="false"
                isWritable="true" isDefinitelyWritable="false"
                isNullable="1" isReadOnly="false"
                isCaseSensitive="false" isSearchable="false" isSigned="true"
                catalog="" schema="" />
</resultSetMetaData>
------------------------------------
```

Oracle's Limitations on ResultSetMetaData.getTableName()

Note that the Oracle implementation of ResultSetMetaData does not provide table names for result set metadata. According to the Oracle documentation (http://www.oracle.com/technology/sample_code/tech/java/codesnippet/jdbc/OracleResultSetMetaData.html), the OracleResultSetMetaData interface does not implement the getSchemaName() and getTableName() methods because the underlying protocol does not make this feasible.

MySQL Database Setup

The client using MySQL database will use the mypictures table described here:

```
mysql> describe mypictures;
+-------+-------------+------+-----+---------+-------+
| Field | Type        | Null | Key | Default | Extra |
+-------+-------------+------+-----+---------+-------+
| id    | int(11)     |      | PRI | 0       |       |
| name  | varchar(20) | YES  |     | NULL    |       |
| photo | blob        | YES  |     | NULL    |       |
+-------+-------------+------+-----+---------+-------+
3 rows in set (0.00 sec)
```

Client Using MySQL

```java
import java.util.*;
import java.io.*;
import java.sql.*;

import jcb.db.*;
import jcb.meta.*;

public class TestMySqlResultSetMetaDataTool {
    public static Connection getConnection() throws Exception {
        String driver = "org.gjt.mm.mysql.Driver";
        String url = "jdbc:mysql://localhost/octopus";
        String username = "root";
        String password = "root";
        Class.forName(driver);  // load MySQL driver
        return DriverManager.getConnection(url, username, password);
    }
    public static void main(String[] args) {
        Connection conn = null;
        Statement stmt = null;
        ResultSet rs = null;
        try {
            conn = getConnection();
            // Create a result set
            stmt = conn.createStatement();
            rs = stmt.executeQuery("SELECT * FROM mypictures");
```

```
            System.out.println("-------- getResultSetMetaData -------------");
            System.out.println("conn="+conn);
            String rsMetaData = ResultSetMetaDataTool.getResultSetMetaData(rs);
            System.out.println(rsMetaData);
            System.out.println("----------------------------------");
        }
        catch(Exception e){
            e.printStackTrace();
            System.exit(1);
        }
        finally {
            DatabaseUtil.close(stmt);
            DatabaseUtil.close(rs);
            DatabaseUtil.close(conn);
        }
    }
}
```

Client Output Using MySQL

```
-------- getResultSetMetaData -------------
conn=com.mysql.jdbc.Connection@1837697
<?xml version='1.0'>
<resultSetMetaData columnCount="3">
    <columnMetaData column="1"
            columnDisplaySize="11" columnLabel="id"
            columnName="id" columnType="4"
            columnTypeName="LONG" columnClassName="java.lang.Integer"
            tableName="mypictures" precision="11" scale="0"
            isAutoIncrement="false" isCurrency="false"
            isWritable="false" isDefinitelyWritable="false"
            isNullable="0" isReadOnly="false"
            isCaseSensitive="false" isSearchable="true" isSigned="true"
            catalog="null" schema="" />
    <columnMetaData column="2"
            columnDisplaySize="20" columnLabel="name"
            columnName="name" columnType="12"
            columnTypeName="VARCHAR" columnClassName="java.lang.String"
            tableName="mypictures" precision="0" scale="0"
            isAutoIncrement="false" isCurrency="false"
            isWritable="false" isDefinitelyWritable="false"
            isNullable="1" isReadOnly="false"
            isCaseSensitive="true" isSearchable="true" isSigned="false"
            catalog="null" schema="" />
```

```
        <columnMetaData column="3"
                columnDisplaySize="65535" columnLabel="photo"
                columnName="photo" columnType="-4"
                columnTypeName="BLOB" columnClassName="java.lang.Object"
                tableName="mypictures" precision="0" scale="0"
                isAutoIncrement="false" isCurrency="false"
                isWritable="false" isDefinitelyWritable="false"
                isNullable="1" isReadOnly="false"
                isCaseSensitive="true" isSearchable="true" isSigned="false"
                catalog="null" schema="" />
</resultSetMetaData>
```

4.8. How Do You Get a Table's Metadata Without Selecting Any Rows?

How do you get table's metadata without selecting any rows? This is possible by selecting required columns without selecting any records or rows. If you are interested in only the ResultSetMetaData (and not the ResultSet itself), then select required columns from a table so that the SQL query's where condition will be false. For example:

```
select id, name from employees where 1 = 0;
```

The condition "1 = 0" (as a boolean expression) is always false; therefore, no data will be selected at all, but you will get the result set metadata information.

The Solution

Our solution generates result set metadata for a given table identified with the tableName parameter. Using tableName, we create the following query (note that Oracle requires the table name to be in uppercase characters, while MySQL does not care):

```
String query = "select * from " + tableName.toUpperCase() + " where 1 = 0";
```

Then, we execute query (note that our query does not select any records from a given table because the where clause is always false) and then call the getResultSetMetaData➥ (ResultSet rs) method. The reason for conversion of table name to uppercase characters is that some databases (such as Oracle) prefer, or even require, table names in uppercase.

```
/**
 * Get table's column names and their associated attributes
 * (type, size, nullable) The result is returned as XML
 * (as a String object);  if table name is null/empty
 * it returns null.
 *
 * @param conn the Connection object.
 * @param tableName the table name.
 * @return result set's metadata as an XML as String object;
```

```
 * this metadata includes column names and their associated
 * attributes: type, size, nullable.
 * @exception Failed to get the result set's metadata as XML.
 */
public static String getTableMetaData(Connection conn,
                                      String tableName)
    throws Exception {
    Statement stmt = null;
    ResultSet rs = null;
    String query = null;
    try {
        if ((conn == null) ||
            (tableName == null) ||
            (tableName.length() == 0)) {
            return null;
        }

        query = "select * from "+ tableName.toUpperCase() + " where 1 = 0";
        stmt = conn.createStatement();
        rs = stmt.executeQuery(query);

        // Retrieves the number, types and properties
        // of this ResultSet object's columns.
        return getResultSetMetaData(rs);
    }
    finally {
        DatabaseUtil.close(rs);
        DatabaseUtil.close((stmt);
    }
}
```

Oracle Database Setup

```
$ sqlplus octopus/octopus
SQL*Plus: Release 9.2.0.1.0 - Production on Wed Feb 26 17:38:26 2003
Copyright (c) 1982, 2002, Oracle Corporation.  All rights reserved.
SQL> describe zdepts;
 Name                 Null?    Type
 ----------------- -------- ------------
 DEPT              NOT NULL VARCHAR2(32)
 NAME              NOT NULL VARCHAR2(32)
 LOCATION          NOT NULL VARCHAR2(64)
 COSTCENTER                 CHAR(32)
```

Client Using an Oracle Table

```java
import java.util.*;
import java.io.*;
import java.sql.*;

import jcb.db.*;
import jcb.meta.*;

public class TestOracleTableResultSetMetaDataTool {

    public static Connection getConnection() throws Exception {
        String driver = "oracle.jdbc.driver.OracleDriver";
        String url = "jdbc:oracle:thin:@localhost:1521:maui";
        String username = "octopus";
        String password = "octopus";
        Class.forName(driver);  // load Oracle driver
        return DriverManager.getConnection(url, username, password);
    }

    public static void main(String[] args) {
        Connection conn = null;
        try {
            conn = getConnection();
            System.out.println("-------- getResultSetMetaData -------------");
            System.out.println("conn="+conn);
            String deptTableName = "zdepts";
            String rsMetaData =
                ResultSetMetaDataTool.getTableMetaData(conn, deptTableName);
            System.out.println(rsMetaData);
            System.out.println("-----------------------------------");
        }
        catch(Exception e){
            e.printStackTrace();
            System.exit(1);
        }
        finally {
            DatabaseUtil.close(conn);
        }
    }
}
```

Output Using an Oracle Table

```
-------- getTableMetaData -------------
conn=oracle.jdbc.driver.OracleConnection@169ca65
<?xml version='1.0'>
<resultSetMetaData columnCount="4">
    <columnMetaData column="1" columnDisplaySize="32"
                columnLabel="DEPT" columnName="DEPT"
                columnType="12" columnTypeName="VARCHAR2"
                columnClassName="java.lang.String" tableName=""
                precision="32" scale="0"
                isAutoIncrement="false" isCurrency="false"
                isWritable="true" isDefinitelyWritable="false"
                isNullable="0" isReadOnly="false"
                isCaseSensitive="true" isSearchable="true"
                isSigned="true" catalog="" schema="" />
    <columnMetaData column="2" columnDisplaySize="32"
                columnLabel="NAME" columnName="NAME"
                columnType="12" columnTypeName="VARCHAR2"
                columnClassName="java.lang.String" tableName=""
                precision="32" scale="0"
                isAutoIncrement="false" isCurrency="false"
                isWritable="true" isDefinitelyWritable="false"
                isNullable="0" isReadOnly="false"
                isCaseSensitive="true" isSearchable="true"
                isSigned="true" catalog="" schema="" />
    <columnMetaData column="3" columnDisplaySize="64"
                columnLabel="LOCATION" columnName="LOCATION"
                columnType="12" columnTypeName="VARCHAR2"
                columnClassName="java.lang.String" tableName=""
                precision="64" scale="0"
                isAutoIncrement="false" isCurrency="false"
                isWritable="true" isDefinitelyWritable="false"
                isNullable="0" isReadOnly="false"
                isCaseSensitive="true" isSearchable="true"
                isSigned="true" catalog="" schema="" />
    <columnMetaData column="4" columnDisplaySize="32"
                columnLabel="COSTCENTER" columnName="COSTCENTER"
                columnType="1" columnTypeName="CHAR"
                columnClassName="java.lang.String" tableName=""
                precision="32" scale="0"
                isAutoIncrement="false" isCurrency="false"
                isWritable="true" isDefinitelyWritable="false"
                isNullable="1" isReadOnly="false"
                isCaseSensitive="true" isSearchable="true"
                isSigned="true" catalog="" schema="" />
</resultSetMetaData>
------------------------------------
```

MySQL Database Setup

```
mysql> describe zperson;
+-------+---------+------+-----+---------+-------+
| Field | Type    | Null | Key | Default | Extra |
+-------+---------+------+-----+---------+-------+
| id    | int(11) | YES  |     | NULL    |       |
| photo | blob    | YES  |     | NULL    |       |
+-------+---------+------+-----+---------+-------+
2 rows in set (0.03 sec)
```

Client Using a MySQL Table

```java
import java.util.*;
import java.io.*;
import java.sql.*;

import jcb.db.*;
import jcb.meta.*;

public class TestMySqlTableResultSetMetaDataTool {

    public static Connection getConnection() throws Exception {
        String driver = "org.gjt.mm.mysql.Driver";
        String url = "jdbc:mysql://localhost/octopus";
        String username = "root";
        String password = "root";
        Class.forName(driver);  // load MySQL driver
        return DriverManager.getConnection(url, username, password);
    }

    public static void main(String[] args) {
        Connection conn = null;
        try {
            conn = getConnection();
            System.out.println("-------- getTableMetaData -------------");
            System.out.println("conn="+conn);
            String deptTableName = "zperson";
            String rsMetaData =
                ResultSetMetaDataTool.getTableMetaData(conn, deptTableName);
            System.out.println(rsMetaData);
            System.out.println("-----------------------------------");
        }
        catch(Exception e){
            e.printStackTrace();
            System.exit(1);
        }
```

```
        finally {
            DatabaseUtil.close(conn);
        }
    }
}
```

Output Using a MySQL Table

```
-------- getTableMetaData -------------
conn=com.mysql.jdbc.Connection@1837697
<?xml version='1.0'>
<resultSetMetaData columnCount="2">
    <columnMetaData column="1" columnDisplaySize="11" columnLabel="id"
                columnName="id" columnType="4" columnTypeName="LONG"
                columnClassName="java.lang.Integer" tableName="ZPERSON"
                precision="11" scale="0" isAutoIncrement="false"
                isCurrency="false" isWritable="false"
                isDefinitelyWritable="false" isNullable="1"
                isReadOnly="false" isCaseSensitive="false"
                isSearchable="true" isSigned="true"
                catalog="null" schema="" />
    <columnMetaData column="2" columnDisplaySize="65535" columnLabel="photo"
                columnName="photo" columnType="-4" columnTypeName="BLOB"
                columnClassName="java.lang.Object" tableName="ZPERSON"
                precision="0" scale="0" isAutoIncrement="false"
                isCurrency="false" isWritable="false"
                isDefinitelyWritable="false" isNullable="1"
                isReadOnly="false" isCaseSensitive="true"
                isSearchable="true" isSigned="false"
                catalog="null" schema="" />
</resultSetMetaData>
------------------------------------
```

4.9. How Do You Retrieve the Column Types from a ResultSet?

In GUI database applications, you must determine the type of a ResultSet's columns in order to validate column values before sending them to the database server. So, to retrieve the column data type from a result set object, let's return the result as a java.util.List, where each element of the list is a java.lang.String, which represents a data type.

The Solution: getTypes()

```
/**
 * Get the column data type from a result set object.
 * @param rs a ResultSet object to process
 * @throws SQLException Failed to get data types from a ResultSet
```

```
 * @return the result as a java.util.List, where each element of the
 *  list is a String object (designates types).
 */
public static java.util.List getTypes(ResultSet rs)
    throws SQLException {
    if (rs == null) {
        return null;
    }

    ResultSetMetaData meta = rs.getMetaData();
    if (meta == null) {
        return null;
    }

    java.util.List types = new java.util.ArrayList();
    for (int i = 1; i <= meta.getColumnCount(); i++){
        String columnType = meta.getColumnTypeName(i);
        types.add(columnType);
    }

    return types;
}
```

Discussion

- The solution presented is a general one: this solution can be applied to any ResultSet object.

- ResultSetMetaData.getColumnCount() returns the total number of columns for a ResultSet object.

- ResultSetMetaData.getColumnTypeName(i) returns the column data type name for the ith position (positions start from 1).

4.10. How Do You Retrieve the Column Name/Data/Type from a ResultSet?

Next we'll see how to retrieve the column name from a result set as well as its associated type and data. To solve this problem, let's return the result as a java.util.List, where each element of the list is a java.util.Map, which represents a retrieved row or record.

The Solution

We'll use two methods:

- getNameAndData(ResultSet rs): Retrieves the column name from a result set as well as its associated data.

- getNameAndType(ResultSet rs): Retrieves the column name from a result set as well as its associated data type.

getNameAndData()

```java
/**
 * Get the column name from a result set as well as its associated data.
 * @param rs a ResultSet object to process
 * @throws SQLException Failed to get name and data from a ResultSet
 * @return the result as a java.util.List (where each element of the
 * list is a java.util.Map, which represents a retrieved row/record).
 */
public static java.util.List getNameAndData(ResultSet rs)
    throws SQLException {
    if (rs == null) {
        return null;
    }

    ResultSetMetaData meta = rs.getMetaData();
    if (meta == null) {
        return null;
    }

    java.util.List rows = new java.util.ArrayList();
    while(rs.next()) {
        Map row = new HashMap();
        for (int i = 1; i <= meta.getColumnCount(); i++){
            String column = meta.getColumnName(i);
            String value = rs.getString(i);
            if (value == null){
                value="";
            }
            row.put(column,value.trim());
        }
        rows.add(row);
    }
    return rows;
}
```

Discussion

- The solution presented is a simplistic one: it assumes that all column types are either VARCHAR or CHAR. For getting values, we invoke ResultSet.getString(), which might not work for some data types such as BLOBs. The revised solution might be to get both the name and data type of each column, and then, based on the data type, invoke ResultSet.getXXX(), where XXX is derived from the data type of a column name.

- ResultSetMetaData.getColumnCount() returns the number of columns returned from a ResultSet object.

- ResultSetMetaData.getColumnName(i) returns the column name for the ith position (positions start from 1).

getNameAndType()

```java
/**
 * Get the column name from a result set as well as its associated data type.
 * @param rs a ResultSet object to process
 * @throws SQLException Failed to get name and data type from a ResultSet
 * @return the result as a java.util.Map, where each element of the
 *  map is a pair of (name, data type).
 */
public static java.util.Map getNameAndType(ResultSet rs)
    throws SQLException {
    if (rs == null) {
        return null;
    }

    ResultSetMetaData meta = rs.getMetaData();
    if (meta == null) {
        return null;
    }

    java.util.Map result = new HashMap();
    for (int i = 1; i <= meta.getColumnCount(); i++){
        String columnName = meta.getColumnName(i);
        String columnType = meta.getColumnTypeName(i);
        result.put(columnName, columnType);
    }

    return result;
}
```

Discussion

- The solution I've presented is a general one, which means you can apply it to any ResultSet object.

- ResultSetMetaData.getColumnName(i) returns the column name for the *i*th position (positions start from 1).

- ResultSetMetaData.getColumnTypeName(i) returns the column data type name for the *i*th position (positions start from 1).

4.11. What Is ResultSet Holdability?

JDBC 3.0 adds support for specifying result set (or cursor) holdability. Result set *holdability* is the ability to specify whether cursors (or a result set as java.sql.ResultSet objects) should be held open or closed at the end of a transaction. A holdable cursor, or result set, is one that does not automatically close when the transaction that contains the cursor is committed. You may improve database performance by including the ResultSet holdability. If ResultSet objects are closed when a commit operation is implicitly or explicitly called, this can also improve performance.

According to Java Database Connectivity, Version 3.0:

> *When the method Connection.commit is called, open ResultSet objects that have been created during the current transaction are closed. With ResultSet holdability, it is possible to exercise greater control on when the ResultSet objects are closed when the commit operation is performed. Using the ResultSet holdability, ResultSet objects that are closed when a commit operation is performed can result in better performance in some applications.*

To specify the holdability of a `ResultSet` object, you must do so when preparing a `java.sql.Statement` (or `java.sql.PreparedStatement` or `java.sql.CallableStatement`) using the `Connection.createStatement()`, `Connection.prepareStatement()`, or `Connection.prepareCall()` method. The `ResultSet` holdability may be one of the following constants (defined in the `ResultSet` interface):

- `HOLD_CURSORS_OVER_COMMIT`: The constant indicating that `ResultSet` objects should not be closed when the method `Connection.commit()` is called.

- `CLOSE_CURSORS_AT_COMMIT`: The constant indicating that `ResultSet` objects should be closed when the method `Connection.commit()` is called.

In general, closing a cursor (as a `ResultSet` object) when a transaction is committed results in better performance.

CHAPTER 5

■ ■ ■

Parameter Metadata

If one is given in a continuum, without first proceeding from a metric, it constitutes a generalization of Riemannian geometry but which still retains the most important derived parameters.

Albert Einstein

This chapter presents `java.sql.ParameterMetaData`, a new interface defined in JDBC 3.0. The `ParameterMetaData` interface contains methods that retrieve information about the parameter markers (indicated with a ?) in a `PreparedStatement` object. `ParameterMetaData` is an object that can be used to get information about the types and properties of the parameters in a `PreparedStatement` object. `ParameterMetaData` describes the number, type, and properties of parameters to prepared statements. The method `PreparedStatement.getParameterMetaData()` returns a `ParameterMetaData` object that describes the parameter markers that appear in the `PreparedStatement` object.

The `ParameterMetaData` interface and the `PreparedStatement.getParameterMetaData()` method are part of the JDBC 3.0 API and are included in J2SE 5.0 (JDK 1.5). For details on `ParameterMetaData`, refer to the JDBC 3.0 final specification. `ParameterMetaData` is an optional interface, and some vendors might not implement it. If the method `PreparedStatement.getParameterMetaData()` returns a `null` object, then it means that `ParameterMetaData` is not implemented.

Note that `CallableStatement.getParameterMetaData()` is a valid method call (`CallableStatement` extends the `PreparedStatement` interface), which should return metadata about the parameters of a "stored procedure" (represented as a `CallableStatement`).

Keep in mind this critical point when reading this chapter: neither MySQL's JDBC driver nor Oracle's JDBC "thin" driver implements the `ParameterMetaData` interface; we will illustrate these cases with an example. To use and understand `ParameterMetaData`, we will use the following databases (both of the following databases support `ParameterMetaData`):

- HSQLDB 100% Java database (`http://hsqldb.sourceforge.net/`), which supports `ParameterMetaData` implementation. HSQLDB is a SQL-based relational database engine written in Java. It has a JDBC driver (`org.hsqldb.jdbcDriver`) and supports a rich subset of ANSI-92 SQL and SQL 99. It offers a small, fast database engine that provides both in-memory and disk-based tables. For using HSQLDB, refer to the HSQLDB User Guide (`http://hsqldb.sourceforge.net/doc/guide/guide.pdf`).

- Derby (Apache's Derby Database, at http://incubator.apache.org/derby/) is a relational database management system (RDBMS) that is based on Java and SQL. You can deploy Derby in a number of different ways:

    - Embedded in a single-user Java application. Derby can be almost invisible to the end user because it requires no administration and runs in the same Java virtual machine (JVM) as the application.

    - Embedded in a multiuser application such as a web server, an application server, or a shared development environment.

    - Embedded in a server framework. You can use the network server with the network client driver or a server of your own choice.

5.1. What Are Dynamic Parameters?

You can prepare SQL queries and statements that are allowed to have dynamic parameters for which the value is not specified when the statement or query is prepared by using PreparedStatement methods in the JDBC API. These parameters, known as *dynamic parameters*, are represented by a ?. The JDBC refers to dynamic parameters as IN (input), INOUT (input and output), or OUT (output) parameters. In SQL, they are always IN (input) parameters. Before you execute queries by PreparedStatement object, you must specify values for all input parameters. The values specified must match the types expected.

Also, dynamic parameters can be used with CallableStatement (this interface extends the PreparedStatement interface) objects (which represents a stored procedure or function in a database server). A CallableStatement object may have any number of IN (input), INOUT (input and output), or OUT (output) parameters.

Next, I provide a dynamic parameter example.

MySQL Database Setup

```
mysql> use octopus;
Database changed
mysql> desc employees;
+-------+-------------+------+-----+---------+-------+
| Field | Type        | Null | Key | Default | Extra |
+-------+-------------+------+-----+---------+-------+
| id    | varchar(8)  |      | PRI |         |       |
| name  | varchar(16) | YES  |     | NULL    |       |
| age   | int(11)     | YES  |     | NULL    |       |
+-------+-------------+------+-----+---------+-------+
3 rows in set (0.01 sec)
```

```
mysql> select * from employees;
+-----+--------+------+
| id  | name   | age  |
+-----+--------+------+
| 88  | Peter  |  80  |
| 77  | Donald |  70  |
| 33  | Mary   |  30  |
| 44  | Monica |  40  |
| 999 | Andre  |  90  |
+-----+--------+------+
5 rows in set (0.00 sec)
```

Using Dynamic Parameters

```java
import java.sql.ResultSet;
import java.sql.PreparedStatement;
import java.sql.Connection;

import jcb.util.DatabaseUtil;
import jcb.db.VeryBasicConnectionManager;

public class DemoDynamicParams {

    public static void main(String[] args) throws Exception {

        ResultSet rs = null;
        Connection conn = null;
        PreparedStatement ps =  null;

        // the following SQL query has two dynamic input parameters:
        // first parameter is for "id" column and second one is for "age" column
        String query =
           "select id, name, age from employees where id < ? and age > ?";

        String dbVendor = args[0];
        try {
           // get a valid connection object
           conn = VeryBasicConnectionManager.getConnection(dbVendor);

           // prepare a SQL statement, which can have parameters; note that
           // a PreparedStatement object may be used any number of times
           ps = conn.prepareStatement(query);

           // specify values for all input parameters
           ps.setInt(1, 100);    // set the first dynamic parameter: id
           ps.setInt(2, 30);     // set the second dynamic parameter: age
```

```
            // now, PreparedStatement object is ready to be executed.
            rs = ps.executeQuery();
            // iterate the result set object
            displayResultSet(rs);

            // NOTE: you may use PreparedStatement as many times as you want
            // here we use it for another set of parameters:
            ps.setInt(1, 110);     // set the first dynamic parameter: id
            ps.setInt(2, 70);      // set the second dynamic parameter: age

            // now, PreparedStatement object is ready to be executed.
            rs = ps.executeQuery();
            // iterate the result set object
            displayResultSet(rs);
        }
        finally {
            // close resources: ResultSet, PreparedStatement, Connection
            DatabaseUtil.close(rs);
            DatabaseUtil.close(ps);
            DatabaseUtil.close(conn);
        }
    }

    public static void displayResultSet(ResultSet rs) throws Exception {
        if (rs == null) {
            return;
        }
        while (rs.next()) {
            int id = rs.getInt(1);
            String name = rs.getString(2);
            int age = rs.getInt(3);
            System.out.println("[id="+id+"][name="+name+"][age="+age+"]");
        }
        System.out.println("-------------");
    }
}
```

Running the Solution for a MySQL Database

```
$ javac DemoDynamicParams.java
$ java DemoDynamicParams mysql
[id=88][name=Peter][age=80]
[id=77][name=Donald][age=70]
[id=44][name=Monica][age=40]
-------------
[id=88][name=Peter][age=80]
-------------
```

Oracle Database Setup

```
SQL> desc employees;
Name                    Null?    Type
---------------------   -------- ------------
ID                      NOT NULL VARCHAR2(10)
NAME                    NOT NULL VARCHAR2(20)
AGE                              NUMBER(38)
SQL> select * from employees;
ID          NAME                      AGE
----------  --------------------  ----------
11          Alex Smith                 25
22          Don Knuth                  65
33          Mary Kent                  35
44          Monica Seles               30
99          Alex Edison
100         Al Sumner                 120
105         Al Sumner                  90

7 rows selected.
```

Running the Solution for an Oracle Database

```
$ java DemoDynamicParams oracle
[id=22][name=Don Knuth][age=65]
[id=33][name=Mary Kent][age=35]
-------------
[id=100][name=Al Sumner][age=120]
[id=105][name=Al Sumner][age=90]
-------------
```

For details on dynamic parameters, you should refer to your database vendor's JDBC and SQL documentations (each vendor might have some restrictions or additions for their dynamic parameters). In general, you can use dynamic parameters anywhere in an expression where their data type can be easily deduced.

5.2. What Is ParameterMetaData?

ParameterMetaData (as an interface) is extracted from a PreparedStatement object using the PreparedStatement.getParameterMetaData() method. The ParameterMetaData interface provides a means to get metadata describing the input parameters (designated as a ? in a SQL statement) to a dynamically prepared statement. The SQL 92 and SQL 99 standards specify a DESCRIBE INPUT statement for dynamic SQL. The JDBC 3.0 specification (included in JDK 1.5) introduces a ParameterMetaData class and methods that correspond to DESCRIBE INPUT support. SQL's DESCRIBE INPUT functionality is similar to ParameterMetaData—all parameter markers used in a prepared or call statement are described with the DESCRIBE INPUT statement, regardless of the mode of the formal parameter. You may use the SQL's DESCRIBE INPUT statement to return input parameter information before a prepared statement is executed.

For example if you have a `PreparedStatement` object, which represents the following SQL query:

```
select id, name, age from employees where id > ? and age < ?
```

then the `ParameterMetaData` object extracted from this `PreparedStatement` object (using `PreparedStatement.getParameterMetaData()`) will have metadata for two parameters:

- id parameter (name="id", type= INTEGER, precision, …)

- age parameter (name="age", type=INTEGER, precision, …)

Figure 5-1 shows the relationships of `PreparedStatement` to `ParameterMetaData`.

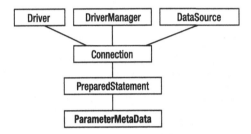

Figure 5-1. *The relationships of PreparedStatement to ParameterMetaData*

5.3. What Is the Definition of ParameterMetaData?

`ParameterMetaData` is an object that can be used to get information about the types and properties of the parameters in a `PreparedStatement` object. J2SE 5.0 defines `ParameterMetaData` as shown in Tables 5-1 and 5-2.

Table 5-1. *ParameterMetaData Field Summary*

Type	Field Name	Description
static int	parameterModeIn	The constant indicating that the parameter's mode is IN.
static int	parameterModeInOut	The constant indicating that the parameter's mode is INOUT.
static int	parameterModeOut	The constant indicating that the parameter's mode is OUT.
static int	parameterModeUnknown	The constant indicating that the mode of the parameter is unknown. (This is an error condition; all parameters must be explicitly defined.)
static int	parameterNoNulls	The constant indicating that a parameter will not allow NULL values.
static int	parameterNullable	The constant indicating that a parameter will allow NULL values.
static int	parameterNullableUnknown	The constant indicating that the nullability of a parameter is unknown.

Table 5-2. *ParameterMetaData Method Summary*

Result Type	Method	Description
String	getParameterClassName (int parameterNumber)	Retrieves the fully qualified name of the Java class whose instances should be passed to the method PreparedStatement.setObject
int	getParameterCount()	Retrieves the number of parameters in the PreparedStatement object for which this ParameterMetaData object contains information
int	getParameterMode (int parameterNumber)	Retrieves the designated parameter's mode
int	getParameterType (int parameterNumber)	Retrieves the designated parameter's SQL type
String	getParameterTypeName (int parameterNumber)	Retrieves the designated parameter's database-specific type name
int	getPrecision (int parameterNumber)	Retrieves the designated parameter's number of decimal digits
int	getScale(int parameterNumber)	Retrieves the designated parameter's number of digits to right of the decimal point
int	isNullable(int parameterNumber)	Retrieves whether null values are allowed in the designated parameter
boolean	isSigned(int parameterNumber)	Retrieves whether values for the designated parameter can be signed numbers

Following the definition, ParameterMetaData methods provide the following types of information:

- The number of parameters (getParameterCount())

- The data types of parameters, including the precision and scale of decimal parameters (getParameterType(int parameterNumber))

- The parameters' database-specific type names (getParameterTypeName(int parameterNumber))

- Whether parameters are nullable (isNullable(int parameterNumber))

- Whether parameters are input, output, or input/output parameters (getParameterMode(int parameterNumber))

- Whether the values of a numeric parameter can be signed (isSigned(int parameterNumber))

- The fully qualified Java class name that the PreparedStatement.setObject() method uses when it sets a parameter value (getParameterClassName(int parameterNumber))

5.4. How Do You Create a ParameterMetaData Object?

The method PrepareStatement.getParameterMetaData() returns a ParameterMetaData object describing the parameter markers that appear in the PreparedStatement object. See java.sql.ParameterMetaData for more information. The PreparedStatement method getParameterMetaData() creates and returns a ParameterMetaData object, as shown in the following code fragment. In this code, the SQL query has only one dynamic input parameter (marked with ?):

```
Connection conn = null;
PreparedStatement pstmt = null;
ParameterMetaData paramMetaData = null;
String query = "select last_name, badge_number from emps where dept = ?";
try {
    conn = getConnection();
    pstmt = con.prepareStatement(query);
    paramMetaData = pstmt.getParameterMetaData();
    if (paramMetaData == null) {
        // db vendor does NOT support ParameterMetaData
    }
    else {
        // db vendor supports ParameterMetaData
        // paramMetaData is not null and you can invoke
        // its methods to get the metadata information
        // on PreparedStatement's input parameters
    }

}
catch(SQLException se) {
    // handle db related exceptions
}
catch(Exception e) {
    // handle non db related exceptions
}
finally {
    // clean up: close PreparedStatement and Connection objects
}
```

The method PreparedStatement.getParameterMetaData() definition is

```
ParameterMetaData getParameterMetaData()
    throws SQLException
```

The method retrieves the number, types, and properties of this PreparedStatement object's parameters. It returns a ParameterMetaData object that contains this information. The method throws a SQLException if a database access error occurs.

To create a ParameterMetaData object, you need to perform these steps:

1. Get a valid database Connection object.

2. Prepare your SQL query with dynamic parameters marked as ?.

3. Invoke the Connection.prepareStatement("Your-SQL-Query") method to create a PreparedStatement object.

4. Invoke the PreparedStatement.getParameterMetaData() method to retrieve a ParameterMetaData object (once a ParameterMetaData is created, then you may invoke its methods to get information on the SQL query's parameters).

Solutions for MySQL and Oracle

Here I will show that MySQL and Oracle drivers do not support ParameterMetaData (if in the future they support this feature, then you may use this code). This example first creates a PreparedStatement object (say pstmt) and then creates a ParameterMetaData object using pstmt.

```java
import java.util.*;
import java.io.*;
import java.sql.*;

import jcb.util.DatabaseUtil;
import jcb.db.VeryBasicConnectionManager;

public class CreateParameterMetaData {

    public static void main(String[] args) {
        String dbVendor = args[0]; // { mysql, oracle }
        Connection conn = null;
        PreparedStatement pstmt = null;
        ParameterMetaData paramMetaData = null;
        String query = "select badge_number, last_name " +
            "from emps where badge_number > ? and dept = ?";
        try {
            conn = VeryBasicConnectionManager.getConnection(dbVendor);
            pstmt = conn.prepareStatement(query);
            paramMetaData = pstmt.getParameterMetaData();
            if (paramMetaData == null) {
              System.out.println("db vendor does NOT support ParameterMetaData");
            }
            else {
              System.out.println("db vendor supports ParameterMetaData");
              // find out the number of dynamic parameters
              int paramCount = paramMetaData.getParameterCount();
              System.out.println("paramCount="+paramCount);
            }
        }
```

```
        catch(Exception e){
            e.printStackTrace();
            System.exit(1);
        }
        finally {
            // release database resources
            DatabaseUtil.close(pstmt);
            DatabaseUtil.close(conn);
        }
    }
}
```

MySQL Database Setup

```
mysql> create table emps (
    ->    badge_number int not null,
    ->    last_name varchar(20),
    ->    dept varchar(10),
    ->    photo BLOB,
    ->    resume TEXT,
    ->
    ->    primary key (badge_number)
    -> );
Query OK, 0 rows affected (0.10 sec)
mysql> desc emps;
+--------------+-------------+------+-----+---------+-------+
| Field        | Type        | Null | Key | Default | Extra |
+--------------+-------------+------+-----+---------+-------+
| badge_number | int(11)     |      | PRI | 0       |       |
| last_name    | varchar(20) | YES  |     | NULL    |       |
| dept         | varchar(10) | YES  |     | NULL    |       |
| photo        | blob        | YES  |     | NULL    |       |
| resume       | text        | YES  |     | NULL    |       |
+--------------+-------------+------+-----+---------+-------+
5 rows in set (0.00 sec)
```

Running the Solution for a MySQL Database

MySQL's JDBC driver does not support ParameterMetaData implementation; therefore, it does not create ParameterMetaData at all.

```
$ javac CreateParameterMetaData.java
$ java CreateParameterMetaData mysql
```

```
com.mysql.jdbc.NotImplemented: Feature not implemented
        at com.mysql.jdbc.ServerPreparedStatement.getParameterMetaData
(ServerPreparedStatement.java:519)
        at CreateParameterMetaData.main(CreateParameterMetaData.java:20)
```

Oracle Database Setup

```
SQL> create table emps (
  2      badge_number int not null primary key,
  3      last_name varchar(20),
  4      dept varchar(10),
  5      photo BLOB,
  6      resume CLOB
  7  );
```

```
Table created.
SQL> desc emps;
 Name                                    Null?    Type
 --------------------------------------- -------- -------------

 BADGE_NUMBER                            NOT NULL NUMBER(38)
 LAST_NAME                                        VARCHAR2(20)
 DEPT                                             VARCHAR2(10)
 PHOTO                                            BLOB
 RESUME                                           CLOB
```

Running the Solution for an Oracle Database

```
$ javac CreateParameterMetaData.java
$ java CreateParameterMetaData oracle
```

```
java.sql.SQLException: Unsupported feature
 at oracle.jdbc.driver.DatabaseError.throwSqlException(DatabaseError.java:125)
 at oracle.jdbc.driver.DatabaseError.throwSqlException(DatabaseError.java:162)
 at oracle.jdbc.driver.DatabaseError.throwSqlException(DatabaseError.java:227)
 at oracle.jdbc.driver.DatabaseError.throwUnsupportedFeatureSqlException(
DatabaseError.java:537)
 at oracle.jdbc.driver.OraclePreparedStatement.getParameterMetaData
(OraclePreparedStatement.java:9086)
 at CreateParameterMetaData.main(CreateParameterMetaData.java:20)
```

The Solution for HSQLDB

```
import java.util.*;
import java.io.*;
import java.sql.*;

import jcb.util.DatabaseUtil;
```

```java
public class CreateParameterMetaData_HSQLDB {
    public static Connection getConnection(String dbName)
        throws Exception {
        // load the HSQL Database Engine JDBC driver
        // hsqldb.jar should be in the class path
        Class.forName("org.hsqldb.jdbcDriver");

        // connect to the database. This will load the
        // db files and start the database if it is not
        // already running. dbName is used to open or
        // create files that hold the state of the db.
        return DriverManager.getConnection("jdbc:hsqldb:"
                                    + dbName,   // filename
                                    "sa",       // username
                                    "");        // password
    }


    public static void main(String[] args) {
        Connection conn = null;
        PreparedStatement pstmt = null;
        ParameterMetaData paramMetaData = null;
        String query = "select id, str_col, num_col " +
            "from sample_table where id > ? and num_col = ?";
        try {
            conn = getConnection("db_file"); // db file name
            System.out.println("conn="+conn);
            pstmt = conn.prepareStatement(query);
            paramMetaData = pstmt.getParameterMetaData();
            if (paramMetaData == null) {
              System.out.println("db vendor does NOT support ParameterMetaData");
            }
            else {
              System.out.println("db vendor supports ParameterMetaData");
              // find out the number of dynamic parameters
              int paramCount = paramMetaData.getParameterCount();
              System.out.println("paramCount="+paramCount);
            }
        }
        catch(Exception e){
            e.printStackTrace();
            System.exit(1);
        }
        finally {
            // release database resources
            DatabaseUtil.close(pstmt);
            DatabaseUtil.close(conn);
        }
    }
}
```

HSQLDB Database Setup

In the following code, mp is an alias name for the database URL and has to be defined in the sqltool.rc file. The environment variable HSQLDB_HOME points to the installation directory of the HSQLDB database.

```
$ java -jar $HSQLDB/hsqldb.jar mp
```

```
JDBC Connection established to a HSQL Database Engine v. 1.7.3 database as 'SA'.

SqlTool v. 1.39.                    (SqlFile processor v. 1.90)
Distribution is permitted under the terms of the HSQLDB license.
(c) 2004 Blaine Simpson and the HSQLDB Development Group.

    \q    to Quit.
    \?    lists Special Commands.
    :?    lists Buffer/Editing commands.
    * ?   lists PL commands (including alias commands).

SPECIAL Commands begin with '\' and execute when you hit ENTER.
BUFFER Commands begin with ':' and execute when you hit ENTER.
COMMENTS begin with '/*' and end with the very next '*/'.
PROCEDURAL LANGUAGE commands begin with '* ' and end when you hit ENTER.
All other lines comprise SQL Statements.
  SQL Statements are terminated by either a blank line (which moves the
  statement into the buffer without executing) or a line ending with ';'
  (which executes the statement).
```

```
sql>
sql> \d sample_table
```

```
name     datatype  width  no-nulls
-------  --------  -----  --------
ID       INTEGER      11  *
STR_COL  VARCHAR     256
NUM_COL  INTEGER      11
```

```
sql>
sql> select * from sample_table;
```

```
ID  STR_COL  NUM_COL
--  -------  -------
 0  Ford         100
 1  Toyota       200
 2  Honda        300
 3  GM           400

4 rows
```

```
sql>
```

Running the Solution for an HSQLDB Database

```
$ javac CreateParameterMetaData_HSQLDB.java
$ java CreateParameterMetaData_HSQLDB
```

```
conn=org.hsqldb.jdbc.jdbcConnection@872380
db vendor supports ParameterMetaData
paramCount=2
```

The Solution for a Derby Database

```java
import java.util.*;
import java.io.*;
import java.sql.*;

import jcb.util.DatabaseUtil;

public class CreateParameterMetaData_Derby {
    public static Connection getConnection()
        throws Exception {
        // in an embedded environment, loading
        // the driver also starts Derby.
        Class.forName("org.apache.derby.jdbc.EmbeddedDriver");

        // connect to the database. This will create the db
        String dbURL = "jdbc:derby:myDB;create=true;user=me;password=mine";
        return DriverManager.getConnection(dbURL);
    }

    public static void main(String[] args) {
        Connection conn = null;
        Statement stmt = null;
        PreparedStatement pstmt = null;
        ParameterMetaData paramMetaData = null;
        String create = "create table sample_table"+
            "(id VARCHAR(10), str_col VARCHAR(20), num_col int)";
        String query = "select id, str_col, num_col " +
            "from sample_table where id > ? and num_col = ?";
        try {
            conn = getConnection();
            System.out.println("conn="+conn);
            stmt = conn.createStatement();
            stmt.executeUpdate(create);
            pstmt = conn.prepareStatement(query);
            paramMetaData = pstmt.getParameterMetaData();
            if (paramMetaData == null) {
              System.out.println("db vendor does NOT support ParameterMetaData");
            }
```

```
        else {
          System.out.println("db vendor supports ParameterMetaData");
          // find out the number of dynamic parameters
          int paramCount = paramMetaData.getParameterCount();
          System.out.println("paramCount="+paramCount);
        }
      }
      catch(Exception e){
        e.printStackTrace();
        System.exit(1);
      }
      finally {
        // release database resources
        DatabaseUtil.close(stmt);
        DatabaseUtil.close(pstmt);
        DatabaseUtil.close(conn);
      }
    }
  }
}
```

Running the Solution for a Derby Database

```
$ java CreateParameterMetaData_Derby
```

```
conn=EmbedConnection
db vendor supports ParameterMetaData
paramCount=2
```

5.5. How Do You Get Information from a ParameterMetaData Object?

After you create a ParameterMetaData object, you may use the ParameterMetaData's methods for getting information on the number, mode, nullability, and type of parameters, as well as other useful related information.

To use a ParameterMetaData object, perform these basic steps:

1. Create a ParameterMetaData object (see Section 5.3).

2. Invoke ParameterMetaData.getParameterCount() to determine the number of parameters in the PreparedStatement. Once you have the number of parameters for a PreparedStatement object, then use the following code snippet to obtain parameter information (the first parameter is 1, the second is 2, etc.):

```
        for (int param=1; param <= numberOfParameters; param++) {
          method-information = ParameterMetaData.<method-name>(param);
        }
```

3. Invoke ParameterMetaData methods on individual parameters.

For example, the following snippet shows how to get the number of parameters and the type of each parameter. Each line of code uses paramMetaData, created in the previous code fragment, to get the number of parameters in the PreparedStatement object pstmt:

```
PreparedStatement pstmt = <a-valid-PreparedStatement-object>;
paramMetaData = pstmt.getParameterMetaData();
if (paramMetaData == null) {
   System.out.println("db vendor does NOT support ParameterMetaData");
}
else {
   System.out.println("db vendor supports ParameterMetaData");
   // find out the number of dynamic parameters
   int paramCount = paramMetaData.getParameterCount();
   System.out.println("paramCount="+paramCount);
   for (int param=1; param <= paramCount; param++) {
      int sqlTypeCode = paramMetaData.getParameterType(param);
      System.out.println("param number="+param);
      System.out.println("param SQL type="+ sqlTypeCode);
   }
}
```

The method ParameterMetaData.getParameterCount() is the only method in the ParameterMetaData interface that takes no parameters. All of the other methods take an integer (Java's int primitive data type) that indicates the position of the parameter to which the information applies. Parameter position numbering starts at one, so the first parameter is 1, the second parameter is 2, and so on. For example, in the following line of code, the method ParameterMetaData.getParameterType() returns the SQL data type of the second parameter (provided that the PreparedStatement that produced ParameterMetaData has at least two parameters):

```
int sqlTypeCode = paramMetaData.getParameterType(2);
if (sqlTypeCode == java.sql.Types.BLOB) {
   // parameter is a SQL type BLOB

   ...
}
else if (sqlTypeCode == java.sql.Types.VARCHAR) {
   // parameter is a SQL type VARCHAR

   ...
}
...
```

The parameter type obtained from the method ParameterMetaData.getParameterType() maps into constants defined in the java.sql.Types class (the Types class defines the constants that are used to identify generic SQL types, called JDBC types).

The Solution for HSQLDB

The following solution shows how to use ParameterMetaData methods to get information about a PreparedStatement object:

```java
import java.util.*;
import java.io.*;
import java.sql.*;

import jcb.util.DatabaseUtil;

public class ExamineParameterMetaData_HSQLDB {
    public static Connection getConnection(String dbName)
        throws Exception {
        // load the HSQL Database Engine JDBC driver
        // hsqldb.jar should be in the class path
        Class.forName("org.hsqldb.jdbcDriver");

        // connect to the database. This will load the
        // db files and start the database if it is not
        // already running. dbName is used to open or
        // create files that hold the state of the db.
        return DriverManager.getConnection("jdbc:hsqldb:"
                                    + dbName,   // filename
                                    "sa",       // username
                                    "");        // password
    }

    public static void main(String[] args) {
        Connection conn = null;
        PreparedStatement pstmt = null;
        ParameterMetaData paramMetaData = null;
        String query = "select id, str_col, num_col " +
            "from sample_table where id > ? and str_col = ? and num_col = ?";
        try {
            conn = getConnection("db_file"); // db file name
            System.out.println("conn="+conn);
            pstmt = conn.prepareStatement(query);
            paramMetaData = pstmt.getParameterMetaData();
            if (paramMetaData == null) {
              System.out.println("db vendor does NOT support ParameterMetaData");
            }
            else {
                System.out.println("db vendor supports ParameterMetaData");
                // find out the number of dynamic parameters
                int paramCount = paramMetaData.getParameterCount();
                System.out.println("paramCount="+paramCount);
                System.out.println("-------------------");
                for (int param=1; param <= paramCount; param++) {
                    System.out.println("param number="+param);
                    int sqlTypeCode = paramMetaData.getParameterType(param);
                    System.out.println("param SQL type code="+ sqlTypeCode);
```

```
                    String paramTypeName = paramMetaData.getParameterTypeName(param);
                    System.out.println("param SQL type name="+ paramTypeName);
                    String paramClassName = paramMetaData.getParameterClassName(param);
                    System.out.println("param class name="+ paramClassName);
                    int paramMode = paramMetaData.getParameterMode(param);

                    System.out.println("param mode="+ paramMode);
                    if (paramMode == ParameterMetaData.parameterModeOut){
                        System.out.println("the parameter's mode is OUT.");
                    }
                    else if (paramMode == ParameterMetaData.parameterModeIn){
                        System.out.println("the parameter's mode is IN.");
                    }
                    else if (paramMode == ParameterMetaData.parameterModeInOut){
                        System.out.println("the parameter's mode is INOUT.");
                    }
                    else {
                        System.out.println("the mode of a parameter is unknown.");
                    }

                    int nullable = paramMetaData.isNullable(param);
                    if (nullable == ParameterMetaData.parameterNoNulls){
                        System.out.println("parameter will not allow NULL values.");
                    }
                    else if (nullable == ParameterMetaData.parameterNullable){
                        System.out.println("parameter will allow NULL values.");
                    }
                    else {
                        System.out.println("nullability of a parameter is unknown.");
                    }
                    System.out.println("-------------------");
                }
            }
        }
        catch(Exception e){
            e.printStackTrace();
            System.exit(1);
        }
        finally {
            // release database resources
            DatabaseUtil.close(pstmt);
            DatabaseUtil.close(conn);
        }
    }
}
```

Running the Solution for HSQLDB

```
$ java ExamineParameterMetaData_HSQLDB
conn=org.hsqldb.jdbc.jdbcConnection@c7e553
db vendor supports ParameterMetaData
paramCount=3
-------------------
param number=1
param SQL type code=4
param SQL type name=INTEGER
param class name=java.lang.Integer
param mode=1
the parameter's mode is IN.
parameter will not allow NULL values.
-------------------
param number=2
param SQL type code=12
param SQL type name=VARCHAR
param class name=java.lang.String
param mode=1
the parameter's mode is IN.
parameter will allow NULL values.
-------------------
param number=3
param SQL type code=4
param SQL type name=INTEGER
param class name=java.lang.Integer
param mode=1
the parameter's mode is IN.
parameter will allow NULL values.
-------------------
```

5.6. How Do You Get XML Information from a ParameterMetaData Object?

In the preceding section, we showed how to get information from a ParameterMetaData object. Now let's modify our solution to return the result as an XML object (as a serialized String object).

The Solution

```java
import java.util.*;
import java.io.*;
import java.sql.*;

import jcb.util.DatabaseUtil;
```

```java
public class ParameterMetaDataAsXML_HSQLDB {
    public static Connection getConnection(String dbName)
        throws Exception {
        // load the HSQL Database Engine JDBC driver
        // hsqldb.jar should be in the class path
        Class.forName("org.hsqldb.jdbcDriver");

        // connect to the database. This will load the
        // db files and start the database if it is not
        // already running. dbName is used to open or
        // create files that hold the state of the db.
        return DriverManager.getConnection("jdbc:hsqldb:"
                                            + dbName,   // filename
                                            "sa",       // username
                                            "");        // password
    }

    public static String getParameterMetaDataAsXML(ParameterMetaData metadata)
        throws SQLException {
        if (metadata == null) {
            return null;
        }

        StringBuilder builder = new StringBuilder();
        int paramCount = metadata.getParameterCount();
        builder.append("<parameterMetaData count=\"");
        builder.append(paramCount);
        builder.append("\">");

        if (paramCount < 1) {
            return builder.toString();
        }

        for (int param=1; param <= paramCount; param++) {
            builder.append("<parameter position=\"");
            builder.append(param);
            builder.append("\">");

            int sqlTypeCode = metadata.getParameterType(param);
            builder.append("<type>");
            builder.append(sqlTypeCode);
            builder.append("</type>");

            String paramTypeName = metadata.getParameterTypeName(param);
            builder.append("<typeName>");
            builder.append(paramTypeName);
            builder.append("</typeName>");
```

```
String paramClassName = metadata.getParameterClassName(param);
builder.append("<className>");
builder.append(paramClassName);
builder.append("</className>");

builder.append("<mode>");
int paramMode = metadata.getParameterMode(param);
if (paramMode == ParameterMetaData.parameterModeOut){
   builder.append("OUT");
}
else if (paramMode == ParameterMetaData.parameterModeIn){
   builder.append("IN");
}
else if (paramMode == ParameterMetaData.parameterModeInOut){
   builder.append("INOUT");
}
else {
   builder.append("UNKNOWN");
}
builder.append("</mode>");

builder.append("<isSigned>");
boolean isSigned = metadata.isSigned(param);
builder.append(isSigned);
builder.append("</isSigned>");

builder.append("<precision>");
int precision = metadata.getPrecision(param);
builder.append(precision);
builder.append("</precision>");

builder.append("<scale>");
int scale = metadata.getScale(param);
builder.append(scale);
builder.append("</scale>");

builder.append("<nullable>");
int nullable = metadata.isNullable(param);
if (nullable == ParameterMetaData.parameterNoNulls){
   builder.append("false");
}
else if (nullable == ParameterMetaData.parameterNullable){
   builder.append("true");
}
else {
   builder.append("UNKOWN");
}
builder.append("</nullable>");
```

```
            builder.append("</parameter>");
        }

        builder.append("</parameterMetaData>");
        return builder.toString();
    }

    public static void main(String[] args) {
        Connection conn = null;
        PreparedStatement pstmt = null;
        ParameterMetaData paramMetaData = null;
        String query = "select id, str_col, num_col " +
            "from sample_table where id > ? and str_col = ? and num_col = ?";
        try {
            conn = getConnection("db_file"); // db file name
            System.out.println("conn="+conn);
            pstmt = conn.prepareStatement(query);
            paramMetaData = pstmt.getParameterMetaData();
            if (paramMetaData == null) {
              System.out.println("db vendor does NOT support ParameterMetaData");
            }
            else {
                String metadataAsXML = getParameterMetaDataAsXML(paramMetaData);
                System.out.println("db vendor supports ParameterMetaData");
                System.out.println(metadataAsXML);
            }
        }
        catch(Exception e){
            e.printStackTrace();
            System.exit(1);
        }
        finally {
            // release database resources
            DatabaseUtil.close(pstmt);
            DatabaseUtil.close(conn);
        }
    }
}
```

Running the Solution for HSQLDB

```
$ javac ParameterMetaDataAsXML_HSQLDB.java
$ java ParameterMetaDataAsXML_HSQLDB
conn=org.hsqldb.jdbc.jdbcConnection@c7e553
db vendor supports ParameterMetaData
```

```
<parameterMetaData count="3">
   <parameter position="1">
      <type>4</type>
      <typeName>INTEGER</typeName>
      <className>java.lang.Integer</className>
      <mode>IN</mode>
      <isSigned>false</isSigned>
      <precision>10</precision>
      <scale>0</scale>
      <nullable>false</nullable>
   </parameter>
   <parameter position="2">
      <type>12</type>
      <typeName>VARCHAR</typeName>
      <className>java.lang.String</className>
      <mode>IN</mode>
      <isSigned>false</isSigned>
      <precision>2147483647</precision>
      <scale>0</scale>
      <nullable>true</nullable>
   </parameter>
   <parameter position="3">
      <type>4</type>
      <typeName>INTEGER</typeName>
      <className>java.lang.Integer</className>
      <mode>IN</mode>
      <isSigned>true</isSigned>
      <precision>10</precision>
      <scale>0</scale>
      <nullable>true</nullable>
   </parameter>
</parameterMetaData>
```

5.7. Why Should You Use ParameterMetadata Wisely?

You should not invoke the PreparedStatement.getParameterMetaData() method very often. Calling this method might slow the performance of your database application. This method call requires a round-trip to the database server to get metadata information about the number of dynamic parameters, data types, and other useful information. If possible, cache the ParameterMetadata objects extracted from PreparedStatement(s). Caching this type of data will improve your application's performance. Note that implementation of the method PreparedStatement.getParameterMetaData() is driver dependent (one implementation might get all parameters in one call versus another driver, which might get metadata per parameter—the latter one will require multiple trips to database server).

5.8. How Do You Get ParameterMetadata from Stored Procedures (Oracle)?

What is a "stored procedure"? A stored procedure or function is a program running in the database server that can take actions based on the input parameters. A stored procedure can have input, output, and input/output parameters. In JDBC, you may use a CallableStatement to invoke a stored procedure. Since CallableStatement extends PreparedStatement, you can invoke CallableStatement.getParameterMetaData() to get metadata information on a stored procedure's parameters. In general, using a stored procedure is faster than doing the same work on a client, because the program runs right inside the database server. Stored procedures are normally written in SQL, Java, or combination of other languages such as PL/SQL (in Oracle).

According to Wikipedia (http://en.wikipedia.org/wiki/Stored_procedure), a stored procedure is "a program (or procedure) which is physically stored within a database. They are usually written in a proprietary database language like PL/SQL for Oracle database. The advantage of a stored procedure is that when it is run, in response to a user request, it is run directly by the database engine, which usually runs on a separate database server. As such, it has direct access to the data it needs to manipulate and only needs to send its results back to the user."

Next, let's set up a stored procedure (called proc3), and invoke it using a CallableStatement. Then, we'll invoke CallableStatement.getParameterMetaData() to get the stored procedure's parameters metadata.

First, define a stored procedure in Oracle that has three parameters:

```
$ sqlplus scott/tiger
SQL*Plus: Release 10.2.0.1.0 - Production on Sun Sep 18 13:30:53 2005
Connected to: Oracle Database 10g Enterprise Edition Release 10.2.0.1.0
SQL> create procedure proc3(
  2                           p1 in varchar2,
  3                           p2 out varchar2,
  4                           p3 in out number
  5                         )
  6  is
  7  begin
  8    -- body-of-stored-procedure-proc3
  9    p2 := p1;
 10    p3 := p3 + 10;
 11  end;
 12  /
Procedure created.
SQL> desc proc3;
PROCEDURE proc3
Argument Name                   Type                     In/Out Default?
-----------------------------   ----------------------   ------ --------
 P1                             VARCHAR2                  IN
 P2                             VARCHAR2                  OUT
 P3                             NUMBER                    IN/OUT
```

```
SQL> var arg1 varchar2(12);
SQL> var arg2 varchar2(12);
SQL> var arg3 number;
SQL> begin :arg1:='abcd'; :arg3 := 6; proc3(:arg1, :arg2, :arg3); end;
  2  .
SQL> run
  1* begin :arg1:='abcd'; :arg3 := 6; proc3(:arg1, :arg2, :arg3); end;
PL/SQL procedure successfully completed.
SQL> print arg1 arg2 arg3
ARG1
--------------------------------
abcd


ARG2
--------------------------------
abcd


ARG3
----------
        16
```

```java
import java.sql.*;
import jcb.util.DatabaseUtil;

public class CallProc3 {

    public static Connection getConnection() throws Exception {
        String driver = "oracle.jdbc.driver.OracleDriver";
        String url = "jdbc:oracle:thin:@localhost:1521:goofy";
        String username = "scott";
        String password = "tiger";
        Class.forName(driver);  // load Oracle driver
        return DriverManager.getConnection(url, username, password);
    }

    public static void main(String[] args) {
        Connection conn = null;
        try {
            //
            // Step-1: get a database connection
            //
            conn = getConnection();
            System.out.println("conn="+conn);
```

```
                //
                // Step-2: identify the stored procedure
                //
                String proc3StoredProcedure = "{ call proc3(?, ?, ?) }";


                //
                // Step-3: prepare the callable statement
                //
                CallableStatement cs = conn.prepareCall(proc3StoredProcedure);


                //
                // Step-4: set input parameters ...
                //
                cs.setString(1, "abcd");      // first input argument
                cs.setInt(3, 10);             // third input argument


                //
                // Step-5: register output parameters ...
                //
                cs.registerOutParameter(2, java.sql.Types.VARCHAR);
                cs.registerOutParameter(3, java.sql.Types.INTEGER);


                //
                // Step-6: execute the stored procedures: proc3
                //
                cs.execute();


                //
                // Step-7: extract the output parameters
                //
                String param2 = cs.getString(2); // get parameter 2 as output
                int param3 = cs.getInt(3);         // get parameter 3 as output
                System.out.println("param2="+param2);
                System.out.println("param3="+param3);
                System.out.println("----------------------------------");
            }
        catch(Exception e){
            e.printStackTrace();
            System.exit(1);
        }
        finally {
            DatabaseUtil.close(conn);
        }
    }
}
```

```
$ javac CallProc3.java
$ java CallProc3
conn=oracle.jdbc.driver.T4CConnection@2a340e
param2=abcd
param3=20
```

Now, we can check to see if a CallableStatement supports ParameterMetaData:

```
//
// Step-5.5: get ParameterMetaData
//
ParameterMetaData pmeta = cs.getParameterMetaData();
if (pmeta == null) {
    System.out.println("Vendor does not support ParameterMetaData");
}
else {
    System.out.println(pmeta.getParameterType(1));
    System.out.println(pmeta.getParameterType(2));
    System.out.println(pmeta.getParameterType(3));
}
```

If you add these lines to the CallProc3 class (call the new class CallProc3WithMetadata) and run the program again, you will get the following error (this means that Oracle does not support the CallableStatement.getParameterMetaData() method):

```
$ javac CallProc3WithMetadata.java
$ java CallProc3WithMetadata
```

```
conn=oracle.jdbc.driver.T4CConnection@2a340e
java.sql.SQLException: Unsupported feature
  at oracle.jdbc.driver.DatabaseError.throwSqlException(DatabaseError.java:125)
  at oracle.jdbc.driver.DatabaseError.throwSqlException(DatabaseError.java:162)
  at oracle.jdbc.driver.DatabaseError.throwSqlException(DatabaseError.java:227)
  at oracle.jdbc.driver.DatabaseError.throwUnsupportedFeatureSqlException(
      DatabaseError.java:537)
  at oracle.jdbc.driver.OraclePreparedStatement.getParameterMetaData(Oracle
      PreparedStatement.java:9086)
  at CallProc3WithMetadata.main(CallProc3WithMetadata.java:49)
```

There is an alternative way that you can get the metadata information on a stored procedure's parameters: you can use Connection.getMetaData(), which will give you a DatabaseMetaData object, and then using that DatabaseMetaData object, you can get the signature of all stored procedures by using the following methods:

```
// retrieves a description of the stored procedures
// available in the given catalog.
ResultSet getProcedures(String catalog,
                        String schemaPattern,
                        String procedureNamePattern)
```

```
// retrieves a description of the given catalog's
// stored procedure parameter and result columns.
ResultSet getProcedureColumns(String catalog,
                              String schemaPattern,
                              String procedureNamePattern,
                              String columnNamePattern)
```

5.9. How Do You Get ParameterMetadata from Stored Procedures (MySQL)?

The current production version of MySQL does not support stored procedures, but the Beta version of MySQL (5.0+ version) does. For details on stored procedures, refer to MySQL's documentation and reference manuals.

Next, let's set up a stored procedure (called simpleproc), and invoke it using a CallableStatement. Then, we'll invoke CallableStatement.getParameterMetaData() to get the stored procedure's parameters metadata.

First, define a very simple stored procedure in MySQL that has one output parameter:

```
mysql> use octopus;
Database changed
mysql> create table test(id varchar(4));
Query OK, 0 rows affected (0.11 sec)
mysql> insert into test(id) values('a');
mysql> insert into test(id) values('b');
mysql> select count(*) from test;
+----------+
| count(*) |
+----------+
|        2 |
+----------+
1 row in set (0.00 sec)
mysql> delimiter //
mysql> CREATE PROCEDURE simpleproc (OUT param1 INT)
    -> BEGIN
    -> SELECT COUNT(*) INTO param1 FROM test;
    -> END
    -> //
Query OK, 0 rows affected (0.08 sec)
mysql> delimiter ;
mysql> describe simpleproc;
ERROR 1146 (42S02): Table 'octopus.simpleproc' doesn't exist
mysql> CALL simpleproc(@out_param1);
Query OK, 0 rows affected (0.05 sec)
mysql> select @out_param1;
```

```
+-------------+
| @out_param1 |
+-------------+
| 2           |
+-------------+
1 row in set (0.00 sec)
mysql> SHOW PROCEDURE STATUS LIKE 'simpleproc'\G
*************************** 1. row ***************************
           Db: octopus
         Name: simpleproc
         Type: PROCEDURE
      Definer: root@localhost
     Modified: 2005-09-18 21:59:09
      Created: 2005-09-18 21:59:09
Security_type: DEFINER
      Comment:
1 row in set (0.03 sec)
```

```java
import java.sql.*;
import jcb.util.DatabaseUtil;

public class CallSimpleProc {

    public static Connection getConnection() throws Exception {
        String driver = "com.mysql.jdbc.Driver";
        String url = "jdbc:mysql://localhost/octopus";
        String username = "root";
        String password = "root";
        Class.forName(driver);  // load MySQL driver
        return DriverManager.getConnection(url, username, password);
    }

    public static void main(String[] args) {
        Connection conn = null;
        try {
            //
            // Step-1: get a database connection
            //
            conn = getConnection();
            System.out.println("conn="+conn);

            //
            // Step-2: identify the stored procedure
            //
            String proc3StoredProcedure = "{ call simpleproc(?) }";
```

```
        //
        // Step-3: prepare the callable statement
        //
        CallableStatement cs = conn.prepareCall(proc3StoredProcedure);

        //
        // Step-4: set input parameters ... NONE
        //

        //
        // Step-5: register output parameters ...
        //
        cs.registerOutParameter(1, java.sql.Types.INTEGER);


        //
        // Step-6: execute the stored procedures: proc3
        //
        cs.execute();

        //
        // Step-7: extract the output parameters
        //
        int param1 = cs.getInt(1);
        System.out.println("param1="+param1);
        System.out.println("-----------------------------------");

        //
        // Step-8: get ParameterMetaData
        //
        ParameterMetaData pmeta = cs.getParameterMetaData();
        if (pmeta == null) {
            System.out.println("Vendor does not support ParameterMetaData");
        }
        else {
            System.out.println(pmeta.getParameterType(1));
        }
    }
    catch(Exception e){
        e.printStackTrace();
        System.exit(1);
    }
    finally {
        DatabaseUtil.close(conn);
    }
    }
}
```

```
$ javac CallSimpleProc.java
$ java CallSimpleProc
conn=com.mysql.jdbc.Connection@17a8913
param1=2
-------------------------------------
com.mysql.jdbc.NotImplemented: Feature not implemented
at com.mysql.jdbc.PreparedStatement.getParameterMetaData
    (PreparedStatement.java:1153)
at CallSimpleProc.main(CallSimpleProc.java:59)
```

As you can see, MySQL's JDBC driver does not support the CallableStatement.getParameterMetaData() method. There is another way that you can get the metadata information on a stored procedure's parameters: you can use Connection.getMetaData(), which will give you a DatabaseMetaData object. Then, using that DatabaseMetaData object, you can get the signature of all stored procedures by using the following methods:

```
// retrieves a description of the stored procedures
// available in the given catalog.
ResultSet getProcedures(String catalog,
                        String schemaPattern,
                        String procedureNamePattern)


// retrieves a description of the given catalog's
// stored procedure parameter and result columns.
ResultSet getProcedureColumns(String catalog,
                              String schemaPattern,
                              String procedureNamePattern,
                              String columnNamePattern)
```

CHAPTER 6

■ ■ ■

Exploring Driver Property Information

Now that we have all this useful information, it would be nice to do something with it.

UNIX Programmer's Manual

This chapter examines the java.sql.DriverPropertyInfo class, which provides Driver properties for making database connection (java.sql.Connection) objects. In this chapter, I will explore the DriverPropertyInfo class by using different JDBC drivers from MySQL and Oracle. The DriverPropertyInfo class is a metadata class, which provides Driver properties for making a database connection. No methods are associated with this class.

In database GUI applications, the database connection information can be provided to users at runtime; the DriverPropertyInfo class enables you to prompt the user for name-value pairs that represent connection-specific properties. The DriverPropertyInfo class is used with the Driver interface's getPropertyInfo() method to determine which values have been specified and which are still needed to establish the database connection.

6.1. What Is DriverPropertyInfo?

The java.sql.DriverPropertyInfo class extends the java.lang.Object class and provides Driver properties for making a database connection. This class is of interest only to advanced programmers who need to interact with a JDBC driver via the method Driver.getPropertyInfo() to discover and supply properties for database connections. The DriverPropertyInfo class provides Driver properties for making a connection.

This class has one public constructor and five public instance attributes. J2SE 5.0 defines them as follows.

DriverPropertyInfo's public constructor has the following signature:

```
/**
 * Constructs a DriverPropertyInfo object with a name and
 * value; other members default to their initial values.
 *
 * @param name the name of the property
 * @param value the current value, which may be null
 */
```

```
public DriverPropertyInfo(String name, String value) {
    this.name = name;
    this.value = value;
}
```

DriverPropertyInfo's constructor requires two strings: the property name and the property value. Here is an example:

```
import java.sql.DriverPropertyInfo;
...
String name = "password";
String value = "mypassword_value";
DriverPropertyInfo driverProperty = new DriverPropertyInfo(name, value);
```

Table 6-1 lists DriverPropertyInfo's public instance attributes.

Table 6-1. *DriverPropertyInfo's Public Instance Attributes*

Name	Type	Description
name	String	The name of the property.
value	String	The value field specifies the current value of the property, based on a combination of the information supplied to the method getPropertyInfo(), the Java environment, and the driver-supplied default values.
choices	String[]	An array of possible values if the value for the field DriverPropertyInfo.value may be selected from a particular set of values; otherwise null.
description	String	A brief description of the property, which may be null.
required	boolean	The required field is true if a value must be supplied for this property during Driver.connect() and false otherwise.

6.2. How Do You Create a DriverPropertyInfo Object?

The java.sql.Driver.getPropertyInfo() method returns an array of DriverPropertyInfo objects (DriverPropertyInfo[]). JDBC's Driver.getPropertyInfo() method allows a GUI tool to determine the database connection properties for which it should prompt a user in order to get enough information to connect to a database. Depending on the values the user has supplied so far, additional values might become necessary. It might be necessary to iterate through several calls to getPropertyInfo(). If no more properties are necessary (i.e., all required parameters are specified), the call returns an array of zero length. In general, Driver.getPropertyInfo() offers java.sql.Connection choices to the user.

How It Works

For most database systems, the properties returned in the DriverPropertyInfo object are connection URL attributes, including a list of booted databases in a system (the databaseName attribute). When a nonzero-length array (DriverPropertyInfo[]) is returned by the Driver.getPropertyInfo() method, each element is a DriverPropertyInfo object representing a connection URL attribute that has not already been specified.

The signature of the `Driver.getPropertyInfo()` method is

```
/**
 * @param url - the URL of the database to which to connect
 * @param info - a proposed list of tag/value pairs that will
 *        be sent on connect open
 * @return Returns an array of DriverPropertyInfo objects
 *         describing possible properties. This array may be
 *         an empty array if no properties are required.
 * @throws SQLException - if a database access error occurs
 */
DriverPropertyInfo[] getPropertyInfo(java.lang.String url,
                            java.util.Properties info)
                            throws java.sql.SQLException
```

I'll describe the `Driver.getPropertyInfo()` method next. This method gets information about the possible properties for this driver. The `getPropertyInfo()` method is intended to allow a generic GUI tool to discover what properties it should prompt the user for in order to get enough information to connect to a database. Note that depending on the values the user has supplied so far, additional values may be required, so it may be necessary to iterate through several calls to the `getPropertyInfo()` method.

According to *JDBC API Tutorial and Reference, Third Edition* (Addison Wesley Publishing, August 1997):

The second argument should be null the first (and generally only) time this method is called. The second argument is included so that it is possible for an application to process input and present the human user with a list of properties from which to choose. Depending on the values the human has supplied so far, it is conceivable that additional values may be needed. In such cases, and assuming that the application has been written to handle the results of multiple calls to getPropertyInfo(), it may be necessary to iterate through several calls to getPropertyInfo(). If the application uses the information it gets to fill in values for a java.util.Properties object, then that object can be supplied to getPropertyInfo() in subsequent calls to the method. The properties returned by this method will often correspond to the properties that are set on a javax.sql.DataSource object for this driver.

The Solution

Here is some example code for a MySQL/Oracle database. This solution displays `Driver` property information as an XML serialized `String` object. In this solution, I check for drivers from Oracle, MySQL, and JDBC-ODBC. You may alter the code and add additional drivers. To do this, modify the `loadDriver()` method.

```java
import java.sql.Driver;
import java.sql.Connection;
import java.sql.DriverManager;
import java.util.Properties;
import java.sql.DriverPropertyInfo;
```

```java
import jcb.util.DatabaseUtil;

public class TestDriverPropertyInfo {

    // list of drivers to be tested.
    public static final String MYSQL_DRIVER =
        "com.mysql.jdbc.Driver";
    public static final String ORACLE_DRIVER =
        "oracle.jdbc.driver.OracleDriver";
    public static final String JDBC_ODBC_BRIDGE_DRIVER =
        "sun.jdbc.odbc.JdbcOdbcDriver";

    public static void loadDriver(String dbVendor) throws Exception {
        if (dbVendor.equalsIgnoreCase("mysql")) {
            Class.forName(MYSQL_DRIVER);  // load MySQL driver
        }
        else if (dbVendor.equalsIgnoreCase("oracle")) {
            Class.forName(ORACLE_DRIVER);  // load Oracle driver
        }
        else if (dbVendor.equalsIgnoreCase("jdbc-odbc")) {
            // load JdbcOdbcDriver
            Class.forName(JDBC_ODBC_BRIDGE_DRIVER);
        }
        else {
            throw new Exception("db vendor not supported");
        }
    }

    public static String getDriverPropertyInfoAsXML
        (DriverPropertyInfo[] properties) throws Exception {

        // If the driver is poorly implemented,
        // a null object may be returned.
        if(properties == null) {
            return null;
        }

        // List all properties.
        StringBuilder buffer = new StringBuilder();
        buffer.append("<driver_property_info>");
        for(int i = 0; i < properties.length; i++) {
            // Get the property metadata
            String name = properties[i].name;
            boolean required = properties[i].required;
            buffer.append("<property  name=\"");
            buffer.append(name);
            buffer.append("\"  required=\"");
```

```java
            buffer.append(required);
            buffer.append("\">");

            String value = properties[i].value;
            buffer.append("<value>");
            buffer.append(value);
            buffer.append("</value>");

            String  description = properties[i].description;
            buffer.append("<description>");
            buffer.append(description);
            buffer.append("</description>");

            String[] choices = properties[i].choices;
            buffer.append("<choices>");

            if(choices != null) {
                for(int j = 0; j < choices.length; j++) {
                    buffer.append("<choice>");
                    buffer.append(choices[j]);
                    buffer.append("</choice>");
                }
            }
            buffer.append("</choices>");
            buffer.append("</property>");

        }
        buffer.append("</driver_property_info>");
        return buffer.toString();
    }

    public static void main(String[] args)throws Exception {
        String dbVendor = args[0]; // { "mysql", "oracle" }
        loadDriver(dbVendor);
        // start with the least amount of information
        // to see the full list of choices; we could also
        // enter with a URL and Properties provided by a user.

        // mysql URL = "jdbc:mysql://localhost/octopus";
        // oracle URL = "jdbc:oracle:thin:@localhost:1521:caspian";
        // JdbcOdbc URL = "jdbc:odbc:northwind";
        String url = args[1]; // database url

        Properties info = new Properties();
        Driver driver = DriverManager.getDriver(url);
        System.out.println("driver="+driver);
```

```
        DriverPropertyInfo[] attributes =
            driver.getPropertyInfo(url, info);
        System.out.println("attributes="+attributes);
        // zero length means a connection attempt can be made

        System.out.println("Resolving properties for: " +
                driver.getClass().getName());
        System.out.println(getDriverPropertyInfoAsXML(attributes));

        // you can insert code here to process the array, e.g.,
        // display all options in a GUI and allow the user to
        // pick and then set the attributes in info or URL.

        // try the connection
        Connection conn = DriverManager.getConnection(url, info);
        System.out.println("----------");
    }
}
```

Running the Solution for a MySQL Database

The following output is formatted to fit the page:

```
$ javac  TestDriverPropertyInfo.java
$ java TestDriverPropertyInfo mysql "jdbc:mysql://localhost/octopus"
```

```
driver=com.mysql.jdbc.Driver@1a46e30
attributes=[Ljava.sql.DriverPropertyInfo;@addbf1
Resolving properties for: com.mysql.jdbc.Driver
<driver_property_info>
    <property  name="HOST"  required="true">
        <value>localhost</value>
        <description>Hostname of MySQL Server</description>
        <choices></choices>
    </property>
    <property  name="PORT"  required="false">
        <value>3306</value>
        <description>Port number of MySQL Server</description>
        <choices></choices>
    </property>
    <property  name="DBNAME"  required="false">
        <value>octopus</value>
        <description>Database name</description>
        <choices></choices>
    </property>
```

```
<property  name="user" required="true">
    <value>null</value>
    <description>Username to authenticate as</description>
    <choices></choices>
</property>
<property  name="password"  required="true">
    <value>null</value>
    <description>Password to use for authentication</description>
    <choices></choices>
</property>
<property  name="autoReconnect"  required="false">
    <value>false</value>
    <description>Should the driver try to re-establish bad
                connections?</description>
    <choices>
        <choice>true</choice><choice>false</choice>
    </choices>
</property>
<property  name="maxReconnects"  required="false">
    <value>3</value>
    <description>Maximum number of reconnects to at
        tempt if autoReconnect is true</description>
    <choices></choices>
</property>
<property  name="initialTimeout"  required="false">
    <value>2</value>
    <description>Initial timeout (seconds)to wait between failed
        connections</description>
     <choices></choices>
</property>
<property  name="profileSql"  required="false">
     <value>false</value>
     <description>Trace queries and their execution/fetch times
        on STDERR (true/false) defaults to false</description>
     <choices><choice>true</choice><choice>false</choice></choices>
</property>
  ...
</driver_property_info>
----------
```

Running the Solution for an Oracle Database

```
$ java TestDriverPropertyInfo oracle "jdbc:oracle:thin:@localhost:1521:caspian"
```

```
driver=oracle.jdbc.driver.OracleDriver@156ee8e
attributes=[Ljava.sql.DriverPropertyInfo;@19b49e6
Resolving properties for: oracle.jdbc.driver.OracleDriver
<driver_property_info>
</driver_property_info>
----------
```

As you can see from the preceding output, the Oracle driver does not properly return an array of DriverPropertyInfo objects, but instead returns an empty array.

Running the Solution for a JDBC-ODBC Configured Database

```
$ java TestDriverPropertyInfo "jdbc-odbc" "jdbc:odbc:northwind"
```

```
driver=sun.jdbc.odbc.JdbcOdbcDriver@757aef
Exception in thread "main" java.sql.SQLException:
[Microsoft][ODBC Driver Manager] Driver does not support this function
        at sun.jdbc.odbc.JdbcOdbc.createSQLException(JdbcOdbc.java:6958)
        at sun.jdbc.odbc.JdbcOdbc.standardError(JdbcOdbc.java:7115)
        at sun.jdbc.odbc.JdbcOdbc.SQLBrowseConnect(JdbcOdbc.java:2552)
        at sun.jdbc.odbc.JdbcOdbcDriver.getConnectionAttributes
        (JdbcOdbcDriver.java:664)
        at sun.jdbc.odbc.JdbcOdbcDriver.getPropertyInfo
        (JdbcOdbcDriver.java:359)
        at TestDriverPropertyInfo.main(TestDriverPropertyInfo.java:97)
```

As the preceding output shows, the JDBC-ODBC bridge driver does not properly return an array of DriverPropertyInfo objects, but instead throws a java.sql.SQLException. The MySQL database driver works better in this respect.

6.3. What Is a Sample Application of DriverPropertyInfo?

The iSQL-Viewer is an open-source JDBC 2.x–compliant database front-end written in Java; for details see http://www.isqlviewer.com/. The iSQL-Viewer provides a table model class, DriverPropertyTableModel, which deals with the DriverPropertyInfo class. For details, see http://www.isqlviewer.com/dev/javadoc/org/isqlviewer/core/model/ DriverPropertyTableModel.html. The iSQL-Viewer's table model has three default columns:

- A boolean column for showing if the value is required, as in DriverPropertyInfo.required.

- A String column for the property name, as in DriverPropertyInfo.name.

- A String column for the property value, as in DriverPropertyInfo.value. This column is also the only editable column and represents the current configure value for the property.

In the iSQL-Viewer environment, there are two places in particular that this model is used:

- In the extended properties section when creating services.

- In the TableFilter classes. This model simplifies creating a java.util.Properties object from the DriverPropertyInfo object contained in the class.

According to the iSQL-Viewer's documentation, "This model simplifies creating a Properties object from the DriverPropertyInfo object contained herein." This class, DriverPropertyTableModel, also provides a unique TableCellEditor that will edit a given value for the Driver property. Since DriverProperties can have a default value and a possible list of choices, the ChoiceEditor will actually change the editable component from a text field to a combobox if necessary. This is what makes the TableCellEditor unique since editors are not row-centric.

6.4. What Connection Properties Should You Supply to a Database Driver in Order to Connect to a Database?

In general, when creating a database connection object (java.sql.Connection), most JDBC drivers should accept three connection properties:

- user (database user)

- password (database user's password)

- hostname (hostname where database resides)

Also, a JDBC driver may accept an arbitrary number of proprietary connection properties. For example, MySQL's JDBC driver (for details on MySQL's connection properties, see http:// mysql.he.net/Downloads/Manual/manual-a4.pdf) can accept over a dozen additional connection properties, such as connectTimeout and useCompression. JDBC drivers can be interrogated for their supported connection properties using the DriverPropertyInfo metadata class. For specific database connection properties, you should consult the vendor's JDBC driver documentation (this documentation should specify all properties and their role in creating the JDBC database connection).

The Solution

This solution identifies which connection properties are required and which ones are optional:

```
import java.sql.Driver;
import java.sql.Connection;
import java.sql.DriverManager;
import java.util.Properties;
import java.sql.DriverPropertyInfo;

import jcb.util.DatabaseUtil;

public class PrintDriverPropertyInfo {
```

```java
// list of drivers to be tested.
public static final String MYSQL_DRIVER =
    "com.mysql.jdbc.Driver";
public static final String ORACLE_DRIVER =
    "oracle.jdbc.driver.OracleDriver";
public static final String JDBC_ODBC_BRIDGE_DRIVER =
    "sun.jdbc.odbc.JdbcOdbcDriver";


public static void loadDriver(String dbVendor) throws Exception {
    if (dbVendor.equalsIgnoreCase("mysql")) {
        Class.forName(MYSQL_DRIVER);  // load MySQL driver
    }
    else if (dbVendor.equalsIgnoreCase("oracle")) {
        Class.forName(ORACLE_DRIVER);  // load Oracle driver
    }
    else if (dbVendor.equalsIgnoreCase("jdbc-odbc")) {
        // load JdbcOdbcDriver
        Class.forName(JDBC_ODBC_BRIDGE_DRIVER);
    }
    else {
        throw new Exception("db vendor not supported");
    }
}


static void printDriverPropertyInfo(DriverPropertyInfo[] properties)
    throws Exception {

    // if the driver is poorly implemented,
    // a null object may be returned.
    if(properties == null) {
        return;
    }

    // list all connection properties.
    for (int i = 0; i < properties.length; i++) {
        // get the property metadata
        String name = properties[i].name;
        String[] choices = properties[i].choices;
        boolean required = properties[i].required;
        String description = properties[i].description;

        // printout property metadata
        System.out.println("" + name +
            " (Required: " + required + ")");
        if(choices == null) {
            System.out.println("  No choices.");
        }
```

```java
        else {
            System.out.print("  Choices are: ");
            for(int j = 0; j < choices.length; j++) {
                System.out.print(" " + choices[j]);
            }
        }

        System.out.println("  Description: " + description);
    }
}

public static void main(String[] args)throws Exception {
    String dbVendor = args[0]; // { "mysql", "oracle", "jdbc-odbc"}
    loadDriver(dbVendor);
    // start with the least amount of information
    // to see the full list of choices; we could also
    // enter with a URL and Properties provided by a user.

    // mysql URL = "jdbc:mysql://localhost/octopus";
    // oracle URL = "jdbc:oracle:thin:@localhost:1521:caspian";
    // JdbcOdbc URL = "jdbc:odbc:northwind";
    String url = args[1]; // database url

    Properties info = new Properties();
    Driver driver = DriverManager.getDriver(url);
    System.out.println("driver="+driver);
    DriverPropertyInfo[] attributes =
        driver.getPropertyInfo(url, info);
    System.out.println("attributes="+attributes);
    // zero length means a connection attempt can be made

    System.out.println("Resolving properties for: " +
            driver.getClass().getName());
    printDriverPropertyInfo(attributes);

    // you can insert code here to process the array, e.g.,
    // display all options in a GUI and allow the user to
    // pick and then set the attributes in info or URL.

    // try the connection
    // Connection conn = DriverManager.getConnection(url, info);
    // System.out.println("conn="+conn);
    System.out.println("----------");
    }
}
```

Running the Solution for a MySQL Database

Because the output was long, I have edited it to fit the page:

```
$ javac PrintDriverPropertyInfo.java
$ java PrintDriverPropertyInfo mysql "jdbc:mysql://localhost/octopus"
```

```
driver=com.mysql.jdbc.Driver@9cab16
attributes=[Ljava.sql.DriverPropertyInfo;@19821f
Resolving properties for: com.mysql.jdbc.Driver
HOST (Required: true)
  No choices.
  Description: Hostname of MySQL Server
PORT (Required: false)
  No choices.
  Description: Port number of MySQL Server
DBNAME (Required: false)
  No choices.
  Description: Database name
user (Required: true)
  No choices.
  Description: Username to authenticate as
password (Required: true)
  No choices.
  Description: Password to use for authentication
autoReconnect (Required: false)
  Choices are:  true false
  Description: Should the driver try to re-establish bad connections?
maxReconnects (Required: false)
  No choices.
  Description: Maximum number of reconnects to attempt if autoReconnect is true
initialTimeout (Required: false)
  No choices.
  Description: Initial timeout (seconds) to wait between failed connections
profileSql (Required: false)
  Choices are:  true false
  Description: Trace queries and their execution/fetch times on
STDERR (true/false) defaults to false
socketTimeout (Required: false)
  No choices.
  Description: Timeout on network socket operations (0 means no timeout)
useSSL (Required: false)
  Choices are:  true false  Description: Use SSL when communicating with the server?
paranoid (Required: false)
  Choices are:  true false
  Description: Expose sensitive information in error messages and clear data
    structures holding sensitive data when possible?
```

useHostsInPrivileges (Required: false)
  Choices are: true false Description: Add '@hostname' to users in
    DatabaseMetaData.getC
olumn/TablePrivileges()
interactiveClient (Required: false)
  Choices are: true false
  Description: Set the CLIENT_INTERACTIVE flag, which tells MySQL to timeout
   connections based on INTERACTIVE_TIMEOUT instead of WAIT_TIMEOUT
useCompression (Required: false)
  Choices are: true false
  Description: Use zlib compression when communicating with the server?
useTimezone (Required: false)
  Choices are: true false
  Description: Convert time/date types between client and server timezones
serverTimezone (Required: false)
  No choices.
  Description: Override detection/mapping of timezone. Used when timezone
  from server doesn't map to Java timezone
connectTimeout (Required: false)
  No choices.
  Description: Timeout for socket connect (in milliseconds), with 0 being no
    timeout. Only works on JDK-1.4 or newer. Defaults to '0'.
secondsBeforeRetryMaster (Required: false)
  No choices.
  Description: How long should the driver wait, when failed over, before attempting
  to reconnect to the master server? Whichever condition is met first,
  'queriesBeforeRetryMaster' or 'secondsBeforeRetryMaster' will cause an attempt to
  be made to reconnect to the master. Time in seconds, defaults
   to 30 queriesBeforeRetryMaster (Required: false)
  No choices.
  Description: Number of queries to issue before falling back to master when
  failed over (when using multi-host failover). Whichever condition is met first,
  'queriesBeforeRetryMaster' or 'secondsBeforeRetryMaster' will cause an attempt
  to be made to reconnect to the master. Defaults to 50.
useStreamLengthsInPrepStmts (Required: false)
  Choices are: true false
  Description: Honor stream length parameter in
  PreparedStatement/ResultSet.setXXXStream() method calls (defaults to 'true')
continueBatchOnError (Required: false)
  Choices are: true false
  Description: Should the driver continue processing batch commands if one
  Statement fails? The JDBC spec allows either way (defaults to 'true').
allowLoadLocalInfile (Required: false)
  Choices are: true false
  Description: Should the driver allow use of 'LOAD DATA LOCAL INFILE...'
  (defaults to 'true').

```
strictUpdates (Required: false)
  Choices are:  true false
  Description: Should the driver do strict checking (all primary keys selected) of
  updatable result sets?...' (defaults to 'true').
ignoreNonTxTables (Required: false)
  Choices are:  true false
  Description: Ignore non-transactional table warning for rollback? (defaults
  to 'false').
reconnectAtTxEnd (Required: false)
  Choices are:  true false
  Description: If autoReconnect is set to true, should the driver attempt
  reconnectionsat the end of every transaction? (true/false, defaults to false)
alwaysClearStream (Required: false)
  Choices are:  true false
  Description: Should the driver clear any remaining data from the input
  stream before issuing a query? Normally not needed
  (approx 1-2%        perf. penalty, true/false,
  defaults to false)
cachePrepStmts (Required: false)
  Choices are:  true false
  Description: Should the driver cache the parsing stage of Prep
aredStatements (true/false, default is 'false')
prepStmtCacheSize (Required: false)
  No choices.
  Description: If prepared statement caching is enabled, how many
  prepared statements
  should be cached? (default is '25')
prepStmtCacheSqlLimit (Required: false)
  No choices.
  Description: If prepared statement caching is enabled, what's the largest SQL the
  driver will cache the parsing for? (in chars, default is '256')
useUnbufferedInput (Required: false)
  No choices.
  Description: Don't use BufferedInputStream for reading data from the server
  true/false (default is 'true')
----------
```

Running the Solution for an ODBC Database

The JDBC-ODBC bridge driver does not properly return an array of DriverPropertyInfo
objects, but instead throws either a NullPointerException or java.sql.SQLException:

```
$ java PrintDriverPropertyInfo "jdbc-odbc" "jdbc:odbc:northwind"
```

```
driver=sun.jdbc.odbc.JdbcOdbcDriver@757aef
Exception in thread "main" java.sql.SQLException:
[Microsoft][ODBC Driver Manager] Driver does not support this function
```

```
at sun.jdbc.odbc.JdbcOdbc.createSQLException(JdbcOdbc.java:6958)
at sun.jdbc.odbc.JdbcOdbc.standardError(JdbcOdbc.java:7115)
at sun.jdbc.odbc.JdbcOdbc.SQLBrowseConnect(JdbcOdbc.java:2552)
at sun.jdbc.odbc.JdbcOdbcDriver.getConnectionAttributes(JdbcOdbcDriver.java:664)
      at sun.jdbc.odbc.JdbcOdbcDriver.getPropertyInfo(JdbcOdbcDriver.java:359)
      at PrintDriverPropertyInfo.main(PrintDriverPropertyInfo.java:85)
```

Running the Solution for an Oracle Database

Oracle's JDBC driver does not implement `Driver.getPropertyInfo()` properly. It just returns an empty array. Here is a section of code from Oracle's JDBC driver:

```
package oracle.jdbc.driver;

import java.sql.*;
import java.util.*;
import oracle.sql.CharacterSetWithConverter;
import oracle.sql.converter.CharacterConverterFactoryOGS;

public class OracleDriver implements Driver {

    public OracleDriver() {
        driverExtensions = new OracleDriverExtension[4];
    }
    ...

    public DriverPropertyInfo[] getPropertyInfo(String s, Properties properties)
        throws SQLException {
        return new DriverPropertyInfo[0];
    }
    ...
}
```

6.5. How Does MySQL's Driver Implement Driver.getPropertyInfo()?

MySQL's Connector/J (the JDBC driver for MySQL databases) implements `Driver.getPropertyInfo()` as follows. I have formatted the syntax to fit the page. The following classes (`com.mysql.jdbc.NonRegistering` and `com.mysql.jdbc.Driver`) work together to implement the `java.sql.Driver` interface. You should study these classes if you are a *driver* developer rather than an *application* developer.

Class Definition for com.mysql.jdbc.NonRegistering

```
package com.mysql.jdbc;

import java.sql.DriverManager;
import java.sql.SQLException;
```

```
public class Driver extends NonRegisteringDriver {

    public Driver()  throws SQLException {
    }

    static  {
        try {
            DriverManager.registerDriver(new Driver());
        }
        catch(SQLException E) {
            throw new RuntimeException("Can't register driver!");
        }
    }
}
```

Class Definition for com.mysql.jdbc.Driver

Here, the String objects have been formatted to fit the page:

```
package com.mysql.jdbc;

import java.sql.*;
import java.util.Properties;
import java.util.StringTokenizer;

public class NonRegisteringDriver implements Driver {

    public NonRegisteringDriver()  throws SQLException {
    }

    public DriverPropertyInfo[] getPropertyInfo(String url, Properties info)
        throws SQLException {
        if(info == null)
            info = new Properties();
        if(url != null && url.startsWith("jdbc:mysql://"))
            info = parseURL(url, info);
        DriverPropertyInfo hostProp =
            new DriverPropertyInfo("HOST", info.getProperty("HOST"));
        hostProp.required = true;
        hostProp.description = "Hostname of MySQL Server";
        DriverPropertyInfo portProp =
            new DriverPropertyInfo("PORT", info.getProperty("PORT", "3306"));
        portProp.required = false;
        portProp.description = "Port number of MySQL Server";
        DriverPropertyInfo dbProp = new
            DriverPropertyInfo("DBNAME", info.getProperty("DBNAME"));
        dbProp.required = false;
        dbProp.description = "Database name";
```

```
DriverPropertyInfo userProp =
    new DriverPropertyInfo("user", info.getProperty("user"));
userProp.required = true;
userProp.description = "Username to authenticate as";
DriverPropertyInfo passwordProp =
    new DriverPropertyInfo("password", info.getProperty("password"));
passwordProp.required = true;
passwordProp.description = "Password to use for authentication";
DriverPropertyInfo autoReconnect = new DriverPropertyInfo("autoReconnect",
    info.getProperty("autoReconnect", "false"));
autoReconnect.required = false;
autoReconnect.choices = (new String[] {
    "true", "false"
});
autoReconnect.description =
    "Should the driver try to re-establish bad connections?";
DriverPropertyInfo maxReconnects = new DriverPropertyInfo("maxReconnects",
    info.getProperty("maxReconnects", "3"));
maxReconnects.required = false;
maxReconnects.description =
    "Maximum number of reconnects to attempt if autoReconnect is true";
DriverPropertyInfo initialTimeout = new DriverPropertyInfo("initialTimeout",
    info.getProperty("initialTimeout", "2"));
initialTimeout.required = false;
initialTimeout.description =
    "Initial timeout (seconds) to wait between failed connections";
DriverPropertyInfo profileSql = new DriverPropertyInfo("profileSql",
    info.getProperty("profileSql", "false"));
profileSql.required = false;
profileSql.choices = (new String[] {
    "true", "false"
});
profileSql.description = "Trace queries and their execution/fetch times on"+
    " STDERR (true/false) defaults to false";
DriverPropertyInfo socketTimeout = new DriverPropertyInfo("socketTimeout",
    info.getProperty("socketTimeout", "0"));
socketTimeout.required = false;
socketTimeout.description =
    "Timeout on network socket operations (0 means no timeout)";
DriverPropertyInfo useSSL = new DriverPropertyInfo("useSSL",
    info.getProperty("useSSL", "false"));
useSSL.required = false;
useSSL.choices = (new String[] {
    "true", "false"
});
```

```
useSSL.description = "Use SSL when communicating with the server?";
DriverPropertyInfo useCompression = new DriverPropertyInfo("useCompression",
    info.getProperty("useCompression", "false"));
useCompression.required = false;
useCompression.choices = (new String[] {
    "true", "false"
});
useCompression.description =
    "Use zlib compression when communicating with the server?";
DriverPropertyInfo paranoid = new DriverPropertyInfo("paranoid",
    info.getProperty("paranoid", "false"));
paranoid.required = false;
paranoid.choices = (new String[] {
    "true", "false"
});
paranoid.description = "Expose sensitive information in error messages and"+
    " clear data structures holding sensitive data when possible?";
DriverPropertyInfo useHostsInPrivileges = new
    DriverPropertyInfo("useHostsInPrivileges",
    info.getProperty("useHostsInPrivileges", "true"));
useHostsInPrivileges.required = false;
useHostsInPrivileges.choices = (new String[] {
    "true", "false"
});
useHostsInPrivileges.description = "Add '@hostname' to users in
    DatabaseMetaData.getColumn/TablePrivileges()";
DriverPropertyInfo interactiveClient = new
    DriverPropertyInfo("interactiveClient",
    info.getProperty("interactiveClient", "false"));
interactiveClient.required = false;
interactiveClient.choices = (new String[] {
    "true", "false"
});
interactiveClient.description =
    "Set the CLIENT_INTERACTIVE flag, which tells MySQL to timeout "+
    "connections based on INTERACTIVE_TIMEOUT instead of WAIT_TIMEOUT";
DriverPropertyInfo useTimezone = new DriverPropertyInfo("useTimezone",
    info.getProperty("useTimezone", "false"));
useTimezone.required = false;
useTimezone.choices = (new String[] {
    "true", "false"
});
useTimezone.description =
    "Convert time/date types between client and server timezones";
DriverPropertyInfo serverTimezone = new DriverPropertyInfo("serverTimezone",
    info.getProperty("serverTimezone", ""));
```

```
serverTimezone.required = false;
serverTimezone.description = "Override detection/mapping of timezone. "+
    "Used when timezone from server doesn't map to Java timezone";
DriverPropertyInfo connectTimeout = new DriverPropertyInfo("connectTimeout",
    info.getProperty("connectTimeout", "0"));
connectTimeout.required = false;
connectTimeout.description = "Timeout for socket connect (in "+
    " milliseconds), with 0 being no timeout. Only works on "+
    "JDK-1.4 or newer. Defaults to '0'.";
DriverPropertyInfo queriesBeforeRetryMaster = new
    DriverPropertyInfo("queriesBeforeRetryMaster",
    info.getProperty("queriesBeforeRetryMaster", "50"));
queriesBeforeRetryMaster.required = false;
queriesBeforeRetryMaster.description = "Number of queries to issue "+
    "before falling back to master when failed over (when using "+
    "multi-host failover). Whichever condition is met first, "+
    "'queriesBeforeRetryMaster' or 'secondsBeforeRetryMaster' will "+
    "cause an attempt to be made to reconnect to the master."+
    "Defaults to 50.";
DriverPropertyInfo secondsBeforeRetryMaster = new
    DriverPropertyInfo("secondsBeforeRetryMaster",
    info.getProperty("secondsBeforeRetryMaster", "30"));
secondsBeforeRetryMaster.required = false;
secondsBeforeRetryMaster.description = "How long should the driver wait, "+
    "when failed over, before attempting to reconnect to the master server? "+
    "Whichever condition is met first, 'queriesBeforeRetryMaster' or "+
    "'secondsBeforeRetryMaster' will cause an attempt to be made "+
    "to reconnect to the master. Time in seconds, defaults to 30";
DriverPropertyInfo useStreamLengthsInPrepStmts = new
    DriverPropertyInfo("useStreamLengthsInPrepStmts",
    info.getProperty("useStreamLengthsInPrepStmts", "true"));
useStreamLengthsInPrepStmts.required = false;
useStreamLengthsInPrepStmts.choices = (new String[] {
    "true", "false"
});
useStreamLengthsInPrepStmts.description = "Honor stream length parameter "+
    "in PreparedStatement/ResultSet.setXXXStream() method calls (defaults "+
    "to 'true')";
DriverPropertyInfo continueBatchOnError = new
    DriverPropertyInfo("continueBatchOnError",
    info.getProperty("continueBatchOnError", "true"));
continueBatchOnError.required = false;
continueBatchOnError.choices = (new String[] {
    "true", "false"
});
```

```
continueBatchOnError.description = "Should the driver continue "+
  "processing batch commands if one statement fails. The JDBC "+
  "spec allows either way (defaults to 'true').";
DriverPropertyInfo allowLoadLocalInfile = new
    DriverPropertyInfo("allowLoadLocalInfile",
    info.getProperty("allowLoadLocalInfile", "true"));
allowLoadLocalInfile.required = false;
allowLoadLocalInfile.choices = (new String[] {
    "true", "false"
});
allowLoadLocalInfile.description = "Should the driver allow use of 'LOAD "+
    "DATA LOCAL INFILE...' (defaults to 'true').";
DriverPropertyInfo strictUpdates = new DriverPropertyInfo("strictUpdates",
    info.getProperty("strictUpdates", "true"));
strictUpdates.required = false;
strictUpdates.choices = (new String[] {
    "true", "false"
});
strictUpdates.description =
    "Should the driver do strict checking (all primary keys selected) "+
    "of updatable result sets?...' (defaults to 'true').";
DriverPropertyInfo ignoreNonTxTables = new
    DriverPropertyInfo("ignoreNonTxTables",
    info.getProperty("ignoreNonTxTables", "false"));
ignoreNonTxTables.required = false;
ignoreNonTxTables.choices = (new String[] {
    "true", "false"
});
ignoreNonTxTables.description = "Ignore non-transactional table warning "+
    "for rollback? (defaults to 'false').";
DriverPropertyInfo clobberStreamingResults = new
    DriverPropertyInfo("clobberStreamingResults",
    info.getProperty("clobberStreamingResults", "false"));
clobberStreamingResults.required = false;
clobberStreamingResults.choices = (new String[] {
    "true", "false"
});
clobberStreamingResults.description = "This will cause a 'streaming' "+
    "ResultSet to be automatically closed, and any outstanding data "+
    "still streaming from the server to be discarded if another query "+
    "is executed before all the data has been read from the server.";
DriverPropertyInfo reconnectAtTxEnd = new
    DriverPropertyInfo("reconnectAtTxEnd",
    info.getProperty("reconnectAtTxEnd", "false"));
reconnectAtTxEnd.required = false;
reconnectAtTxEnd.choices = (new String[] {
    "true", "false"
});
```

```
reconnectAtTxEnd.description = "If autoReconnect is set to true, should "+
    "the driver attempt reconnections at the end of every transaction? "+
    " (true/false,  defaults to false)";
DriverPropertyInfo alwaysClearStream = new
    DriverPropertyInfo("alwaysClearStream",
    info.getProperty("alwaysClearStream", "false"));
alwaysClearStream.required = false;
alwaysClearStream.choices = (new String[] {
    "true", "false"
});
alwaysClearStream.description = "Should the driver clear any remaining "+
    "data from the input stream before issuing a query? Normally not "+
    "needed (approx 1-2%\tperf. penalty, true/false, defaults to false)";
DriverPropertyInfo cachePrepStmts = new DriverPropertyInfo("cachePrepStmts",
    info.getProperty("cachePrepStmts", "false"));
cachePrepStmts.required = false;
cachePrepStmts.choices = (new String[] {
    "true", "false"
});
cachePrepStmts.description = "Should the driver cache the parsing stage "+
    "of PreparedStatements (true/false, default is 'false')";
DriverPropertyInfo prepStmtCacheSize = new
    DriverPropertyInfo("prepStmtCacheSize",
    info.getProperty("prepStmtCacheSize", "25"));
prepStmtCacheSize.required = false;
prepStmtCacheSize.description = "If prepared statement caching is "+
 "enabled, how many prepared statements should be cached? "+
 "(default is '25')";
DriverPropertyInfo prepStmtCacheSqlLimit = new
    DriverPropertyInfo("prepStmtCacheSqlLimit",
    info.getProperty("prepStmtCacheSqlLimit", "256"));
prepStmtCacheSqlLimit.required = false;
prepStmtCacheSqlLimit.description = "If prepared statement caching is "+
    "enabled, what's the largest SQL the driver will cache the "+
    "parsing for? (in chars, default is '256')";
DriverPropertyInfo useUnbufferedInput = new
    DriverPropertyInfo("useUnbufferedInput",
    info.getProperty("useUnbufferedInput", "true"));
useUnbufferedInput.required = false;
useUnbufferedInput.description = "Don't use BufferedInputStream for "+
    "reading data from the server true/false (default is 'true')";

DriverPropertyInfo dpi[] = {
    hostProp, portProp, dbProp, userProp, passwordProp,
    autoReconnect, maxReconnects, initialTimeout, profileSql,
    socketTimeout, useSSL, paranoid, useHostsInPrivileges,
    interactiveClient, useCompression, useTimezone, serverTimezone,
```

```
            connectTimeout, secondsBeforeRetryMaster,
            queriesBeforeRetryMaster, useStreamLengthsInPrepStmts,
            continueBatchOnError, allowLoadLocalInfile, strictUpdates,
            ignoreNonTxTables, reconnectAtTxEnd, alwaysClearStream,
            cachePrepStmts, prepStmtCacheSize, prepStmtCacheSqlLimit,
            useUnbufferedInput
        };
        return dpi;
    }

        ...

}
```

CHAPTER 7

■ ■ ■

RowSet Metadata

A relation is in second normal form if the relation depends on the key, the whole key, and nothing but the key, so help me Codd.

Edgar "Ted" Codd

This chapter provides information on javax.sql.RowSetMetaData (derived from the ResultSetMetaData interface) object, which contains information about the columns in a javax.sql.RowSet object. An application can use RowSetMetaData methods to find out how many columns the rowset contains and what kind of data each column can contain. In order to understand RowSetMetaData, we need to understand RowSet and its derived objects. I will present a couple of examples on RowSet creation and then look at the details of RowSetMetaData object. A RowSet object is a JavaBeans component because it has properties and participates in the JavaBeans event (the RowSetListener interface) notification mechanism.

Java (standard J2SE 5.0) and Sun Microsystems provide the following packages, which deal with rowset concepts and the associated metadata:

- javax.sql: Provides the API for server-side data source access and processing from the Java programming language.

- javax.sql.rowset: Contains standard interfaces and base classes for JDBC RowSet implementations.

- javax.sql.rowset.serial: Provides utility classes to allow serializable mappings between SQL types and data types in the Java programming language.

- javax.sql.rowset.spi: Contains the standard classes and interfaces that a third-party vendor has to use in its implementation of a synchronization provider.

- com.sun.rowset: Provides five standard implementations of the standard JDBC RowSet implementation interface definitions (Sun's reference implementation of rowsets). This package is not included in J2SE 5.0.

- com.sun.rowset.providers: Serves as a repository for the RowSet reference implementations of the SyncProvider abstract class (Sun's reference implementation of rowsets). This package is not included in J2SE 5.0.

For details on RowSet, visit the following websites:

- Sun's website on rowsets: http://java.sun.com/j2se/1.5.0/docs/guide/jdbc/getstart/rowsetImpl.html

- JDBC's rowset reference implementations: http://today.java.net/today/2004/10/15/jdbcRowsets.pdf

Overall, RowSet (which extends ResultSet) provides a richer API than ResultSet:

- It provides "connected" and "disconnected" semantics: a connected rowset maintains its connection to its data source.

- It provides insert, update, and delete APIs: you may insert, update, and delete rows from a given RowSet object.

- It provides a mapping of the input/output of RowSet to and from XML: a simple API is provided to get or set data and metadata in XML format.

- RowSets are JavaBeans: therefore, they have proper setXXX() and getXXX() methods.

7.1. What Is a RowSet Object?

The javax.sql package provides the rowset API, which makes it easy to handle data sets from virtually any data source as JavaBeans components. A RowSet object represents a set of rows returned by a database server as a result of running a SQL query or opening a table. According to *JDBC API Tutorial and Reference, Third Edition* (Addison-Wesley Professional, 2003), "a RowSet object is a container for tabular data, encapsulating a set of zero or more rows that have been retrieved from a data source. In a basic implementation of the RowSet interface, the rows are retrieved from a JDBC data source, but a 'row set' may be customized so that its data can also be from a spreadsheet, a flat file, or any other data source with a tabular format. A RowSet object extends the ResultSet interface, which means that it can be scrollable, can be updatable, and can do anything a ResultSet object can do."

Different kinds of rowsets (these are all interfaces and extend the RowSet) are provided by J2SE 5.0 (I will provide details on these different rowsets in the following questions and answers):

- **Cached rowset** (javax.sql.CachedRowSet): A CachedRowSet object is special in that it can operate without being connected to its data source—that is, it is a disconnected RowSet object (disconnected rowsets are those that do not maintain a connection with their data sources).

- **JDBC rowset** (javax.sql.JdbcRowSet): A wrapper around a ResultSet object that makes it possible to use the result set as a JavaBeans component. Thus, a JdbcRowSet object can be one of the beans that a tool makes available for composing an application. A JdbcRowSet is a connected rowset.

- **Web rowset** (javax.sql.WebRowSet): A WebRowSet object is very special because in addition to offering all of the capabilities of a CachedRowSet object, it can write itself as an XML document and can also read that XML document to convert itself back to a WebRowSet object.

- **Filtered rowset** (`javax.sql.FilteredRowSet`): There are occasions when a `RowSet` object has a need to provide a degree of filtering to its contents. One possible solution is to provide a query language for all standard `RowSet` implementations; however, this is not a practical approach for lightweight components such as disconnected `RowSet` objects. The `FilteredRowSet` interface seeks to address this need without supplying a heavy-weight query language along with the processing that such a query language would require.

- **Join rowset** (`javax.sql.JoinRowSet`): The `JoinRowSet` interface provides a mechanism for combining related data from different `RowSet` objects into one `JoinRowSet` object, which represents a SQL `JOIN`. In other words, a `JoinRowSet` object acts as a container for the data from `RowSet` objects that form a SQL `JOIN` relationship.

- **Synchronized Resolver rowset** (`javax.sql.rowset.spi.SyncResolver`): A `SyncResolver` object is a specialized `RowSet` object that implements the `SyncResolver` interface. It may operate as either a connected `RowSet` object (an implementation of the `JdbcRowSet` interface) or a connected `RowSet` object (an implementation of the `CachedRowSet` interface or one of its subinterfaces).

The following is taken from the J2SE 5.0 documentation:

The RowSet interface provides a set of JavaBeans properties that allow a RowSet instance to be configured to connect to a JDBC data source and read some data from the data source. A group of setter methods (setInt(), setBytes(), setString(), and so on) provide a way to pass input parameters to a rowset's command property. This command is the SQL query the rowset uses when it gets its data from a relational database, which is generally the case. The RowSet interface supports JavaBeans events, allowing other components in an application to be notified when an event occurs on a rowset, such as a change in its value. The RowSet interface is unique in that it is intended to be implemented using the rest of the JDBC API. In other words, a RowSet implementation is a layer of software that executes "on top" of a JDBC driver. Implementations of the RowSet interface can be provided by anyone, including JDBC driver vendors who want to provide a RowSet implementation as part of their JDBC products.

And the following is taken from *JDBC API Tutorial and Reference*:

*Rowsets may be either **connected** or **disconnected**. A connected RowSet object maintains a connection to its data source the entire time it is in use, whereas a disconnected rowset is connected to its data source only while it is reading data from the data source or writing data to it. While the rowset is disconnected, it does not need a JDBC driver or the full implementation of the JDBC API. This makes it very lean and therefore an ideal container for sending a set of data to a thin client. The client can, if it chooses, make updates to the data and send the rowset back to the application server. On the server, the disconnected RowSet object uses its reader to make a connection to the data source and write data back to it. Exactly how this is done depends on how the reader is implemented. Typically, the reader delegates making a connection and reading/writing data to the JDBC driver.*

A rowset may be *disconnected* from a data source, that is, function without maintaining an open connection to a data source the whole time it is in use. In addition, a rowset can be serialized, which means that it can be sent to a remote object over a network (e.g., RMI Server).

According to the J2SE 5.0 documentation, the RowSet interface works with various other classes and interfaces behind the scenes. These can be grouped into three categories:

- Event notification

  - RowSetListener: A RowSet object is a JavaBeans component because it has properties and participates in the JavaBeans event notification mechanism. The RowSetListener interface is implemented by a component that wants to be notified about events that occur to a particular RowSet object. Such a component registers itself as a listener with a rowset via the RowSet.addRowSetListener() method. When the RowSet object changes one or all of its rows, or moves its cursor, it also notifies each listener that is registered with it. The listener reacts by carrying out its implementation of the notification method called on it.

  - RowSetEvent: As part of its internal notification process, a RowSet object creates an instance of RowSetEvent and passes it to the listener. The listener can use this RowSetEvent object to find out which rowset had the event.

- Metadata

  - RowSetMetaData: This interface, derived from the ResultSetMetaData interface, provides information about the columns in a RowSet object. An application can use RowSetMetaData methods to find out how many columns the rowset contains and what kind of data each column can contain. The RowSetMetaData interface provides methods for setting the information about columns, but an application would not normally use these methods. When an application calls the RowSet method execute, the RowSet object will contain a new set of rows, and its RowSetMetaData object will have been internally updated to contain information about the new columns.

- The Reader/Writer facility: A RowSet object that implements the RowSetInternal interface can call on the RowSetReader object associated with it to populate itself with data. It can also call on the RowSetWriter object associated with it to write any changes to its rows back to the data source from which it originally got the rows. A rowset that remains connected to its data source does not need to use a reader and writer because it can simply operate on the data source directly.

  - RowSetInternal: By implementing the RowSetInternal interface, a RowSet object gets access to its internal state and is able to call on its reader and writer. A rowset keeps track of the values in its current rows and of the values that immediately preceded the current ones, referred to as the *original* values. A rowset also keeps track of (1) the parameters that have been set for its command and (2) the connection that was passed to it, if any. A rowset uses the RowSetInternal methods behind the scenes to get access to this information. An application does not normally invoke these methods directly.

- `RowSetReader`: A disconnected `RowSet` object that has implemented the `RowSetInternal` interface can call on its reader (the `RowSetReader` object associated with it) to populate it with data. When an application calls the `RowSet.execute()` method, that method calls on the rowset's reader to do much of the work. Implementations can vary widely, but generally a reader makes a connection to the data source, reads data from the data source and populates the rowset with it, and closes the connection. A reader may also update the `RowSetMetaData` object for its rowset. The rowset's internal state is also updated, either by the reader or directly by the method `RowSet.execute()`.

- `RowSetWriter`: A disconnected `RowSet` object that has implemented the `RowSetInternal` interface can call on its writer (the `RowSetWriter` object associated with it) to write changes back to the underlying data source. Implementations may vary widely, but generally, a writer will (1) make a connection to the data source, (2) check to see whether there is a conflict, that is, whether a value that has been changed in the rowset has also been changed in the data source, (3) write the new values to the data source if there is no conflict, and (4) close the connection.

The `RowSet` interface may be implemented in any number of ways, and anyone may write an implementation. Developers are encouraged to use their imaginations in coming up with new ways to use rowsets.

7.2. What Are the Relationships Between Key Classes and Interfaces for Rowsets?

Figure 7-1 show the relationships between key classes and interfaces for rowsets.
We can observe the following from Figure 7-1:

- `RowSet` is a foundation interface for all rowset objects (`CachedRowSet`, `WebRowSet`, etc.).

- `RowSet` extends `ResultSet` and `RowSetMetaData` extends `ResultSetMetaData`.

- Every rowset object has an internal object (called `InternalRowSet`) that enables reading and writing to data sources.

- The `RowSet` interface supports JavaBeans events (by using `RowSetEvent`), allowing other components in an application to be notified when an event (such as adding, deleting, or updating a row or record) occurs on a rowset, such as a change in its value.

For details on the relationship of rowsets, refer to the online publication *JDBC Specification 3.0, Final Release*, by Jon Ellis, Linda Ho, and Maydene Fisher.

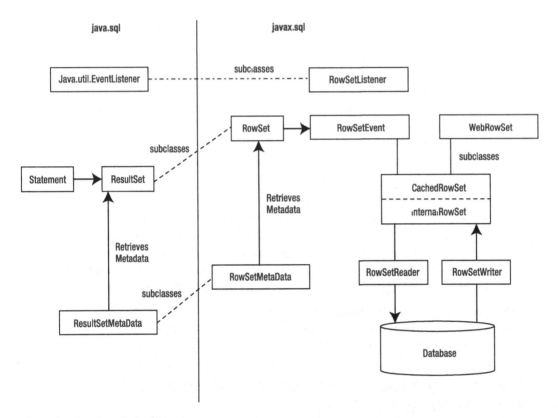

Figure 7-1. *RowSet relationships*

7.3. What Is a JdbcRowSet?

JdbcRowSet (javax.sql.JdbcRowSet interface) is a connected rowset that serves mainly as a thin wrapper around a ResultSet object to make a JDBC driver look like a JavaBeans component. According to J2SE 5.0 documentation, "a JdbcRowSet object can be one of the Beans that a tool makes available for composing an application. Because a JdbcRowSet is a connected rowset, that is, it continually maintains its connection to a database using a JDBC technology-enabled driver, it also effectively makes the driver a JavaBeans component." JdbcRowSet is defined as follows:

```
package javax.sql.rowset;

import javax.sql.RowSet;
import javax.sql.rowset.Joinable;

public interface JdbcRowSet
    extends RowSet, Joinable {
    ...
}
```

Because JdbcRowSet is always connected to its database, an instance of JdbcRowSet can simply take calls invoked on it and in turn call them on its ResultSet object. As a consequence, a result set can, for example, be a component in a Swing application. Another advantage of a JdbcRowSet object is that it can be used to make a ResultSet object scrollable and updatable. All RowSet objects are by default scrollable and updatable. If the driver and database being used do not support scrolling or updating of result sets, an application can populate a JdbcRowSet object with the data of a ResultSet object and then operate on the JdbcRowSet object as if it were the ResultSet object.

The following code fragment illustrates creating a JdbcRowSet object, setting its properties, and executing the command string in its command property:

```java
import java.sql.Connection;            // database connection object
import java.sql.rowset.JdbcRowSet;     // JdbcRowSet definition
import com.sun.rowset.JdbcRowSetImpl;  // Sun's reference impl. of JdbcRowSet
...
Connection conn = null;
JdbcRowSet jrs = null;
String query = "SELECT author, title FROM books";
try {
    conn = getConnection();
    jrs = new JdbcRowSetImpl(conn);
    jrs.setCommand(query);
    jrs.execute();
    ...
}
catch(SQLException se) {
    // handle database exceptions
}
catch(Exception e) {
    // handle other exceptions
}
finally {
    // close resources
}
```

At this point, jrs contains all of the selected data in the books table. After creating a JdbcRowSet object, you may use ResultSet methods because it is effectively operating on a ResultSet object. It can navigate the rows in jrs, retrieve column values, update column values, insert new rows, and so on. For example, to process results, you may write the following to iterate all rows:

```java
while (jrs.next()) {
    System.out.println("author: " + jrs.getString(1));
    System.out.println("title: " + jrs.getString(2));
}
```

In this example, the next three lines of code go to the fifth row and retrieve the value in the first and second columns using ResultSet methods:

```
jrs.absolute(5);
String author = jrs.getString(1);
String title = jrs.getString(2);
```

Once you create a JdbcRowSet object, then you can extract its metadata by using this code (note that the method getMetaData() is a ResultSet method that returns a ResultSetMetaData object, so it must be cast to a RowSetMetaData object before it can be assigned to rsMetaData):

```
RowSetMetaData rsMetaData = (RowSetMetaData) jrs.getMetaData();
If (rsMetaData == null) {
    // vendor has not implemented the RowSetMetaData interface
}
else {
    // you can invoke RowSetMetaData methods to get JdbcRowSet's metadata
    int numberOfColumns = rsMetaData.getColumnCount();
    ...
}
```

For rowset objects, you may pass input parameters (similar to PreparedStatement objects). The following code fragment shows what an application might do: it sets the rowset's command, sets the command's parameters, and executes the command. Simply by calling the execute method, jrs populates itself with the requested data from the table CUSTOMERS:

```
Connection conn = getConnection();
JdbcRowSet jrs = new JdbcRowSetImpl(conn);
jrs.setCommand("SELECT  author, title FROM books where author = ?");
jrs.setString(1, "Knuth");
jrs.execute();
```

Sun's reference implementation class, com.sun.rowset.JdbcRowSetImpl, which is defined next, has four constructors. In order to understand the JdbcRowSetImpl class, we need to understand the BaseRowSet class—the superclass for the JdbcRowSetImpl class.

BaseRowSet Class Definition

```
package javax.sql.rowset;
public abstract class BaseRowSet
    extends Object
    implements Serializable, Cloneable {
    ...
}
```

According to the JDBC 3.0 Specification (implemented in JDK 1.5), the BaseRowSet is an abstract class providing a RowSet object with its basic functionality. The basic functions include having properties and sending event notifications, which all JavaBeans components must implement. The BaseRowSet class provides the core functionality for all RowSet implementations, and all standard implementations may use this class in combination with one or more RowSet interfaces in order to provide a standard vendor-specific implementation. To clarify, all implementations must implement at least one of the RowSet interfaces (JdbcRowSet,

CachedRowSet, JoinRowSet, FilteredRowSet, or WebRowSet). This means that any implementation that extends the BaseRowSet class must also implement one of the RowSet interfaces.

The BaseRowSet class provides the following:

- Properties

  - Fields for storing current properties

  - Methods for getting and setting properties

- Event notification

- A complete set of setter methods for setting the parameters in a RowSet object's command

- Streams

  - Fields for storing stream instances

  - Constants for indicating the type of a stream

JdbcRowSetImpl Class Definition

```
package com.sun.rowset;

public class JdbcRowSetImpl
    extends javax.sql.rowset.BaseRowSet
    implements javax.sql.rowset.JdbcRowSet, javax.sql.rowset.Joinable {
    ...
}
```

Here, the javax.sql.rowset.Joinable interface provides the methods for getting and setting a match column, which is the basis for forming the SQL JOIN formed by adding RowSet objects to a JoinRowSet object.

JdbcRowSetImpl Class Constructors

- JdbcRowSetImpl(): Constructs a default JdbcRowSet object

- JdbcRowSetImpl(java.sql.Connection con): Constructs a default JdbcRowSet object given a valid Connection object

- JdbcRowSetImpl(java.sql.ResultSet res): Constructs a JdbcRowSet object using the given valid ResultSet object

- JdbcRowSetImpl(String url, String user, String password): Constructs a default JdbcRowSet object using the URL, username, and password arguments supplied

7.4. What Is a CachedRowSet?

CachedRowSet (javax.sql.CachedRowSet) object is a disconnected (from the database) ResultSet object. CachedRowSet is a JavaBean, and this means that like any other JavaBean, implementations of javax.sql.CachedRowSet may be serialized. This allows for CachedRowSet objects to be serialized, sent to remote clients, updated, and then sent back to the server (including the database server). For example, a CachedRowSet object can be used as the data model for a Java servlet or JavaServer Pages (JSP) entry or edit form.

The following is taken from the J2SE 5.0 documentation:

A CachedRowSet object is a container for rows of data that caches its rows in memory, which makes it possible to operate without always being connected to its data source. Further, it is a JavaBeans component and is scrollable, updatable, and serializable. A CachedRowSet object typically contains rows from a result set, but it can also contain rows from any file with a tabular format, such as a spread sheet. The reference implementation (com.sun.rowset.CachedRowSetImpl class) supports getting data only from a ResultSet object, but developers can extend the SyncProvider implementations to provide access to other tabular data sources.

A CachedRowSet object can be used as the data model for a Java server-side entry or edit form. An application can modify the data in a CachedRowSet object, and those modifications can then be propagated back to the source of the data.

According to J2SE 5.0 documentation, a CachedRowSet object is'

. . . a disconnected rowset, which means that it makes use of a connection to its data source only briefly. It connects to its data source while it is reading data to populate itself with rows and again while it is propagating changes back to its underlying data source. The rest of the time, a CachedRowSet object is disconnected, including while its data is being modified. Being disconnected makes a RowSet object much leaner and therefore much easier to pass to another component. For example, a disconnected RowSet object can be serialized and passed over the wire to a thin client such as a personal digital assistant (PDA).

Therefore, a CachedRowSet object is special in that it can operate without being connected to its data source—that is, it is a disconnected RowSet object. It gets the name "CachedRowSet" from the fact that it stores (caches) its data in memory so that it can operate on its own data rather than on the data stored in a database.

CachedRowSet is defined as

```
package javax.sql.rowset;

import javax.sql.RowSet;
import javax.sql.rowset.Joinable;

public interface CachedRowSet
    extends RowSet, Joinable {

    ""

}
```

To create a CachedRowSet object, use its JavaBeans properties. The CachedRowSet properties allow it to connect to a database and retrieve data on its own. Table 7-1 describes some of the properties necessary to initialize a CachedRowSet without a preexisting database connection.

Table 7-1. *CachedRowSet Properties*

Property	Description
Username	Database username
Password	Database user password
URL	Database JDBC URL such as jdbc:odbc:myPayroll
Command	SQL query statement

The following code fragment illustrates creating a CachedRowSet object, setting its properties, and executing the command string in its command property:

```
import java.sql.Connection;              // database connection object
import java.sql.ResultSet;               // result set object
import java.sql.Statement;               // statement object
import java.sql.rowset.CachedRowSet;     // JdbcRowSet definition
import com.sun.rowset.CachedRowSetImpl;  // Sun's reference impl. of CachedRowSet
import jcb.util.DatabaseUtil;            // a utility class to close resources
...
String query = "select author, title from books";
Connection conn = null;
Statement stmt = null;
ResultSet rs = null;
CachedRowSet crs = null;
try {
   conn = getConnection();
   stmt = conn.createStatement();
   rs = stmt.executeQuery(query);

   // create CachedRowSet and populate
   crs = new CachedRowSetImpl();
   crs.populate(rs); // populate using a ResultSet object
   // here you may use crs (a CachedRowSet object)
}
catch (SQLException e) {
   // handle exception
   e.printStackTrace();
   ...
}
finally {
   // note that the connection is being closed
   DatabaseUtil.close(rs);
   DatabaseUtil.close(stmt);
   DatabaseUtil.close(conn);
}
```

```
// here you can use CachedRowSet without being connected to database:
if (crs != null) {
   while (crs.next()) {
      String author = crs.getString(1);
      String title = crs.getString(2);
   }
}
```

At this point, crs contains all of the selected data in the books table. After creating a CachedRowSet object, you may use ResultSet methods because the CachedRowSet object is effectively operating on a ResultSet object. We can navigate the rows in crs (by using the next() method), retrieve column values, update column values, insert new rows, and so on. For example, the next three lines of code go to the third row and retrieve the value in the first and second columns using ResultSet methods. You might be wondering whether this allows going back to any row, and the answer is yes. You also might be wondering what happens if any updates are done to this CachedRowSet object. If you do not commit changes to your database, then changes will not be reflected on the database at all.

```
crs.absolute(3);
String author = jrs.getString(1);
String title = jrs.getString(2);
```

Once you create a CachedRowSet object, then you can extract its metadata by using this code:

```
RowSetMetaData rsMetaData = (RowSetMetaData) crs.getMetaData();
If (rsMetaData == null) {
   // vendor has not implemented the RowSetMetaData interface
}
else {
   // you can invoke RowSetMetaData methods to get JdbcRowSet's metadata
   int numberOfColumns = rsMetaData.getColumnCount();
   ...
}
```

Sun's reference implementation class, com.sun.rowset.CachedRowSetImpl, which is defined next, has two constructors.

CachedRowSetImpl Class Definition

```
package com.sun.rowset;

public class CachedRowSetImpl
   extends javax.sql.rowset.BaseRowSet
   implements javax.sql.RowSet,
               javax.sql.rowset.CachedRowSet,
               javax.sql.RowSetInternal,
               java.io.Serializable,
               java.lang.Cloneable {
   ...
}
```

CachedRowSetImpl Class Constructors

- CachedRowSetImpl(): Constructs a new default CachedRowSetImpl object with the capacity to hold 100 rows

- CachedRowSetImpl(java.util.Hashtable env): Provides a CachedRowSetImpl instance with the same default properties as the zero parameter constructor

You can make changes to a CachedRowSet object (i.e., its data) and then commit the changes back into the database. Therefore, for a given CachedRowSet object, you can not only read its data, but you can also propagate changes back to the database. For example, the following code segment updates a CachedRowSet object, and then commits changes back into its data source:

```
crs.absolute(3);
crs.updateString(1, "Donald E. Knuth");
crs.updateRow();
commitToDatabase(crs);
```

where the commitToDatabase() method is defined as

```
import java.sql.Connection;
import java.sql.SQLException;
import javax.sql.rowset.CachedRowSet;
import jcb.util.DatabaseUtil;  // for closing resources
...
public static boolean commitToDatabase(CachedRowSet crs) {
   if (crs == null) {
      // there is nothing to commit
      return true;
   }

   Connection conn = null;
   try {
      conn = getConnection();
      // propagate changes and close connection
      crs.acceptChanges(conn);

      return true;

   }
   catch (SQLException se) {
      // handle exception
      return false;
   }
   catch (Exception e) {
      // handle exception
      return false;
   }
   finally {
      DatabaseUtil.close(conn);
   }
}
```

To use a CachedRowSet object with JavaServer Pages (JSP), see the article "Get Disconnected with CachedRowSet," at http://www.javaworld.com/javaworld/jw-02-2001/jw-0202-cachedrow_p.html.

The Oracle database imposes some constraints on CachedRowSet objects: all the constraints that apply to an updatable result set are applicable here except serialization, since OracleCachedRowSet is serializable. The SQL query has the following constraints:

- It references only a single table in the database.

- It contains no join operations.

- It selects the primary key of the table it references.

In addition, a SQL query should also satisfy these conditions if inserts are to be performed:

- It selects all of the non-nullable columns in the underlying table.

- It selects all columns that do not have a default value.

7.5. What Is a WebRowSet?

A WebRowSet (javax.sql.WebRowSet) object is a disconnected rowset that caches its data in memory in the same manner as a CachedRowSet object. A WebRowSet object is special because in addition to offering all the capabilities of a CachedRowSet object, it can write itself as an XML document and can also read that XML document to convert itself back to a WebRowSet object. Due to its XML support, WebRowSet is an ideal object format for web services. WebRowSet is also ideal for just painting a data for a single web page—a large-sized WebRowSet might introduce performance problems. Therefore, for better performance, you should keep its size as small as possible.

XML is the language through which disparate enterprises can communicate with each other, and has become the standard for web services communication. As a consequence, a WebRowSet object fills a real need by making it easy for web services to send and receive data from a database in the form of an XML document.

According to J2SE 5.0 documentation, WebRowSet describes the standard XML document format required when describing a RowSet object in XML and must be used by all standard implementations of the WebRowSet interface to ensure interoperability. In addition, the WebRowSet schema uses specific SQL/XML schema annotations, thus ensuring greater cross-platform interoperability. This is an effort currently under way at the ISO organization. The SQL/XML definition is available at http://standards.iso.org/iso/9075/2002/12/sqlxml.xsd.

The schema definition describes the internal data of a RowSet object in three distinct areas:

- **Properties**: These properties describe the standard synchronization provider properties in addition to the more general RowSet properties.

- **Metadata**: This area describes the metadata associated with the tabular structure governed by a WebRowSet object. The metadata described is closely aligned with the metadata accessible in the underlying java.sql.ResultSet interface.

- **Data**: This area describes the original data (the state of data since the last population or last synchronization of the WebRowSet object) and the current data. By keeping track of the delta between the original data and the current data, a WebRowSet maintains the ability to synchronize changes in its data back to the originating data source.

The Creation and Population of WebRowSet

You can create a WebRowSet object and its associated metadata by using the following code fragments. Before creating a WebRowSet object, I set up a database table:

```
mysql> use octopus;
Database changed
mysql> desc employees;
+-------+-------------+------+-----+---------+-------+
| Field | Type        | Null | Key | Default | Extra |
+-------+-------------+------+-----+---------+-------+
| id    | varchar(3)  |      | PRI |         |       |
| name  | varchar(16) | YES  |     | NULL    |       |
| age   | int(11)     | YES  |     | NULL    |       |
+-------+-------------+------+-----+---------+-------+
3 rows in set (0.00 sec)
mysql> select * from employees;
+----+--------------+------+
| id | name         | age  |
+----+--------------+------+
| 88 | Peter Pan    | NULL |
| 77 | Donald Duck  | NULL |
| 33 | Mary Kent    |   35 |
| 44 | Monica Seles |   30 |
+----+--------------+------+
4 rows in set (0.00 sec)
mysql>
```

First, you need to create an empty WebRowSet object:

```
import javax.sql.rowset.WebRowSet;
import com.sun.rowset.WebRowSetImpl;
...
WebRowSet wrs = new WebRowSetImpl();
```

After creating an empty WebRowSet object, you can populate it:

```
import java.sql.Connection;
import jcb.util.DatabaseUtil;
import jcb.db.VeryBasicConnectionManager;
...
Connection conn = VeryBasicConnectionManager.getConnection("mysql");
wrs.setCommand("SELECT id, name, age FROM employees");
wrs.execute(conn);
```

Alternatively, you can populate the WebRowSet object from a ResultSet object:

```
// load MySQL JDBC Driver and return a connection
Connection conn = VeryBasicConnectionManager.getConnection("mysql");

// use a statement to gather data from the database
Statement stmt = conn.createStatement();
String query = "SELECT id, name, age FROM employees";
WebRowSet wrs = new WebRowSetImpl();

// execute the query
ResultSet resultSet = stmt.executeQuery(query);
wrs.populate(rs);
```

Getting RowSetMetaData from a WebRowSet Object

After populating a WebRowSet object, you can get its metadata by using this code:

```
import javax.sql.RowSetMetaData;
...
RowSetMetaData rsMetaData = (RowSetMetaData) wrs;
If (rsMetaData == null) {
   // db vendor does not support WebRowSet's metadata
}
else {
   // db vendor does support WebRowSet's metadata
   // you may invoke RowSetMetaData methods
   int numberOfColumns = rsMetaData.getColumnCount();

   ...
}
```

Updating a WebRowSet Object

To update a WebRowSet object, you may update your desired rows (by using WebRowSet.updateXXX() methods) and then invoke the WebRowSet.acceptChanges() method. The following code fragment updates the first two rows in the WebRowSet object wrs:

```
// wrs is initialized with its original and current values
wrs.execute();

// set the cursor to the first row
wrs.first();
wrs.updateString(2, "Jane Doe");
wrs.updateInt(3, 45);
wrs.updateRow();
// the current value of the first row has been updated
```

```
// set the cursor to the second row
wrs.relative(1);
wrs.updateString(2, "Toni Duncan");
wrs.updateInt(3, 55);
wrs.updateRow();
// the current value of the second row has been updated

wrs.acceptChanges();
// the original value has been set to the current value
// and the database has been updated
```

Representing a WebRowSet Object as an XML Object

Writing a WebRowSet object to an XML document can be accomplished by using the WebRowSet.writeXml() method, which can take either an OutputStream object (if we want to write in bytes) or a Writer object (if we want to write in characters). This code snippet writes to a file called emps.xml using a FileWriter object:

```
String filename = "c:\\myrowset\\emps.xml";            // Windows
// String filename = "/home/alex/myrowset/emps.xml";   // UNIX
java.io.FileWriter writer = new java.io.FileWriter(filename);
wrs.writeXml(writer);
```

The created emps.xml file will have three sections:

- Properties

- Metadata

- Data

A generated XML document will contain a properties section, which will contain information about our connection, including the command associated with our WebRowSet object—SELECT id, name, age FROM employees—as well as other important information. The properties section of a WebRowSet object is depicted here (extracted from emps.xml):

```
<properties>
  <command>SELECT id, name, age FROM employees</command>
  <concurrency>1008</concurrency>
  <datasource><null/></datasource>
  <escape-processing>true</escape-processing>
  <fetch-direction>1000</fetch-direction>
  <fetch-size>0</fetch-size>
  <isolation-level>2</isolation-level>
  <key-columns></key-columns>
  <map></map>
  <max-field-size>0</max-field-size>
  <max-rows>0</max-rows>
  <query-timeout>0</query-timeout>
  <read-only>true</read-only>
```

```
<rowset-type>ResultSet.TYPE_SCROLL_INSENSITIVE</rowset-type>
<show-deleted>false</show-deleted>
<table-name>employees</table-name>
<url><null/></url>
<sync-provider>
  <sync-provider-name>com.sun.rowset.providers.RIOptimisticProvider
  </sync-provider-name>
  <sync-provider-vendor>Sun Microsystems Inc.</sync-provider-vendor>
  <sync-provider-version>1.0</sync-provider-version>
  <sync-provider-grade>2</sync-provider-grade>
  <data-source-lock>1</data-source-lock>
</sync-provider>
</properties>
```

The metadata section contains metadata about the structure of the columns that our WebRowSet object consists of. For each rowset's column we have a `<column-definition>` element that describes the structure of the underlying column. The metadata section of a WebRowSet object is depicted here (extracted from emps.xml):

```
<metadata>
  <column-count>3</column-count>
  <column-definition>
    <column-index>1</column-index>
    <auto-increment>false</auto-increment>
    <case-sensitive>false</case-sensitive>
    <currency>false</currency>
    <nullable>0</nullable>
    <signed>false</signed>
    <searchable>true</searchable>
    <column-display-size>10</column-display-size>
    <column-label>id</column-label>
    <column-name>id</column-name>
    <schema-name></schema-name>
    <column-precision>10</column-precision>
    <column-scale>0</column-scale>
    <table-name>employees</table-name>
    <catalog-name>octopus</catalog-name>
    <column-type>12</column-type>
    <column-type-name>VARCHAR</column-type-name>
  </column-definition>
  <column-definition>
    <column-index>2</column-index>
    <auto-increment>false</auto-increment>
    <case-sensitive>false</case-sensitive>
    <currency>false</currency>
    <nullable>1</nullable>
    <signed>false</signed>
```

```
    <searchable>true</searchable>
    <column-display-size>20</column-display-size>
    <column-label>name</column-label>
    <column-name>name</column-name>
    <schema-name></schema-name>
    <column-precision>20</column-precision>
    <column-scale>0</column-scale>
    <table-name>employees</table-name>
    <catalog-name>octopus</catalog-name>
    <column-type>12</column-type>
    <column-type-name>VARCHAR</column-type-name>
  </column-definition>
  <column-definition>
    <column-index>3</column-index>
    <auto-increment>false</auto-increment>
    <case-sensitive>false</case-sensitive>
    <currency>false</currency>
    <nullable>1</nullable>
    <signed>true</signed>
    <searchable>true</searchable>
    <column-display-size>11</column-display-size>
    <column-label>age</column-label>
    <column-name>age</column-name>
    <schema-name></schema-name>
    <column-precision>11</column-precision>
    <column-scale>0</column-scale>
    <table-name>employees</table-name>
    <catalog-name>octopus</catalog-name>
    <column-type>4</column-type>
    <column-type-name>INTEGER</column-type-name>
  </column-definition>
</metadata>
```

The data section of a WebRowSet object is depicted here (extracted from emps.xml):

```
<data>
  <currentRow>
    <columnValue>88</columnValue>
    <columnValue>Peter Pan</columnValue>
    <columnValue><null/></columnValue>
  </currentRow>
  <currentRow>
    <columnValue>77</columnValue>
    <columnValue>Donald Duck</columnValue>
    <columnValue><null/></columnValue>
  </currentRow>
```

```
    <currentRow>
      <columnValue>33</columnValue>
      <columnValue>Mary Kent</columnValue>
      <columnValue>35</columnValue>
    </currentRow>
    <currentRow>
      <columnValue>44</columnValue>
      <columnValue>Monica Seles</columnValue>
      <columnValue>30</columnValue>
    </currentRow>
  </data>
```

The Solution

Here, I put all of the pieces together as a single program, which shows how to create a WebRowSet object and populate it from a database:

```java
import java.io.*;
import java.sql.*;
import javax.sql.*;

import javax.sql.rowset.WebRowSet;
import com.sun.rowset.WebRowSetImpl;

import jcb.util.DatabaseUtil;
import jcb.db.VeryBasicConnectionManager;

public class DemoWebRowSet {
   WebRowSet webRS = null;

   public static void main(String[] args) {
       String dbVendor = args[0]; // {"mysql", "oracle", "odbc"}
       DemoWebRowSet demo = new DemoWebRowSet();
       Connection conn = null;
       try {
           conn = VeryBasicConnectionManager.getConnection(dbVendor);
           demo.populateRowSet(conn);
           // note that WebRowSet is a "disconnected" object
           DatabaseUtil.close(conn);
           demo.writeXML();
       }
       catch (Exception e) {
          e.printStackTrace();
       }
   }
```

```java
    void populateRowSet(Connection conn) throws Exception {
        ResultSet rs = null;
        Statement stmt = null;
        try {
            stmt = conn.createStatement();
            String query = "SELECT id, name, age FROM employees";
            rs = stmt.executeQuery(query);

            webRS = new WebRowSetImpl();
            webRS.setCommand(query);
            webRS.execute(conn);
        }
        finally {
            DatabaseUtil.close(rs);
            DatabaseUtil.close(stmt);
        }
    }

    void writeXML() throws Exception {
        if (webRS == null) {
            System.out.println("No data found");
            return;
        }

        String filename = "c:\\temp\\emps.xml";              // Windows
        // String filename = "/home/alex/myrowset/emps.xml";  // UNIX
        java.io.FileWriter writer = new java.io.FileWriter(filename);
        webRS.writeXml(writer);
    }
}
```

Running the Solution for a MySQL Database

```
$ javac DemoWebRowSet.java
$ java DemoWebRowSet mysql
$ type c:\temp\emps.xml
<?xml version="1.0"?>
<webRowSet xmlns="http://java.sun.com/xml/ns/jdbc"
xmlns:xsi="http://www.w3.org/2001/XMLSchema-instance"
xsi:schemaLocation="http://java.sun.com/xml/ns/jdbc/webrowset.xsd">
  <properties> … </properties>
  <metadata> … </metadata>
  <data> … </data>
</webRowSet>
```

Oracle Database Setup

```
SQL> desc employees;
Name                                            Null?    Type
----------------------------------------------- -------- ----------------
ID                                              NOT NULL VARCHAR2(10)
NAME                                            NOT NULL VARCHAR2(20)
AGE                                                      NUMBER(38)
SQL> select * from employees;
ID          NAME                    AGE
----------  --------------------    ----------
11          Alex Smith               25
22          Don Knuth                65
33          Mary Kent                35
44          Monica Seles             30
99          Alex Edison
```

Running the Solution for an Oracle Database

```
$ javac DemoWebRowSet.java
$ java DemoWebRowSet oracle

$ type c:\temp\emps.xml
<?xml version="1.0"?>
<webRowSet xmlns="http://java.sun.com/xml/ns/jdbc"
xmlns:xsi="http://www.w3.org/2001/XMLSchema-instance"
xsi:schemaLocation="http://java.sun.com/xml/ns/jdbc/webrowset.xsd">
  <properties>
    <command>SELECT id, name, age FROM employees</command>
    <concurrency>1008</concurrency>
    <datasource><null/></datasource>
    <escape-processing>true</escape-processing>
    <fetch-direction>1000</fetch-direction>
    <fetch-size>0</fetch-size>
    <isolation-level>2</isolation-level>
    <key-columns>
    </key-columns>
    <map>
    </map>
    <max-field-size>0</max-field-size>
    <max-rows>0</max-rows>
    <query-timeout>0</query-timeout>
    <read-only>true</read-only>
    <rowset-type>ResultSet.TYPE_SCROLL_INSENSITIVE</rowset-type>
    <show-deleted>false</show-deleted>
    <table-name>employees</table-name>
    <url><null/></url>
```

```
  <sync-provider>
    <sync-provider-name>
     com.sun.rowset.providers.RIOptimisticProvider</sync-provider-name>
    <sync-provider-vendor>Sun Microsystems Inc.</sync-provider-vendor>
    <sync-provider-version>1.0</sync-provider-version>
    <sync-provider-grade>2</sync-provider-grade>
    <data-source-lock>1</data-source-lock>
  </sync-provider>
</properties>
<metadata>
  <column-count>3</column-count>
  <column-definition>
    <column-index>1</column-index>
    <auto-increment>false</auto-increment>
    <case-sensitive>true</case-sensitive>
    <currency>false</currency>
    <nullable>0</nullable>
    <signed>true</signed>
    <searchable>true</searchable>
    <column-display-size>10</column-display-size>
    <column-label>ID</column-label>
    <column-name>ID</column-name>
    <schema-name></schema-name>
    <column-precision>10</column-precision>
    <column-scale>0</column-scale>
    <table-name></table-name>
    <catalog-name></catalog-name>
    <column-type>12</column-type>
    <column-type-name>VARCHAR2</column-type-name>
  </column-definition>
  <column-definition>
    <column-index>2</column-index>
    <auto-increment>false</auto-increment>
    <case-sensitive>true</case-sensitive>
    <currency>false</currency>
    <nullable>0</nullable>
    <signed>true</signed>
    <searchable>true</searchable>
    <column-display-size>20</column-display-size>
    <column-label>NAME</column-label>
    <column-name>NAME</column-name>
    <schema-name></schema-name>
    <column-precision>20</column-precision>
    <column-scale>0</column-scale>
    <table-name></table-name>
    <catalog-name></catalog-name>
    <column-type>12</column-type>
```

```xml
        <column-type-name>VARCHAR2</column-type-name>
      </column-definition>
      <column-definition>
        <column-index>3</column-index>
        <auto-increment>false</auto-increment>
        <case-sensitive>false</case-sensitive>
        <currency>true</currency>
        <nullable>1</nullable>
        <signed>true</signed>
        <searchable>true</searchable>
        <column-display-size>22</column-display-size>
        <column-label>AGE</column-label>
        <column-name>AGE</column-name>
        <schema-name></schema-name>
        <column-precision>38</column-precision>
        <column-scale>0</column-scale>
        <table-name></table-name>
        <catalog-name></catalog-name>
        <column-type>2</column-type>
        <column-type-name>NUMBER</column-type-name>
      </column-definition>
    </metadata>
    <data>
      <currentRow>
        <columnValue>11</columnValue>
        <columnValue>Alex Smith</columnValue>
        <columnValue>25</columnValue>
      </currentRow>
      <currentRow>
        <columnValue>22</columnValue>
        <columnValue>Don Knuth</columnValue>
        <columnValue>65</columnValue>
      </currentRow>
      <currentRow>
        <columnValue>33</columnValue>
        <columnValue>Mary Kent</columnValue>
        <columnValue>35</columnValue>
      </currentRow>
      <currentRow>
        <columnValue>44</columnValue>
        <columnValue>Monica Seles</columnValue>
        <columnValue>30</columnValue>
      </currentRow>
      <currentRow>
        <columnValue>99</columnValue>
        <columnValue>Alex Edison</columnValue>
```

```
        <columnValue><null/></columnValue>
      </currentRow>
    </data>
  </webRowSet>
```

7.6. What Is a FilteredRowSet?

The FilteredRowSet (javax.sql.FilteredRowSet) is a disconnected rowset, which enables you to retrieve a custom view of database data using a filter (filtering logic) that takes a snapshot of, but doesn't alter, your table. The FilteredRowset interface extends the WebRowSet interface, which in turn extends the javax.sql.Rowset interface. The FilteredRowSet enables you to narrow down the number of rows in a disconnected object based on filtering logic you provide without requiring an ongoing connection to your database. How do you filter rowsets? You have at least two options:

- Use the WHERE clause in a SQL's SELECT statement (this option can be applied once and cannot be repeated for a disconnected rowset object). This might be a good option for connected rowsets such as JdbcRowSet—it will not work for disconnected rowsets.

- Use the Predicate (javax.sql.rowset.Predicate) interface (this option can be applied many times to a disconnected object). You may implement the Predicate interface for filtering your desired rowsets dynamically.

The following is taken from the J2SE 5.0 documentation:

There are occasions when a RowSet object has a need to provide a degree of filtering to its contents. One possible solution is to provide a query language for all standard RowSet implementations; however, this is an impractical approach for lightweight components such as disconnected RowSet objects. The FilteredRowSet interface seeks to address this need without supplying a heavyweight query language along with the processing that such a query language would require. A JDBC FilteredRowSet standard implementation implements the RowSet interfaces and extends the CachedRowSet class. The CachedRowSet class provides a set of protected cursor manipulation methods, which a FilteredRowSet implementation can override to supply filtering support.

What is the Predicate interface? According to J2SE 5.0 documentation:

The Predicate interface is a standard interface that applications can implement to define the filter they wish to apply to a FilteredRowSet object. A FilteredRowSet object consumes implementations of this interface and enforces the constraints defined in the implementation of the method evaluate. A FilteredRowSet object enforces the filter constraints in a bi-directional manner: It outputs only rows that are within the constraints of the filter; and conversely, it inserts, modifies, or updates only rows that are within the constraints of the filter.

The Predicate interface has the following methods:

- boolean evaluate(Object value, int column): This method is called by a FilteredRowSet object to check whether the value lies within the filtering criterion (or criteria if multiple constraints exist) set using the setFilter() method.

- boolean evaluate(Object value, String columnName): This method is called by the FilteredRowSet object to check whether the value lies within the filtering criteria set using the setFilter method.

- boolean evaluate(RowSet rs): This method is typically called a FilteredRowSet object's internal methods (not public) that control the RowSet object's cursor moving from one row to the next.

How does a FilteredRowSet object use a Predicate object? The FilteredRowSet interface has two specific methods for dealing with Predicate objects:

- Predicate getFilter(): Retrieves the active filter for this FilteredRowSet object

- void setFilter(Predicate p): Applies the given Predicate object to this FilteredRowSet object

With some basic examples, I will show you how to use a FilteredRowSet object and set a simple filter for filtering rowsets.

MySQL Database Setup

```
mysql> use octopus;
Database changed
mysql> desc employees;
+-------+-------------+------+-----+---------+-------+
| Field | Type        | Null | Key | Default | Extra |
+-------+-------------+------+-----+---------+-------+
| id    | varchar(8)  |      | PRI |         |       |
| name  | varchar(16) | YES  |     | NULL    |       |
| age   | int(11)     | YES  |     | NULL    |       |
+-------+-------------+------+-----+---------+-------+
3 rows in set (0.00 sec)
mysql> select * from employees;
+-----+--------+------+
| id  | name   | age  |
+-----+--------+------+
| 88  | Peter  |   80 |
| 77  | Donald |   70 |
| 33  | Mary   |   30 |
| 44  | Monica |   40 |
| 999 | Andre  |   90 |
+-----+--------+------+
5 rows in set (0.20 sec)
```

Implementing Predicate

```
import java.sql.SQLException;
import javax.sql.RowSet;
import javax.sql.rowset.Predicate;
import javax.sql.rowset.FilteredRowSet;

public class AgeFilter implements Predicate {
    private int lowAge;
    private int highAge;
    private int columnIndex;
    private String columnName;

    public AgeFilter(int lowAge, int highAge, int columnIndex, String columnName) {
        this.lowAge = lowAge;
        this.highAge = highAge;
        this.columnName = columnName;
        this.columnIndex = columnIndex;
    }

    public AgeFilter(int lowAge, int highAge, int columnIndex) {
        this(lowAge, highAge, columnIndex, "age");
    }

    public boolean evaluate(Object value, String columnName) {
        boolean evaluation = true;
        if (columnName.equalsIgnoreCase(this.columnName)) {
            int columnValue = ((Integer)value).intValue();
            if ((columnValue >= this.lowAge) && (columnValue <= this.highAge)) {
                evaluation = true;
            }
            else {
                evaluation = false;
            }
        }
        return evaluation;
    }


    public boolean evaluate(Object value, int columnNumber) {
        boolean evaluation = true;
        if (columnIndex == columnNumber) {
            int columnValue = ((Integer)value).intValue();
            if ((columnValue >= this.lowAge) && (columnValue <= this.highAge)) {
                evaluation = true;
            }
```

```
                    else {
                        evaluation = false;
                    }
                }
                return evaluation;
        }

        public boolean evaluate(RowSet rs) {
            if (rs == null) {
                return false;
            }

            FilteredRowSet frs = (FilteredRowSet) rs;
            boolean evaluation = false;
            try {
                int columnValue = frs.getInt(this.columnIndex);
                if ((columnValue >= this.lowAge) && (columnValue <= this.highAge)) {
                    evaluation = true;
                }
            }
            catch (SQLException e) {
                return false;
            }
            return evaluation;
        }
}
```

Using Predicate with a FilteredRowSet

```java
import java.sql.Connection;
import java.sql.DriverManager;
import java.sql.Statement;
import java.sql.ResultSet;
import java.sql.SQLException;

import javax.sql.RowSet;
import javax.sql.rowset.FilteredRowSet;

import com.sun.rowset.FilteredRowSetImpl;
import com.sun.rowset.CachedRowSetImpl;

public class DemoFilteredRowSet {

    public static void main(String args[]) {
        try {
            // load the MYSQL driver
            Class.forName("com.mysql.jdbc.Driver");
```

```java
        // establish a connection to MySQL database
        FilteredRowSet frs = new FilteredRowSetImpl();
        frs.setUsername("root");
        frs.setPassword("root");
        frs.setUrl("jdbc:mysql://localhost/octopus");
        frs.setCommand("SELECT id, name, age FROM employees");
        frs.execute();

        // display records in (un)filtered rowset
        System.out.println("--- Unfiltered RowSet: ---");
        displayRowSet(frs);

        // create a filter that restricts entries in
        // the age column to be between 70 and 100
        AgeFilter filter = new AgeFilter(70, 100, 3);


        // set the filter.
        frs.setFilter(filter);

        // go to the beginning of the Rowset
        System.out.println("--- Filtered RowSet: ---");

        // Moves the cursor to the front of this FilteredRowSet
        // object, just before the first row.
        frs.beforeFirst();
        // show filtered data
        displayRowSet(frs);
    }
    catch (Exception e) {
        e.printStackTrace();
    }
}

static void displayRowSet(RowSet rs) throws SQLException {
    while (rs.next()) {
        System.out.println(rs.getRow() + " - " +
                rs.getString("id") + ":" +
                rs.getString("name") + ":" + rs.getInt("age"));
    }
}
}
```

Using a FilteredRowSet with a MySQL Database

```
$ javac DemoFilteredRowSet.java
$ javac AgeFilter.java
$ java DemoFilteredRowSet
--- Unfiltered RowSet: ---
1 - 88:Peter:80
2 - 77:Donald:70
3 - 33:Mary:30
4 - 44:Monica:40
5 - 999:Andre:90
--- Filtered RowSet: ---
1 - 88:Peter:80
2 - 77:Donald:70
5 - 999:Andre:90
```

7.7. How Do You Get Metadata from a FilteredRowSet Object?

The FilteredRowSet (javax.sql.FilteredRowSet) is a disconnected rowset, which enables you to retrieve a custom view of database data using a filter (filtering logic) that takes a snapshot of, but doesn't alter, your table. The FilteredRowset interface extends the WebRowSet interface, which in turn extends the javax.sql.Rowset interface. The FilteredRowSet enables you to narrow down the number of rows in a disconnected object based on filtering logic you provide without requiring an ongoing connection to your database. How do you filter rowsets? You have at least two options, which I'll describe next.

First, you create an empty FilteredRowset object:

```
import javax.sql.rowset.FilteredRowSet;
import com.sun.rowset.FilteredRowSetImpl;
import java.sql.Connection;

import jcb.util.DatabaseUtil;
import jcb.db.VeryBasicConnectionManager;
...
FilteredRowSet frs = new FilteredRowSetImpl();
```

After creating an empty FilteredRowSet object, you can populate it:

```
Connection conn = VeryBasicConnectionManager.getConnection("mysql");
frs.setCommand("SELECT id, name, age FROM employees");
frs.execute(conn);
```

Alternatively, you can populate the FilteredRowSet object from a ResultSet object:

```
// load MySQL JDBC Driver and return a connection
Connection conn = VeryBasicConnectionManager.getConnection("mysql");
```

```
// use a statement to gather data from the database
Statement stmt = conn.createStatement();
String query = "SELECT id, name, age FROM employees";
FilteredRowSet frs = new FilteredRowSetImpl();

// execute the query
ResultSet resultSet = stmt.executeQuery(query);
frs.populate(rs);
```

After populating a FilteredRowSet object, you can apply an additional filter to restrict the selected rows or records by using the setFilter() method:

```
// create a filter that restricts entries in
// the age column to be between 70 and 100
AgeFilter filter = new AgeFilter(70, 100, 3);

// set the filter.
frs.beforeFirst();
frs.setFilter(filter);
```

Customized Predicates

Some vendors provide a customized filter to be used by FilteredRowSet objects. For example, BEA WebLogic Server provides a SQLPredicate class (weblogic.jdbc.rowset.SQLPredicate), which directly implements the javax.sql.rowset.Predicate interface and provides the following constructor:

```
        public SQLPredicate(String selector)
```

Using this class, you can create customized filters and predicates:

```
import javax.sql.rowset.Predicate;
import javax.sql.rowset.FilteredRowSet;
import weblogic.jdbc.rowset.SQLPredicate;

...

FilteredRowSet frs = …

...

// SET CUSTOMIZED FILTER
// use SQLPredicate class to create a SQLPredicate object,
// then pass the object in the setFilter method to filter the RowSet.
Predicate filter = new SQLPredicate("age >= 103");
frs.setFilter(filter);
```

The SQLPredicate class borrows its grammar from the JMS selector grammar, which is very similar to the grammar for a SQL SELECT WHERE clause.

Extracting Metadata from a FilteredRowSet Object

After populating a WebRowSet object, you can get its metadata by using the following:

```
import javax.sql.RowSetMetaData;
…
RowSetMetaData rsMetaData = (RowSetMetaData) frs;
If (rsMetaData == null) {
   // db vendor does not support FilteredRowSet's metadata
}
else {
   // db vendor does support FilteredRowSet's metadata
   // you may invoke RowSetMetaData methods
   int numberOfColumns = rsMetaData.getColumnCount();
   …
}
```

Representing a FilteredRowSet Object as an XML Document

Writing a FilteredRowSet object to an XML document can be accomplished by using the FilteredRowSet.writeXml() method, which can take in either an OutputStream object (if we want to write in bytes) or a Writer object (if we want to write in characters). The code snippet that follows writes to a file called emps.xml using a FileWriter object:

```
String filename = "c:\\myrowset\\emps.xml";              // Windows
// String filename = "/home/alex/myrowset/emps.xml";  // UNIX
java.io.FileWriter writer = new java.io.FileWriter(filename);
frs.writeXml(writer);
```

The JoinRowSet is a disconnected rowset object, which extends the WebRowSet interface (which is also a disconnected rowset). JoinRowSet mimics the concept of a SQL JOIN. A JOIN combines records or rows from two or more tables in a relational database. According to Wikipedia (http://en.wikipedia.org), "A **join** combines records from two or more tables in a relational database. In the Structured Query Language (SQL), there are two types of joins: 'inner' and 'outer'. Outer joins are subdivided further into left outer joins, right outer joins, and full outer joins." To understand the JoinRowSet interface better, I set up some database tables to be used by JoinRowSet objects.

MySQL Database Setup

```
mysql> use octopus;
Database changed
mysql> desc employees;
+--------+-------------+------+-----+---------+-------+
| Field  | Type        | Null | Key | Default | Extra |
+--------+-------------+------+-----+---------+-------+
| id     | varchar(10) | NO   | PRI |         |       |
| name   | varchar(20) | YES  |     | NULL    |       |
| age    | int(11)     | YES  |     | NULL    |       |
| dept   | int(11)     | NO   |     |         |       |
+--------+-------------+------+-----+---------+-------+
```

```
4 rows in set (0.01 sec)
mysql> desc departments;
+----------+-------------+------+-----+---------+-------+
| Field    | Type        | Null | Key | Default | Extra |
+----------+-------------+------+-----+---------+-------+
| dept     | int(11)     | NO   | PRI |         |       |
| location | varchar(12) | YES  |     | NULL    |       |
+----------+-------------+------+-----+---------+-------+
2 rows in set (0.01 sec)
mysql> select * from employees;
+----+--------+------+------+
| id | name   | age  | dept |
+----+--------+------+------+
| 11 | Alex   |   25 | 1111 |
| 44 | Monica |   30 | 1111 |
| 88 | Jeff   |   45 | 2222 |
| 99 | Bob    | NULL | 2222 |
+----+--------+------+------+
4 rows in set (0.00 sec)
mysql> select * from departments;
+------+-----------+
| dept | location  |
+------+-----------+
| 1111 | Detroit   |
| 2222 | Sunnyvale |
| 3333 | San Jose  |
+------+-----------+
3 rows in set (0.01 sec)
```

The following query verifies that a join is basically a Cartesian product that is followed by a predicate to filter the results:

```
mysql> select employees.id, employees.name, departments.location
        from employees, departments;
+----+--------+-----------+
| id | name   | location  |
+----+--------+-----------+
| 11 | Alex   | Detroit   |
| 11 | Alex   | Sunnyvale |
| 11 | Alex   | San Jose  |
| 44 | Monica | Detroit   |
| 44 | Monica | Sunnyvale |
| 44 | Monica | San Jose  |
| 88 | Jeff   | Detroit   |
| 88 | Jeff   | Sunnyvale |
| 88 | Jeff   | San Jose  |
| 99 | Bob    | Detroit   |
| 99 | Bob    | Sunnyvale |
| 99 | Bob    | San Jose  |
+----+--------+-----------+
12 rows in set (0.00 sec)
```

You can filter the result of the JOIN operation. In the following SQL query, note that the INNER JOIN statement was issued using the on employees.dept = departments.dept clause. This JOIN operation effectively combined the data contained in two tables (employees and departments) based on a common attribute (the "dept" value). Using a JoinRowSet object, the SQL JOIN operation will be performed using a match column of "dept". To be a match column, the column of interest needs to be residing in the employees and departments tables, which are being joined.

```
mysql> select employees.id, employees.name, departments.location
          from employees, departments
              where employees.dept = departments.dept;
+----+--------+-----------+
| id | name   | location  |
+----+--------+-----------+
| 11 | Alex   | Detroit   |
| 44 | Monica | Detroit   |
| 88 | Jeff   | Sunnyvale |
| 99 | Bob    | Sunnyvale |
+----+--------+-----------+
4 rows in set (0.00 sec)
```

We will use this database object to show how to create a JoinRowSet object. JoinRowSet is capable of doing a SQL JOIN operation. Let's see how.

First, create CachedRowSet objects for both tables:

```
// load the Driver
Class.forName("com.mysql.jdbc.Driver");

// create a CachedRowSet for employees
CachedRowSet employees = new CachedRowSetImpl();
employees.setUsername("root");
employees.setPassword("root");
employees.setUrl("jdbc:mysql://localhost/octopus");
employees.setCommand("SELECT * FROM employees");
employees.execute();

// create a CachedRowSet for departments
CachedRowSet departments = new CachedRowSetImpl();
departments.setUsername("root");
departments.setPassword("root");
departments. setUrl("jdbc:mysql://localhost/octopus");
departments.setCommand("SELECT * FROM departments");
departments.execute();
```

Next, we perform a JOIN operation:

```
JoinRowSet join = new JoinRowSetImpl(),
join.addRowSet(employees,"dept");
join.addRowSet(departments,"dept");
```

There is an alternative method to doing a JOIN operation: you can use the Joinable interface to accomplish the same thing:

```
JoinRowSet join = new JoinRowSetImpl();
((Joinable)employees).setMatchColumn("dept");
((Joinable)departments).setMatchColumn("dept");
join.addRowSet(employees);
join.addRowSet(departments);
```

After performing our offline JOIN, you can traverse our JoinRowSet object using getter methods like we do with ResultSet objects. Here's this iteration in the code:

```
// display records in JoinRowSet object
while (join.next()) {
   String id = join.getString(1);
   String name = join.getString(2);
   String location = join.getString(3);
}
```

Extracting Metadata from a JoinRowSet Object

After creating a JoinRowSet object, you can get its metadata by using the following:

```
import javax.sql.RowSetMetaData;
...
RowSetMetaData rsMetaData = (RowSetMetaData) join;
If (rsMetaData == null) {
   // db vendor does not support JoinRowSet's metadata
}
else {
   // db vendor does support JoinRowSet's metadata
   // you may invoke RowSetMetaData methods
   int numberOfColumns = rsMetaData.getColumnCount();
   ...
}
```

7.8. What Is a SyncResolver?

SyncResolver (javax.sql.rowset.spi.SyncResolver) is a "synchronized resolver" rowset, which extends the RowSet interface. According to the J2SE 5.0 documentation, SyncResolver

> ... defines a framework that allows applications to use a manual decision tree to decide what should be done when a synchronization conflict occurs. Although it is not mandatory for applications to resolve synchronization conflicts manually, this framework provides the means to delegate to the application when conflicts arise. Note that a conflict is a situation where the RowSet object's original values for a row do not match the values in the data source, which indicates that the data source row has been modified since the last synchronization. Note also that a RowSet object's original values are the values it had just prior to the last synchronization, which are not necessarily its initial values.

According to the J2SE 5.0 documentation, a SyncResolver object is a specialized RowSet object that implements the SyncResolver interface. It *may* operate as either a connected RowSet object (an implementation of the JdbcRowSet interface) or a disconnected RowSet object (an implementation of the CachedRowSet interface or one of its subinterfaces). The reference implementation for SyncResolver implements the CachedRowSet interface, but other implementations may choose to implement the JdbcRowSet interface to satisfy particular needs.

What is a synchronization conflict and when does it occur? When you change (update, insert, or delete) your RowSet object and you want to commit changes back to your data source, if there are problems, then these will be reported back to the client code. These problems are called "synchronization conflicts" (because you are trying to synchronize your rowset with data source data). Four types of conflicts (defined as static int) have been identified by the SyncResolver, and I have listed them here (for details on these types of conflicts, refer to the JDBC 3.0 Specification and consult the documentation for the driver you are working with):

- static int DELETE_ROW_CONFLICT: Indicates that a conflict occurred while the RowSet object was attempting to delete a row in the data source.

- static int INSERT_ROW_CONFLICT: Indicates that a conflict occurred while the RowSet object was attempting to insert a row into the data source.

- static int NO_ROW_CONFLICT: Indicates that *no* conflict occurred while the RowSet object was attempting to update, delete, or insert a row in the data source.

- static int UPDATE_ROW_CONFLICT: Indicates that a conflict occurred while the RowSet object was attempting to update a row in the data source.

According to the J2SE 5.0 documentation, the reference implementation provides a means by which an application can choose to resolve conflicts on a case-by-case basis. After the writer (a class that implements the RowSetWriter interface) finds all the conflicts, it throws a SyncProviderException object. An application can catch that exception and use it to create a SyncResolver object, a specialized kind of RowSet object. A SyncResolver object mirrors the RowSet object experiencing the conflicts, having the same number of rows and columns; however, it contains only the data that is in conflict. The SyncResolver object retrieves each conflict value in a row, comparing the value in the data source with the value in the RowSet object. After a decision is made as to which value should persist for each conflict in the row, the SyncResolver object sets those values with the method setResolvedValue. The SyncResolver object then goes to the next conflict and repeats the process until there are no more conflicts.

The following example (adapted from the J2SE 5.0 documentation) shows how to use a SyncResolver object:

```
import javax.sql.rowSet.CachedRowSet;
import javax.sql.rowset.spi.SyncResolver
import javax.sql.rowset.spi.SyncProviderException;
. . .
CachedRowSet crs = …;
try {
    . . .
    crs.acceptChanges(con);
    . . .
}
catch (SyncProviderException spe) {

    SyncResolver resolver = spe.getSyncResolver();
    If (resolver == null) {
       // vendor has not implemented SyncResolver
       // not much can be done here.
    }
    else {
       // vendor has implemented SyncResolver
       Object crsValue;      // value in the RowSet object
       Object resolverValue: // value in the SyncResolver object
       Object resolvedValue: // value to be persisted

       while(resolver.nextConflict()) {
           if(resolver.getStatus() == SyncResolver.UPDATE_ROW_CONFLICT) {
               int row = resolver.getRow();
               crs.absolute(row);

               int colCount = crs.getMetaData().getColumnCount();
               for(int j = 1; j <= colCount; j++) {
                  if (resolver.getConflictValue(j) != null) {
                     crsValue = crs.getObject(j);
                     resolverValue = resolver.getConflictValue(j);
                     . . .
                     // compare crsValue and resolverValue to determine
                     // which should be the resolved value (the value to persist)
                     resolvedValue = crsValue;

                     resolver.setResolvedValue(j, resolvedValue);
                  }
               }
           }
       } // while
    } //else
}
```

7.9. How Do You Create a RowSet Object?

Before you can create a RowSet object, you need to provide implementation classes for the RowSet interface, or you can use the reference implementations provided by Sun (http://java.sun.com/products/jdbc/download.html#rowset1_0_1). To use Sun's reference implementations, you need to download the reference implementations of RowSet and include the rowset.jar file in your CLASSPATH environment variable.

Sun's reference implementation has two packages:

- com.sun.rowset: Provides five standard implementations of the standard JDBC RowSet implementation interface definitions:

  - CachedRowSetImpl: The standard implementation of the CachedRowSet interface

  - FilteredRowSetImpl: The standard implementation of the FilteredRowSet interface

  - JdbcRowSetImpl: The standard implementation of the JdbcRowSet interface

  - JoinRowSetImpl: The standard implementation of the JoinRowSet interface providing a SQL JOIN between RowSet objects

  - WebRowSetImpl: The standard implementation of the WebRowSet interface

- com.sun.rowset.providers: Stores the RowSet reference implementations of the SyncProvider abstract class:

  - RIOptimisticProvider: The reference implementation of a JDBC Rowset synchronization provider providing optimistic synchronization with a relational data store using any JDBC technology-enabled driver

  - RIXMLProvider: A reference implementation of a JDBC RowSet synchronization provider with the ability to read and write rowsets in well-formed XML using the standard WebRowSet schema

In order to create RowSet, JdbcRowSet, or CachedRowSet objects, you need to use the classes provided in the com.sun.rowset and com.sun.rowset.providers packages provided by Sun's reference implementation.

MySQL Database Setup

```
mysql> use octopus;
Database changed
mysql> desc ztest;
+-------+-------------+------+-----+---------+-------+
| Field | Type        | Null | Key | Default | Extra |
+-------+-------------+------+-----+---------+-------+
| id    | varchar(10) |      | PRI |         |       |
| name  | varchar(20) | YES  |     | NULL    |       |
+-------+-------------+------+-----+---------+-------+
2 rows in set (0.00 sec)
mysql> select * from ztest;
```

```
+----+------+
| id | name |
+----+------+
| 11 | alex |
| 22 | bob  |
| 33 | mary |
+----+------+
3 rows in set (0.00 sec)
```

Create a JdbcRowSet Object

To create a JdbcRowSet object, we use two classes: ExampleListener and JdbcRowSetExample. The ExampleListener class implements the RowSetListener interface. (RowSetListener is an interface that must be implemented by a component that wants to be notified when a significant event happens in the life of a RowSet object. A component becomes a listener by being registered with a RowSet object via the method RowSet.addRowSetListener.) Sun's reference implementation of the JdbcRowSet interface, the JdbcRowSetImpl class, provides an implementation of the default constructor. A new instance is initialized with default values, which can be set with new values as needed. A new instance is not really functional until its execute() method is called. In general, this method does the following:

- Establishes a connection with a database

- Creates a PreparedStatement object and sets any of its placeholder parameters

- Executes the statement to create a ResultSet object

The following is a basic class, which implements the RowSetListener interface:

```java
import javax.sql.RowSetEvent;
import javax.sql.RowSetListener;

public class ExampleListener implements RowSetListener {
  public void cursorMoved(RowSetEvent event) {
    System.out.println("ExampleListener notified of cursorMoved event");
    System.out.println(event.toString());
  }

  public void rowChanged(RowSetEvent event) {
    System.out.println("ExampleListener notified of rowChanged event");
    System.out.println(event.toString());
  }

  public void rowSetChanged(RowSetEvent event) {
    System.out.println("ExampleListener notified of rowSetChanged event");
    System.out.println(event.toString());
  }
}
```

The following, JdbcRowSetExample, is a class, which shows how to use the JdbcRowSet interface. This class also uses the ExampleListener class defined earlier.

```java
import java.sql.ResultSet;
import java.sql.Connection;
import java.sql.SQLException;
import java.sql.DriverManager;

import javax.sql.rowset.JdbcRowSet;
import com.sun.rowset.JdbcRowSetImpl;

import jcb.util.DatabaseUtil;
import jcb.db.VeryBasicConnectionManager;

public class JdbcRowSetExample {

   JdbcRowSet jdbcRS;

   public static void main(String[] args) {
     String dbVendor = args[0]; // {"mysql", "oracle", "odbc"}
     JdbcRowSetExample jrse = new JdbcRowSetExample();
     Connection conn = null;
     try {
        conn = VeryBasicConnectionManager.getConnection(dbVendor);
        // populate jdbcRS object from a given Connection object
        // and add some simple listener events
        jrse.populateRowSet(conn);
        // show events while iterating jdbcRS object
        jrse.createEvents();
     }
     catch (Exception e) {
         // handle exception
         e.printStackTrace();
     }
     finally {
        DatabaseUtil.close(jrse.jdbcRS);
        DatabaseUtil.close(conn);
     }
   }

   void populateRowSet(Connection conn)
      throws ClassNotFoundException, SQLException {
      jdbcRS = new JdbcRowSetImpl(conn);
      jdbcRS.setType(ResultSet.TYPE_SCROLL_INSENSITIVE);
      String sql = "SELECT * FROM ztest";
      jdbcRS.setCommand(sql);
      jdbcRS.execute();
      jdbcRS.addRowSetListener(new ExampleListener());
   }
```

```
    void createEvents()
      throws SQLException, ClassNotFoundException {
      while (jdbcRS.next()) {
         //each call to next, generates a cursorMoved event
         System.out.println("id="+jdbcRS.getString(1));
         System.out.println("name="+jdbcRS.getString(2));
         System.out.println("-----------");
      }
   }
}
```

Running the Solution for a MySQL Database

```
$ javac JdbcRowSetExample.java
$ java JdbcRowSetExample mysql
ExampleListener notified of cursorMoved event
javax.sql.RowSetEvent[source=com.sun.rowset.JdbcRowSetImpl@ef22f8]
id=11
name=alex
-----------
ExampleListener notified of cursorMoved event
javax.sql.RowSetEvent[source=com.sun.rowset.JdbcRowSetImpl@ef22f8]
id=22
name=bob
-----------
ExampleListener notified of cursorMoved event
javax.sql.RowSetEvent[source=com.sun.rowset.JdbcRowSetImpl@ef22f8]
id=33
name=mary
-----------
ExampleListener notified of cursorMoved event
javax.sql.RowSetEvent[source=com.sun.rowset.JdbcRowSetImpl@ef22f8]
```

7.10. What Is a RowSetMetaData Object?

javax.sql.RowSetMetaData (which extends java.sql.ResultSetMetaData) manages a RowSet's metadata information. According to the J2SE 5.0 documentation, RowSetMetaData is an object that contains information about the columns in a RowSet object. This interface is an extension of the ResultSetMetaData interface with methods for setting the values in a RowSetMetaData object. When a RowSetReader object reads data into a RowSet object, it creates a RowSetMetaData object and initializes it using the methods in the RowSetMetaData interface. Then the reader passes the RowSetMetaData object to the rowset.

The RowSetMetaDataImpl class implements three interfaces: Serializable, ResultSetMetaData, and RowSetMetaData. According to the J2SE 5.0 documentation, the RowSetMetaDataImpl class provides implementations for the methods that set and get metadata information about a RowSet object's columns. A RowSetMetaDataImpl object keeps track of the number of columns in the rowset and maintains an internal array of column attributes for each column. A RowSet object creates a RowSetMetaDataImpl object internally in order to set and retrieve information about its columns. All metadata in a RowSetMetaDataImpl object should be considered as unavailable until the RowSet object that it describes is populated. Therefore, any RowSetMetaDataImpl method that retrieves information is defined as having unspecified behavior when it is called before the RowSet object contains data.

7.11. How Do You Create a RowSetMetaData Object?

To create (materialize) a RowSetMetaData object, you need to create a RowSet object (or descendent objects such as a WebRowSet or JdbcRowSet object) and then invoke the getMetaData() method on that object. The following code snippet shows how to create a RowSetMetaData object:

```
// materialize a rowset object
Connection conn = getConnection();
WebRowSet webRS = new WebRowSetImpl();
String sqlQuery = " select a, b, c from mytable";
webRS.setCommand(sqlQuery);
webRS.execute(conn);
// then get a RowSetMetaData object
RowSetMetaData rsMD =  (RowSetMetaData) webRS.getMetaData();
System.out.println("rsMD="+rsMD);
if (rsMD == null) {
    System.out.println("vendor does not support RowSetMetaData");
}
else {
    int columnCount = rsMD.getColumnCount();
    System.out.println("columnCount="+columnCount);
}
```

You need to cast RowSet.getMetaData() to the RowSetMetaData object, because RowSet does not have a method that returns a RowSetMetaData object (note that getMetaData() is inherited from the ResultSetMetaData interface). Next, we set up sample databases for MySQL and ODBC (using Microsoft Access on Windows XP). Then we apply our solution to these databases.

MySQL Database Setup

```
mysql> use octopus;
Database changed
mysql> desc ztest;
+-------+-------------+------+-----+---------+-------+
| Field | Type        | Null | Key | Default | Extra |
+-------+-------------+------+-----+---------+-------+
| id    | varchar(10) |      | PRI |         |       |
| name  | varchar(20) | YES  |     | NULL    |       |
+-------+-------------+------+-----+---------+-------+
2 rows in set (0.00 sec)
mysql> select * from ztest;
```

```
+----+------+
| id | name |
+----+------+
| 11 | alex |
| 22 | bob  |
| 33 | mary |
+----+------+
3 rows in set (0.00 sec)
```

ODBC Database Setup

Using the ODBC Data Source Administrator, create a data source. Call it odbc and create a table called ztest (similar to the MySQL table in the previous section).

The Solution

Here is a simple class to create a RowSetMetaData object. Note the following line of code:

```
RowSetMetaData rsMD =  (RowSetMetaData) webRS.getMetaData();
```

WebRowSet.getMetaData() returns a ResultSetMetaData, which has to be cast to the RowSetMetaData object.

```java
import java.sql.Connection;
import javax.sql.RowSetMetaData;
import javax.sql.rowset.WebRowSet;
import com.sun.rowset.WebRowSetImpl;

import jcb.util.DatabaseUtil;
import jcb.db.VeryBasicConnectionManager;

public class CreateRowSetMetaData {

    public static void main(String[] args) {
        String dbVendor = args[0]; // {"mysql", "oracle", "odbc"}
        CreateRowSetMetaData wrse = new CreateRowSetMetaData();
        WebRowSet webRS=null;
        Connection conn = null;
        try {
            // create and populate a rowset object
            conn = VeryBasicConnectionManager.getConnection(dbVendor);
            webRS = populateRowSet(conn);

            // create RowSetMetaData object
            RowSetMetaData rsMD =  (RowSetMetaData) webRS.getMetaData();
            System.out.println("rsMD="+rsMD);
            if (rsMD == null) {
                System.out.println("vendor does not support RowSetMetaData");
            }
```

```
            else {
                int columnCount = rsMD.getColumnCount();
                System.out.println("columnCount="+columnCount);
            }
        }
        catch (Exception e) {
            e.printStackTrace();
        }
        finally {
            DatabaseUtil.close(conn);
        }
    }

    static WebRowSet populateRowSet(Connection conn)
        throws Exception {
        System.out.println("Querying database for track data...");
        String sqlQuery = "SELECT * FROM ztest";
        System.out.println("sqlQuery="+sqlQuery);

        WebRowSet webRS = new WebRowSetImpl();
        webRS.setCommand(sqlQuery);
        webRS.execute(conn);
        return webRS;
    }
}
```

Running the Solution for a MySQL Database

```
$ javac CreateRowSetMetaData.java
$ java CreateRowSetMetaData mysql
Querying database for track data...
sqlQuery=SELECT * FROM ztest
rsMD=javax.sql.rowset.RowSetMetaDataImpl@119cca4
columnCount=2
```

Running the Solution for an ODBC Database

```
$ javac CreateRowSetMetaData.java
$ java CreateRowSetMetaData odbc
Querying database for track data...
sqlQuery=SELECT * FROM ztest
java.lang.UnsupportedOperationException at
sun.jdbc.odbc.JdbcOdbcDatabaseMetaData.locatorsUpdateCopy
(JdbcOdbcDatabaseMetaData.java:4051)
...
```

7.12. What Is a WebRowSet Object?

The WebRowSet interface extends the CachedRowSet interface and therefore has all of the same capabilities. An implementation of the CachedRowSet interface (which is disconnected and able to operate without a driver) is designed to work especially well with a thin client for passing data in a distributed application or for making a result set scrollable and updatable. Many other RowSet implementations can be designed for other purposes. WebRowSet adds the ability to read and write a rowset in XML format (the ideal format for a web services application). The WebRowSet interface is also a very interesting object from the metadata point of view, because when you convert it to XML, there is a complete section on metadata.

A WebRowSetImpl object uses a WebRowSetXmlReader object to read a rowset in XML format and a WebRowSetXmlWriter object to write a rowset in XML format. The XML version contains a WebRowSetImpl object's metadata as well as its data.

The standard WebRowSet XML schema definition is available at http://java.sun.com/xml/ns/jdbc/webrowset.xsd. It describes the standard XML document format required when describing a RowSet object in XML and must be used for all standard implementations of the WebRowSet interface to ensure interoperability.

The schema definition describes the internal data of a RowSet object in three distinct areas:

- **Properties**: These properties describe the standard synchronization provider properties in addition to the more general RowSet properties.

- **Metadata**: This area describes the metadata associated with the tabular structure governed by a WebRowSet object. The metadata described is closely aligned with the metadata accessible in the underlying java.sql.ResultSet interface.

- **Data**: This area describes the original data (the state of data since the last population or last synchronization of the WebRowSet object) and the current data. By keeping track of the delta between the original data and the current data, a WebRowSet maintains the ability to synchronize changes in its data back to the originating data source.

7.13. How Do You Create a WebRowSet Object?

Before you can create a RowSet object, you need to provide implementation classes for the RowSet interface, or you may use the reference implementations provided by Sun (http://java.sun.com/products/jdbc/download.html#rowset1_0_1). To use Sun's reference implementations, you need to download the reference implementations of RowSet and include the rowset.jar file in your CLASSPATH environment variable. Sun's reference implementation provides the com.sun.rowset.WebRowSetImpl class, which implements the WebRowSet interface (the standard implementation of the WebRowSet interface).

MySQL Database Setup

```
mysql> use octopus;
Database changed
mysql> desc ztest;
+-------+-------------+------+-----+---------+-------+
| Field | Type        | Null | Key | Default | Extra |
+-------+-------------+------+-----+---------+-------+
| id    | varchar(10) |      | PRI |         |       |
| name  | varchar(20) | YES  |     | NULL    |       |
+-------+-------------+------+-----+---------+-------+
2 rows in set (0.00 sec)
mysql> select * from ztest;
+----+------+
| id | name |
+----+------+
| 11 | alex |
| 22 | bob  |
| 33 | mary |
+----+------+
3 rows in set (0.00 sec)
```

Create a WebRowSet Object

To create a WebRowSet object, we use the WebRowSetExample class, which does the following:

- Create a WebRowSet object:

    ```
    webRS = new WebRowSetImpl();
    ```

- Set the SQL query for getting the result from the database:

    ```
    webRS.setCommand(sqlQuery);
    ```

- Pass the Connection object to the execute() method to fill up the WebRowSet object:

    ```
    webRS.execute(conn);
    import java.io.*;
    import java.sql.*;
    import javax.sql.*;

    import javax.sql.rowset.WebRowSet;
    import com.sun.rowset.WebRowSetImpl;

    import jcb.util.DatabaseUtil;
    import jcb.db.VeryBasicConnectionManager;

    public class WebRowSetExample {
        WebRowSet webRS;
    ```

```java
public static void main(String[] args) {
    String dbVendor = args[0]; // {"mysql", "oracle", "odbc"}
    String id = args[1];        // PK to ztest table
    WebRowSetExample wrse = new WebRowSetExample();
    Connection conn = null;
    try {
        conn = VeryBasicConnectionManager.getConnection(dbVendor);
        wrse.populateRowSet(conn, id);
        wrse.writeXml(id);
    }
    catch (Exception e) {
        e.printStackTrace();
    }
}

void populateRowSet(Connection conn, String id)
    throws Exception {
    ResultSet rs = null;
    Statement stmt = null;
    try {
        stmt = conn.createStatement();
        String sqlCount = "SELECT count(*) FROM ztest WHERE " +
            "id='" + id + "'";
        System.out.println("sqlCount="+sqlCount);
        rs = stmt.executeQuery(sqlCount);
        int count = 0;
        if (rs.next()) {
            count = rs.getInt(1);
        }

        webRS = null;
        if (count > 0) {
            System.out.println("Found " + count + " IDs for id " + id);
            System.out.println("Querying database for track data...");
            String sqlQuery = "SELECT * FROM ztest WHERE " + "id='" +
                            id + "'";
            System.out.println("sqlQuery="+sqlQuery);

            webRS = new WebRowSetImpl();
            webRS.setCommand(sqlQuery);
            webRS.execute(conn);
            RowSetMetaData rsMD = (RowSetMetaData) webRS.getMetaData();
            System.out.println("rsMD="+rsMD);
        }
    }
```

```
        finally {
           DatabaseUtil.close(rs);
           DatabaseUtil.close(stmt);
           DatabaseUtil.close(conn);
        }
    }

    void writeXml(String id) throws SQLException, IOException {
        if (webRS == null) {
            System.out.println("No emp data found for id="+id);
            return;
        }
        FileWriter fw = null;
        try {
            File file = new File(id + ".xml");
            fw = new FileWriter(file);
            System.out.println("Writing db data to file " +
                               file.getAbsolutePath());
            webRS.writeXml(fw);

            // convert XML to a String object
            StringWriter sw = new StringWriter();
            webRS.writeXml(sw);
            System.out.println("==============");
            System.out.println(sw.toString());
            System.out.println("==============");
        }
        finally {
            fw.flush();
            fw.close();
        }
    }
}
```

Running the Solution for a MySQL Database

According to http://today.java.net/today/2004/10/15/jdbcRowsets.pdf, "The metadata section of the XML document describing a WebRowSet object contains information about the columns in that WebRowSet object." The following XML output shows what this section looks like for the WebRowSet object webRS. Because webRS has two columns, the XML document describing it has two <column-definition> elements. Each <column-definition> element has subelements giving information about the column being described.

A WebRowSet object in XML has three sections: Properties, Metadata, and Data. Here, for readability purposes, I have partitioned output of the program into Properties, Metadata, and Data:

```
$ javac WebRowSetExample.java
$ java WebRowSetExample mysql 11
```

```
sqlCount=SELECT count(*) FROM ztest WHERE id='11'
Found 1 IDs for id 11
Querying database for track data...
sqlQuery=SELECT * FROM ztest WHERE id='11'
Writing db data to file C:\mp\book\src\client\rowset\11.xml
==============
<?xml version="1.0"?>
<webRowSet xmlns="http://java.sun.com/xml/ns/jdbc"
xmlns:xsi="http://www.w3.org/2001/XMLSchema-instance"
xsi:schemaLocation="http://java.sun.com/xml/ns/jdbc
http://java.sun.com/xml/ns/jdbc/webrowset.xsd">
  <properties>
    ...
  </properties>
  <metadata>
    ...
  </metadata>
  <data>
    ...
  </data>
</webRowSet>


==============
```

The Properties section (`<properties>` shown here) contains information about our connection, including our SQL command associated to our WebRowSet:

```
<properties>
    <command>SELECT * FROM ztest WHERE id=&apos;11&apos;</command>
    <concurrency>1008</concurrency>
    <datasource><null/></datasource>
    <escape-processing>true</escape-processing>
    <fetch-direction>1000</fetch-direction>
    <fetch-size>0</fetch-size>
    <isolation-level>2</isolation-level>
    <key-columns>
    </key-columns>
    <map>
    </map>
    <max-field-size>0</max-field-size>
    <max-rows>0</max-rows>
    <query-timeout>0</query-timeout>
    <read-only>true</read-only>
```

```
<rowset-type>ResultSet.TYPE_SCROLL_INSENSITIVE</rowset-type>
<show-deleted>true</show-deleted>
<table-name>ztest</table-name>
<url><null/></url>
<sync-provider>
  <sync-provider-name>
    com.sun.rowset.providers.RIOptimisticProvider
  </sync-provider-name>
  <sync-provider-vendor>Sun Microsystems Inc.</sync-provider-vendor>
  <sync-provider-version>1.0</sync-provider-version>
  <sync-provider-grade>2</sync-provider-grade>
  <data-source-lock>1</data-source-lock>
</sync-provider>
</properties>
```

The Metadata section (`<metadata>` shown here) contains metadata about the structure of the columns that our WebRowSet object consists of:

```
<metadata>
  <column-count>2</column-count>
  <column-definition>
    <column-index>1</column-index>
    <auto-increment>false</auto-increment>
    <case-sensitive>false</case-sensitive>
    <currency>false</currency>
    <nullable>0</nullable>
    <signed>false</signed>
    <searchable>true</searchable>
    <column-display-size>30</column-display-size>
    <column-label>id</column-label>
    <column-name>id</column-name>
    <schema-name></schema-name>
    <column-precision>30</column-precision>
    <column-scale>0</column-scale>
    <table-name>ztest</table-name>
    <catalog-name>octopus</catalog-name>
    <column-type>12</column-type>
    <column-type-name>VARCHAR</column-type-name>
  </column-definition>
  <column-definition>
    <column-index>2</column-index>
    <auto-increment>false</auto-increment>
    <case-sensitive>false</case-sensitive>
    <currency>false</currency>
    <nullable>1</nullable>
    <signed>false</signed>
```

```
      <searchable>true</searchable>
      <column-display-size>60</column-display-size>
      <column-label>name</column-label>
      <column-name>name</column-name>
      <schema-name></schema-name>
      <column-precision>60</column-precision>
      <column-scale>0</column-scale>
      <table-name>ztest</table-name>
      <catalog-name>octopus</catalog-name>
      <column-type>12</column-type>
      <column-type-name>VARCHAR</column-type-name>
    </column-definition>
  </metadata>
```

The Data section (<data> shown here) contains data about the contents of the columns that our WebRowSet object consists of:

```
<data>
  <currentRow>
    <columnValue>11</columnValue>
    <columnValue>alex</columnValue>
  </currentRow>
</data>
```

7.14. How Do You Get WebRowSet's Metadata as XML?

Let's say that you want to only get the metadata of a WebRowSet object without retrieving any data from the database server. To get only the metadata, you need to send a valid SQL query, which returns only metadata without getting any data; for example, you may send the following SQL query:

```
select  *  from  ztest  where 1 = 0;
```

We know that this SQL query will not retrieve any data (because the Boolean expression 1 = 0 will be always false), but all of the metadata for the ztest table will be captured.

MySQL Database Setup

```
mysql> use octopus;
Database changed
mysql> desc ztest;
+-------+-------------+------+-----+---------+-------+
| Field | Type        | Null | Key | Default | Extra |
+-------+-------------+------+-----+---------+-------+
| id    | varchar(10) |      | PRI |         |       |
| name  | varchar(20) | YES  |     | NULL    |       |
+-------+-------------+------+-----+---------+-------+
```

```
2 rows in set (0.00 sec)
mysql> select * from ztest;
+----+------+
| id | name |
+----+------+
| 11 | alex |
| 22 | bob  |
| 33 | mary |
+----+------+
3 rows in set (0.00 sec)
```

Create WebRowSet's Metadata

```java
import java.io.*;
import java.sql.*;
import javax.sql.*;

import javax.sql.rowset.WebRowSet;
import com.sun.rowset.WebRowSetImpl;

import jcb.util.DatabaseUtil;
import jcb.db.VeryBasicConnectionManager;

public class WebRowSetMetaDataExample {
    WebRowSet webRS;

    public static void main(String[] args) {
        String dbVendor = args[0]; // {"mysql", "oracle", "odbc"}
        WebRowSetMetaDataExample wrse = new WebRowSetMetaDataExample();
        Connection conn = null;
        try {
            conn = VeryBasicConnectionManager.getConnection(dbVendor);
            wrse.populateRowSet(conn);
            wrse.writeXml();
        }
        catch (Exception e) {
            e.printStackTrace();
        }
        finally {
            DatabaseUtil.close(conn);
        }
    }

    void populateRowSet(Connection conn) throws Exception {
        System.out.println("Querying database for metadata only...");
        String sqlQuery = "SELECT * FROM ztest WHERE 1=0";
        System.out.println("sqlQuery="+sqlQuery);
```

```
        webRS = new WebRowSetImpl();
        webRS.setCommand(sqlQuery);
        webRS.execute(conn);
    }

    void writeXml() throws SQLException, IOException {
        if (webRS == null) {
            System.out.println("No data found.");
            return;
        }
        FileWriter fw = null;
        try {
            File file = new File("metadata.xml");
            fw = new FileWriter(file);
            System.out.println("Writing db data to file " + file.getAbsolutePath());
            webRS.writeXml(fw);

            // convert xml to a String object
            StringWriter sw = new StringWriter();
            webRS.writeXml(sw);
            System.out.println("==============");
            System.out.println(sw.toString());
            System.out.println("==============");
        }
        finally {
            fw.flush();
            fw.close();
        }
    }
}
```

Running the Solution for a MySQL Database

As you can observe, the <data> tag is empty:

```
$ javac WebRowSetMetaDataExample.java
$ java WebRowSetMetaDataExample mysql
Querying database for metadata only...
sqlQuery=SELECT * FROM ztest WHERE 1=0
Writing db data to file C:\mp\book\src\client\rowset\metadata.xml
==============
<?xml version="1.0"?>
<webRowSet xmlns="http://java.sun.com/xml/ns/jdbc"
xmlns:xsi="http://www.w3.org/2001/XMLSchema-instance"
xsi:schemaLocation="http://java.sun.com/xml/ns/jdbc
http://java.sun.com/xml/ns/jdbc/webrowset.xsd">
  <properties>
    <command>SELECT * FROM ztest WHERE 1=0</command>
```

```
<concurrency>1008</concurrency>
<datasource><null/></datasource>
<escape-processing>true</escape-processing>
<fetch-direction>1000</fetch-direction>
<fetch-size>0</fetch-size>
<isolation-level>2</isolation-level>
<key-columns>
</key-columns>
<map>
</map>
<max-field-size>0</max-field-size>
<max-rows>0</max-rows>
<query-timeout>0</query-timeout>
<read-only>true</read-only>
<rowset-type>ResultSet.TYPE_SCROLL_INSENSITIVE</rowset-type>
<show-deleted>true</show-deleted>
<table-name>ztest</table-name>
<url><null/></url>
<sync-provider>
  <sync-provider-name>
    com.sun.rowset.providers.RIOptimisticProvider
  </sync-provider-name>
  <sync-provider-vendor>Sun Microsystems Inc.</sync-provider-vendor>
  <sync-provider-version>1.0</sync-provider-version>
  <sync-provider-grade>2</sync-provider-grade>
  <data-source-lock>1</data-source-lock>
</sync-provider>
</properties>
<metadata>
  <column-count>2</column-count>
  <column-definition>
    <column-index>1</column-index>
    <auto-increment>false</auto-increment>
    <case-sensitive>false</case-sensitive>
    <currency>false</currency>
    <nullable>0</nullable>
    <signed>false</signed>
    <searchable>true</searchable>
    <column-display-size>30</column-display-size>
    <column-label>id</column-label>
    <column-name>id</column-name>
    <schema-name></schema-name>
    <column-precision>30</column-precision>
    <column-scale>0</column-scale>
    <table-name>ztest</table-name>
    <catalog-name>octopus</catalog-name>
    <column-type>12</column-type>
```

```
      <column-type-name>VARCHAR</column-type-name>
    </column-definition>
    <column-definition>
      <column-index>2</column-index>
      <auto-increment>false</auto-increment>
      <case-sensitive>false</case-sensitive>
      <currency>false</currency>
      <nullable>1</nullable>
      <signed>false</signed>
      <searchable>true</searchable>
      <column-display-size>60</column-display-size>
      <column-label>name</column-label>
      <column-name>name</column-name>
      <schema-name></schema-name>
      <column-precision>60</column-precision>
      <column-scale>0</column-scale>
      <table-name>ztest</table-name>
      <catalog-name>octopus</catalog-name>
      <column-type>12</column-type>
      <column-type-name>VARCHAR</column-type-name>
    </column-definition>
  </metadata>
  <data>
  </data>
</webRowSet>


==============
```

Running the Solution for an ODBC Database

```
$ java WebRowSetMetaDataExample odbc
Querying database for metadata only...
sqlQuery=SELECT * FROM ztest WHERE 1=0
java.lang.UnsupportedOperationException at
sun.jdbc.odbc.JdbcOdbcDatabaseMetaData.locatorsUpdateCopy
(JdbcOdbcDatabaseMetaData.java:4051)
```

7.15. How Do You Retrieve Metadata from RowSetMetaData?

A JDBC application can get metadata information about the columns in a RowSet object (such as CachedRowSet or WebRowSet) by invoking ResultSetMetaData and RowSetMetaData methods on a RowSetMetaData object. The following code fragment, in which webRS is a WebRowSet object, illustrates the process. The first line creates a WebRowSet object. The second line creates a RowSetMetaData object with information about the columns in webRS. The method getMetaData(), inherited from the ResultSet interface, returns a ResultSetMetaData object, which is cast to a RowSetMetaData object before being assigned to the variable rsMD. The third line finds out how many columns rsMD has, and the fourth line gets the JDBC type of values stored in the second column of webRS.

```
WebRowSet webRS = <get-a-WebRowSet-object>;                 // 1
RowSetMetaData rsMD = (RowSetMetaData) webRS.getMetaData();  // 2
int columnCount = rsMD.getColumnCount();                     // 3
int type = rsMD.getColumnType(2);                            // 4
```

According to the J2SE 5.0 documentation (http://java.sun.com/j2se/1.5.0/docs/api/javax/sql/rowset/CachedRowSet.html), the RowSetMetaData interface differs from the ResultSetMetaData interface in two ways:

- **It includes** setter **methods**: A RowSet object uses these methods internally when it is populated with data from a different ResultSet object.

- **It contains fewer** getter **methods**: Some ResultSetMetaData methods do not apply to a RowSet object. For example, methods retrieving whether a column value is writable or read only do not apply because all of a RowSet object's columns will be writable or read only, depending on whether or not the rowset is updatable.

Note In order to return a RowSetMetaData object, JDBC driver implementations must override the getMetaData() method defined in java.sql.ResultSet and return a RowSetMetaData object.

7.16. How Can You Create a Custom RowSetMetaData Object?

JDBC provides a basic class (javax.sql.rowset.RowSetMetaDataImpl) for implementing a custom RowSetMetaData object. This means that implementations almost have to be proprietary. The JDBC RowSet package is the most commonly available and offers the sun.jdbc.rowset.RowSetMetaDataImpl class.

After instantiation of RowSetMetaDataImpl, any of the RowSetMetaData setter methods may be used. The minimum needed for a RowSet to function is to set the column count (RowSetMetaData.setColumnCount()) for a row and the column type (RowSetMetaData.setColumnType()) for each column in the row.

For example, the following code segment will populate two columns called id and name with three rows. After populating the CachedRowSet object, we commit the inserted records back to a designated data source.

```
import java.sql.Types;
import javax.sql.RowSetMetaData;
import javax.sql.RowSetMetaDataImpl ;
import javax.sql.rowset.CachedRowSet;
import com.sun.rowset.CachedRowSetImpl;
…
// create a custom-made RowSetMetaData object
RowSetMetaData rsMD = new RowSetMetaDataImpl();
rsMD.setColumnCount(2);
rsMD.setColumnName(1, "id");
rsMD.setColumnType(1, Types.VARCHAR);
rsMD.setColumnName(2, "name");
```

```
rsMD.setColumnType(2, Types.VARCHAR);
// sets the designated column's table name, if any, to the given String.
rsMD.setTableName(1, "ztest");
rsMD.setTableName(2, "ztest");

// use a custom-made RowSetMetaData object for CachedRowSet object
CachedRowSet crs = new CachedRowSetImpl();
crs.setMetaData(rsMD);

crs.moveToInsertRow();
crs.updateString(1, "1111");
crs.updateString(2, "alex");
crs.insertRow();

crs.updateString(1, "2222");
crs.updateString(2, "jane");
crs.insertRow();

//
// if you want to commit changes from a CachedRowSet object
// to your desired data source, then you must create a Connection object.
//
Connection conn = getConnection();
// when the method acceptChanges() is executed, the CachedRowSet
// object's writer, a RowSetWriterImpl object, is called behind the
// scenes to write the changes made to the rowset to the underlying
// data source. The writer is implemented to make a connection to
// the data source and write updates to it.
crs.acceptChanges(conn);
```

The Solution

The following solution creates a custom-made RowSet metadata object. This provides a lot of freedom to RowSet developers to tailor their metadata according to the application's data requirements.

```
import java.sql.Types;
import java.sql.Connection;
import javax.sql.RowSetMetaData;
import javax.sql.rowset.RowSetMetaDataImpl;
import javax.sql.rowset.CachedRowSet;
import com.sun.rowset.CachedRowSetImpl;

import jcb.util.DatabaseUtil;
import jcb.db.VeryBasicConnectionManager;

public class CreateCustomRowSetMetaData {
```

```java
public static void main(String[] args) {
    String dbVendor = args[0]; // {"mysql", "oracle", "odbc"}
    CachedRowSet crs = null;
    Connection conn = null;
    RowSetMetaData rsMD = null;
    try {
        // create a custom-made RowSetMetaData object
        rsMD = createRowSetMetaData();

        // use a custom-made RowSetMetaData object for CachedRowSet object
        crs = new CachedRowSetImpl();
        crs.setMetaData(rsMD);

        crs.moveToInsertRow();
        crs.updateString(1, "1111");
        crs.updateString(2, "alex");
        crs.insertRow();

        crs.moveToInsertRow();
        crs.updateString(1, "2222");
        crs.updateString(2, "jane");
        crs.insertRow();

        // if you want to commit changes from a CachedRowSet
        // object to your desired data source, then you must
        // create a Connection object.
        conn = VeryBasicConnectionManager.getConnection(dbVendor);

        // moves the cursor to the remembered cursor position, usually
        // the current row. This method has no effect if the cursor is
        // not on the insert row.
        crs.moveToCurrentRow();

        // when the method acceptChanges() is executed, the CachedRowSet
        // object's writer, a RowSetWriterImpl object, is called behind the
        // scenes to write the changes made to the rowset to the underlying
        // data source. The writer is implemented to make a connection to
        // the data source and write updates to it.
        crs.acceptChanges(conn);
    }
    catch (Exception e) {
        e.printStackTrace();
    }
    finally {
        DatabaseUtil.close(conn);
    }
}
```

```
static RowSetMetaData createRowSetMetaData()
    throws Exception {
    // create a custom made RowSetMetaData object
    RowSetMetaData rsMD = new RowSetMetaDataImpl();
    rsMD.setColumnCount(2);
    rsMD.setColumnName(1, "id");
    rsMD.setColumnType(1, Types.VARCHAR);
    rsMD.setColumnName(2, "name");
    rsMD.setColumnType(2, Types.VARCHAR);
    // sets the designated column's table name, if any, to the given String.
    rsMD.setTableName(1, "ztest");
    rsMD.setTableName(2, "ztest");
    return rsMD;
  }
}
```

The MySQL Database Before Running the Solution

```
mysql> desc ztest;
+-------+-------------+------+-----+---------+-------+
| Field | Type        | Null | Key | Default | Extra |
+-------+-------------+------+-----+---------+-------+
| id    | varchar(10) |      | PRI |         |       |
| name  | varchar(20) | YES  |     | NULL    |       |
+-------+-------------+------+-----+---------+-------+
2 rows in set (0.06 sec)
mysql> select * from ztest;
+----+------+
| id | name |
+----+------+
| 11 | alex |
| 22 | bob  |
| 33 | mary |
+----+------+
3 rows in set (0.00 sec)
```

The MySQL Database After Running the Solution

```
$ javac CreateCustomRowSetMetaData.java
$ java CreateCustomRowSetMetaData mysql
mysql> select * from ztest;
```

```
+------+------+
| id   | name |
+------+------+
| 11   | alex |
| 22   | bob  |
| 33   | mary |
| 1111 | alex |
| 2222 | jane |
+------+------+
5 rows in set (0.00 sec)
```

7.17. How Can You Instantiate and Load a New CachedRowSet Object from a Non-JDBC Source?

You want to create a new CachedRowSet object from a non-JDBC source (such as a file or a spreadsheet). To do so, follow these steps:

1. Create an object that implements javax.sql.RowSetReader, which loads the data from a non-JDBC source.

2. Create an object that implements javax.sql.RowSetWriter, which writes the data to a data source (this can be a JDBC data source or a non-JDBC data source).

3. Register classes created in steps 1 and 2.

4. Instantiate a CachedRowset object with registered classes.

5. Invoke CachedRowset.execute() to load the data.

6. Invoke CachedRowset.acceptChanges() to write the data.

Before creating a CachedRowSet object, a RowSetMetaData object must be created, set up with a description of the data, and attached to the CachedRowset object before loading the actual data from a non-JDBC source. Next, I discuss these steps in detail.

Creating an Object That Implements javax.sql.RowSetReader

This step involves creating a class that implements the javax.sql.RowSetReader interface, which loads the data from a non-JDBC source. According to the J2SE documentation, RowSetReader is the facility that a disconnected RowSet object calls on to populate itself with rows of data. A reader (an object implementing the RowSetReader interface) may be registered with a RowSet object that supports the reader/writer paradigm. When the RowSet object's execute() method is called, it in turn calls the reader's readData() method.

The RowSetReader interface has only one method:

```
void readData(RowSetInternal caller)
// Reads the new contents of the calling RowSet object.
```

The following class (CustomRowSetReader) implements the RowSetReader interface, which loads the data into a CachedRowSet object from a non-JDBC source. According to JDK 1.5, RowSetInternal is an interface that a RowSet object implements in order to present itself to

a RowSetReader or RowSetWriter object. The RowSetInternal interface contains methods that
let the reader or writer access and modify the internal state of the rowset.

```java
import java.sql.*;
import javax.sql.*;
import javax.sql.rowset.*;
import com.sun.rowset.*;

public class CustomRowSetReader implements RowSetReader {

    public CustomRowSetReader() {
        System.out.println("CustomRowSetReader: constructor.");
    }

    public void readData(RowSetInternal caller) throws SQLException {
        System.out.println("--- CustomRowSetReader: begin. ---");
        if (caller == null) {
            System.out.println("CustomRowSetReader: caller is null.");
            return;
        }

        CachedRowSet crs = (CachedRowSet) caller;

        RowSetMetaData rsmd = new RowSetMetaDataImpl();

        rsmd.setColumnCount(3);

        rsmd.setColumnType(1, Types.VARCHAR);
        rsmd.setColumnType(2, Types.INTEGER);
        rsmd.setColumnType(3, Types.VARCHAR);

        rsmd.setColumnName(1, "col1");
        rsmd.setColumnName(2, "col2");
        rsmd.setColumnName(3, "col3");

        crs.setMetaData( rsmd );
        System.out.println("CustomRowSetReader: crs.setMetaData( rsmd );");

        crs.moveToInsertRow();

        crs.updateString( 1, "StringCol11" ); // value for row 1 column 1
        crs.updateInt( 2, 1 );                // value for row 1 column 2
        crs.updateString( 3, "StringCol31" ); // value for row 1 column 3
        crs.insertRow();
        System.out.println("CustomRowSetReader: crs.insertRow() 1");
```

```
        crs.updateString( 1, "StringCol12" ); // value for row 2 column 1
        crs.updateInt( 2, 2 );                 // value for row 2 column 2
        crs.updateString( 3, "StringCol32" ); // value for row 2 column 3
        crs.insertRow();
        System.out.println("CustomRowSetReader: crs.insertRow() 2");

        crs.moveToCurrentRow();
        crs.beforeFirst();
        displayRowSet(crs);
        crs.beforeFirst();
        System.out.println("CustomRowSetReader: end.");
    } // end readData

    static void displayRowSet(RowSet rs) throws SQLException {
        while (rs.next()) {
            System.out.println(rs.getRow() + " - " +
                        rs.getString("col1") + ":" +
                        rs.getInt("col2") + ":" + rs.getString("col3"));
        }
    }
}
```

Creating an Object That Implements javax.sql.RowSetWriter

This step involves creating a class that implements the javax.sql.RowSetWriter interface,
which writes the data from a CachedRowSet object to a data source. According to the J2SE
documentation, an object that implements the RowSetWriter interface, called a writer, may
be registered with a RowSet object that supports the reader/writer paradigm. If a disconnected
RowSet object modifies some of its data, and it has a writer associated with it, it may be implemented so that it calls on the writer's writeData method internally to write the updates back
to the data source. In order to do this, the writer must first establish a connection with the
rowset's data source. If the data to be updated has already been changed in the data source,
there is a conflict, in which case the writer will not write the changes to the data source. The
algorithm that the writer uses for preventing or limiting conflicts depends entirely on its
implementation.

The RowSetWriter interface has only one method:

```
    boolean writeData(RowSetInternal caller)
    // Writes the changes in this RowSetWriter object's rowset
    // back to the data source from which it got its data.
```

The following class (CustomRowSetWriter) implements the RowSetWriter interface, which
reads the data from a CachedRowSet object and writes it to a data source:

```
import java.sql.*;
import javax.sql.*;
import javax.sql.rowset.*;
import com.sun.rowset.*;
```

```java
public class CustomRowSetWriter implements RowSetWriter {

  public CustomRowSetWriter() {
      System.out.println("CustomRowSetWriter: constructor.");
  }

  public boolean writeData(RowSetInternal caller) throws SQLException {
      System.out.println("--- CustomRowSetWriter: begin. ---");
      if (caller == null) {
          System.out.println("CustomRowSetWriter: caller is null.");
          return false;
      }

      CachedRowSet crs = (CachedRowSet) caller;
      // for now do not write any data
      return true;
  }
}
```

Registering Classes Created in Steps 1 and 2

To register your custom RowSetReader and RowSetWriter, you have to implement the javax.sql.rowset.spi.SyncProvider. SyncProvider is the synchronization mechanism that provides reader and writer capabilities for disconnected RowSet objects. A SyncProvider implementation is a class that extends the SyncProvider abstract class.

The MySyncProvider class registers our custom RowSetReader and RowSetWriter:

```java
import javax.sql.RowSetReader;
import javax.sql.RowSetWriter;
import javax.sql.rowset.spi.SyncProvider;


public class MySyncProvider extends SyncProvider {

    private int dataSourceLock;

    /**
     * creates a default SyncProvider object.
     */
    public MySyncProvider() {
        System.out.println("MySyncProvider: constructor.");
        this.dataSourceLock = SyncProvider.DATASOURCE_NO_LOCK;
    }

    /**
     * Returns the current data source lock severity level active
     * in this SyncProvider implementation.
     */
```

```java
    public int  getDataSourceLock() {
        return this.dataSourceLock;
    }

    /**
     * Returns a constant indicating the grade of synchronization a
     * RowSet object can expect from this SyncProvider object.
     */
    public int getProviderGrade() {
        return SyncProvider.GRADE_NONE;
    }

    /**
     * Returns the unique identifier for this SyncProvider object.
     */
    public String  getProviderID() {
        String id = getClass().getName();
        System.out.println("--- MySyncProvider: getProviderID() ="+id);
        return id; //"MySyncProvider";
    }

    /**
     * Returns a javax.sql.RowSetReader object, which can be used to
     * populate a RowSet object with data.
     */
    public RowSetReader  getRowSetReader() {
        System.out.println("--- MySyncProvider: getRowSetReader() ---");
        return new CustomRowSetReader();
    }

    /**
     * Returns a javax.sql.RowSetWriter object, which can be used to
     * write a RowSet object's data back to the underlying data source.
     */
    public RowSetWriter  getRowSetWriter() {
        System.out.println("--- MySyncProvider: getRowSetWriter() ---");
        return new CustomRowSetWriter();
    }

    /**
     * Returns the vendor name of this SyncProvider instance
     */
    public String getVendor() {
        return "custom-made";
    }
```

```java
/**
 * Returns the release version of this SyncProvider instance.
 */
public String getVersion() {
    return "1.0";
}

/**
 * Sets a lock on the underlying data source at the level
 * indicated by datasourceLock.
 */
public void  setDataSourceLock(int dataSourceLock) {
    this.dataSourceLock = dataSourceLock;
}

/**
 * Returns whether this SyncProvider implementation can perform
 * synchronization between a RowSet object and the SQL VIEW in
 * the data source from which the RowSet object got its data.
 */
public int supportsUpdatableView() {
    return SyncProvider.NONUPDATABLE_VIEW_SYNC;
}
}
```

Instantiating a CachedRowset Object with Registered Classes

To instantiate a CachedRowSet object with registered classes, we need to pass the MySyncProvider object to a constructor of the CachedRowSetImpl class (a Sun reference implementation of the cachedRowSet interface).

```java
CachedRowSet crs;
...
try {
    SyncFactory.registerProvider("MySyncProvider");
    Hashtable env = new Hashtable();
    env.put(SyncFactory.ROWSET_SYNC_PROVIDER, "MySyncProvider");
    crs = new CachedRowSetImpl(env);
    ...
```

Invoking CachedRowset.execute() to Load the Data

We next invoke the method CachedRowset.execute():

```java
crs.execute();  // load data from custom RowSetReader
```

Invoking CachedRowset.acceptChanges() to Write the Data

Finally, we invoke CachedRowset.acceptChanges() to commit changes back to the database.

I've provided a complete solution here. This solution puts together the steps I defined earlier to create a custom RowSet object. You have complete freedom in creating your RowSet object (you even tailor your custom RowSet's metadata).

```java
import java.util.Hashtable;
import java.sql.Types;
import java.sql.SQLException;
import javax.sql.RowSetReader;
import javax.sql.RowSetInternal;
import javax.sql.RowSetMetaData;
import javax.sql.rowset.RowSetMetaDataImpl;
import javax.sql.rowset.CachedRowSet;
import com.sun.rowset.CachedRowSetImpl;
import javax.sql.rowset.spi.SyncFactory;

public class DemoCustomRowSet {

  CachedRowSet crs;
  String stringColumn1;
  String stringColumn3;
  int intColumn2;


  public DemoCustomRowSet() {
    try {
      SyncFactory.registerProvider("MySyncProvider");
      Hashtable env = new Hashtable();
      env.put(SyncFactory.ROWSET_SYNC_PROVIDER, "MySyncProvider");
      crs = new CachedRowSetImpl(env);
      crs.execute();  // load data from custom RowSetReader

      System.out.println("Fetching from RowSet...");
      while(crs.next())  {
        displayData();
      }

      if(crs.isAfterLast() == true)  {
        System.out.println("We have reached the end");
        System.out.println("crs row: " + crs.getRow());
      }

      System.out.println("And now backwards...");

      while(crs.previous()) {
        displayData();
      }  // end while previous
```

```java
        if(crs.isBeforeFirst()) {
            System.out.println("We have reached the start");
        }

        crs.first();
        if(crs.isFirst()) {
            System.out.println("We have moved to first");
        }

        System.out.println("crs row: " + crs.getRow());

        if(!crs.isBeforeFirst()) {
            System.out.println("We aren't before the first row.");
        }

        crs.last();
        if(crs.isLast())  {
            System.out.println("...and now we have moved to the last");
        }

        System.out.println("crs row: " + crs.getRow());

        if(!crs.isAfterLast()) {
          System.out.println("we aren't after the last.");
        }

    } // end try
    catch (SQLException e) {
      e.printStackTrace();
      System.err.println("SQLException: " + e.getMessage());
    }

} // end constructor

public void displayData() throws SQLException {
    stringColumn1 = crs.getString(1);
    if(crs.wasNull()) {
        System.out.println("stringColumn1 is null");
    }
    else {
        System.out.println("stringColumn1: " + stringColumn1);
    }

    intColumn2 = crs.getInt(2);
    if (crs.wasNull()) {
        System.out.println("intColumn2 is null");
    }
```

```java
        else {
            System.out.println("intColumn2: " + intColumn2);
        }

        stringColumn3 = crs.getString(3);
        if(crs.wasNull()) {
            System.out.println("stringColumn3 is null");
        }
        else {
            System.out.println("stringColumn3: " + stringColumn3);
        }

    }  // end displayData

    public static void main(String args[]) {
      DemoCustomRowSet test = new DemoCustomRowSet();
    }

} // end class DemoCustomRowSet
```

CHAPTER 8

■ ■ ■

Web Access to Metadata, Part 1

Only two things are infinite, the universe and human stupidity, and I'm not sure about the former.

Albert Einstein

In building web-based database applications (such as SQL adapters and connectors), metadata plays the key role. If you do not depend on metadata, then you have to "hard-code" your metadata, and if you hard-code your metadata, then maintenance of such an application or system will be impossible (because the moment the database schema changes, then your application or system will collapse). JDBC enables you to discover database metadata at runtime.

With database metadata, you can invoke a SQL query, find a list of tables, or execute a stored procedure. If you are interested in the various approaches to building web-based applications that access database metadata through JDBC, then this chapter is for you. In this hands-on chapter, you will learn the basics of this process using the Java servlets approach. This chapter shows you how to access database metadata from Java servlets. Our focus will be basic access to database (such as Oracle and MySQL) metadata. We will not concentrate on web frameworks such as Apache's Struts or Cocoon (these topics have their respected books on the market).

This chapter will answer the following types of questions by using Java servlets and JDBC:

- How do you get a list of tables or views for a given database?

- How do you get a list of column names or types for a given table or view?

- How do you get a list of stored procedures for a given database?

- What is the signature of a stored procedure?

- What are the PK/FK columns for a given table?

- How do you get `ResultSet`'s metadata?

All of these questions will be answered in the context of a web browser, JDBC, and Java servlets (as illustrated in a moment). Before answering these questions, we will briefly take a look at Java servlets and then answer these questions.

For presenting web access to database metadata, I will be using Apache's Tomcat servlet container (http://tomcat.apache.org/). Apache Tomcat is the servlet container used in the

307

official reference implementation for the Java servlet and JavaServer Pages technologies. For demonstration purposes, I will put all Java servlets (`.class` files) under the following directory (I used "octopus" as a web application name):

```
<tomcat-installed-directory>/webapps/octopus/WEB-INF/classes/
```

All Java servlets in this chapter will be able to emit its output as XML or HTML. To save space, I will show the output as XML only (you may try the HTML output by setting `format=html` in your servlet calls).

8.1. How Do Web Clients and Servers Communicate?

How do web clients (browsers such as Microsoft's Internet Explorer and Mozilla's Firefox) and servers (servlet containers—such as Apache Tomcat—or application servers—such as IBM's WebSphere) communicate? In the Java world, the web protocol HTTP (Hypertext Transfer Protocol), HTML (Hypertext Markup Language) forms, and Java servlets enable this communication. A web client sends an HTTP request, and the server receives the request, analyzes it, and sends back a proper HTTP response (dynamic content as another HTML message).

Java servlets are the central component of web applications and include servlet containers, request and response processing, sessions, redirection, and forward and include actions. Essentially, a servlet receives the request and then sends the response as another HTML message. We will focus on accessing databases using the JDBC API. Also, servlets may be used to authenticate users and control their access to server-side resources (such as data or metadata).

According to "Servlet Best Practices, Part 1" (`http://www.onjava.com/lpt/a/2825`), since their introduction in 1996 servlets have dominated the server-side Java landscape and have become the standard way to interface Java to the Web. They are the foundation technology on which Java developers build web applications and, increasingly, web services. This chapter discusses best practices for servlet-based communication using JDBC development and deployment.

According to Sun (`http://java.sun.com/products/servlet/`), Java servlet technology provides web developers with a simple, consistent mechanism for extending the functionality of a web server and for accessing existing business systems. You can think of a servlet as an applet that runs on the server side—without a face or presentation. Java servlets have made many web applications possible. Servlets have access to the entire family of Java APIs, including the JDBC API to access enterprise databases.

As we will observe (by examining questions and answers in this chapter), JDBC provides a powerful, comprehensive interface for accessing databases from Java programs and servlets. The JDBC API allows any Java program—even an applet and servlet—to connect to a relational database management system (RDBMS) and perform queries and transactions. Servlets and JDBC are ideal for creating "dynamic contents."

Using JDBC from a Java servlet involves a three-tier distributed application, consisting of a user interface (the web browser), business logic (a series of Java servlets), and database access. The user interface is an HTML file in a browser. The middle tier is a Java servlet that handles requests from the client web browser and provides access to the third tier, a database accessed via JDBC. Figure 8-1 presents a basic model (three-tier model) for accessing database metadata.

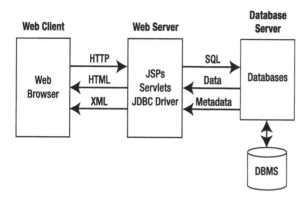

Figure 8-1. *A basic model to access database metadata*

Our basic model (typically used by many web-based applications) for accessing database and database metadata has three tiers:

- **Tier 1**: The web browser
- **Tier 2**: The servlet/web server
- **Tier 3**: The database server

Tier 1: The Web Browser

The first tier uses a web browser (such as Firefox or Internet Explorer), which is the default client for Internet applications. Client can use an HTML form for user input and the results of the database query (as dynamic content) are returned as an HTML/XML page.

Tier 2: The Servlet Container

The second tier is implemented with a servlet container (such as Tomcat, BEA's WebLogic Server, or WebSphere) running Java servlets or JavaServer Pages (JSP).

The Java servlet is able to receive the user's request (the web browser sends an HTTP request) and access the database (using the JDBC API) and database metadata (using the JDBC API) and return the result as an HTML/XML page.

Tier 3: The Database Server

The third tier is the back-end database server. The Java servlet can access information in the database provided that a JDBC driver is available. JDBC drivers are available for most widely used databases (such as Oracle, MySQL, DB2, Sybase, etc.). A servlet can use one or many databases, either directly or indirectly.

8.2. What Is a Java Servlet in a Nutshell?

In a nutshell, a servlet is a web component that generates dynamic content. Servlets are small, platform-independent Java classes compiled to an architecture-neutral bytecode that can be loaded dynamically into and run by a servlet container or an application server. Servlets interact with web clients (i.e., web browsers) via a request-response paradigm (see Figure 8-2) implemented by the servlet container. This request-response model is based on the behavior of HTTP.

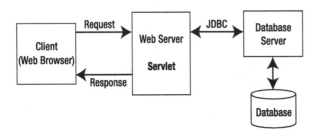

Figure 8-2. *The Java servlet's request-response paradigm*

What is a Java servlet? A servlet is an extension to a web server and is used for generating dynamic web content. A servlet gets an HTTP request from a client, such as a web browser; processes the request; and returns the HTTP response to the client. The response typically contains HTML code, XML, or an image (binary data) that is displayed by the web browser. A Java servlet enables dynamic web content from a static web page. Much in the same way other existing scripting languages like CGI or ASP can generate dynamic content based on input given to it by a user, so too does a Java servlet. The advantage of a Java servlet over these other existing scripting languages is its portability. Java was specifically designed so that an application could be written once and run on any operating systems with a virtual machine. Java servlets take this concept further by extending it into the field of server-side scripting.

Servlets are small Java classes that run in a server application (hence the name "servlets," similar to "applets" on the client side) to answer client requests. Servlets are not tied to a specific client-server protocol, but they are most commonly used with HTTP and the word "servlet" is often used in the meaning of "HTTP servlet."

Servlets make use of the Java classes in these packages:

- `javax.servlet`: The basic Servlet framework

- `javax.servlet.http`: Extensions of the servlet framework for servlets that answer HTTP requests

Typical uses for HTTP servlets include

- Processing and/or storing data submitted by an HTML form

- Providing dynamic content, for example, returning the results of a database query to the client (as HTML, XML)

- Managing state information on top of the stateless HTTP, for example, for an online shopping cart system that manages shopping carts for many concurrent customers and maps every request to the right customer

A *Java servlet engine* is the Java application that executes the Java servlet. It is a mechanism by which a Java application can be written to provide dynamic web content. For example, Tomcat (http://jakarta.apache.org/tomcat/) has a servlet engine that you can use to execute Java servlets.

8.3. What Is CGI?

The Common Gateway Interface (CGI) is a standard for interfacing external applications with information servers, such as HTTP or web servers. A plain HTML document that the web daemon retrieves is static, which means it exists in a constant state: a text file that doesn't change. A CGI (http://www.cgi101.com/book/) program, on the other hand, is executed in real time so that it can output dynamic information. CGI is a proven architecture, but it has had some major limitations that create significant problems when you are trying to develop enterprise-wide web solutions:

- Difficulty in maintaining state and session connection (there is no session concept; therefore a state cannot be kept).

- Performance bottlenecks (resource-intensive scripts could cause performance problems).

- Can involve proprietary APIs.

- Malicious scripts could crash the HTTP server; CGI scripts run as a separate process from the HTTP server, which isolates the server from most script errors; however, operating system errors do exist, and scripts that crash UNIX systems can be found on the Web.

- In general, compared to Java programs, CGI scripts are unreadable.

There is a newer architecture (Java servlets—a servlet is a small Java class) that not only solves these problems but also provides code portability, plus the ability to allow your server-side application to interface with a wide range of relational databases. This architecture is using JDBC with Java servlets to replace CGI.

8.4. How Does a Java Servlet Work?

A servlet is a web component that generates dynamic content. Servlets are small, platform-independent Java classes compiled to an architecture-neutral bytecode that can be loaded dynamically into and run by a servlet container. Servlets interact with web clients via a request-response paradigm implemented by the servlet container. This request-response model is based on the behavior of HTTP. Servlets allow state, can use the JDBC API, and have a significant performance increase because they have no heavy process startup and initialization for each client request as CGI does.

According to Sun (http://www.sun.com), a servlet is a Java programming language class used to extend the capabilities of servers that host applications accessed via a request-response programming model. Although servlets can respond to any type of request, they are commonly used to extend the applications hosted by web servers. For such applications, Java servlet technology (Figure 8-3) defines HTTP-specific servlet classes. The javax.servlet and javax.servlet.http packages provide interfaces and classes for writing servlets. All servlets must implement the Servlet interface, which defines life-cycle methods.

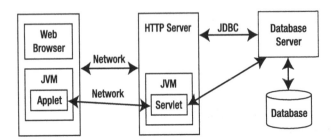

Figure 8-3. *Web and java servlet technology*

Servlets can be used for any number of web-related applications. Let's look at a few examples. Developing e-commerce "store clients" has become one of the most common uses for Java servlets. A servlet can build an online catalog based on the contents of a database. It can then present this catalog to the customer using dynamic HTML. The customer will choose the items to be ordered, enter the shipping and billing information, and then submit the data to the servlet. When the servlet receives the posted data, it will process the orders and place them in the database for fulfillment. Every one of these processes can be easily implemented using Java servlets.

Servlets can be used to deploy websites that open up large legacy systems on the Internet. Many companies have massive amounts of data stored on large mainframe systems. These businesses do not want to re-architect their systems, so they choose to provide inexpensive web interfaces into them. Because you have the entire JDK at your disposal and security provided by the servlet container, you can use servlets to interface with these systems using anything from Transmission Control Protocol/Internet Protocol (TCP/IP) to Common Object Request Broker Architecture (CORBA).

The following is a skeleton of a servlet:

```java
import java.net.*;
import java.io.*;
import java.util.*;
import javax.servlet.*;
import javax.servlet.http.*;
import java.sql.*;

public class MyDatabaseServlet extends HttpServlet {

    public void init(ServletConfig config) throws ServletException
        // handle the initialization: when a servlet is first loaded,
        // the servlet container calls its init() method exactly once.
        ...
    }

    public void doGet(HttpServletRequest request,
                      HttpServletResponse response)
        throws ServletException, IOException {
        // handle the HTTP GET method
        ...
    }
```

```
    public void doPost(HttpServletRequest request,
                       HttpServletResponse response)
        throws ServletException, IOException {
        // handle the HTTP POST method
        ...
    }

    public void destroy() {
            // called by the servlet container to indicate to a
            // servlet that the servlet is being taken out of service.
            ...
    }

    // other private methods

} // end MyDatabaseServlet
```

HttpServlet (defined in the javax.servlet.http package) is an abstract class to be subclassed to create an HTTP servlet suitable for a website. A subclass of HttpServlet must override at least one method, usually one of these:

- doGet(), for HTTP GET requests

- doPost(), for HTTP POST requests

- doPut(), for HTTP PUT requests

- doDelete(), for HTTP DELETE requests

- init() and destroy(), to manage resources that are held for the life of the servlet

- getServletInfo(), which the servlet uses to provide information about itself

Figure 8-4 shows one of the most common ways of using a Java servlet. A user (1) requests (using a web browser or other means) some information by filling out an HTML form containing a link to a servlet and clicking the Submit (by invoking a GET or POST operation) button (2). The server (3) locates the requested servlet (4). The servlet then executes the doGet() or doPost() method and gathers the information needed (by using some databases (5) or other resources such as file systems) to satisfy the user's request and constructs a web page (6) containing the information (this can be HTML, XML, etc.). Finally, that web page is displayed on the user's browser (7).

For details on Java servlets, refer to the following websites:

- http://www.apl.jhu.edu/~hall/java/Servlet-Tutorial/

- http://java.sun.com/docs/books/tutorial/index.html

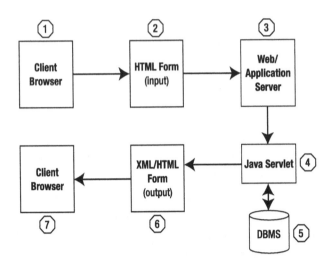

Figure 8-4. *Most common way of using a Java servlet*

8.5. How Does a Servlet Talk to a Servlet Container?

When a web server calls a servlet, it loads the servlet's .class file (if it has not already been loaded) and calls one of the servlet's methods (doGet(), doPost(), etc.). The method takes two parameters, an HttpServletRequest (request) and an HttpServletResponse (response), and uses these two classes to send content back to the user/client (a web browser). Four methods are available to servlet developers for producing content:

- doHead(): Returns the headers identified by the request URL. This method is called by the servlet container to process a HEAD request. There may be many threads calling this method simultaneously:

```
public void doHead(HttpServletRequest request, HttpServletResponse response)
    throws IOException {
    response.setContentLength(120);        // set the content length
    response.setContentType("text/html");  // set the content type
}
```

- service(): Provides an HTTP service:

```
public void service(HttpServletRequest request, HttpServletResponse response)
```

- doGet(): Retrieves the resource identified by the request URL:

```
public void doGet(HttpServletRequest request, HttpServletResponse response)
```

- doPost(): Sends data of unlimited length to the servlet container:

```
public void doPost(HttpServletRequest request, HttpServletResponse response)
```

service() is the generic servlet request method. If you write your servlet using service(), you can ignore the other options. The doGet() and doPost() methods are more specialized: they are used for handling HTTP GET and POST requests. If you place your application code in doGet(), your servlet will only respond to GET requests.

8.6. What Are the Advantages of Java Servlets?

Java servlets have the following advantages over other server extension mechanisms:

- They typically run inside multithreaded servlet containers that can handle multiple requests concurrently (you have the option to run them single-threaded).

- They are generally much faster than CGI scripts because a different process model is used (the servlets are not created for every request; they are created once and can handle any number of requests).

- They use a standard API that is supported by many servlet containers.

- They have all the advantages of the Java programming language, including Java threads (Java language provides natural concurrent programming support) and ease of development and platform independence.

- They can access the large set of APIs available for the Java platform.

- They are extensible—you can inherit all your functionality from the base classes made available to you.

- They are portable—they run on all platforms (such as UNIX, Linux, Mac, Windows).

- They can be integrated into most servlet containers.

- They can run stand-alone in a servlet runner.

- Exception handling is built in.

- Security is built in.

- They are a single technology solution for applications.

- They can be interfaced to most other systems (such as JDBC).

8.7. What Is the Life Cycle of a Servlet?

What really goes on inside a Java servlet and container? Figure 8-5 shows a step-by-step summary.

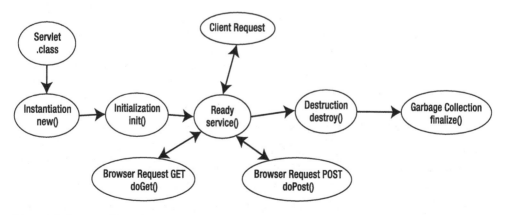

Figure 8-5. *Java servlet and container*

1. Use your favorite text editor (or any Java IDE) to create your Java servlet, SERVLET-NAME.java.

2. Using the Java compiler (javac), compile SERVLET-NAME.java (the output of this step is SERVLET-NAME.class).

3. Place the SERVLET-NAME.class file into your .../WEB-INF/classes directory (for details, see Tomcat's directory structure or your desired web application server).

4. Start the web/application server (this might load some or even all of the servlets depending on how the servlet container is configured).

5. A web/application server loads and initializes the servlet: when the first client requests a service from a servlet, then Java servlet (a .class file—in this case, SERVLET-NAME.class) is loaded.

■**Note** A servlet container starts the servlet .class files when the server starts or upon first request, depending on how the container is configured.

---

6. After the .class files are loaded, they stay resident in memory until the servlet container is shut down.

7. The servlet's init() (i.e., initialization) method is run. The init() method is used to initialize global data structures and databases for the life of the servlet (for example, to set up counters, establish database connections, and initialize any objects within memory that the servlet will need).

8. After the servlet is loaded and initialized, it is ready for service (now clients can send requests to that servlet).

9. The servlet handles zero or more client requests: each client request initializes a separate service object. It is closed as soon as the request is finished.

10. Web browsers make requests in two ways (POST and GET), and servlets have support for both GET (handled by the doGet() method) and POST (handled by the doPost() method).

    • Using the GET method (the servlet executes the doGet() method), variables that the browser is sending from forms are sent as an extension of the URL (this is known as URL rewriting; http://www.tiger.com/book/servlet/getEmp?name=alex).

    • The POST method (the servlet executes the doPost() method) sends the variables in the actual request sent to the server. POST is the preferred method by most programmers since it does put information on the URL line.

11. The server removes the servlet: when the web/application server is shut down or is restarted, the destroy() method will be executed. The purpose of this method is to "clean up" (such as closing database connections or closing log files).

12. Java uses automatic garbage collection (Java will automatically detect the unneeded objects).

8.8. What Is a Very Simple Servlet Example Using JDBC?

Here I provide a very simple servlet, which can access MySQL and Oracle databases. This servlet accepts one parameter, which is the database vendor (vendor). Based on this parameter (the possible values are mysql and oracle), this servlet creates a database Connection object, and finally displays all data from the employees table in an HTML table format.

MySQL Database Setup

```
mysql> select * from employees;
+-----+--------+------+
| id  | name   | age  |
+-----+--------+------+
| 88  | Peter  |  80  |
| 77  | Donald |  70  |
| 33  | Mary   |  30  |
| 44  | Monica |  40  |
| 999 | Andre  |  90  |
+-----+--------+------+
5 rows in set (0.15 sec)
```

Oracle Database Setup

```
SQL> select * from employees;
ID         NAME                 AGE
---------- -------------------- ----------
11         Alex Smith           25
22         Don Knuth            65
33         Mary Kent            35
44         Monica Seles         30
99         Alex Edison          80
100        Al Sumner            70
105        Al Sumner            90

7 rows selected.
```

The Solution As a Servlet

```java
import java.io.PrintWriter;
import java.io.IOException;

import java.sql.*;
import javax.servlet.*;
import javax.servlet.http.*;

import jcb.util.DatabaseUtil;
import jcb.db.VeryBasicConnectionManager;

public class MyDatabaseServlet extends HttpServlet {
```

```java
public void doGet(HttpServletRequest request,
                  HttpServletResponse response)
    throws ServletException, IOException {
    String query = "SELECT id, name, age FROM employees";
    ResultSet rs = null;
    Statement stmt = null;
    Connection conn = null;
    try {
        String dbVendor = request.getParameter("vendor").trim();
        conn = VeryBasicConnectionManager.getConnection(dbVendor);
        stmt = conn.createStatement();
        rs = stmt.executeQuery(query);
        printResultSet(response, rs );
    }
    catch(Exception e) {
        printError(response, e.getMessage());
    }
    finally {
        DatabaseUtil.close(rs);
        DatabaseUtil.close(stmt);
        DatabaseUtil.close(conn);
    }

} // end doGet

private static void printResultSet(HttpServletResponse response,
                                   ResultSet rs)
    throws Exception  {
    PrintWriter out = response.getWriter();
    StringBuffer buffer = new StringBuffer();
    buffer.append("<html><body><table border=1 cellspacing=0 cellpadding=0>");
    buffer.append("<TR><TH>id</TH><TH>name</TH><TH>age</TH></TR>");
    while (rs.next()) {
        int id = rs.getInt(1);
        String name = rs.getString(2);
        int age = rs.getInt(3);
        buffer.append("<TR><TD>"+id+"</TD><TD>"+name+
                    "</TD><TD>"+age+"</TD></TR>");
    }
    buffer.append("</table></body></html>");
    out.println(buffer.toString());
}
```

```java
    private static void printError(HttpServletResponse response,
                                   String message) {
        try {
            PrintWriter out = response.getWriter();
            StringBuffer buffer = new StringBuffer();
            buffer.append("<html><body>");
            buffer.append(message);
            buffer.append("</body></html>");
            out.println(buffer);
        }
        catch(Exception ignore) {
            // here I ignored the exception, but you can
            // modify the code to do more here …
        }
    }
}
```

Invoking MyDatabaseServlet for MySQL

Figure 8-6 shows how to invoke MyDatabaseServlet with a single parameter (where the parameter name is vendor and its value is mysql).

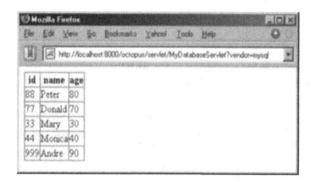

Figure 8-6. *Invoking MyDatabaseServlet for MySQL*

Invoking MyDatabaseServlet for Oracle

Figure 8-7 shows how to invoke MyDatabaseServlet with a single parameter (where the parameter name is vendor and its value is oracle).

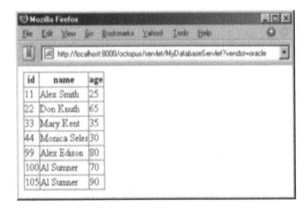

Figure 8-7. *Invoking MyDatabaseServlet for Oracle*

8.9. How Do You Get a List of Table Types for a Database?

Table type is defined as a type of table for storing data and database objects. Each database vendor may have a different set of table types. For example, MySQL's table types are TABLE, VIEW, and LOCAL TEMPORARY and Oracle's table types are TABLE, VIEW, and SYNONYM. You can use the DatabaseMetaData.getTableTypes() method to retrieve a list of the table types available in the given catalog (database). Here is the signature of the DatabaseMetaData.getTableTypes() method:

```
ResultSet getTableTypes() throws SQLException
```

This method retrieves the table types available for a given database, with the results ordered by table type. Possible table types are TABLE, VIEW, SYSTEM TABLE, GLOBAL TEMPORARY, LOCAL TEMPORARY, ALIAS, and SYNONYM. The method returns a ResultSet object in which each row has a single String column that is a table type. This method returns the result as a ResultSet object, which is not very useful for web-based applications. Therefore, we will convert the ResultSet object to HTML/XML, which can be quite useful to web-based applications.

Next I present a Java servlet (GetTableTypes), which will be able to get table types as HTML or XML. Here is the signature of the servlet:

```
GetTableTypes?vendor=<vendor-name>&format=<HTML-or-XML>
```

You may add additional parameters to suit your database application. Here, I use vendor to act as a database selector. So, to get the table information as XML or HTML for a MySQL or Oracle database, you may invoke it as

```
GetTableTypes?vendor=mysql&format=xml
GetTableTypes?vendor=mysql&format=html
GetTableTypes?vendor=oracle&format=xml
GetTableTypes?vendor=oracle&format=html
```

The Solution

In our solution, we use the DatabaseMetaData.getTableTypes() method to solve the problem. This servlet (GetTableTypes) will display the result as XML or HTML.

```java
import java.sql.*;
import javax.servlet.*;
import javax.servlet.http.*;

import java.util.List;
import java.util.ArrayList;

import java.io.PrintWriter;
import java.io.IOException;

import jcb.util.DatabaseUtil;
import jcb.db.VeryBasicConnectionManager;

public class GetTableTypes extends HttpServlet {

    public void doGet(HttpServletRequest request,
                      HttpServletResponse response)
        throws ServletException, IOException {
        Connection conn = null;
        try {
            String dbVendor = request.getParameter("vendor").trim();
            String outputFormat = request.getParameter("format").trim();
            conn = VeryBasicConnectionManager.getConnection(dbVendor);
            List<String> tableTypes = getTableTypes(conn);
            if (outputFormat.equals("xml")) {
                printXML(response, tableTypes);
            }
            else {
                printHTML(response, tableTypes);
            }
        }
        catch(Exception e) {
            printError(response, e.getMessage());
        }
        finally {
            DatabaseUtil.close(conn);
        }

    } // end doGet

    private static void printHTML(HttpServletResponse response,
                                  List<String> tableTypes)
        throws Exception  {
        response.setContentType("text/html");
        PrintWriter out = response.getWriter();
        StringBuilder buffer = new StringBuilder();
        buffer.append("<html><body><table border=1 cellspacing=0 cellpadding=0>");
        buffer.append("<TR><TH>Table Type</TH></TR>");
        for (int i=0; i < tableTypes.size(); i++) {
```

```java
            buffer.append("<TR><TD>");
            buffer.append(tableTypes.get(i));
            buffer.append("</TD></TR>");
        }
        buffer.append("</table></body></html>");
        out.println(buffer.toString());
    }
    private static void printXML(HttpServletResponse response,
                                 List<String> tableTypes)
        throws Exception  {
        response.setContentType("text/xml");
        PrintWriter out = response.getWriter();
        StringBuilder buffer = new StringBuilder();
        buffer.append("<?xml version=\"1.0\" encoding=\"ISO-8859-1\"?>");
        buffer.append("<tableTypes>");
        for (int i=0; i < tableTypes.size(); i++) {
            buffer.append("<type>");
            buffer.append(tableTypes.get(i));
            buffer.append("</type>");
        }
        buffer.append("</tableTypes>");
        out.println(buffer.toString());
    }

    private static void printError(HttpServletResponse response,
                                   String message) {
        try {
            PrintWriter out = response.getWriter();
            StringBuffer buffer = new StringBuffer();
            buffer.append("<html><body>");
            buffer.append(message);
            buffer.append("</body></html>");
            out.println(buffer);
        }
        catch(Exception ignore) {
        }
    }

    /**
     * Get the table names for a given connection object.
     * @param conn the Connection object
     * @return the list of table names as a List.
     * @exception Failed to get the table names from the database.
     */
    public static List<String> getTableTypes(Connection conn)
        throws Exception {
        ResultSet rs = null;
```

```java
    try {
        DatabaseMetaData meta = conn.getMetaData();
        if (meta == null) {
            return null;
        }

        rs = meta.getTableTypes();
        if (rs == null) {
            return null;
        }

        List<String> list = new ArrayList<String>();
        System.out.println("getTableTypes(): --------------");
        while (rs.next()) {
            String type = rs.getString(1);
            System.out.println("type="+type);
            if (type != null) {
                list.add(type);
            }
        }
        System.out.println("--------------");
        return list;
    }
    finally {
        DatabaseUtil.close(rs);
    }
    }
}
```

Invoking GetTableTypes for MySQL

Figure 8-8 shows how to run the solution for the MySQL database.

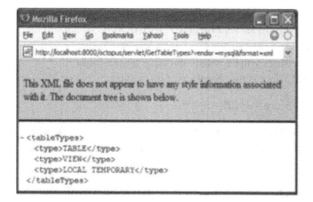

Figure 8-8. *Invoking GetTableTypes for MySQL (XML output)*

Invoking GetTableTypes for Oracle

Figure 8-9 shows how to run the solution for the Oracle database.

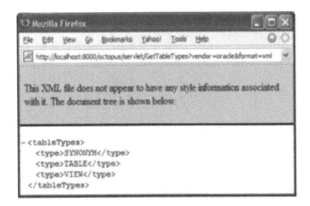

Figure 8-9. *Invoking GetTableTypes for Oracle (XML output)*

8.10. How Do You Get a List of Table Names for a Database?

Each database has a finite set of tables, views, and other objects (such as indexes and stored procedures). JDBC enables you to get a list of tables for a specific database. You can use `DatabaseMetaData.getTables()` to retrieve a description of the tables available in the given catalog (database). Only table descriptions matching the catalog, schema, table name, and type criteria are returned. They are ordered by `TABLE_TYPE`, `TABLE_SCHEM`, and `TABLE_NAME`. The signature of `DatabaseMetaData.getTables()` is

```
ResultSet getTables(String catalog,
                    String schemaPattern,
                    String tableNamePattern,
                    String[] types)
                    throws SQLException
```

This method returns the result as a `ResultSet` object, which is not very useful for web-based applications. Therefore, we will convert the `ResultSet` object to HTML or XML, which can be quite useful to web-based applications.

I present a Java servlet (`GetTables`), which will be able to get table names (plus other metadata information) as HTML or XML. Here is the signature of the servlet:

```
GetTables?vendor=<vendor-name>&format=<HTML-or-XML>
```

You may add additional parameters to suit your database application. Here, I use `vendor` to act as a database selector. So, to get the table information as XML for a MySQL database, you may invoke it as

```
GetTables?vendor=mysql&format=xml
GetTables?vendor=mysql&format=html
GetTables?vendor=oracle&format=xml
GetTables?vendor=oracle&format=html
```

MySQL Database Setup

```
mysql> use octopus;
Database changed
mysql> show tables;
+--------------------+
| Tables_in_octopus  |
+--------------------+
| departments        |
| employees          |
| employees_original |
| test               |
| test1              |
| test2              |
+--------------------+
6 rows in set (0.00 sec)
```

Oracle Database Setup

```
$ sqlplus.exe scott/tiger
SQL*Plus: Release 10.2.0.1.0 - Production on Tue Sep 20 20:19:45 2005
Connected to: Oracle Database 10g Enterprise Edition Release 10.2.0.1.0 - Production
SQL> select object_name from user_objects where object_type = 'TABLE';
OBJECT_NAME
-----------
DEPT
EMP
BONUS
SALGRADE
```

The Solution

We treat MySQL and Oracle differently, because Oracle's driver returns extra tables (the tables not created by the database user) for DatabaseMetaData.getTables(). To eliminate this problem, for Oracle's tables I use the following SQL query:

```
select object_name from user_objects where object_type = 'TABLE'
```

Because of all of these differences, I provide an additional method (getOracleTableNames()) to handle Oracle's special case. This again proves that the "vendor" factor is crucial for handling data and metadata for JDBC applications. Here is a complete solution (the GetTables servlet) for getting table names:

```
import java.sql.*;
import javax.servlet.*;
import javax.servlet.http.*;

import java.util.List;
import java.util.ArrayList;
```

```java
import java.io.PrintWriter;
import java.io.IOException;

import jcb.util.DatabaseUtil;
import jcb.db.VeryBasicConnectionManager;

public class GetTables extends HttpServlet {

    private static final String  ORACLE_TABLES =
        "select object_name from user_objects where object_type = 'TABLE'";
    private static final String[] DB_TABLE_TYPES = { "TABLE" };
    private static final String COLUMN_NAME_TABLE_NAME = "TABLE_NAME";

    public void doGet(HttpServletRequest request,
                      HttpServletResponse response)
        throws ServletException, IOException {
        Connection conn = null;
        try {
            String dbVendor = request.getParameter("vendor").trim();
            String outputFormat = request.getParameter("format").trim();
            conn = VeryBasicConnectionManager.getConnection(dbVendor);
            List<String> tables = null;

            if (dbVendor.equals("oracle")) {
                tables = getOracleTableNames(conn);
            }
            else {
                tables = getTableNames(conn);
            }

            if (tables == null) {
                printError(response, "NO-TABLES-FOUND");
                return;
            }

            if (outputFormat.equals("xml")) {
                printXML(response, tables);
            }
            else {
                printHTML(response, tables);
            }
        }
        catch(Exception e) {
            printError(response, e.getMessage());
        }
        finally {
            DatabaseUtil.close(conn);
        }

    } // end doGet
```

```java
private static void printHTML(HttpServletResponse response,
                             List<String> tables)
    throws Exception  {
    response.setContentType("text/html");
    PrintWriter out = response.getWriter();
    StringBuilder buffer = new StringBuilder();
    buffer.append("<html><body><table border=1 cellspacing=0 cellpadding=0>");
    buffer.append("<TR><TH>Table Name</TH></TR>");
    for (int i=0; i < tables.size(); i++) {
        buffer.append("<TR><TD>");
        buffer.append(tables.get(i));
        buffer.append("</TD></TR>");
    }
    buffer.append("</table></body></html>");
    out.println(buffer.toString());
}
private static void printXML(HttpServletResponse response,
                             List<String> tables)
    throws Exception  {
    response.setContentType("text/xml");
    PrintWriter out = response.getWriter();
    StringBuilder buffer = new StringBuilder();
    buffer.append("<?xml version=\"1.0\" encoding=\"ISO-8859-1\"?>");
    buffer.append("<tables>");
    for (int i=0; i < tables.size(); i++) {
        buffer.append("<name>");
        buffer.append(tables.get(i));
        buffer.append("</name>");
    }
    buffer.append("</tables>");
    out.println(buffer.toString());
}

private static void printError(HttpServletResponse response,
                               String message) {
    try {
        PrintWriter out = response.getWriter();
        StringBuffer buffer = new StringBuffer();
        buffer.append("<html><body>");
        buffer.append(message);
        buffer.append("</body></html>");
        out.println(buffer);
    }
    catch(Exception ignore) {
    }
}
```

```
/**
 * Get the Oracle table names for a given connection object.
 * If you use getTableNames() for an Oracle database, you
 * will get lots of auxiliary tables, which belong to the user,
 * but the user is not interested in seeing them.
 *
 * @param conn the Connection object
 * @return the list of table names as a List.
 * @exception Failed to get the table names from the database.
 */
public static List<String> getOracleTableNames(Connection conn)
    throws Exception {
    Statement stmt = null;
    ResultSet rs = null;
    try {
        stmt = conn.createStatement();
        rs = stmt.executeQuery(ORACLE_TABLES);
        if (rs == null) {
            return null;
        }

        List<String> list = new ArrayList<String>();
        while (rs.next()) {
            String tableName = DatabaseUtil.getTrimmedString(rs, 1);
            System.out.println("tableName="+tableName);
            if (tableName != null) {
                list.add(tableName);
            }
        }

        return list;
    }
    finally {
        DatabaseUtil.close(rs);
        DatabaseUtil.close(stmt);
    }
}


/**
 * Get the table names for a given connection object.
 * @param conn the Connection object
 * @return the list of table names as a List.
 * @exception Failed to get the table names from the database.
 */
```

```java
    public static List<String> getTableNames(Connection conn)
      throws Exception {
      ResultSet rs = null;
      try {
          DatabaseMetaData meta = conn.getMetaData();
          if (meta == null) {
              return null;
          }

          rs = meta.getTables(null, null, null, DB_TABLE_TYPES);
          if (rs == null) {
              return null;
          }

          List<String> list = new ArrayList<String>();
          System.out.println("getTableNames(): --------------");
          while (rs.next()) {
              String tableName =
                  DatabaseUtil.getTrimmedString(rs, COLUMN_NAME_TABLE_NAME);
              System.out.println("tableName="+tableName);
              if (tableName != null) {
                  list.add(tableName);
              }
          }
          System.out.println("--------------");
          return list;
      }
      finally {
          DatabaseUtil.close(rs);
      }
  }
}
```

Invoking GetTables for MySQL

Figure 8-10 shows how to run the solution for the MySQL database.

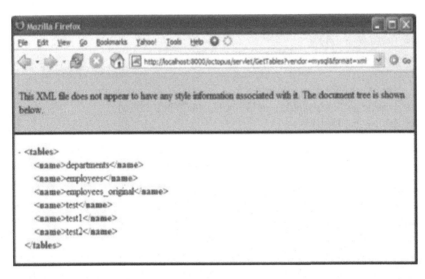

Figure 8-10. *Invoking GetTables for MySQL (XML output)*

Invoking GetTables for Oracle

Figure 8-11 shows how to run the solution for the Oracle database.

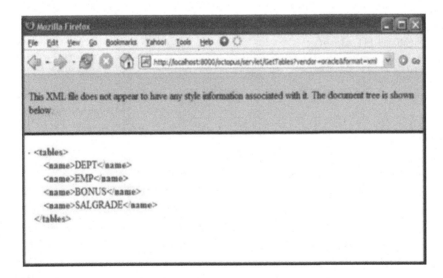

Figure 8-11. *Invoking GetTables for Oracle (XML output)*

Invoking GetTables to Handle Errors

Figure 8-12 shows how to run the solution for handling errors.

Figure 8-12. *Invoking GetTables to handle errors*

8.11. How Do You Get a List of View Names for a Database?

What is a view? According to Wikipedia, "In database theory, a view is a virtual or logical table composed of the result set of a pre-compiled query. Unlike ordinary tables in a relational database, a view is not part of the physical schema: it is a dynamic, virtual table computed or collated from data in the database. Changing the data in a view alters the data stored in the database."

Both MySQL (version 5+) and Oracle support the creation and use of database views.

Oracle Database Setup

```
SQL> desc employees;
 Name                                      Null?    Type
 ----------------------------------------- -------- -------------
 ID                                        NOT NULL VARCHAR2(10)
 NAME                                      NOT NULL VARCHAR2(20)
 AGE                                                NUMBER(38)
SQL> select * from employees;
ID         NAME                 AGE
---------- -------------------- ----------
11         Alex Smith            25
22         Don Knuth             65
33         Mary Kent             35
44         Monica Seles          30
99         Alex Edison           80
100        Al Sumner             70
105        Al Sumner             90

7 rows selected.
SQL> select object_name from user_objects where object_type ='VIEW';
no rows selected
SQL> create view emp55plus as
  2    select name, age from employees where age > 55;
View created.
```

```
SQL> desc emp55plus;
 Name                                      Null?    Type
 ---------------------------------------- -------- -------------
 NAME                                      NOT NULL VARCHAR2(20)
 AGE                                                NUMBER(38)
SQL> select * from emp55plus;
NAME                      AGE
-------------------- ----------
Don Knuth                  65
Alex Edison                80
Al Sumner                  70
Al Sumner                  90
SQL> create view empids as
  2  select id from employees;
View created.
SQL> desc empids;
 Name                                      Null?    Type
 ---------------------------------------- -------- -------------
 ID                                        NOT NULL VARCHAR2(10)
SQL> select * from empids;
ID
----------
100
105
11
22
33
44
99

7 rows selected.
SQL> select object_name from user_objects where object_type ='VIEW';
OBJECT_NAME
-----------------------------------------------------------------------
EMP55PLUS
EMPIDS
SQL>SQL> commit;
Commit complete.
```

MySQL Database Setup

```
mysql> use octopus;
Database changed
mysql> desc employees;
+-------+-------------+------+-----+---------+-------+
| Field | Type        | Null | Key | Default | Extra |
+-------+-------------+------+-----+---------+-------+
| id    | varchar(8)  | NO   | PRI |         |       |
| name  | varchar(16) | YES  |     | NULL    |       |
| age   | int(11)     | YES  |     | NULL    |       |
+-------+-------------+------+-----+---------+-------+
3 rows in set (0.00 sec)
mysql> select * from employees;
+-----+--------+------+
| id  | name   | age  |
+-----+--------+------+
| 88  | Peter  |   80 |
| 77  | Donald |   70 |
| 33  | Mary   |   30 |
| 44  | Monica |   40 |
| 999 | Andre  |   90 |
+-----+--------+------+
5 rows in set (0.00 sec)
mysql> create view emps55plus as select name, age from employees
    -> where age > 55;
Query OK, 0 rows affected (0.39 sec)
mysql> desc emps55plus;
+-------+-------------+------+-----+---------+-------+
| Field | Type        | Null | Key | Default | Extra |
+-------+-------------+------+-----+---------+-------+
| name  | varchar(16) | YES  |     | NULL    |       |
| age   | int(11)     | YES  |     | NULL    |       |
+-------+-------------+------+-----+---------+-------+
2 rows in set (0.02 sec)
mysql> select * from emps55plus;
+--------+------+
| name   | age  |
+--------+------+
| Peter  |   80 |
| Donald |   70 |
| Andre  |   90 |
+--------+------+
3 rows in set (0.00 sec)
```

The Solution

```java
import java.io.PrintWriter;
import java.io.IOException;

import java.sql.*;
import javax.servlet.*;
import javax.servlet.http.*;

import java.util.List;
import java.util.ArrayList;

import jcb.util.DatabaseUtil;
import jcb.db.VeryBasicConnectionManager;
import jcb.meta.DatabaseMetaDataTool;

public class GetViews extends HttpServlet {

    private static final String  ORACLE_VIEWS =
        "select object_name from user_objects where object_type = 'VIEW'";
    private static final String[] DB_VIEW_TYPES =
        { "VIEW" };
    private static final String COLUMN_NAME_VIEW_NAME =
        "TABLE_NAME";

    public void doGet(HttpServletRequest request,
                      HttpServletResponse response)
        throws ServletException, IOException {
        Connection conn = null;
        try {
            String dbVendor = request.getParameter("vendor").trim();
            String outputFormat = request.getParameter("format").trim();
            conn = VeryBasicConnectionManager.getConnection(dbVendor);
            List<String> views = null;

            if (dbVendor.equals("oracle")) {
                views = getOracleViewNames(conn);
            }
            else {
                views = getViewNames(conn);
            }

            if (views == null) {
                printError(response, "NO-VIEWS-FOUND");
                return;
            }
```

```java
            if (outputFormat.equals("xml")) {
                printXML(response, views);
            }
            else {
                printHTML(response, views);
            }
        }
        catch(Exception e) {
            printError(response, e.getMessage());
        }
        finally {
            DatabaseUtil.close(conn);
        }

    } // end doGet

    private static void printHTML(HttpServletResponse response,
                                  List<String> views)
        throws Exception  {
        response.setContentType("text/html");
        PrintWriter out = response.getWriter();
        StringBuilder buffer = new StringBuilder();
        buffer.append("<html><body><table border=1 cellspacing=0 cellpadding=0>");
        buffer.append("<TR><TH>View Name</TH></TR>");
        for (int i=0; i < views.size(); i++) {
            buffer.append("<TR><TD>");
            buffer.append(views.get(i));
            buffer.append("</TD></TR>");
        }
        buffer.append("</table></body></html>");
        out.println(buffer.toString());
    }
    private static void printXML(HttpServletResponse response,
                                 List<String> views)
        throws Exception  {
        response.setContentType("text/xml");
        PrintWriter out = response.getWriter();
        StringBuilder buffer = new StringBuilder();
        buffer.append("<?xml version=\"1.0\" encoding=\"ISO-8859-1\"?>");
        buffer.append("<views>");
        for (int i=0; i < views.size(); i++) {
            buffer.append("<name>");
            buffer.append(views.get(i));
            buffer.append("</name>");
        }
        buffer.append("</views>");
        out.println(buffer.toString());
    }
```

```java
    private static void printError(HttpServletResponse response,
                                   String message) {
        try {
            PrintWriter out = response.getWriter();
            StringBuffer buffer = new StringBuffer();
            buffer.append("<html><body>");
            buffer.append(message);
            buffer.append("</body></html>");
            out.println(buffer);
        }
        catch(Exception ignore) {
        }
    }


    /**
     * Get the Oracle table names for a given connection object.
     * If you use getViewNames() for an Oracle database, you
     * will get lots of auxiliary tables, which belong to the user,
     * but the user is not interested in seeing them.
     *
     * @param conn the Connection object
     * @return the list of table names as a List.
     * @exception Failed to get the table names from the database.
     */
    public static List<String> getOracleViewNames(Connection conn)
        throws Exception {
        Statement stmt = null;
        ResultSet rs = null;
        try {
            stmt = conn.createStatement();
            rs = stmt.executeQuery(ORACLE_VIEWS);
            if (rs == null) {
                return null;
            }

            List<String> list = new ArrayList<String>();
            while (rs.next()) {
                String viewName = DatabaseUtil.getTrimmedString(rs, 1);
                System.out.println("viewName="+viewName);
                if (viewName != null) {
                    list.add(viewName);
                }
            }
```

```java
                return list;
            }
            finally {
                DatabaseUtil.close(rs);
                DatabaseUtil.close(stmt);
            }
        }


    /**
     * Get the table names for a given connection object.
     * @param conn the Connection object
     * @return the list of table names as a List.
     * @exception Failed to get the table names from the database.
     */
    public static List<String> getViewNames(Connection conn)
        throws Exception {
        ResultSet rs = null;
        try {
            DatabaseMetaData meta = conn.getMetaData();
            if (meta == null) {
                return null;
            }

            rs = meta.getTables(null, null, null, DB_VIEW_TYPES);
            if (rs == null) {
                return null;
            }

            List<String> list = new ArrayList<String>();
            System.out.println("getViewNames(): --------------");
            while (rs.next()) {
                String viewName =
                    DatabaseUtil.getTrimmedString(rs, COLUMN_NAME_VIEW_NAME);
                System.out.println("viewName="+viewName);
                if (viewName != null) {
                    list.add(viewName);
                }
            }
            System.out.println("--------------");
            return list;
        }
        finally {
            DatabaseUtil.close(rs);
        }
    }
}
```

Invoking GetViews for MySQL

Figure 8-13 shows how to run the solution for the MySQL database.

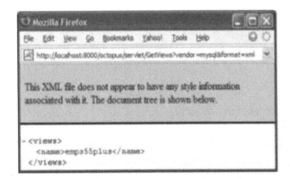

Figure 8-13. *Invoking GetViews for MySQL (XML output)*

Invoking GetViews for Oracle

Figure 8-14 shows how to run the solution for the Oracle database.

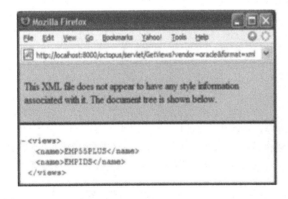

Figure 8-14. *Invoking GetViews for Oracle (XML output)*

8.12. How Do You Get a List of Tables and Views for a Database?

Each database has a finite set of tables, views, and other objects (such as indexes and stored procedures). JDBC enables you to get a list of combined tables and views for a specific database. You can use `DatabaseMetaData.getTables()` to retrieve a description of the tables and views available in the given catalog (database). Only table and view descriptions matching the catalog, schema, table/view name, and type criteria are returned. They are ordered by `TABLE_TYPE`, `TABLE_SCHEM`, and `TABLE_NAME`. The signature of `DatabaseMetaData.getTables()` is

```
ResultSet getTables(String catalog,
                    String schemaPattern,
                    String tableNamePattern,
                    String[] types)
                    throws SQLException
```

This method returns the result as a ResultSet object, which is not very useful for web-based applications. Therefore, we will convert the ResultSet object to HTML/XML, which can be quite useful to web-based applications. In invoking this method, you need to pass the correct information for the types parameter. To get both tables and views, you must pass {"TABLE", "VIEW"} for the types parameter.

Next I present a Java servlet (GetTablesAndViews), which will be able to get table/view names (plus other metadata information) as HTML or XML. Here is the signature of the servlet:

```
GetTablesAndViews?vendor=<vendor-name>&format=<HTML-or-XML>
```

You may add other parameters to suit your database application. Here, I use vendor to act as a database selector. So, to get the table information as XML for a MySQL database, you may invoke it as

```
GetTablesAndViews?vendor=mysql&format=xml
GetTablesAndViews?vendor=mysql&format=html
GetTablesAndViews?vendor=oracle&format=xml
GetTablesAndViews?vendor=oracle&format=html
```

MySQL Database Setup

```
mysql> use octopus;
Database changed
mysql> create table emps_table (
    ->     badge_number varchar(5) not null,
    ->     name varchar(20) not null,
    ->     email varchar(20) not null,
    ->     primary key (badge_number)
    -> );
Query OK, 0 rows affected (0.12 sec)
mysql> create table roles_table (
    ->     role varchar(5) not null,
    ->     description varchar(25) not null,
    ->     primary key (role)
    -> );
Query OK, 0 rows affected (0.07 sec)
mysql> create table emps_roles (
    ->   badge_number varchar(5) not null,
    ->   role varchar(5) not null,
    ->   PRIMARY KEY (badge_number, role)
    -> );
Query OK, 0 rows affected (0.06 sec)
```

```
mysql> show tables;
+-------------------+
| Tables_in_octopus |
+-------------------+
| emps_roles        |
| emps_table        |
| roles_table       |
+-------------------+
3 rows in set (0.00 sec)
mysql> create view admin_roles as select role, description
    ->    from roles_table where role like 'admin%';
Query OK, 0 rows affected (0.03 sec)
mysql> desc admin_roles;
+-------------+-------------+------+-----+---------+-------+
| Field       | Type        | Null | Key | Default | Extra |
+-------------+-------------+------+-----+---------+-------+
| role        | varchar(5)  | NO   |     |         |       |
| description | varchar(25) | NO   |     |         |       |
+-------------+-------------+------+-----+---------+-------+
2 rows in set (0.02 sec)
mysql> create view yahoo_emails as select * from emps_table
    ->    where email like '%@yahoo.com';
Query OK, 0 rows affected (0.01 sec)
mysql> desc yahoo_emails;
+--------------+-------------+------+-----+---------+-------+
| Field        | Type        | Null | Key | Default | Extra |
+--------------+-------------+------+-----+---------+-------+
| badge_number | varchar(5)  | NO   |     |         |       |
| name         | varchar(20) | NO   |     |         |       |
| email        | varchar(20) | NO   |     |         |       |
+--------------+-------------+------+-----+---------+-------+
3 rows in set (0.02 sec)
mysql> show tables;
+-------------------+
| Tables_in_octopus |
+-------------------+
| admin_roles       |
| emps_roles        |
| emps_table        |
| roles_table       |
| yahoo_emails      |
+-------------------+
5 rows in set (0.00 sec)
```

Oracle Database Setup

```
$ sqlplus.exe scott/tiger
SQL> create view my_view as select * from emp where empno > 1000;
View created.
SQL> desc my_view;
 Name                                      Null?    Type
 ----------------------------------------- -------- --------------
 EMPNO                                     NOT NULL NUMBER(4)
 ENAME                                              VARCHAR2(10)
 JOB                                                VARCHAR2(9)
 MGR                                                NUMBER(4)
 HIREDATE                                           DATE
 SAL                                                NUMBER(7,2)
 COMM                                               NUMBER(7,2)
 DEPTNO                                             NUMBER(2)
SQL> desc bonus;
 Name                                      Null?    Type
 ----------------------------------------- -------- --------------
 ENAME                                              VARCHAR2(10)
 JOB                                                VARCHAR2(9)
 SAL                                                NUMBER
 COMM                                               NUMBER
SQL> create view big_salary as select * from bonus where sal > 200000;
View created.
SQL> desc big_salary;
 Name                                      Null?    Type
 ----------------------------------------- -------- --------------
 ENAME                                              VARCHAR2(10)
 JOB                                                VARCHAR2(9)
 SAL                                                NUMBER
 COMM                                               NUMBER
SQL> select object_name, object_type from user_objects
where object_type = 'TABLE' or object_type = 'VIEW';
OBJECT_NAME OBJECT_TYPE
----------- -----------
DEPT        TABLE
EMP         TABLE
BONUS       TABLE
SALGRADE    TABLE
MYTABLE     TABLE
BIG_SALARY  VIEW
MY_VIEW     VIEW

7 rows selected.
```

The Solution

We treat MySQL and Oracle differently, because Oracle's driver returns extra tables for
DatabaseMetaData.getTables(). To eliminate this problem, for Oracle's tables and views,
I use the following SQL query:

```
select object_name, object_type
    from user_objects
        where object_type = 'TABLE' or object_type = 'VIEW'
```

Because of all these differences, I provide an additional method
(getOracleTableAndViewNames()) to handle Oracle's special case. This again proves that the database "vendor" factor is a crucial one for handling data and metadata for JDBC applications. Here
is a complete solution (the GetTablesAndViews servlet) for getting tables and views:

```java
import java.io.PrintWriter;
import java.io.IOException;

import java.sql.*;
import javax.servlet.*;
import javax.servlet.http.*;

import java.util.Map;
import java.util.Map.Entry;
import java.util.HashMap;

import jcb.util.DatabaseUtil;
import jcb.db.VeryBasicConnectionManager;

public class GetTablesAndViews extends HttpServlet {

    private static final String  ORACLE_TABLES_AND_VIEWS =
        "select object_name, object_type from user_objects "+
        "where object_type = 'TABLE' or object_type = 'VIEW'";
    private static final String[] DB_TABLE_AND_VIEW_TYPES =
        { "TABLE", "VIEW" };
    private static final String COLUMN_NAME_TABLE_NAME = "TABLE_NAME";
    private static final String COLUMN_NAME_TABLE_TYPE = "TABLE_TYPE";

    public void doGet(HttpServletRequest request,
                      HttpServletResponse response)
        throws ServletException, IOException {
        Connection conn = null;
        try {
            String dbVendor = request.getParameter("vendor").trim();
            String outputFormat = request.getParameter("format").trim();
            conn = VeryBasicConnectionManager.getConnection(dbVendor);
            Map<String, String> tablesAndViews = null;
```

```
        if (dbVendor.equals("oracle")) {
            tablesAndViews = getOracleTablesAndViews(conn);
        }
        else {
            tablesAndViews = getTablesAndViews(conn);
        }

        if (tablesAndViews == null) {
            printError(response, "NO-TABLES-OR-VIEWS-FOUND");
            return;
        }

        if (outputFormat.equals("xml")) {
            printXML(response, tablesAndViews);
        }
        else {
            printHTML(response, tablesAndViews);
        }
    }
    catch(Exception e) {
        printError(response, e.getMessage());
    }
    finally {
        DatabaseUtil.close(conn);
    }

} // end doGet

private static void printHTML(HttpServletResponse response,
                             Map<String, String> tablesAndViews)
    throws Exception  {
    response.setContentType("text/html");
    PrintWriter out = response.getWriter();
    StringBuilder buffer = new StringBuilder();
    buffer.append("<html><body><table border=1 cellspacing=0 cellpadding=0>");
    buffer.append("<TR><TH>Table/View Name</TH><TH>Type</TH></TR>");
    for (Map.Entry<String, String> e : tablesAndViews.entrySet()) {
        buffer.append("<TR><TD>");
        buffer.append(e.getKey());
        buffer.append("</TD><TD>");
        buffer.append(e.getValue());
        buffer.append("</TD></TR>");
    }
    buffer.append("</table></body></html>");
    out.println(buffer.toString());
}
```

```
private static void printXML(HttpServletResponse response,
                            Map<String, String> tablesAndViews)
    throws Exception  {
    response.setContentType("text/xml");
    PrintWriter out = response.getWriter();
    StringBuilder buffer = new StringBuilder();
    buffer.append("<?xml version=\"1.0\" encoding=\"ISO-8859-1\"?>");
    buffer.append("<tables_and_views>");
    for (Map.Entry<String, String> e : tablesAndViews.entrySet()) {
        buffer.append("<name type=\"");
        buffer.append(e.getValue());
        buffer.append("\">");
        buffer.append(e.getKey());
        buffer.append("</name>");
    }
    buffer.append("</tables_and_views>");
    out.println(buffer.toString());
}

private static void printError(HttpServletResponse response,
                              String message) {
    try {
        PrintWriter out = response.getWriter();
        StringBuffer buffer = new StringBuffer();
        buffer.append("<html><body>");
        buffer.append(message);
        buffer.append("</body></html>");
        out.println(buffer);
    }
    catch(Exception ignore) {
    }
}


/**
 * Get the Oracle table names for a given connection object.
 * If you use getTableNames() for an Oracle database, you
 * will get lots of auxiliary tables, which belong to the user,
 * but the user is not interested in seeing them.
 *
 * @param conn the Connection object
 * @return the list of table names as a List.
 * @exception Failed to get the table names from the database.
 */
```

```java
public static Map<String, String> getOracleTablesAndViews(Connection conn)
    throws Exception {
    Statement stmt = null;
    ResultSet rs = null;
    try {
        stmt = conn.createStatement();
        rs = stmt.executeQuery(ORACLE_TABLES_AND_VIEWS);
        if (rs == null) {
            return null;
        }

        Map<String, String> list = new HashMap<String, String>();
        while (rs.next()) {
            String name = DatabaseUtil.getTrimmedString(rs, 1);
            String type = DatabaseUtil.getTrimmedString(rs, 2);
            //System.out.println("name="+name);
            if (name != null) {
                list.put(name, type);
            }
        }

        return list;
    }
    finally {
        DatabaseUtil.close(rs);
        DatabaseUtil.close(stmt);
    }
}


/**
 * Get the table names for a given connection object.
 * @param conn the Connection object
 * @return the list of table names as a List.
 * @exception Failed to get the table names from the database.
 */
public static Map<String, String> getTablesAndViews(Connection conn)
    throws Exception {
    ResultSet rs = null;
    try {
        DatabaseMetaData meta = conn.getMetaData();
        if (meta == null) {
            return null;
        }
```

```
            rs = meta.getTables(null, null, null, DB_TABLE_AND_VIEW_TYPES);
            if (rs == null) {
                return null;
            }

            Map<String, String> list = new HashMap<String, String>();
            while (rs.next()) {
                String name =
                    DatabaseUtil.getTrimmedString(rs, COLUMN_NAME_TABLE_NAME);
                String type =
                    DatabaseUtil.getTrimmedString(rs, COLUMN_NAME_TABLE_TYPE);
                if (name != null) {
                    list.put(name, type);
                }
            }
            return list;
        }
        finally {
            DatabaseUtil.close(rs);
        }
    }
}
```

Invoking GetTablesAndViews for MySQL

Figure 8-15 shows how to run the solution for the MySQL database.

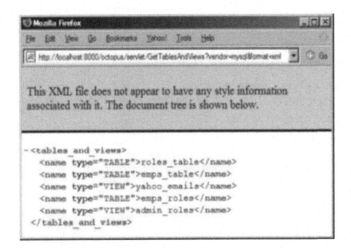

Figure 8-15. *Invoking GetTablesAndViews for MySQL (XML output)*

Invoking GetTablesAndViews for Oracle

Figure 8-16 shows how to run the solution for the Oracle database.

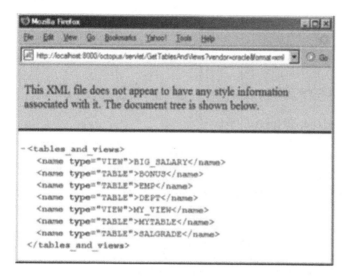

Figure 8-16. *Invoking GetTablesAndViews for Oracle (XML output)*

8.13. How Do You Get a List of SQL's Keywords?

Each database has a finite set of SQL keywords. JDBC enables you to get a list of these keywords for a specific database. You can use `DatabaseMetaData.getSQLKeywords()` to retrieve a set of SQL keywords.

Next I present a Java servlet (`GetSQLKeywords`), which will be able to get a list of SQL keywords as HTML or XML. Here is the signature of the servlet:

```
GetSQLKeywords?vendor=<vendor-name>&format=<HTML-or-XML>
```

You may add other parameters to suit your database application. Here, I use vendor to act as a database selector. So, to get the table information as XML for a MySQL database, you may invoke it as

```
GetSQLKeywords?vendor=mysql&format=xml
GetSQLKeywords?vendor=mysql&format=html
GetSQLKeywords?vendor=oracle&format=xml
GetSQLKeywords?vendor=oracle&format=html
```

The Solution

```
import java.sql.*;
import javax.servlet.*;
import javax.servlet.http.*;
```

```java
import java.util.List;
import java.util.ArrayList;
import java.util.StringTokenizer;

import java.io.PrintWriter;
import java.io.IOException;

import jcb.util.DatabaseUtil;
import jcb.db.VeryBasicConnectionManager;

public class GetSQLKeywords extends HttpServlet {

    public void doGet(HttpServletRequest request,
                      HttpServletResponse response)
        throws ServletException, IOException {
        Connection conn = null;
        try {
            String dbVendor = request.getParameter("vendor").trim();
            String outputFormat = request.getParameter("format").trim();
            conn = VeryBasicConnectionManager.getConnection(dbVendor);
            List<String> sqlKeywords = getSQLKeywords(conn);
            if (outputFormat.equals("xml")) {
                printXML(response, sqlKeywords);
            }
            else {
                printHTML(response, sqlKeywords);
            }
        }
        catch(Exception e) {
            printError(response, e.getMessage());
        }
        finally {
            DatabaseUtil.close(conn);
        }

    } // end doGet

    private static void printHTML(HttpServletResponse response,
                                  List<String> sqlKeywords)
        throws Exception  {
        response.setContentType("text/html");
        PrintWriter out = response.getWriter();
        StringBuilder buffer = new StringBuilder();
        buffer.append("<html><body><table border=1 cellspacing=0 cellpadding=0>");
        buffer.append("<TR><TH>SQL Keywords</TH></TR>");
```

```java
        for (int i=0; i < sqlKeywords.size(); i++) {
            buffer.append("<TR><TD>");
            buffer.append(sqlKeywords.get(i));
            buffer.append("</TD></TR>");
        }
        buffer.append("</table></body></html>");
        out.println(buffer.toString());
    }

    private static void printXML(HttpServletResponse response,
                                 List<String> sqlKeywords)
        throws Exception  {
        response.setContentType("text/xml");
        PrintWriter out = response.getWriter();
        StringBuilder buffer = new StringBuilder();
        buffer.append("<?xml version=\"1.0\" encoding=\"ISO-8859-1\"?>");
        buffer.append("<sqlKeywords>");
        for (int i=0; i < sqlKeywords.size(); i++) {
            buffer.append("<keyword>");
            buffer.append(sqlKeywords.get(i));
            buffer.append("</keyword>");
        }
        buffer.append("</sqlKeywords>");
        out.println(buffer.toString());
    }

    private static void printError(HttpServletResponse response,
                                   String message) {
        try {
            PrintWriter out = response.getWriter();
            StringBuffer buffer = new StringBuffer();
            buffer.append("<html><body>");
            buffer.append(message);
            buffer.append("</body></html>");
            out.println(buffer);
        }
        catch(Exception ignore) {
        }
    }

    /**
     * Get the table names for a given connection object.
     * @param conn the Connection object
     * @return the list of table names as a List.
     * @exception Failed to get the table names from the database.
     */
```

```
public static List<String> getSQLKeywords(Connection conn)
    throws Exception {
    DatabaseMetaData meta = conn.getMetaData();
    if (meta == null) {
        return null;
    }

    String sqlKeywords = meta.getSQLKeywords();
    if ((sqlKeywords == null) || (sqlKeywords.length() == 0)) {
        return null;
    }

    List<String> list = new ArrayList<String>();
    // SQL keywords are separated by ","
    StringTokenizer st = new StringTokenizer(sqlKeywords, ",");
    while(st.hasMoreTokens()) {
        list.add(st.nextToken().trim());
    }
    System.out.println("--------------");
    return list;
    }
}
```

Invoking GetSQLKeywords for MySQL

Figure 8-17 shows how to run the solution for the MySQL database.

Figure 8-17. *Invoking GetSQLKeywords for MySQL (XML output)*

Invoking GetTablesAndViews for Oracle

Figure 8-18 shows how to run the solution for the Oracle database.

Figure 8-18. *Invoking GetSQLKeywords for Oracle (XML output)*

8.14. How Do You Get a Table's Primary Key Columns?

The primary key (PK) of a relational table uniquely identifies each row or record in the table. The PK can be comprised of one or more non-null columns. For database applications (including web-based applications), you need to know the PK columns before inserting new records (to make sure that the PK columns cannot be NULL).

The DatabaseMetaData.getPrimaryKeys() method retrieves a table's PK columns and its signature is

```
ResultSet getPrimaryKeys(String catalog,
                         String schema,
                         String table)
                         throws SQLException
```

This method retrieves a description of the given table's primary key columns. The result is returned as a ResultSet object and they are ordered by COLUMN_NAME. If a database access error occurs, then this method throws SQLException.

Each primary key column description has the columns shown in Table 8-1.

Table 8-1. *Primary Key Columns*

Column Name	Column Type	Description
TABLE_CAT	String	Table catalog (may be null)
TABLE_SCHEM	String	Table schema (may be null)
TABLE_NAME	String	Table name
COLUMN_NAME	String	Column name
KEY_SEQ	short	Sequence number within primary key
PK_NAME	String	Primary key name (may be null)

Parameters

- catalog: A catalog name; it must match the catalog name as it is stored in the database. "" retrieves those without a catalog; null means that the catalog name should not be used to narrow the search.

- schema: A schema name; it must match the schema name as it is stored in the database. "" retrieves those without a schema; null means that the schema name should not be used to narrow the search.

- table: A table name; it must match the table name as it is stored in the database.

As you can observe, this method returns its result as a ResultSet object (each row is a primary key column description), which is not very useful for web-based applications.

Next I present a Java servlet (GetPKColumns), which will be able to get a table's primary key columns (along with other related metadata information) as HTML or XML. Here is the signature of the servlet:

```
GetPKColumns?vendor=<vendor-name>&table=<table-name>&format=<HTML-or-XML>
```

You may add other parameters to suit your database application. Here, I use vendor to act as a database selector. So, to get the employee table's primary key columns information as XML for a MySQL database, you may invoke it as

```
GetPKColumns?vendor=mysql&table=employees&format=xml
```

The other possibilities are

```
GetPKColumns?vendor=mysql&table=employees&format=html
GetPKColumns?vendor=oracle&table=employees&format=xml
GetPKColumns?vendor=oracle&table=employees&format=html
```

MySQL Database Setup

```
mysql> use octopus;
Database changed
mysql> create table mytable (
          id varchar(10) not null,
          name varchar(20) not null,
```

```
            age integer,
            primary key (id, name)
);
Query OK, 0 rows affected (0.08 sec)
mysql> desc mytable;
+-------+-------------+------+-----+---------+-------+
| Field | Type        | Null | Key | Default | Extra |
+-------+-------------+------+-----+---------+-------+
| id    | varchar(10) | NO   | PRI |         |       |
| name  | varchar(20) | NO   | PRI |         |       |
| age   | int(11)     | YES  |     | NULL    |       |
+-------+-------------+------+-----+---------+-------+
3 rows in set (0.03 sec)
```

Oracle Database Setup

```
SQL> create table mytable(
        id varchar2(10) not null,
        name varchar(20) not null,
        age number,
        primary key (id, name)
);
Table created.
SQL> desc mytable;
 Name                                     Null?    Type
 ---------------------------------------- -------- ------------
 ID                                       NOT NULL VARCHAR2(10)
 NAME                                     NOT NULL VARCHAR2(20)
 AGE                                               NUMBER
```

The Solution

```java
import java.sql.*;
import javax.servlet.*;
import javax.servlet.http.*;

import java.util.List;
import java.util.ArrayList;
import java.util.StringTokenizer;

import java.io.PrintWriter;
import java.io.IOException;

import jcb.util.DatabaseUtil;
import jcb.db.VeryBasicConnectionManager;

public class GetPKColumns extends HttpServlet {
```

```java
public void doGet(HttpServletRequest request,
                  HttpServletResponse response)
    throws ServletException, IOException {
    ResultSet primaryKeys = null;
    Connection conn = null;
    try {
        String dbVendor = request.getParameter("vendor").trim();
        String table = request.getParameter("table").trim();
        String outputFormat = request.getParameter("format").trim();
        conn = VeryBasicConnectionManager.getConnection(dbVendor);
        primaryKeys = getPrimaryKeys(conn, table);
        if (outputFormat.equals("xml")) {
            printXML(response, primaryKeys);
        }
        else {
            printHTML(response, primaryKeys);
        }
    }
    catch(Exception e) {
        printError(response, e.getMessage());
    }
    finally {
        DatabaseUtil.close(primaryKeys);
        DatabaseUtil.close(conn);
    }

} // end doGet

private static void printHTML(HttpServletResponse response,
                              ResultSet primaryKeys)
    throws Exception  {
    response.setContentType("text/html");
    PrintWriter out = response.getWriter();
    StringBuilder buffer = new StringBuilder();
    buffer.append("<html><body><table border=1 cellspacing=0 cellpadding=0>");
    buffer.append("<TR><TH>Catalog</TH>");
    buffer.append("<TH>Schema</TH>");
    buffer.append("<TH>Table Name</TH>");
    buffer.append("<TH>Column Name</TH>");
    buffer.append("<TH>Key Sequence</TH>");
    buffer.append("<TH>PK Name</TH></TR>");
    while (primaryKeys.next()) {
        buffer.append("<TR><TD>");
        buffer.append(primaryKeys.getString("TABLE_CAT"));
        buffer.append("</TD><TD>");
        buffer.append(primaryKeys.getString("TABLE_SCHEM"));
```

```
            buffer.append("</TD><TD>");
            buffer.append(primaryKeys.getString("TABLE_NAME"));
            buffer.append("</TD><TD>");
            buffer.append(primaryKeys.getString("COLUMN_NAME"));
            buffer.append("</TD><TD>");
            buffer.append(primaryKeys.getShort("KEY_SEQ"));
            buffer.append("</TD><TD>");
            buffer.append(primaryKeys.getString("PK_NAME"));
            buffer.append("</TD></TR>");
        }
        buffer.append("</table></body></html>");
        out.println(buffer.toString());
    }


    private static void printXML(HttpServletResponse response,
                                 ResultSet primaryKeys)
        throws Exception  {
        response.setContentType("text/xml");
        PrintWriter out = response.getWriter();
        StringBuilder buffer = new StringBuilder();
        buffer.append("<?xml version=\"1.0\" encoding=\"ISO-8859-1\"?>");
        buffer.append("<primaryKeys>");
        while (primaryKeys.next()) {
            buffer.append("<pkColumn><catalog>");
            buffer.append(primaryKeys.getString("TABLE_CAT"));
            buffer.append("</catalog><schema>");
            buffer.append(primaryKeys.getString("TABLE_SCHEM"));
            buffer.append("</schema><tableName>");
            buffer.append(primaryKeys.getString("TABLE_NAME"));
            buffer.append("</tableName><columnName>");
            buffer.append(primaryKeys.getString("COLUMN_NAME"));
            buffer.append("</columnName><keySEQ>");
            buffer.append(primaryKeys.getShort("KEY_SEQ"));
            buffer.append("</keySEQ><pkName>");
            buffer.append(primaryKeys.getString("PK_NAME"));
            buffer.append("</pkName></pkColumn>");
        }
        buffer.append("</primaryKeys>");
        out.println(buffer.toString());
    }


    private static void printError(HttpServletResponse response,
                                   String message) {
        try {
            PrintWriter out = response.getWriter();
            StringBuffer buffer = new StringBuffer();
```

```java
            buffer.append("<html><body>");
            buffer.append(message);
            buffer.append("</body></html>");
            out.println(buffer);
        }
        catch(Exception ignore) {
        }
    }



    /**
     * Retrieves a description of the given table's primary key columns.
     * @param conn the Connection object
     * @param tableName name of a table in the database.
     * @return the list of PK columns as a ResultSet object
     * @exception Failed to get the Primary Keys for a given table.
     */
    public static ResultSet getPrimaryKeys(Connection conn,
                                              String tableName)
        throws Exception {
        if ((tableName == null) || (tableName.length() == 0)) {
            return null;
        }

        DatabaseMetaData meta = conn.getMetaData();
        if (meta == null) {
            return null;
        }

        //
        // The Oracle database stores its table names as
        // uppercase; if you pass a table name in lowercase
        // characters, it will not work. MySQL database does
        // not care if the table name is uppercase/lowercase.
        //
        return meta.getPrimaryKeys(null, null, tableName.toUpperCase());
    }
}
```

Invoking GetPKColumns for MySQL

Figure 8-19 shows how to run the solution for the MySQL database.

Figure 8-19. *Invoking GetPKColumns for MySQL (XML output)*

Invoking GetPKColumns for Oracle

Figure 8-20 shows how to run the solution for the Oracle database.

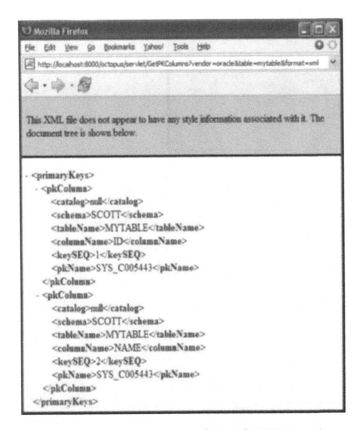

Figure 8-20. *Invoking GetPKColumns for Oracle (XML output)*

8.15. How Do You Get a Table's Columns?

A relational table has a finite set of columns (column names must be unique and each might have a different data type). In GUI database applications, in order to manipulate a relational table, you need to understand column names and types. Also, for a web-based application, you need to know the primary key (PK) columns before inserting new records (to make sure that the PK columns cannot be NULL).

The DatabaseMetaData.getColumns() method retrieves a description of table columns available in the specified catalog. The method's signature is

```
ResultSet getColumns(String catalog,
                     String schemaPattern,
                     String tableNamePattern,
                     String columnNamePattern)
                     throws SQLException
```

Only column descriptions matching the catalog, schema, table, and column name criteria are returned. They are ordered by TABLE_SCHEM, TABLE_NAME, and ORDINAL_POSITION.

Each column description has the columns shown in Table 8-2.

Table 8-2. *Column Descriptions*

Column Name	Column Type	Description
TABLE_CAT	String	Table catalog (may be null).
TABLE_SCHEM	String	Table schema (may be null).
TABLE_NAME	String	Table name.
COLUMN_NAME	String	Column name.
DATA_TYPE	int	SQL type from java.sql.Types.
TYPE_NAME	String	Data source–dependent type name; for a UDT, the type name is fully qualified.
COLUMN_SIZE	int	Column size. For char or date types, this is the maximum number of characters; for numeric or decimal types, this is precision.
BUFFER_LENGTH		Is not used.
DECIMAL_DIGITS	int	The number of fractional digits.
NUM_PREC_RADIX	int	Radix (typically either 10 or 2).
NULLABLE	int	Specifies whether NULL is allowed: columnNoNulls: Might not allow NULL values. columnNullable: Definitely allows NULL values. columnNullableUnknown: Nullability unknown.
REMARKS	String	Comment describing the column (may be null).
COLUMN_DEF	String	The default value (may be null).
SQL_DATA_TYPE	int	Unused.
SQL_DATETIME_SUB	int	Unused.
CHAR_OCTET_LENGTH	int	For char types, the maximum number of bytes in the column.
ORDINAL_POSITION	int	The index of columns in the table (starting at 1).
IS_NULLABLE	String	NO means the column definitely does not allow NULL values; YES means the column might allow NULL values. An empty string means nullability is unknown.
SCOPE_CATLOG	String	A catalog of the table that is the scope of a reference attribute (null if DATA_TYPE isn't REF).
SCOPE_SCHEMA	String	A schema of the table that is the scope of a reference attribute (null if the DATA_TYPE isn't REF).
SCOPE_TABLE	String	The name of the table that is the scope of a reference attribute (null if the DATA_TYPE isn't REF).
SOURCE_DATA_TYPE	short	The source type of a distinct type or user-generated Ref or SQL type from java.sql.Types (null if DATA_TYPE isn't DISTINCT or user-generated REF).

The parameters are

- catalog: A catalog name; it must match the catalog name as it is stored in the database. "" retrieves those without a catalog; null means that the catalog name should not be used to narrow the search.

- schemaPattern: A schema name pattern; it must match the schema name as it is stored in the database. "" retrieves those without a schema; null means that the schema name should not be used to narrow the search.

- tableNamePattern: A table name pattern; it must match the table name as it is stored in the database.

- columnNamePattern: A column name pattern; it must match the column name as it is stored in the database.

As you can see, this method returns its result as a ResultSet object (each row is a detailed column description), which is not very useful for web-based applications.

Next I present a Java servlet (GetColumns), which will be able to get a table's columns (as well as other related metadata information) as HTML or XML. Here is the signature of the servlet:

```
GetColumns?vendor=<vendor-name>&table=<table-name>&format=<HTML-or-XML>
```

You may add other parameters to suit your database application. Here, I use vendor to act as a database selector. So, to get the employee table's columns information as XML for a MySQL database, you may invoke it as

```
GetColumns?vendor=mysql&table=employees&format=xml
```

The other possibilities are

```
GetColumns?vendor=mysql&table=employees&format=html
GetColumns?vendor=oracle&table=employees&format=xml
GetColumns?vendor=oracle&table=employees&format=html
```

MySQL Database Setup

```
mysql> use octopus;
Database changed
mysql> create table mytable (
          id varchar(10) not null,
          name varchar(20) not null,
          age integer,
          primary key (id, name)
);
Query OK, 0 rows affected (0.08 sec)
```

```
mysql> desc mytable;
+-------+-------------+------+-----+---------+-------+
| Field | Type        | Null | Key | Default | Extra |
+-------+-------------+------+-----+---------+-------+
| id    | varchar(10) | NO   | PRI |         |       |
| name  | varchar(20) | NO   | PRI |         |       |
| age   | int(11)     | YES  |     | NULL    |       |
+-------+-------------+------+-----+---------+-------+
3 rows in set (0.03 sec)
```

Oracle Database Setup

```
SQL> create table mytable(
        id varchar2(10) not null,
        name varchar(20) not null,
        age number,
        primary key (id, name)
);
Table created.
SQL> desc mytable;
 Name                                      Null?    Type
 ----------------------------------------- -------- ------------
 ID                                        NOT NULL VARCHAR2(10)
 NAME                                      NOT NULL VARCHAR2(20)
 AGE                                                NUMBER
```

The Solution

```java
import java.sql.*;
import javax.servlet.*;
import javax.servlet.http.*;

import java.io.PrintWriter;
import java.io.IOException;

import jcb.util.DatabaseUtil;
import jcb.db.VeryBasicConnectionManager;

public class GetColumns extends HttpServlet {

    public void doGet(HttpServletRequest request,
                      HttpServletResponse response)
        throws ServletException, IOException {
        ResultSet columns = null;
        Connection conn = null;
```

```java
try {
    String dbVendor = request.getParameter("vendor").trim();
    String table = request.getParameter("table").trim();
    String outputFormat = request.getParameter("format").trim();
    conn = VeryBasicConnectionManager.getConnection(dbVendor);
    columns = getColumns(conn, table);
    if (outputFormat.equals("xml")) {
        printXML(response, columns);
    }
    else {
        printHTML(response, columns);
    }
}
catch(Exception e) {
    printError(response, e.getMessage());
}
finally {
    DatabaseUtil.close(columns);
    DatabaseUtil.close(conn);
}

} // end doGet

private static void printHTML(HttpServletResponse response,
                             ResultSet columns)
    throws Exception  {
    response.setContentType("text/html");
    PrintWriter out = response.getWriter();
    StringBuilder buffer = new StringBuilder();
    buffer.append("<html><body><table border=1 cellspacing=0 cellpadding=0>");
    buffer.append("<TR><TH>Catalog</TH>");
    buffer.append("<TH>Schema</TH>");
    buffer.append("<TH>Table Name</TH>");
    buffer.append("<TH>Column Name</TH>");
    buffer.append("<TH>Data Type</TH>");
    buffer.append("<TH>Type Name</TH>");
    buffer.append("<TH>Column Size</TH>");
    buffer.append("<TH>Is Nullable?</TH>");
    buffer.append("<TH>Is Nullable?</TH>");
    buffer.append("<TH>Ordinal Position</TH></TR>");
    while (columns.next()) {
        buffer.append("<TR><TD>");
        buffer.append(columns.getString("TABLE_CAT"));
        buffer.append("</TD><TD>");
        buffer.append(columns.getString("TABLE_SCHEM"));
        buffer.append("</TD><TD>");
        buffer.append(columns.getString("TABLE_NAME"));
```

```java
            buffer.append("</TD><TD>");
            buffer.append(columns.getString("COLUMN_NAME"));
            buffer.append("</TD><TD>");
            buffer.append(columns.getShort("DATA_TYPE"));
            buffer.append("</TD><TD>");
            buffer.append(columns.getString("TYPE_NAME"));
            buffer.append("</TD><TD>");
            buffer.append(columns.getString("COLUMN_SIZE"));
            buffer.append("</TD><TD>");
            int nullable = columns.getInt("NULLABLE");
            if (nullable == DatabaseMetaData.columnNullable) {
                buffer.append("true");
            }
            else if (nullable == DatabaseMetaData.columnNoNulls) {
                buffer.append("false");
            }
            else {
                buffer.append("unknown");
            }
            buffer.append("</TD><TD>");
            buffer.append(columns.getString("IS_NULLABLE"));
            buffer.append("</TD><TD>");
            buffer.append(columns.getString("ORDINAL_POSITION"));
            buffer.append("</TD></TR>");
        }
        buffer.append("</table></body></html>");
        out.println(buffer.toString());
    }

    private static void printXML(HttpServletResponse response,
                                 ResultSet columns)
        throws Exception  {
        response.setContentType("text/xml");
        PrintWriter out = response.getWriter();
        StringBuilder buffer = new StringBuilder();
        buffer.append("<?xml version=\"1.0\"?>");
        buffer.append("<columns>");
        while (columns.next()) {
            buffer.append("<column><catalog>");
            buffer.append(columns.getString("TABLE_CAT"));
            buffer.append("</catalog><schema>");
            buffer.append(columns.getString("TABLE_SCHEM"));
            buffer.append("</schema><tableName>");
            buffer.append(columns.getString("TABLE_NAME"));
            buffer.append("</tableName><columnName>");
            buffer.append(columns.getString("COLUMN_NAME"));
```

```java
        buffer.append("</columnName><dataType>");
        buffer.append(columns.getShort("DATA_TYPE"));
        buffer.append("</dataType><typeName>");
        buffer.append(columns.getString("TYPE_NAME"));
        buffer.append("</typeName><columnSize>");
        buffer.append(columns.getString("COLUMN_SIZE"));
        buffer.append("</columnSize><nullable>");
        int nullable = columns.getInt("NULLABLE");
        if (nullable == DatabaseMetaData.columnNullable) {
            buffer.append("true");
        }
        else if (nullable == DatabaseMetaData.columnNoNulls) {
            buffer.append("false");
        }
        else {
            buffer.append("unknown");
        }
        buffer.append("</nullable><isNullable>");
        buffer.append(columns.getString("IS_NULLABLE"));
        buffer.append("</isNullable><ordinalPosition>");
        buffer.append(columns.getString("ORDINAL_POSITION"));
        buffer.append("</ordinalPosition></column>");
    }
    buffer.append("</columns>");
    out.println(buffer.toString());
}

private static void printError(HttpServletResponse response,
                               String message) {
    try {
        PrintWriter out = response.getWriter();
        StringBuffer buffer = new StringBuffer();
        buffer.append("<html><body>");
        buffer.append(message);
        buffer.append("</body></html>");
        out.println(buffer);
    }
    catch(Exception ignore) {
    }
}
```

```java
/**
 * Retrieves a description of the given table's columns.
 * @param conn the Connection object
 * @param tableName name of a table in the database.
 * @return the list of columns as a ResultSet object
 * @exception Failed to get the table's columns.
 */
public static ResultSet getColumns(Connection conn,
                                   String tableName)
    throws Exception {
    if ((tableName == null) || (tableName.length() == 0)) {
        return null;
    }

    DatabaseMetaData meta = conn.getMetaData();
    if (meta == null) {
        return null;
    }

    //
    // The Oracle database stores its table names as
    // uppercase; if you pass a table name in lowercase
    // characters, it will not work. MySQL database does
    // not care if the table name is uppercase/lowercase.
    //
    return meta.getColumns(null, null, tableName.toUpperCase(), null);
}
}
```

Invoking GetColumns for MySQL

Figure 8-21 shows how to run the solution for the MySQL database.

Figure 8-21. *Invoking GetColumns for MySQL (XML output)*

Invoking GetColumns for Oracle

Figure 8-22 shows how to run the solution for the Oracle database.

Figure 8-22. *Invoking GetColumns for Oracle (XML output)*

8.16. How Do You Get a View's Columns?

To get a database view's columns, you can use the GetColumns servlet and, for the table parameter, pass the name of your desired database view name. Next, I'll show you how to the get the columns of views from MySQL and Oracle databases.

MySQL Database Setup

```
mysql> show tables;
+-------------------+
| Tables_in_octopus |
+-------------------+
| emps_roles        |
| emps_table        |
| roles_table       |
+-------------------+
3 rows in set (0.00 sec)
mysql> create view admin_roles as select role, description
    ->    from roles_table where role like 'admin%';
Query OK, 0 rows affected (0.03 sec)
mysql> desc admin_roles;
+-------------+-------------+------+-----+---------+-------+
| Field       | Type        | Null | Key | Default | Extra |
+-------------+-------------+------+-----+---------+-------+
| role        | varchar(5)  | NO   |     |         |       |
| description | varchar(25) | NO   |     |         |       |
+-------------+-------------+------+-----+---------+-------+
2 rows in set (0.02 sec)
```

Oracle Database Setup

```
SQL> desc dept;
 Name                                      Null?    Type
 ----------------------------------------- -------- ------------
 DEPTNO                                    NOT NULL NUMBER(2)
 DNAME                                              VARCHAR2(14)
 LOC                                                VARCHAR2(13)
SQL> select * from dept;
    DEPTNO DNAME          LOC
---------- -------------- -------------
        10 ACCOUNTING     NEW YORK
        20 RESEARCH       DALLAS
        30 SALES          CHICAGO
        40 OPERATIONS     BOSTON
SQL> create view deptPlus20 as select DEPTNO, DNAME from dept where DEPTNO > 20;
View created.
SQL> select * from deptPlus20;
    DEPTNO DNAME
---------- --------------
        30 SALES
        40 OPERATIONS
```

Invoking GetColumns for MySQL

Figure 8-23 shows how to run the solution for the MySQL database.

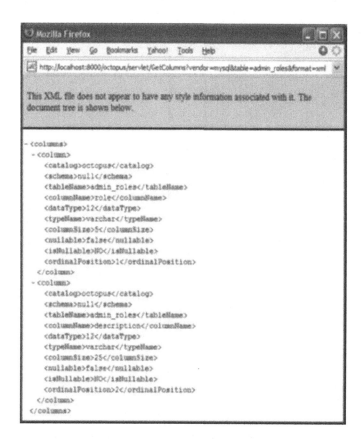

Figure 8-23. *Invoking GetColumns for MySQL (XML output)*

Invoking GetColumns for Oracle

Figure 8-24 shows how to run the solution for the Oracle database.

Figure 8-24. *Invoking GetColumns for Oracle (XML output)*

8.17. How Do You Get Stored Procedure Names?

According to JDBC tutorial (http://java.sun.com/docs/books/tutorial/jdbc):

> *A stored procedure is a group of SQL statements that form a logical unit and perform a particular task. Stored procedures are used to encapsulate a set of operations or queries to execute on a database server. For example, operations on an employee database (hire, fire, promote, lookup) could be coded as stored procedures executed by application code. Stored procedures can be compiled and executed with different parameters and results, and they may have any combination of input, output, and input/output parameters. Stored procedures are supported by most DBMSs, but there is a fair amount of variation in their syntax and capabilities.*

In order to execute a stored procedure, you need to know its name and its associated signature—the number of parameters, the type of each parameter, the mode of each parameter (IN, OUT, IN/OUT), and the result type.

Oracle Database Setup

```
SQL> select * from employees;
ID          NAME                 AGE
----------  -------------------- ----------
11          Alex Smith           25
22          Don Knuth            65
33          Mary Kent            35
44          Monica Seles         30
99          Alex Edison          80
100         Al Sumner            70
105         Al Sumner            90

7 rows selected.
SQL> CREATE OR REPLACE  FUNCTION getEmployeesCount RETURN INTEGER IS
  2       empCount INTEGER;
  3  BEGIN
  4       SELECT count(*) INTO empCount FROM employees;
  5       RETURN empCount;
  6  END getEmployeesCount;
  7  /
Function created.
SQL> var myCount number;
SQL> exec :myCount := getEmployeesCount;
PL/SQL procedure successfully completed.
SQL> print myCount;
   MYCOUNT
----------
        7
SQL> create procedure raiseAge(id_Param number, increment_Param number) is
  2     cursor empCursor (myid number) is
  3             select id from EMPLOYEES where id = myid
  4                     for update of age;
  5
  6     emp_id number(8);
  7  begin
  8     open empCursor(id_Param);
  9     loop
 10             fetch empCursor into emp_id;
 11             exit when empCursor%NOTFOUND;
 12             update EMPLOYEES set age = age + increment_Param
 13                     where current of empCursor;
 14     end loop;
```

```
15      close empCursor;
16      commit;
17   end raiseAge;
18   /
Procedure created.
SQL> describe raiseAge;
PROCEDURE raiseAge
 Argument Name                     Type                      In/Out Default?
 ----------------------------- ----------------------- ------ --------
 ID_PARAM                          NUMBER                    IN
 INCREMENT_PARAM                   NUMBER                    IN
SQL> select * from employees where id =11;
ID         NAME                    AGE
---------- -------------------- ----------
11         Alex Smith               25
SQL> execute raiseAge(11, 3);
PL/SQL procedure successfully completed.
SQL> select * from employees where id =11;
ID         NAME                    AGE
---------- -------------------- ----------
11         Alex Smith               28
SQL> commit;
SQL> select * from employees where id =44;
ID         NAME                    AGE
---------- -------------------- ----------
44         Monica Seles             30
SQL> execute raiseAge(44, 7);
PL/SQL procedure successfully completed.
SQL> select * from employees where id =44;
ID         NAME                    AGE
---------- -------------------- ----------
44         Monica Seles             37
```

MySQL Database Setup

```
$ mysql -u root -proot
Welcome to the MySQL monitor.  Commands end with ; or \g.
Your MySQL connection id is 4 to server version: 5.0.12-beta-nt
mysql> use octopus;
Database changed
mysql> delimiter //
mysql> CREATE PROCEDURE simpleproc (OUT param1 INT)
    -> BEGIN
    ->   SELECT COUNT(*) INTO param1 FROM employees;
    -> END
    -> //
```

```
Query OK, 0 rows affected (0.38 sec)
mysql> select * from employees;
+-----+--------+------+
| id  | name   | age  |
+-----+--------+------+
| 88  | Peter  |  80  |
| 77  | Donald |  70  |
| 33  | Mary   |  30  |
| 44  | Monica |  40  |
| 999 | Andre  |  90  |
+-----+--------+------+
5 rows in set (0.00 sec)
mysql> select count(*) from employees;
+----------+
| count(*) |
+----------+
|        5 |
+----------+
1 row in set (0.00 sec)
mysql> CALL simpleproc(@a);
Query OK, 0 rows affected (0.40 sec)
mysql> SELECT @a;
+------+
| @a   |
+------+
| 5    |
+------+
1 row in set (0.00 sec)
mysql> show create procedure simpleproc;
+------------+----------+------------------------------------------------------------------+
| Procedure  | sql_mode | Create Procedure                                                 |
+------------+----------+------------------------------------------------------------------+
| simpleproc |          | CREATE PROCEDURE `octopus`.`simpleproc`(OUT param1 INT)           |
|            |          | BEGIN                                                            |
|            |          |     SELECT COUNT(*) INTO param1 FROM employees;                  |
|            |          | END                                                              |
+------------+----------+------------------------------------------------------------------+
1 row in set (0.00 sec)
mysql> delimiter //
mysql> CREATE PROCEDURE createEmp (IN idParam INTEGER, IN ageParam INTEGER)
    -> BEGIN
    ->    DECLARE variable1 CHAR(10);
    ->    IF idParam > 50 THEN
    ->        SET variable1 = 'duck';
    ->     ELSE
    ->        SET variable1 = 'dragon';
    ->    END IF;
```

```
    ->      INSERT INTO employees(id, name, age)
    ->          VALUES (idParam, variable1, ageParam);
    -> END
    -> //
Query OK, 0 rows affected (0.01 sec)
mysql> delimiter ;
mysql> show create procedure createEmp;
+-----------+----------+-----------------------------------------------------+
| Procedure | sql_mode | Create Procedure                                    |
+-----------+----------+-----------------------------------------------------+
| createEmp |          | CREATE PROCEDURE `octopus`.`createEmp`               |
|           |          |         (IN idParam INTEGER,                         |
|           |          |          IN ageParam INTEGER)                        |
|           |          | BEGIN                                                |
|           |          |   DECLARE variable1 CHAR(10);                        |
|           |          |     IF idParam > 50 THEN                             |
|           |          |       SET variable1 = 'duck';                        |
|           |          |     ELSE                                             |
|           |          |       SET variable1 = 'dragon';                      |
|           |          |     END IF;                                           |
|           |          |     INSERT INTO employees(id, name, age)             |
|           |          |         VALUES (idParam, variable1, ageParam);       |
|           |          | END                                                  |
+-----------+----------+-----------------------------------------------------+
1 row in set (0.00 sec)
mysql> CALL createEmp(51, 72);
Query OK, 1 row affected (0.01 sec)
mysql> select * from employees;
+-----+--------+------+
| id  | name   | age  |
+-----+--------+------+
| 88  | Peter  |   80 |
| 77  | Donald |   70 |
| 33  | Mary   |   30 |
| 44  | Monica |   40 |
| 999 | Andre  |   90 |
| 51  | duck   |   72 |
+-----+--------+------+
6 rows in set (0.00 sec)
mysql> CALL createEmp(41, 20);
Query OK, 1 row affected (0.00 sec)
```

```
mysql> select * from employees;
+-----+--------+------+
| id  | name   | age  |
+-----+--------+------+
| 88  | Peter  |  80  |
| 77  | Donald |  70  |
| 33  | Mary   |  30  |
| 44  | Monica |  40  |
| 999 | Andre  |  90  |
| 51  | duck   |  72  |
| 41  | dragon |  20  |
+-----+--------+------+
7 rows in set (0.00 sec)
```

The Solution

```java
import java.io.PrintWriter;
import java.io.IOException;

import java.sql.*;
import javax.servlet.*;
import javax.servlet.http.*;

import jcb.util.DatabaseUtil;
import jcb.db.VeryBasicConnectionManager;

public class GetStoredProcedures extends HttpServlet {

    private static final String  STORED_PROCEDURE_RETURNS_RESULT =
        "procedureReturnsResult";
    private static final String  STORED_PROCEDURE_NO_RESULT =
        "procedureNoResult";
    private static final String  STORED_PROCEDURE_RESULT_UNKNOWN =
        "procedureResultUnknown";

    public void doGet(HttpServletRequest request,
                      HttpServletResponse response)
        throws ServletException, IOException {
        Connection conn = null;
        ResultSet storedProcedures = null;
        try {
            String dbVendor = request.getParameter("vendor").trim();
            String outputFormat = request.getParameter("format").trim();
            conn = VeryBasicConnectionManager.getConnection(dbVendor);
```

```java
        if (dbVendor.equals("mysql")) {
            String catalog = request.getParameter("catalog").trim();
            storedProcedures = getStoredProcedures(conn,
                                              catalog, // catalog,
                                              "%",     // schema Pattern,
                                              "%");    // proc. Pattern
        }
        else if (dbVendor.equals("oracle")) {
            String schema = request.getParameter("schema").trim();
            storedProcedures = getStoredProcedures(conn,
                                              null,   // catalog
                                              schema, // schema Pattern,
                                              "%");   // proc. Pattern
        }
        else {
            printError(response, "unknown db vendor");
            return;
        }

        if (outputFormat.equals("xml")) {
            printXML(response, storedProcedures);
        }
        else {
            printHTML(response, storedProcedures);
        }

    }
    catch(Exception e) {
        printError(response, e.getMessage());
    }
    finally {
        DatabaseUtil.close(storedProcedures);
        DatabaseUtil.close(conn);
    }

} // end doGet

private static void printHTML(HttpServletResponse response,
                              ResultSet storedProcedures)
    throws Exception  {
    response.setContentType("text/html");
    PrintWriter out = response.getWriter();
    StringBuilder buffer = new StringBuilder();
    buffer.append("<html><body><table border=1 cellspacing=0 cellpadding=0>");
    buffer.append("<TR><TH>Procedure Name</TH>");
    buffer.append("<TH>Procedure Type</TH></TR>");
```

```java
        while (storedProcedures.next()) {
            buffer.append("<TR><TD>");
            buffer.append(storedProcedures.getString("PROCEDURE_NAME"));
            buffer.append("</TD><TD>");
            int type = storedProcedures.getInt("PROCEDURE_TYPE");
            buffer.append(getStoredProcedureType(type));
            buffer.append("</TD><TR>");
        }
        buffer.append("</table></body></html>");
        out.println(buffer.toString());
    }

    private static void printXML(HttpServletResponse response,
                                 ResultSet storedProcedures)
        throws Exception  {
        response.setContentType("text/xml");
        PrintWriter out = response.getWriter();
        StringBuilder buffer = new StringBuilder();
        buffer.append("<?xml version=\"1.0\" encoding=\"UTF-8\"?>");
        buffer.append("<storedProcedures>");
        while (storedProcedures.next()) {
            buffer.append("<procedure name=\"");
            buffer.append(storedProcedures.getString("PROCEDURE_NAME"));
            buffer.append("\" type=\"");
            int type = storedProcedures.getInt("PROCEDURE_TYPE");
            buffer.append(getStoredProcedureType(type));
            buffer.append("\"/>");
        }
        buffer.append("</storedProcedures>");
        out.println(buffer.toString());
    }

    private static void printError(HttpServletResponse response,
                                   String message) {
        try {
            PrintWriter out = response.getWriter();
            StringBuilder buffer = new StringBuilder();
            buffer.append("<html><body>");
            buffer.append(message);
            buffer.append("</body></html>");
            out.println(buffer.toString());
        }
        catch(Exception ignore) {
        }
    }
```

```java
/**
 * Get the stored-procedures names.
 * @param conn the Connection object
 * @catalog database catalog name
 * @schemaPattern database schema pattern
 * @procedureNamePattern database procedure name pattern
 * @return a table of stored procedures names
 * as a ResultSet object.
 * Each element of XML document will have the name and
 * type of a stored procedure.
 *
 */
public static ResultSet getStoredProcedures
    (java.sql.Connection conn,
     String catalog,
     String schemaPattern,
     String procedureNamePattern)
    throws Exception {

    DatabaseMetaData meta = conn.getMetaData();
    if (meta == null) {
        return null;
    }

    return meta.getProcedures(catalog,
                              schemaPattern,
                              procedureNamePattern);
}

private static String getStoredProcedureType(int spType) {
    if (spType == DatabaseMetaData.procedureReturnsResult) {
        return STORED_PROCEDURE_RETURNS_RESULT;
    }
    else if (spType == DatabaseMetaData.procedureNoResult) {
        return STORED_PROCEDURE_NO_RESULT;
    }
    else {
        return STORED_PROCEDURE_RESULT_UNKNOWN;
    }
}
}
```

Invoking GetStoredProcedures for MySQL

Figure 8-25 shows how to run the solution for the MySQL database.

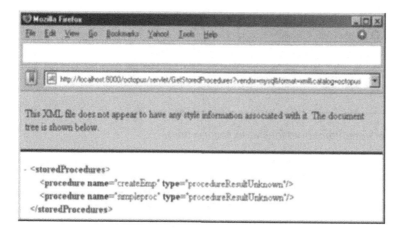

Figure 8-25. *Invoking GetStoredProcedures for MySQL (XML output)*

Invoking GetStoredProcedures for Oracle

Figure 8-26 shows how to run the solution for the Oracle database.

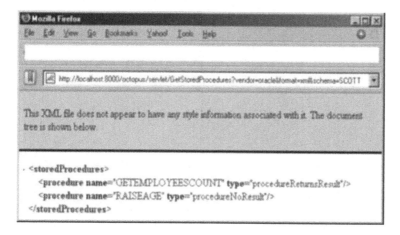

Figure 8-26. *Invoking GetStoredProcedures for Oracle (XML output)*

Invoking GetStoredProcedures for Unknown Vendor

Figure 8-27 shows how to run the solution for an unknown database vendor.

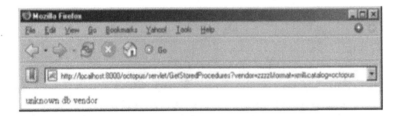

Figure 8-27. *Invoking GetStoredProcedures for an unknown vendor*

CHAPTER 9

Web Access to Metadata, Part 2

I have a dream that one day this nation will rise up, live out the true meaning of its creed—we hold these truths to be self-evident, that all men are created equal.

Martin Luther King Jr.

This chapter continues our discussion from Chapter 8, focusing on web access to metadata for stored procedures, RowSet objects, tables, and column privileges.

For presenting web access to database metadata, I will be using Apache's Tomcat servlet container (http://tomcat.apache.org/). Apache Tomcat is the servlet container that is used in the official reference implementation for the Java Servlet and JavaServer Pages technologies. For demonstration purposes, I will put all Java servlets (.class files) under the following directory:

```
<tomcat-installed-directory>/webapps/octopus/WEB-INF/classes/
```

All Java servlets in this chapter will be able to emit their output as XML or HTML. To save space, I will show the output as XML only (you may try the HTML output by setting format=html in your servlet calls).

9.1. How Do You Get the Signature of a Stored Procedure?

To invoke a stored procedure or function from a web-based application, you need to know the details of all of the parameters and result types for your stored procedures or functions. To get a signature of a stored procedure or function, you can use the DatabaseMetaData. getProcedureColumns() method, which retrieves a description of the given catalog's stored procedure parameter and result columns. The getProcedureColumns() method signature is as follows:

```
ResultSet getProcedureColumns(String catalog,
                              String schemaPattern,
                              String procedureNamePattern,
                              String columnNamePattern)
                              throws SQLException
```

When using this method, you have to be very careful to pass the right parameters. For example, the Oracle JDBC driver does not care about the catalog parameter at all and ignores it completely. On the other hand, the MySQL JDBC driver ignores the schema pattern (the schemaPattern parameter).

Only descriptions matching the schema, procedure, and parameter name criteria are returned. They are ordered by PROCEDURE_SCHEM and PROCEDURE_NAME. Within this, the return value, if any, is first. Next are the parameter descriptions in call order. The column descriptions follow in column number order. Each row in the ResultSet is a parameter description or column description with the fields shown in Table 9-1.

Table 9-1. *ResultSet Columns for getProcedureColumns()*

Name	Type	Description
PROCEDURE_CAT	String	Procedure catalog (may be null)
PROCEDURE_SCHEM	String	Procedure schema (may be null)
PROCEDURE_NAME	String	Procedure name
COLUMN_NAME	String	Column/parameter name
COLUMN_TYPE	Short	Kind of column/parameter: procedureColumnUnknown: Unknown procedureColumnIn: IN parameter procedureColumnInOut: INOUT parameter procedureColumnOut: OUT parameter procedureColumnReturn: Procedure return value procedureColumnResult: Result column in ResultSet
DATA_TYPE	int	SQL type from java.sql.Types
TYPE_NAME	String	SQL type name; for a UDT type the type name is fully qualified
PRECISION	int	Precision
LENGTH	int	Length in bytes of data
SCALE	short	Scale
RADIX	short	Radix
NULLABLE	short	Specifies whether it can contain NULL: procedureNoNulls: Does not allow NULL values procedureNullable: Allows NULL values procedureNullableUnknown: Nullability unknown
REMARKS	String	Comment describing the parameter or column

Note Some databases may not return the column descriptions for a procedure. Additional columns beyond REMARKS can be defined by the database.

The parameters are as follows:

- catalog: A catalog name; must match the catalog name as it is stored in the database. "" retrieves those without a catalog; null means that the catalog name should not be used to narrow the search.

- schemaPattern: A schema name pattern; must match the schema name as it is stored in the database. "" retrieves those without a schema; null means that the schema name should not be used to narrow the search.

- procedureNamePattern: A procedure name pattern; must match the procedure name as it is stored in the database.

- columnNamePattern: A column name pattern; must match the column name as it is stored in the database.

Oracle Database Setup

```
SQL> create procedure raiseAge(id_Param number, increment_Param number) is
  2      cursor empCursor (myid number) is
  3              select id from EMPLOYEES where id = myid
  4                      for update of age;
  5
  6      emp_id number(8);
  7  begin
  8      open empCursor(id_Param);
  9      loop
 10              fetch empCursor into emp_id;
 11              exit when empCursor%NOTFOUND;
 12              update EMPLOYEES set age = age + increment_Param
 13                      where current of empCursor;
 14      end loop;
 15      close empCursor;
 16      commit;
 17  end raiseAge;
 18  /
Procedure created.
SQL> describe raiseAge;
PROCEDURE raiseAge
 Argument Name                   Type                    In/Out Default?
 ------------------------------- ----------------------- ------ --------
 ID_PARAM                        NUMBER                  IN
 INCREMENT_PARAM                 NUMBER                  IN
SQL> select * from employees where id =11;
ID         NAME                 AGE
---------- -------------------- ----------
11         Alex Smith                   25
SQL> execute raiseAge(11, 3);
PL/SQL procedure successfully completed.
SQL> select * from employees where id =11;
ID         NAME                 AGE
---------- -------------------- ----------
11         Alex Smith                   28
SQL> commit;
Commit complete.
```

```
SQL> select * from employees where id =44;
ID         NAME                  AGE
---------- --------------------- ----------
44         Monica Seles          30
SQL> execute raiseAge(44, 7);
PL/SQL procedure successfully completed.
SQL> select * from employees where id =44;
ID         NAME                  AGE
---------- --------------------- ----------
44         Monica Seles          37
SQL>
```

MySQL Database Setup

```
mysql> delimiter //
mysql> CREATE PROCEDURE createEmp (IN idParam INTEGER, IN ageParam INTEGER)
    -> BEGIN
    ->    DECLARE variable1 CHAR(10);
    ->    IF idParam > 50 THEN
    ->        SET variable1 = 'duck';
    ->     ELSE
    ->        SET variable1 = 'dragon';
    ->    END IF;
    ->    INSERT INTO employees(id, name, age)
    ->        VALUES (idParam, variable1, ageParam);
    -> END
    -> //
Query OK, 0 rows affected (0.01 sec)
mysql> delimiter ;
mysql> show create procedure createEmp;
+-----------+----------+----------------------------------------------------+
| Procedure | sql_mode | Create Procedure                                   |
+-----------+----------+----------------------------------------------------+
| createEmp |          | CREATE PROCEDURE `octopus`.`createEmp`             |
|           |          |         (IN idParam INTEGER,                       |
|           |          |          IN ageParam INTEGER)                      |
|           |          | BEGIN                                              |
|           |          |   DECLARE variable1 CHAR(10);                      |
|           |          |      IF idParam > 50 THEN                          |
|           |          |          SET variable1 = 'duck';                   |
|           |          |       ELSE                                         |
|           |          |          SET variable1 = 'dragon';                 |
|           |          |      END IF;                                       |
|           |          |      INSERT INTO employees(id, name, age)          |
|           |          |          VALUES (idParam, variable1, ageParam);    |
|           |          |   END                                              |
+-----------+----------+----------------------------------------------------+
1 row in set (0.00 sec)
```

```
mysql> CALL createEmp(51, 72);
Query OK, 1 row affected (0.01 sec)
mysql> select * from employees;
+-----+--------+------+
| id  | name   | age  |
+-----+--------+------+
| 88  | Peter  |  80  |
| 77  | Donald |  70  |
| 33  | Mary   |  30  |
| 44  | Monica |  40  |
| 999 | Andre  |  90  |
| 51  | duck   |  72  |
+-----+--------+------+
6 rows in set (0.00 sec)
mysql> CALL createEmp(41, 20);
Query OK, 1 row affected (0.00 sec)
mysql> select * from employees;
+-----+--------+------+
| id  | name   | age  |
+-----+--------+------+
| 88  | Peter  |  80  |
| 77  | Donald |  70  |
| 33  | Mary   |  30  |
| 44  | Monica |  40  |
| 999 | Andre  |  90  |
| 51  | duck   |  72  |
| 41  | dragon |  20  |
+-----+--------+------+
7 rows in set (0.00 sec)
```

The Solution

```java
import java.sql.*;
import javax.servlet.*;
import javax.servlet.http.*;

import java.io.PrintWriter;
import java.io.IOException;

import java.sql.*;
import javax.servlet.*;
import javax.servlet.http.*;

import jcb.util.DatabaseUtil;
import jcb.db.VeryBasicConnectionManager;

public class GetSPColumns extends HttpServlet {
```

```java
private static final String  STORED_PROCEDURE_RETURNS_RESULT =
    "procedureReturnsResult";
private static final String  STORED_PROCEDURE_NO_RESULT =
    "procedureNoResult";
private static final String  STORED_PROCEDURE_RESULT_UNKNOWN =
    "procedureResultUnknown";

public void doGet(HttpServletRequest request,
                  HttpServletResponse response)
    throws ServletException, IOException {
    Connection conn = null;
    ResultSet storedProcedureColumns = null;
    try {
        String dbVendor = request.getParameter("vendor").trim();
        String outputFormat = request.getParameter("format").trim();
        String procedure = request.getParameter("procedure").trim();
        conn = VeryBasicConnectionManager.getConnection(dbVendor);
        if (dbVendor.equals("mysql")) {
            String catalog = request.getParameter("catalog").trim();
            storedProcedureColumns =
                getStoredProcedureColumns(conn,
                                          catalog, // catalog,
                                          "%",     // schema Pattern,
                                          "%");    // proc. Pattern
        }
        else if (dbVendor.equals("oracle")) {
            String schema = request.getParameter("schema").trim();
            storedProcedureColumns =
                getStoredProcedureColumns(conn,
                                          null,   // catalog
                                          schema, // schema Pattern,
                        "%"+procedure+"%");     // proc. Pattern
        }
        else {
            printError(response, "unknown db vendor");
            return;
        }

        if (outputFormat.equals("xml")) {
            printXML(response, storedProcedureColumns);
        }
        else {
            printHTML(response, storedProcedureColumns);
        }
```

```
        }
        catch(Exception e) {
            printError(response, e.getMessage());
        }
        finally {
            DatabaseUtil.close(storedProcedureColumns);
            DatabaseUtil.close(conn);
        }

    } // end doGet

    private static void printHTML(HttpServletResponse response,
                                 ResultSet spColumns)
        throws Exception  {
        response.setContentType("text/html");
        PrintWriter out = response.getWriter();
        StringBuilder buffer = new StringBuilder();
        buffer.append("<html><body><table border=1 cellspacing=0 cellpadding=0>");
        buffer.append("<TR><TH>Catalog</TH>");
        buffer.append("<TH>Schema</TH>");
        buffer.append("<TH>Procedure Name</TH>");
        buffer.append("<TH>Column Name</TH>");
        buffer.append("<TH>Column Type</TH>");
        buffer.append("<TH>Data Type</TH>");
        buffer.append("<TH>Type Name</TH>");
        buffer.append("<TH>Nullable</TH></TR>");
        while (spColumns.next()) {
            buffer.append("<TR><TD>");
            buffer.append(spColumns.getString("PROCEDURE_CAT"));
            buffer.append("</TD><TD>");
            buffer.append(spColumns.getString("PROCEDURE_SCHEM"));
            buffer.append("</TD><TD>");
            buffer.append(spColumns.getString("PROCEDURE_NAME"));
            buffer.append("</TD><TD>");
            buffer.append(spColumns.getString("COLUMN_NAME"));
            buffer.append("</TD><TD>");
            short columnType = spColumns.getShort("COLUMN_TYPE");
            buffer.append(getColumnType(columnType));
            buffer.append("</TD><TD>");
            buffer.append(spColumns.getString("DATA_TYPE"));
            buffer.append("</TD><TD>");
            buffer.append(spColumns.getString("TYPE_NAME"));
            buffer.append("</TD><TD>");
            buffer.append(spColumns.getShort("NULLABLE"));
            buffer.append("</TD><TR>");
        }
```

```java
        buffer.append("</table></body></html>");
        out.println(buffer.toString());
    }


    private static void printXML(HttpServletResponse response,
                                 ResultSet spColumns)
        throws Exception  {
        response.setContentType("text/xml");
        PrintWriter out = response.getWriter();
        StringBuilder buffer = new StringBuilder();
        buffer.append("<?xml version=\"1.0\" encoding=\"UTF-8\"?>");
        buffer.append("<storedProcedureColumns>");
        while (spColumns.next()) {
            buffer.append("<column><catalog>");
            buffer.append(spColumns.getString("PROCEDURE_CAT"));
            buffer.append("</catalog><schema>");
            buffer.append(spColumns.getString("PROCEDURE_SCHEM"));
            buffer.append("</schema><procedureName>");
            buffer.append(spColumns.getString("PROCEDURE_NAME"));
            buffer.append("</procedureName><columnName>");
            buffer.append(spColumns.getString("COLUMN_NAME"));
            buffer.append("</columnName><columnType>");
            short columnType = spColumns.getShort("COLUMN_TYPE");
            buffer.append(getColumnType(columnType));
            buffer.append("</columnType><dataType>");
            buffer.append(spColumns.getString("COLUMN_NAME"));
            buffer.append("</dataType><typeName>");
            buffer.append(spColumns.getString("TYPE_NAME"));
            buffer.append("</typeName><nullable>");
            buffer.append(spColumns.getShort("NULLABLE"));
            buffer.append("</nullable></column>");
        }
        buffer.append("</storedProcedureColumns>");
        out.println(buffer.toString());
    }


    private static void printError(HttpServletResponse response,
                                   String message) {
        try {
            PrintWriter out = response.getWriter();
            StringBuilder buffer = new StringBuilder();
            buffer.append("<html><body>");
            buffer.append(message);
            buffer.append("</body></html>");
            out.println(buffer.toString());
        }
```

```java
        catch(Exception ignore) {
        }
}

/**
 * Get the stored-procedures names.
 * @param conn the Connection object
 * @catalog database catalog name
 * @schemaPattern database schema pattern
 * @procedureNamePattern database procedure name pattern
 * @return a table of stored procedures names
 * as a ResultSet object.
 * Each element of XML document will have the name and
 * type of a stored procedure.
 *
 */
public static ResultSet getStoredProcedureColumns
    (java.sql.Connection conn,
     String catalog,
     String schemaPattern,
     String procedureNamePattern)
     throws Exception {

     DatabaseMetaData meta = conn.getMetaData();
     if (meta == null) {
         return null;
     }

     return meta.getProcedureColumns(catalog,
                                     schemaPattern,
                                     procedureNamePattern,
                                     "%");
}

private static String getColumnType(short columnType) {
    if (columnType == DatabaseMetaData.procedureColumnIn) {
        return "IN parameter";
    }
    else if (columnType == DatabaseMetaData.procedureColumnInOut) {
        return "INOUT parameter";
    }
    else if (columnType == DatabaseMetaData.procedureColumnOut) {
        return "OUT parameter";
    }
    else if (columnType == DatabaseMetaData.procedureColumnReturn) {
        return "procedure return value";
    }
```

```
            else if (columnType == DatabaseMetaData.procedureColumnResult) {
                return "result column in ResultSet";
            }
            else {
                return "nobody knows";
            }
        }
    }
}
```

Invoking GetSPColumns for MySQL

Figure 9-1 shows how to run the solution for the MySQL database.

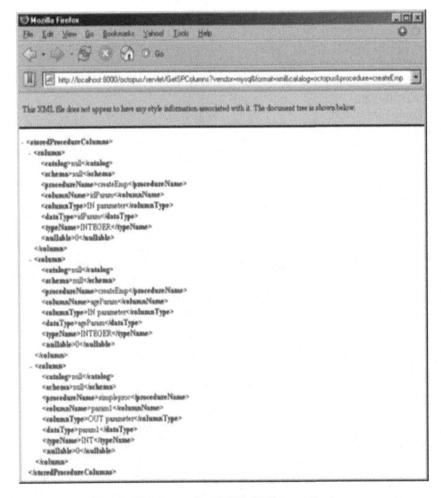

Figure 9-1. *Invoking GetSPColumns for MySQL (XML output)*

Invoking GetSPColumns for Oracle

Figure 9-2 shows how to run the solution for the Oracle database.

Figure 9-2. *Invoking GetSPColumns for Oracle (XML output)*

9.2. How Do You Get Database Catalogs?

If you want to provide catalog and schema services to database applications, then you might need to provide catalog and schema values to client applications. The words "catalog" and "schema" have different meanings, depending on the database vendor. Again, the vendor parameter is very important in understanding the semantics of catalogs and schemas. Oracle treats "schema" as a database name, while MySQL treats "catalog" as a database name. So, in order to get the names of databases from Oracle, you must use getSchemas(); to get the names of databases from MySQL, you must use getCatalogs(). If you use getCatalogs() for an Oracle database, or getSchemas() for MySQL, it returns nothing (as null objects). In the JDBC API, getSchemas() claims that it returns a set of two columns (table schema and table catalog), but in reality it just returns table schema, as a first column of the result set. Once again, this proves at least two points:

- You have to test your code against different databases; that is, databases can have different semantics by using the same JDBC API.

- When you define connections, make sure that the vendor parameter is defined. By knowing who the database vendor is, you can invoke the correct methods.

MySQL Database Setup

```
$ mysql -u root -proot
Welcome to the MySQL monitor.  Commands end with ; or \g.
Your MySQL connection id is 36 to server version: 5.0.12-beta-nt

Type 'help;' or '\h' for help. Type '\c' to clear the buffer.
mysql> show databases;
+--------------------+
| Database           |
+--------------------+
| information_schema |
| deanza             |
| mysql              |
| octopus            |
| test               |
+--------------------+
5 rows in set (0.00 sec)
```

Oracle Database Setup

In Oracle, the DBA_USERS table describes all users (in Oracle, "user" is semantically equivalent to a "schema") of the database. To save space, I have edited the output.

```
$ sqlplus system/password
SQL*Plus: Release 10.2.0.1.0 - Production on Sun Sep 25 00:11:49 2005
Connected to: Oracle Database 10g Enterprise Edition Release 10.2.0.1.0 - Production
SQL> select username from dba_users;
USERNAME
-----------
MGMT_VIEW
SYS
SYSTEM
DBSNMP
SYSMAN
XDB
SCOTT
...ANONYMOUS
...
HR

27 rows selected.
```

The Solution

```java
import java.io.PrintWriter;
import java.io.IOException;

import java.sql.*;
import javax.servlet.*;
import javax.servlet.http.*;

import java.util.List;
import java.util.ArrayList;

import jcb.util.DatabaseUtil;
import jcb.db.VeryBasicConnectionManager;

public class GetCatalogs extends HttpServlet {

    public void doGet(HttpServletRequest request,
                      HttpServletResponse response)
        throws ServletException, IOException {
        Connection conn = null;
        try {
            String dbVendor = request.getParameter("vendor").trim();
            String outputFormat = request.getParameter("format").trim();
            conn = VeryBasicConnectionManager.getConnection(dbVendor);
            List<String> catalogs = getCatalogs(conn);
            if (outputFormat.equals("xml")) {
                printXML(response, catalogs);
            }
            else {
                printHTML(response, catalogs);
            }
        }
        catch(Exception e) {
            printError(response, e.getMessage());
        }
        finally {
            DatabaseUtil.close(conn);
        }
    } // end doGet

    private static void printHTML(HttpServletResponse response,
                                  List<String> tables)
        throws Exception  {
        response.setContentType("text/html");
        PrintWriter out = response.getWriter();
        StringBuilder buffer = new StringBuilder();
```

```
        buffer.append("<html><body><table border=1 cellspacing=0 cellpadding=0>");
        buffer.append("<TR><TH>Catalogs</TH></TR>");
        for (int i=0; i < tables.size(); i++) {
            buffer.append("<TR><TD>");
            buffer.append(tables.get(i));
            buffer.append("</TD></TR>");
        }
        buffer.append("</table></body></html>");
        out.println(buffer.toString());
    }
    private static void printXML(HttpServletResponse response,
                                 List<String> catalogs)
        throws Exception  {
        response.setContentType("text/xml");
        PrintWriter out = response.getWriter();
        StringBuilder buffer = new StringBuilder();
        buffer.append("<?xml version=\"1.0\" encoding=\"ISO-8859-1\"?>");
        buffer.append("<catalogs>");
        for (int i=0; i < catalogs.size(); i++) {
            buffer.append("<name>");
            buffer.append(catalogs.get(i));
            buffer.append("</name>");
        }
        buffer.append("</catalogs>");
        out.println(buffer.toString());
    }

    private static void printError(HttpServletResponse response,
                                   String message) {
        try {
            PrintWriter out = response.getWriter();
            StringBuffer buffer = new StringBuffer();
            buffer.append("<html><body>");
            buffer.append(message);
            buffer.append("</body></html>");
            out.println(buffer);
        }
        catch(Exception ignore) {
        }
    }

    /**
     * Get Catalogs: Retrieves the catalog names available in
     * this database.  The results are ordered by catalog name.
     *
```

```java
 * @param conn the Connection object
 * @return list of all catalogs.
 * @exception Failed to get the Get Catalogs.
 */
public static List<String> getCatalogs(Connection conn)
    throws Exception {
    ResultSet catalogs = null;
    try {
        DatabaseMetaData meta = conn.getMetaData();
        if (meta == null) {
            return null;
        }

        catalogs = meta.getCatalogs();
        if (catalogs == null) {
            return null;
        }

        List<String> list = new ArrayList<String>();
        while (catalogs.next()) {
            String catalog = catalogs.getString(1); //"TABLE_CATALOG"
            if (catalog != null) {
                list.add(catalog);
            }
        }
        return list;
    }
    finally {
        DatabaseUtil.close(catalogs);
    }
}

}
```

Invoking GetCatalogs for MySQL

Figure 9-3 shows how to run the solution for the MySQL database.

Figure 9-3. *Invoking GetCatalogs for MySQL (XML output)*

Invoking GetCatalogs for Oracle

Figure 9-4 shows how to run the solution for the Oracle database.

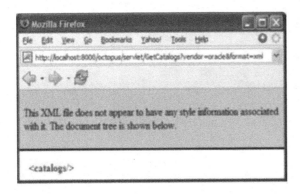

Figure 9-4. *Invoking GetCatalogs for Oracle (XML output)*

9.3. How Do You Get Database Schemas?

Oracle treats "schema" as a database name, while MySQL treats "catalog" as a database name. So, in order to get the names of databases from Oracle, you must use getSchemas(); to get the names of databases from MySQL, you must use getCatalogs(). If you use getCatalogs() for an Oracle database, or getSchemas() for MySQL, it returns nothing (as null objects). In the

JDBC API, getSchemas() claims that it returns a set of two columns (table schema and table catalog), but in reality it just returns table schema, as a first column of the result set. Once again, this proves at least two points:

- You have to test your code against different databases; that is, databases can have different semantics by using the same JDBC API.

- When you define connections, make sure that the vendor parameter is defined. By knowing who the database vendor is, you can invoke the correct methods.

MySQL Database Setup

```
$ mysql -u root -proot
Welcome to the MySQL monitor.  Commands end with ; or \g.
Your MySQL connection id is 36 to server version: 5.0.12-beta-nt

Type 'help;' or '\h' for help. Type '\c' to clear the buffer.
mysql> show databases;
+--------------------+
| Database           |
+--------------------+
| information_schema |
| deanza             |
| mysql              |
| octopus            |
| test               |
+--------------------+
5 rows in set (0.00 sec)
```

Oracle Database Setup

In Oracle, the DBA_USERS table describes all users (in Oracle, "user" is semantically equivalent to a "schema") of the database. Partial output is shown for some SQL queries.

```
$ sqlplus system/password
SQL*Plus: Release 10.2.0.1.0 - Production on Sun Sep 25 00:11:49 2005
SQL> Select username from dba_users;
USERNAME
-----------
MGMT_VIEW
SYS
SYSTEM
DBSNMP
SYSMAN
XDB
SCOTT
...
```

```
DIP
OE
HR

27 rows selected.
```

The Solution

```java
import java.io.PrintWriter;
import java.io.IOException;

import java.sql.*;
import javax.servlet.*;
import javax.servlet.http.*;

import java.util.List;
import java.util.ArrayList;

import jcb.util.DatabaseUtil;
import jcb.db.VeryBasicConnectionManager;

public class GetSchemas extends HttpServlet {

    public void doGet(HttpServletRequest request,
                      HttpServletResponse response)
        throws ServletException, IOException {
        Connection conn = null;
        try {
            String dbVendor = request.getParameter("vendor").trim();
            String outputFormat = request.getParameter("format").trim();
            conn = VeryBasicConnectionManager.getConnection(dbVendor);
            List<String> schemas = getSchemas(conn);
            if (outputFormat.equals("xml")) {
                printXML(response, schemas);
            }
            else {
                printHTML(response, schemas);
            }
        }
        catch(Exception e) {
            printError(response, e.getMessage());
        }
        finally {
            DatabaseUtil.close(conn);
        }
    } // end doGet
```

```java
private static void printHTML(HttpServletResponse response,
                             List<String> schemas)
    throws Exception  {
    response.setContentType("text/html");
    PrintWriter out = response.getWriter();
    StringBuilder buffer = new StringBuilder();
    buffer.append("<html><body><table border=1 cellspacing=0 cellpadding=0>");
    buffer.append("<TR><TH>Schemas</TH></TR>");
    for (int i=0; i < schemas.size(); i++) {
        buffer.append("<TR><TD>");
        buffer.append(schemas.get(i));
        buffer.append("</TD></TR>");
    }
    buffer.append("</table></body></html>");
    out.println(buffer.toString());
}
private static void printXML(HttpServletResponse response,
                             List<String> schemas)
    throws Exception  {
    response.setContentType("text/xml");
    PrintWriter out = response.getWriter();
    StringBuilder buffer = new StringBuilder();
    buffer.append("<?xml version=\"1.0\" encoding=\"ISO-8859-1\"?>");
    buffer.append("<schemas>");
    for (int i=0; i < schemas.size(); i++) {
        buffer.append("<name>");
        buffer.append(schemas.get(i));
        buffer.append("</name>");
    }
    buffer.append("</schemas>");
    out.println(buffer.toString());
}


private static void printError(HttpServletResponse response,
                               String message) {
    try {
        PrintWriter out = response.getWriter();
        StringBuffer buffer = new StringBuffer();
        buffer.append("<html><body>");
        buffer.append(message);
        buffer.append("</body></html>");
        out.println(buffer);
    }
    catch(Exception ignore) {
    }
}
```

```java
/**
 * Get Schemas: Retrieves the catalog names available in
 * this database.  The results are ordered by catalog name.
 *
 * @param conn the Connection object
 * @return list of all schemas.
 * @exception Failed to get the Get Schemas.
 */
public static List<String> getSchemas(Connection conn)
    throws Exception {
    ResultSet schemas = null;
    try {
        DatabaseMetaData meta = conn.getMetaData();
        if (meta == null) {
            return null;
        }

        schemas = meta.getSchemas();
        if (schemas == null) {
            return null;
        }

        List<String> list = new ArrayList<String>();
        while (schemas.next()) {
            String schema = schemas.getString(1); //"TABLE_CATALOG"
            if (schema != null) {
                list.add(schema);
            }
        }
        return list;
    }
    finally {
        DatabaseUtil.close(schemas);
    }
}

}
```

Invoking GetSchemas for MySQL

Figure 9-5 shows how to run the solution for the MySQL database.

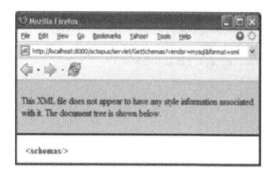

Figure 9-5. *Invoking GetSchemas for MySQL (XML output)*

Invoking GetSchemas for Oracle

Figure 9-6 shows how to run the solution for the Oracle database.

Figure 9-6. *Invoking GetSchemas for Oracle (XML output)*

9.4. What Are the Exported Keys for a Table?

To retrieve a description of the foreign key columns that reference the given table's primary key columns (the foreign keys exported by a table), you can use the DatabaseMetaData. getExportedKeys() method. This method returns its result as a ResultSet object (which is not very useful for web-based applications). For web-based applications, it is better to return the result as HTML or XML.

The signature of DatabaseMetaData's .getExportedKeys() is as follows:

```
ResultSet getExportedKeys(String catalog,
                          String schema,
                          String table)
                          throws SQLException
```

This method retrieves a description of the foreign key columns that reference the given table's primary key columns (the foreign keys exported by a table). They are ordered by FKTABLE_CAT, FKTABLE_SCHEM, FKTABLE_NAME, and KEY_SEQ. Each foreign key column description has the columns shown in Table 9-2.

Table 9-2. *ResultSet Columns for getExportedKeys()*

Name	Type	Description
PKTABLE_CAT	String	Primary key table catalog (may be null).
PKTABLE_SCHEM	String	Primary key table schema (may be null).
PKTABLE_NAME	String	Primary key table name.
PKCOLUMN_NAME	String	Primary key column name.
FKTABLE_CAT	String	Foreign key table catalog (may be null) being exported (may be null).
FKTABLE_SCHEM	String	Foreign key table schema (may be null) being exported (may be null).
FKTABLE_NAME	String	Foreign key table name being exported.
FKCOLUMN_NAME	String	Foreign key column name being exported.
KEY_SEQ	short	Sequence number within foreign key.
UPDATE_RULE	short	Specifies what happens to the foreign key when the primary key is updated: importedNoAction: Do not allow update of the primary key if it has been imported importedKeyCascade: Change the imported key to agree with the primary key update. importedKeySetNull: Change the imported key to NULL if its primary key has been updated. importedKeySetDefault: Change the imported key to default values if its primary key has been updated. importedKeyRestrict: Same as importedKeyNoAction (for ODBC 2.*x* compatibility).

Name	Type	Description
DELETE_RULE	short	Specifies what happens to the foreign key when the primary key is deleted: importedKeyNoAction: Do not allow deletion of the primary key if it has been imported. importedKeyCascade: Delete rows that import a deleted key. importedKeySetNull: Change the imported key to NULL if its primary key has been deleted. importedKeyRestrict: Same as importedKeyNoAction (for ODBC 2.*x* compatibility). importedKeySetDefault: Change the imported key to the default if its primary key has been deleted.
FK_NAME	String	Foreign key name (may be null).
PK_NAME	String	Primary key name (may be null).
DEFERRABILITY	short	Specifies whether the evaluation of foreign key constraints be deferred until commit: importedKeyInitiallyDeferred: See SQL-92 for definition. importedKeyInitiallyImmediate: See SQL-92 for definition. importedKeyNotDeferrable: See SQL-92 for definition.

The parameters are

- catalog: A catalog name; must match the catalog name as it is stored in this database. "" retrieves those without a catalog; null means that the catalog name should not be used to narrow the search.

- schema: A schema name; must match the schema name as it is stored in the database. "" retrieves those without a schema; null means that the schema name should not be used to narrow the search.

- table: A table name; must match the table name as it is stored in this database.

Oracle Database Setup

Let's create two tables (dept_table and emp_table) and define the PK and FK. Also, keep in mind that that if you violate the PK and FK rules, the SQL INSERT operation will fail.

```
$ sqlplus scott/tiger
SQL*Plus: Release 10.1.0.2.0 - Production on Tue Aug 24 14:17:06 2004
Copyright (c) 1982, 2004, Oracle.  All rights reserved.
SQL> create table dept_table (
  2    dept varchar2(2) not null primary key,
  3    location varchar2(8)
  4  );
Table created.
```

```
SQL> desc dept_table;
 Name                                      Null?    Type
 ----------------------------------------- -------- -----------
 DEPT                                      NOT NULL VARCHAR2(2)
 LOCATION                                           VARCHAR2(8)
SQL> create table emp_table (
  2     id varchar2(5) not null primary key,
  3     name varchar2(10),
  4     dept varchar2(2) not null references dept_table(dept)
  5  );
Table created.
SQL> desc emp_table;
 Name                                      Null?    Type
 ----------------------------------------- -------- ------------
 ID                                        NOT NULL VARCHAR2(5)
 NAME                                               VARCHAR2(10)
 DEPT                                      NOT NULL VARCHAR2(2)
SQL> insert into dept_table(dept, location) values('11', 'Boston');
SQL> insert into dept_table(dept, location) values('22', 'Detroit');
SQL> insert into emp_table(id, name, dept) values('55555', 'Alex', '11');
SQL> insert into emp_table(id, name, dept) values('66666', 'Mary', '22');
SQL> select * from dept_table;
DEPT LOCATION
---- --------
11   Boston
22   Detroit
SQL> select * from emp_table;
ID    NAME       DEPT
----- ---------- ----
55555 Alex       11
66666 Mary       22
SQL> insert into emp_table(id, name, dept) values('77777', 'Bob', '33');
insert into emp_table(id, name, dept) values('77777', 'Bob', '33')
*
ERROR at line 1:
ORA-02291: integrity constraint (SCOTT.SYS_C005465) violated - parent key not
Found
```

■**Note** Since dept 33 is not defined in the dept_table, Oracle gives an error.

```
SQL> select * from emp_table;
ID     NAME        DEPT
-----  ----------  ----
55555  Alex          11
66666  Mary          22
SQL> commit;
```

MySQL Database Setup

Only MySQL's InnoDB table types support the concept of foreign keys (note that MyISAM table types do not support foreign keys).

```
$ mysql --user=root --password=root
Welcome to the MySQL monitor.  Commands end with ; or \g.
Your MySQL connection id is 130 to server version: 4.0.18-nt
mysql> use octopus;
Database changed
mysql> create table dept_table (
    -> dept char(2) not null,
    -> location varchar(8),
    -> PRIMARY KEY(dept)
    -> ) TYPE=InnoDB;
Query OK, 0 rows affected (0.15 sec)
mysql> create table emp_table (
    -> dept char(2) not null,
    -> id varchar(5) not null,
    -> name varchar(10),
    -> PRIMARY KEY(id),
    -> INDEX dept_index (dept),
    -> CONSTRAINT fk_dept FOREIGN KEY(dept) REFERENCES dept_table(dept)
    -> ) TYPE=InnoDB;
Query OK, 0 rows affected (0.11 sec)
mysql> insert into dept_table(dept, location) values('11', 'Boston');
mysql> insert into dept_table(dept, location) values('22', 'Detroit');
mysql> insert into emp_table(id, name, dept) values('55555', 'Alex', '11');
mysql> insert into emp_table(id, name, dept) values('66666', 'Mary', '22');
mysql> insert into emp_table(id, name, dept) values('77777', 'Bob', '33');
ERROR 1216: Cannot add or update a child row: a foreign key constraint fails
mysql> select * from emp_table;
+------+-------+------+
| dept | id    | name |
+------+-------+------+
| 11   | 55555 | Alex |
| 22   | 66666 | Mary |
+------+-------+------+
2 rows in set (0.00 sec)
```

```
mysql> select * from dept_table;
+------+----------+
| dept | location |
+------+----------+
| 11   | Boston   |
| 22   | Detroit  |
+------+----------+
2 rows in set (0.00 sec)
```

The Solution

```java
import java.sql.*;
import javax.servlet.*;
import javax.servlet.http.*;

import java.io.PrintWriter;
import java.io.IOException;

import java.sql.*;
import javax.servlet.*;
import javax.servlet.http.*;

import jcb.util.DatabaseUtil;
import jcb.db.VeryBasicConnectionManager;

public class GetExportedKeys extends HttpServlet {

    public void doGet(HttpServletRequest request,
                      HttpServletResponse response)
        throws ServletException, IOException {
        Connection conn = null;
        ResultSet exportedKeys = null;
        try {
            String dbVendor = request.getParameter("vendor").trim();
            String outputFormat = request.getParameter("format").trim();
            String table = request.getParameter("table").trim();
            conn = VeryBasicConnectionManager.getConnection(dbVendor);

            if (dbVendor.equals("mysql")) {
                String catalog = request.getParameter("catalog").trim();
                exportedKeys = getExportedKeys(conn,
                                               catalog, // catalog,
                                               null,    // schema
                                               table);
            }
```

```
            else if (dbVendor.equals("oracle")) {
                String schema = request.getParameter("schema").trim();
                exportedKeys = getExportedKeys(conn,
                                               null,   // catalog,
                                               schema, // schema
                                               table);
            }
            else {
                printError(response, "unknown db vendor");
                return;
            }

            if (outputFormat.equals("xml")) {
                printXML(response, exportedKeys);
            }
            else {
                printHTML(response, exportedKeys);
            }

        }
        catch(Exception e) {
            e.printStackTrace();
            printError(response, e.getMessage());
        }
        finally {
            DatabaseUtil.close(exportedKeys);
            DatabaseUtil.close(conn);
        }

    } // end doGet


    private static void printHTML(HttpServletResponse response,
                                  ResultSet exportedKeys)
        throws Exception  {
        response.setContentType("text/html");
        PrintWriter out = response.getWriter();
        StringBuilder buffer = new StringBuilder();
        buffer.append("<html><body><table border=1 cellspacing=0 cellpadding=0>");
        buffer.append("<TR><TH>PK Catalog</TH>");
        buffer.append("<TH>PK Schema</TH>");
        buffer.append("<TH>PK Table</TH>");
        buffer.append("<TH>PK Column</TH>");
        buffer.append("<TH>FK Catalog</TH>");
        buffer.append("<TH>FK Schema</TH>");
        buffer.append("<TH>FK Table</TH>");
```

```java
                    buffer.append("<TH>FK Column</TH>");
                    buffer.append("<TH>FK Seq.</TH>");
                    buffer.append("<TH>Update Rule</TH>");
                    buffer.append("<TH>Delete Rule</TH>");
                    buffer.append("<TH>FK Name</TH>");
                    buffer.append("<TH>PK Name</TH>");
                    buffer.append("<TH>Deferrability</TH></TR>");
                    while (exportedKeys.next()) {
                        buffer.append("<TR><TD>");
                        buffer.append(exportedKeys.getString("PKTABLE_CAT"));
                        buffer.append("</TD><TD>");
                        buffer.append(exportedKeys.getString("PKTABLE_SCHEM"));
                        buffer.append("</TD><TD>");
                        buffer.append(exportedKeys.getString("PKTABLE_NAME"));
                        buffer.append("</TD><TD>");
                        buffer.append(exportedKeys.getString("PKCOLUMN_NAME"));
                        buffer.append("</TD><TD>");
                        buffer.append(exportedKeys.getString("FKTABLE_CAT"));
                        buffer.append("</TD><TD>");
                        buffer.append(exportedKeys.getString("FKTABLE_SCHEM"));
                        buffer.append("</TD><TD>");
                        buffer.append(exportedKeys.getString("FKTABLE_NAME"));
                        buffer.append("</TD><TD>");
                        buffer.append(exportedKeys.getString("FKCOLUMN_NAME"));
                        buffer.append("</TD><TD>");
                        buffer.append(exportedKeys.getShort("KEY_SEQ"));
                        buffer.append("</TD><TD>");
                        short updateRule = exportedKeys.getShort("UPDATE_RULE");
                        buffer.append(getUpdateRule(updateRule));
                        buffer.append("</TD><TD>");
                        short deleteRule = exportedKeys.getShort("DELETE_RULE");
                        buffer.append(getDeleteRule(deleteRule));
                        buffer.append("</TD><TD>");
                        buffer.append(exportedKeys.getString("FK_NAME"));
                        buffer.append("</TD><TD>");
                        buffer.append(exportedKeys.getString("PK_NAME"));
                        buffer.append("</TD><TD>");
                        short deferrability = exportedKeys.getShort("DEFERRABILITY");
                        buffer.append(getDeferrability(deferrability));
                        buffer.append("</TD><TR>");
                    }
                    buffer.append("</table></body></html>");
                    out.println(buffer.toString());
                }
```

```java
private static void printXML(HttpServletResponse response,
                            ResultSet exportedKeys)
    throws Exception  {
    response.setContentType("text/xml");
    PrintWriter out = response.getWriter();
    StringBuilder buffer = new StringBuilder();
    buffer.append("<?xml version=\"1.0\" encoding=\"UTF-8\"?>");
    buffer.append("<exported_keys>");
    while (exportedKeys.next()) {
        buffer.append("<exported_key><pk_table_catalog>");
        buffer.append(exportedKeys.getString("PKTABLE_CAT"));
        buffer.append("</pk_table_catalog><pk_table_schema>");
        buffer.append(exportedKeys.getString("PKTABLE_SCHEM"));
        buffer.append("</pk_table_schema><pk_table_name>");
        buffer.append(exportedKeys.getString("PKTABLE_NAME"));
        buffer.append("</pk_table_name><pk_column_name>");
        buffer.append(exportedKeys.getString("PKCOLUMN_NAME"));
        buffer.append("</pk_column_name><fk_table_catalog>");
        buffer.append(exportedKeys.getString("FKTABLE_CAT"));
        buffer.append("</fk_table_catalog><fk_table_schema>");
        buffer.append(exportedKeys.getString("FKTABLE_SCHEM"));
        buffer.append("</fk_table_schema><fk_table_name>");
        buffer.append(exportedKeys.getString("FKTABLE_NAME"));
        buffer.append("</fk_table_name><fk_column_name>");
        buffer.append(exportedKeys.getString("FKCOLUMN_NAME"));
        buffer.append("</fk_column_name><key_sequence>");
        buffer.append(exportedKeys.getString("KEY_SEQ"));
        buffer.append("</key_sequence><update_rule>");
        short updateRule = exportedKeys.getShort("UPDATE_RULE");
        buffer.append(getUpdateRule(updateRule));
        buffer.append("</update_rule><delete_rule>");
        short deleteRule = exportedKeys.getShort("DELETE_RULE");
        buffer.append(getDeleteRule(deleteRule));
        buffer.append("</delete_rule><fk_name>");
        buffer.append(exportedKeys.getString("FK_NAME"));
        buffer.append("</fk_name><pk_name>");
        buffer.append(exportedKeys.getString("PK_NAME"));
        buffer.append("</pk_name><deferrability>");
        short deferrability = exportedKeys.getShort("DEFERRABILITY");
        buffer.append(getDeferrability(deferrability));
        buffer.append("</deferrability></exported_key>");
    }
    buffer.append("</exported_keys>");
    out.println(buffer.toString());
}
```

```java
    private static void printError(HttpServletResponse response,
                                   String message) {
        try {
            PrintWriter out = response.getWriter();
            StringBuilder buffer = new StringBuilder();
            buffer.append("<html><body>");
            buffer.append(message);
            buffer.append("</body></html>");
            out.println(buffer.toString());
        }
        catch(Exception ignore) {
        }
    }


    /**
     * Get the stored-procedures names.
     * @param conn the Connection object
     * @catalog database catalog name
     * @schemaPattern database schema pattern
     * @procedureNamePattern database procedure name pattern
     * @return a table of stored procedures names
     * as a ResultSet object.
     * Each element of XML document will have the name and
     * type of a stored procedure.
     *
     */
    public static ResultSet getExportedKeys(Connection conn,
                                            String catalog,
                                            String schema,
                                            String table)
        throws Exception {

        if (table == null) {
            return null;
        }

        DatabaseMetaData meta = conn.getMetaData();
        if (meta == null) {
            return null;
        }

        return meta.getExportedKeys(catalog, schema, table.toUpperCase());
    }
```

```java
private static String getUpdateRule(short updateRule) {
   if (updateRule == DatabaseMetaData.importedKeyNoAction) {
       return "importedKeyNoAction";
   }
   else if (updateRule == DatabaseMetaData.importedKeyCascade) {
       return "importedKeyCascade";
   }
   else if (updateRule == DatabaseMetaData.importedKeySetNull) {
       return "importedKeySetNull";
   }
   else if (updateRule == DatabaseMetaData.importedKeySetDefault) {
       return "importedKeySetDefault";
   }
   else if (updateRule == DatabaseMetaData.importedKeyRestrict) {
       return "importedKeyRestrict";
   }
   else {
       return "nobody knows";
   }
}

private static String getDeleteRule(short deleteRule) {
   if (deleteRule == DatabaseMetaData.importedKeyNoAction) {
       return "importedKeyNoAction";
   }
   else if (deleteRule == DatabaseMetaData.importedKeyCascade) {
       return "importedKeyCascade";
   }
   else if (deleteRule == DatabaseMetaData.importedKeySetNull) {
       return "importedKeySetNull";
   }
   else if (deleteRule == DatabaseMetaData.importedKeyRestrict) {
       return "importedKeyRestrict";
   }
   else if (deleteRule == DatabaseMetaData.importedKeySetDefault) {
       return "importedKeySetDefault";
   }
   else {
       return "nobody knows";
   }
}

private static String getDeferrability(short deferrability) {
   if (deferrability == DatabaseMetaData.importedKeyInitiallyDeferred) {
       return "importedKeyInitiallyDeferred";
   }
```

```
        else if (deferrability == DatabaseMetaData.importedKeyInitiallyImmediate) {
            return "importedKeyInitiallyImmediate";
        }
        else if (deferrability == DatabaseMetaData.importedKeyNotDeferrable) {
            return "importedKeyNotDeferrable";
        }
        else {
            return "nobody knows";
        }
    }
}
```

Invoking GetExportedKeys for MySQL

Figure 9-7 shows how to run the solution for the MySQL database.

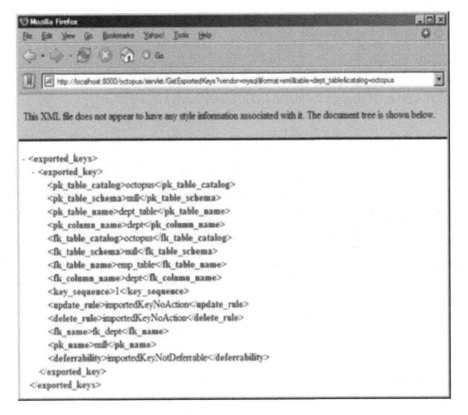

Figure 9-7. *Invoking GetExportedKeys for MySQL (XML output)*

Invoking GetExportedKeys for Oracle

Figure 9-8 shows how to run the solution for the Oracle database.

Figure 9-8. *Invoking GetExportedKeys for Oracle (XML output)*

9.5. What Foreign Keys Are Used in a Table?

DatabaseMetaData.getImportedKeys() returns a ResultSet object with data about foreign key columns, tables, sequence, and update and delete rules. DatabaseMetaData's getImportedKeys() returns a ResultSet that retrieves a description of the primary key columns for that object that are referenced by a table's foreign key columns (the primary keys imported by a table). The ResultSet object's records are ordered by column names PKTABLE_CAT, PKTABLE_SCHEM, PKTABLE_NAME, and KEY_SEQ.

A primary key (PK) is a column or set of columns that uniquely identifies a row/record in a table. A foreign key (FK) is one or more columns in one table that are used as a primary key in another table. First, I show these concepts in a simple example, and then I develop a JDBC solution and a test client program to show these relationships using DatabaseMetaData. getImportedKeys().

Oracle Database Setup

Let's create two tables (dept_table and emp_table) and define the PK and FK. Keep in mind that if you violate the PK and FK rules, then the SQL INSERT operation will fail.

```
SQL> create table emps_table (
    badge_number varchar(5) not null,
    name varchar2(20) not null,
    email varchar2(20) not null,
    primary key (badge_number)
);


SQL> create table roles_table (
    role varchar2(5) not null,
    description varchar2(25) not null,
    primary key (role)
);


SQL> create table emps_roles (
  badge_number varchar2(5) not null,
  role varchar2(5) not null,
  CONSTRAINT pk_badge_number_role PRIMARY KEY (badge_number, role)
);


SQL> alter table emps_roles add constraint fk_column_badge_number
    FOREIGN KEY (badge_number references emps_table(badge_number);

SQL> alter table emps_roles add constraint fk_column_role
    FOREIGN KEY (role) references roles_table(role);

insert into roles_table(role, description) values('dba', 'database administrator');
insert into roles_table(role, description) values('mgr', 'database manager');
insert into roles_table(role, description) values('dev', 'database developer');

insert into emps_table(badge_number, name, email)
    values('11111', 'Alex', 'alex@yahoo.com');

insert into emps_table(badge_number, name, email)
    values('22222', 'Mary', 'mary@yahoo.com');

insert into emps_roles(badge_number, role)
    values('11111', 'mgr');
insert into emps_roles(badge_number, role)
    values('11111', 'dev');
insert into emps_roles(badge_number, role)
    values('22222', 'dba');
```

```
SQL> select * from roles_table;
ROLE  DESCRIPTION
----- ----------------------
dba   database administrator
mgr   database manager
dev   database developer
SQL> select * from emps_table;
BADGE  NAME  EMAIL
-----  ----  --------------
11111  Alex  alex@yahoo.com
22222  Mary  mary@yahoo.com
SQL> select * from emps_roles;
BADGE  ROLE
-----  -----
11111  dev
11111  mgr
22222  dba
SQL> commit;
Commit complete.
```

The signature of `DatabaseMetaData.getImportedKeys()` is

```
public ResultSet getImportedKeys(String catalog,
                                 String schema,
                                 String table)
                  throws SQLException
```

This method retrieves a description of the primary key columns that are referenced by a table's foreign key columns (the primary keys imported by a table). They are ordered by `PKTABLE_CAT`, `PKTABLE_SCHEM`, `PKTABLE_NAME`, and `KEY_SEQ`.

Each primary key column description has the columns shown in Table 9-3.

Table 9-3. *ResultSet Columns for getImportedKeys()*

Name	Type	Description
PKTABLE_CAT	String	Primary key table catalog being imported (may be null).
PKTABLE_SCHEM	String	Primary key table schema being imported (may be null).
PKTABLE_NAME	String	Primary key table name being imported.
PKCOLUMN_NAME	String	Primary key column name being imported.
FKTABLE_CAT	String	Foreign key table catalog (may be null).
FKTABLE_SCHEM	String	Foreign key table schema (may be null).
FKTABLE_NAME	String	Foreign key table name.
FKCOLUMN_NAME	String	Foreign key column name.
KEY_SEQ	short	Sequence number within a foreign key.

Continued

Table 9-3. *Continued*

Name	Type	Description
UPDATE_RULE	short	Specifies what happens to a foreign key when the primary key is updated: importedNoAction: Do not allow the update of the primary key if it has been imported. importedKeyCascade: Change the imported key to agree with the primary key update. importedKeySetNull: Change the imported key to NULL if its primary key has been updated. importedKeySetDefault: Change the imported key to default values if its primary key has been update. importedKeyRestrict: Same as importedKeyNoAction (for ODBC 2.*x* compatibility).
DELETE_RULE	short	Specifies what happens to the foreign key when the primary key is deleted: importedKeyNoAction: Do not allow deletion of the primary key if it has been imported. importedKeyCascade: Delete rows that import a deleted key. importedKeySetNull: Change the imported key to NULL if its primary key has been deleted. importedKeyRestrict: Same as importedKeyNoAction (for ODBC 2.*x* compatibility). importedKeySetDefault: Change the imported key to the default if its primary key has been deleted.
FK_NAME	String	Foreign key name (may be null).
PK_NAME	String	Primary key name (may be null).
DEFERRABILITY	short	Specifies whether the evaluation of foreign key constraints can be deferred until commit: importedKeyInitiallyDeferred: See SQL-92 for definition. importedKeyInitiallyImmediate: See SQL-92 for definition. importedKeyNotDeferrable: See SQL-92 for definition.

The parameters are

- catalog: A catalog name; must match the catalog name as it is stored in the database. "" retrieves those without a catalog; null means that the catalog name should not be used to narrow the search.

- schema: A schema name; must match the schema name as it is stored in the database. "" retrieves those without a schema; null means that the schema name should not be used to narrow the search.

- table: A table name; must match the table name as it is stored in the database.

MySQL Database Setup

In the current version of MySQL (version 4.0.18), only InnoDB table types support the foreign key concept. According to MySQL, starting with MySQL 5.1, foreign keys will be supported for all table types, not just InnoDB. Let's create two tables (dept_table and emp_table) and define the PK and FK. Keep in mind that if you violate the PK and FK rules, the SQL INSERT operation will fail.

```
$ mysql --user=root --password=root
Welcome to the MySQL monitor.  Commands end with ; or \g.
Your MySQL connection id is 1 to server version: 4.0.18-nt
mysql> use octopus;
Database changed
mysql> create table emps_table (
    ->        badge_number varchar(5) not null,
    ->        name varchar(20) not null,
    ->        email varchar(20) not null,
    ->
    ->        primary key (badge_number)
    -> ) TYPE=InnoDB;
Query OK, 0 rows affected (0.24 sec)
mysql> create table roles_table (
    ->        role varchar(5) not null,
    ->        description varchar(25) not null,
    ->
    ->        primary key (role)
    -> ) TYPE=InnoDB;
Query OK, 0 rows affected (0.13 sec)
mysql> create table emps_roles (
    ->        badge_number varchar(5) not null,
    ->        role varchar(5) not null,
    ->
    ->        primary key (badge_number, role),
    ->        INDEX badge_number_index (badge_number),
    ->        foreign key (badge_number) references emps_table(badge_number),
    ->        INDEX role_index (role),
    ->        foreign key (role) references roles_table(role)
    -> ) TYPE=InnoDB;
Query OK, 0 rows affected (0.24 sec)
mysql> insert into roles_table(role, description)
       values('dba', 'database administrator');

mysql> insert into roles_table(role, description)
       values('mgr', 'database manager');

mysql> insert into roles_table(role, description)
       values('dev', 'database developer');

mysql> insert into emps_table(badge_number, name, email)
       values('11111', 'Alex', 'alex@yahoo.com');

mysql> insert into emps_table(badge_number, name, email)
       values('22222', 'Mary', 'mary@yahoo.com');
```

```
mysql> insert into emps_roles(badge_number, role)
    values('11111', 'mgr');

mysql> insert into emps_roles(badge_number, role)
    values('11111', 'dev');

mysql> insert into emps_roles(badge_number, role)
    values('22222', 'dba');

mysql> insert into emps_roles(badge_number, role) values('22222', 'a');
ERROR 1216: Cannot add or update a child row: a foreign key constraint fails
mysql> insert into emps_roles(badge_number, role) values('2222', 'a');
ERROR 1216: Cannot add or update a child row: a foreign key constraint fails
mysql> select * from emps_table;
+--------------+------+-----------------+
| badge_number | name | email           |
+--------------+------+-----------------+
| 11111        | Alex | alex@yahoo.com  |
| 22222        | Mary | mary@yahoo.com  |
+--------------+------+-----------------+
2 rows in set (0.02 sec)
mysql> select * from roles_table;
+------+------------------------+
| role | description            |
+------+------------------------+
| dba  | database administrator |
| dev  | database developer     |
| mgr  | database manager       |
+------+------------------------+
3 rows in set (0.00 sec)
mysql> select * from emps_roles;
+--------------+------+
| badge_number | role |
+--------------+------+
| 11111        | dev  |
| 11111        | mgr  |
| 22222        | dba  |
+--------------+------+
3 rows in set (0.00 sec)
```

The Solution

```
import java.sql.*;
import javax.servlet.*;
import javax.servlet.http.*;
```

```java
import java.io.PrintWriter;
import java.io.IOException;

import java.sql.*;
import javax.servlet.*;
import javax.servlet.http.*;

import jcb.util.DatabaseUtil;
import jcb.db.VeryBasicConnectionManager;

public class GetForeignKeys extends HttpServlet {

    public void doGet(HttpServletRequest request,
                      HttpServletResponse response)
        throws ServletException, IOException {
        Connection conn = null;
        ResultSet foreignKeys = null;
        try {
            String dbVendor = request.getParameter("vendor").trim();
            String outputFormat = request.getParameter("format").trim();
            String table = request.getParameter("table").trim();
            conn = VeryBasicConnectionManager.getConnection(dbVendor);

            if (dbVendor.equals("mysql")) {
                String catalog = request.getParameter("catalog").trim();
                foreignKeys = getForeignKeys(conn,
                                             catalog, // catalog,
                                             null,    // schema
                                             table);
            }
            else if (dbVendor.equals("oracle")) {
                String schema = request.getParameter("schema").trim();
                foreignKeys = getForeignKeys(conn,
                                             null,   // catalog,
                                             schema, // schema
                                             table);
            }
            else {
                printError(response, "unknown db vendor");
                return;
            }

            if (outputFormat.equals("xml")) {
                printXML(response, foreignKeys);
            }
            else {
                printHTML(response, foreignKeys);
            }
```

```
        }
    catch(Exception e) {
        e.printStackTrace();
        printError(response, e.getMessage());
    }
    finally {
        DatabaseUtil.close(foreignKeys);
        DatabaseUtil.close(conn);
    }

} // end doGet


private static void printHTML(HttpServletResponse response,
                             ResultSet foreignKeys)
    throws Exception  {
    response.setContentType("text/html");
    PrintWriter out = response.getWriter();
    StringBuilder buffer = new StringBuilder();
    buffer.append("<html><body><table border=1 cellspacing=0 cellpadding=0>");
    buffer.append("<TR><TH>PK Catalog</TH>");
    buffer.append("<TH>PK Schema</TH>");
    buffer.append("<TH>PK Table</TH>");
    buffer.append("<TH>PK Column</TH>");
    buffer.append("<TH>FK Catalog</TH>");
    buffer.append("<TH>FK Schema</TH>");
    buffer.append("<TH>FK Table</TH>");
    buffer.append("<TH>FK Column</TH>");
    buffer.append("<TH>FK Seq.</TH>");
    buffer.append("<TH>Update Rule</TH>");
    buffer.append("<TH>Delete Rule</TH>");
    buffer.append("<TH>FK Name</TH>");
    buffer.append("<TH>PK Name</TH>");
    buffer.append("<TH>Deferrability</TH></TR>");
    while (foreignKeys.next()) {
        buffer.append("<TR><TD>");
        buffer.append(foreignKeys.getString("PKTABLE_CAT"));
        buffer.append("</TD><TD>");
        buffer.append(foreignKeys.getString("PKTABLE_SCHEM"));
        buffer.append("</TD><TD>");
        buffer.append(foreignKeys.getString("PKTABLE_NAME"));
        buffer.append("</TD><TD>");
        buffer.append(foreignKeys.getString("PKCOLUMN_NAME"));
        buffer.append("</TD><TD>");
        buffer.append(foreignKeys.getString("FKTABLE_CAT"));
        buffer.append("</TD><TD>");
        buffer.append(foreignKeys.getString("FKTABLE_SCHEM"));
```

```java
                buffer.append("</TD><TD>");
                buffer.append(foreignKeys.getString("FKTABLE_NAME"));
                buffer.append("</TD><TD>");
                buffer.append(foreignKeys.getString("FKCOLUMN_NAME"));
                buffer.append("</TD><TD>");
                buffer.append(foreignKeys.getShort("KEY_SEQ"));
                buffer.append("</TD><TD>");
                short updateRule = foreignKeys.getShort("UPDATE_RULE");
                buffer.append(getUpdateRule(updateRule));
                buffer.append("</TD><TD>");
                short deleteRule = foreignKeys.getShort("DELETE_RULE");
                buffer.append(getDeleteRule(deleteRule));
                buffer.append("</TD><TD>");
                buffer.append(foreignKeys.getString("FK_NAME"));
                buffer.append("</TD><TD>");
                buffer.append(foreignKeys.getString("PK_NAME"));
                buffer.append("</TD><TD>");
                short deferrability = foreignKeys.getShort("DEFERRABILITY");
                buffer.append(getDeferrability(deferrability));
                buffer.append("</TD><TR>");
        }
        buffer.append("</table></body></html>");
        out.println(buffer.toString());
}

private static void printXML(HttpServletResponse response,
                             ResultSet foreignKeys)
    throws Exception {
    response.setContentType("text/xml");
    PrintWriter out = response.getWriter();
    StringBuilder buffer = new StringBuilder();
    buffer.append("<?xml version=\"1.0\" encoding=\"UTF-8\"?>");
    buffer.append("<exported_keys>");
    while (foreignKeys.next()) {
        buffer.append("<exported_key><pk_table_catalog>");
        buffer.append(foreignKeys.getString("PKTABLE_CAT"));
        buffer.append("</pk_table_catalog><pk_table_schema>");
        buffer.append(foreignKeys.getString("PKTABLE_SCHEM"));
        buffer.append("</pk_table_schema><pk_table_name>");
        buffer.append(foreignKeys.getString("PKTABLE_NAME"));
        buffer.append("</pk_table_name><pk_column_name>");
        buffer.append(foreignKeys.getString("PKCOLUMN_NAME"));
        buffer.append("</pk_column_name><fk_table_catalog>");
        buffer.append(foreignKeys.getString("FKTABLE_CAT"));
        buffer.append("</fk_table_catalog><fk_table_schema>");
        buffer.append(foreignKeys.getString("FKTABLE_SCHEM"));
        buffer.append("</fk_table_schema><fk_table_name>");
```

```java
                buffer.append(foreignKeys.getString("FKTABLE_NAME"));
                buffer.append("</fk_table_name><fk_column_name>");
                buffer.append(foreignKeys.getString("FKCOLUMN_NAME"));
                buffer.append("</fk_column_name><key_sequence>");
                buffer.append(foreignKeys.getString("KEY_SEQ"));
                buffer.append("</key_sequence><update_rule>");
                short updateRule = foreignKeys.getShort("UPDATE_RULE");
                buffer.append(getUpdateRule(updateRule));
                buffer.append("</update_rule><delete_rule>");
                short deleteRule = foreignKeys.getShort("DELETE_RULE");
                buffer.append(getDeleteRule(deleteRule));
                buffer.append("</delete_rule><fk_name>");
                buffer.append(foreignKeys.getString("FK_NAME"));
                buffer.append("</fk_name><pk_name>");
                buffer.append(foreignKeys.getString("PK_NAME"));
                buffer.append("</pk_name><deferrability>");
                short deferrability = foreignKeys.getShort("DEFERRABILITY");
                buffer.append(getDeferrability(deferrability));
                buffer.append("</deferrability></exported_key>");
            }
        buffer.append("</exported_keys>");
        out.println(buffer.toString());
    }

    private static void printError(HttpServletResponse response,
                                   String message) {

        try {
            PrintWriter out = response.getWriter();
            StringBuilder buffer = new StringBuilder();
            buffer.append("<html><body>");
            buffer.append(message);
            buffer.append("</body></html>");
            out.println(buffer.toString());
        }
        catch(Exception ignore) {
        }
    }

    /**
     * Get the Foreign Keys.
     * @param conn the Connection object
     * @catalog database catalog name
     * @schemaPattern database schema pattern
     * @procedureNamePattern database procedure name pattern
     * @return a table of Foreign Keys as a ResultSet object.
     *
     */
```

```java
public static ResultSet getForeignKeys(Connection conn,
                                       String catalog,
                                       String schema,
                                       String table)
    throws Exception {

    if (table == null) {
        return null;
    }

    DatabaseMetaData meta = conn.getMetaData();
    if (meta == null) {
        return null;
    }

    return meta.getImportedKeys(catalog, schema, table.toUpperCase());
}


private static String getUpdateRule(short updateRule) {
    if (updateRule == DatabaseMetaData.importedKeyNoAction) {
        return "importedKeyNoAction";
    }
    else if (updateRule == DatabaseMetaData.importedKeyCascade) {
        return "importedKeyCascade";
    }
    else if (updateRule == DatabaseMetaData.importedKeySetNull) {
        return "importedKeySetNull";
    }
    else if (updateRule == DatabaseMetaData.importedKeySetDefault) {
        return "importedKeySetDefault";
    }
    else if (updateRule == DatabaseMetaData.importedKeyRestrict) {
        return "importedKeyRestrict";
    }
    else {
        return "nobody knows";
    }
}

private static String getDeleteRule(short deleteRule) {
    if (deleteRule == DatabaseMetaData.importedKeyNoAction) {
        return "importedKeyNoAction";
    }
    else if (deleteRule == DatabaseMetaData.importedKeyCascade) {
        return "importedKeyCascade";
    }
```

```java
        else if (deleteRule == DatabaseMetaData.importedKeySetNull) {
            return "importedKeySetNull";
        }
        else if (deleteRule == DatabaseMetaData.importedKeyRestrict) {
            return "importedKeyRestrict";
        }
        else if (deleteRule == DatabaseMetaData.importedKeySetDefault) {
            return "importedKeySetDefault";
        }
        else {
            return "nobody knows";
        }
    }

    private static String getDeferrability(short deferrability) {
        if (deferrability == DatabaseMetaData.importedKeyInitiallyDeferred) {
            return "importedKeyInitiallyDeferred";
        }
        else if (deferrability == DatabaseMetaData.importedKeyInitiallyImmediate) {
            return "importedKeyInitiallyImmediate";
        }
        else if (deferrability == DatabaseMetaData.importedKeyNotDeferrable) {
            return "importedKeyNotDeferrable";
        }
        else {
            return "nobody knows";
        }
    }
}
```

Invoking GetForeignKeys for MySQL

Figure 9-9 shows how to run the solution for the MySQL database.

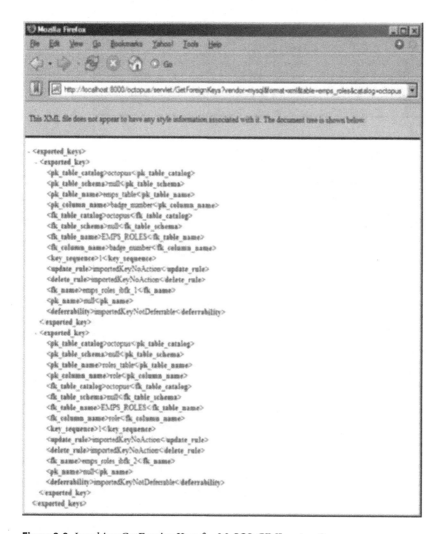

Figure 9-9. *Invoking GetForeignKeys for MySQL (XML output)*

Invoking GetForeignKeys for Oracle

Figure 9-10 shows how to run the solution for the Oracle database.

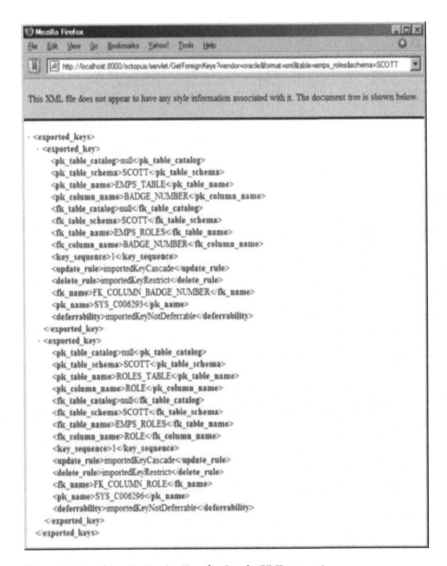

Figure 9-10. *Invoking GetForeignKeys for Oracle (XML output)*

9.6. What Are the Available SQL Types Used by a Database?

To get the list of available SQL data types used by a database, you can use the
DatabaseMetaData.getTypeInfo() method, which retrieves a description of all the standard
SQL types supported by this database. This method returns the result as a ResultSet object,
which is not very useful for web-based applications. The results of this method are ordered by
DATA_TYPE and then by how closely the data type maps to the corresponding JDBC SQL type.

The signature of DatabaseMetaData.getTypeInfo() is

```
ResultSet getTypeInfo()
                throws SQLException
```

This method retrieves a description of all the standard SQL types supported by this database. They are ordered by DATA_TYPE and then by how closely the data type maps to the corresponding JDBC SQL type.

Each type description has the columns shown in Table 9-4.

Table 9-4. *ResultSet Columns for getTypeInfo()*

Name	Type	Description
TYPE_NAME	String	Type name
DATA_TYPE	int	SQL data type from java.sql.Types
PRECISION	int	Maximum precision
LITERAL_PREFIX	String	Prefix used to quote a literal (may be null)
LITERAL_SUFFIX	String	Suffix used to quote a literal (may be null)
CREATE_PARAMS	String	Parameters used in creating the type (may be null)
NULLABLE	short	Specifies whether you can use NULL for this type: typeNoNulls: Does not allow NULL values typeNullable:Allows NULL values typeNullableUnknown: Nullability unknown
CASE_SENSITIVE	boolean	Specifies whether it is case sensitive
SEARCHABLE	short	Specifies whether you can use WHERE based on this type: typePredNone: No support typePredChar: Only supported with WHERE .. LIKE typePredBasic: Supported except for WHERE .. LIKE typeSearchable: Supported for all WHERE ..
UNSIGNED_ATTRIBUTE	boolean	Specifies whether it is unsigned
FIXED_PREC_SCALE	boolean	Specifies whether it can be a money value
AUTO_INCREMENT	boolean	Specifies whether it can be used for an auto-increment value
LOCAL_TYPE_NAME	String	Localized version of type name (may be null)
MINIMUM_SCALE	short	Minimum scale supported
MAXIMUM_SCALE	short	Maximum scale supported
SQL_DATA_TYPE	int	Unused
SQL_DATETIME_SUB	int	Unused
NUM_PREC_RADIX	int	Usually 2 or 10

The Solution

```
import java.io.PrintWriter;
import java.io.IOException;

import java.sql.*;
import javax.servlet.*;
import javax.servlet.http.*;
```

```java
import java.util.List;
import java.util.ArrayList;

import jcb.util.DatabaseUtil;
import jcb.db.VeryBasicConnectionManager;

public class GetTypes extends HttpServlet {

    public void doGet(HttpServletRequest request,
                      HttpServletResponse response)
        throws ServletException, IOException {
        ResultSet types = null;
        Connection conn = null;
        try {
            String dbVendor = request.getParameter("vendor").trim();
            String outputFormat = request.getParameter("format").trim();
            conn = VeryBasicConnectionManager.getConnection(dbVendor);
            types = getTypes(conn);
            if (outputFormat.equals("xml")) {
                printXML(response, types);
            }
            else {
                printHTML(response, types);
            }
        }
        catch(Exception e) {
            printError(response, e.getMessage());
        }
        finally {
            DatabaseUtil.close(types);
            DatabaseUtil.close(conn);
        }

    } // end doGet

    private static void printHTML(HttpServletResponse response,
                                  ResultSet types)
        throws Exception {
        response.setContentType("text/html");
        PrintWriter out = response.getWriter();
        StringBuilder buffer = new StringBuilder();
        buffer.append("<html><body><table border=1 cellspacing=0 cellpadding=0>");
        buffer.append("<TR><TH>Type Name</TH>");
        buffer.append("<TH>Data Type</TH></TR>");
```

```java
        while (types.next()) {
            buffer.append("<TR><TD>");
            buffer.append(types.getString("TYPE_NAME"));
            buffer.append("</TD><TD>");
            buffer.append(types.getString("DATA_TYPE"));
            buffer.append("</TD><TR>");
        }
        buffer.append("</table></body></html>");
        out.println(buffer.toString());
    }

    private static void printXML(HttpServletResponse response,
                                 ResultSet types)
        throws Exception  {
        response.setContentType("text/xml");
        PrintWriter out = response.getWriter();
        StringBuilder buffer = new StringBuilder();
        buffer.append("<?xml version=\"1.0\" encoding=\"UTF-8\"?>");
        buffer.append("<types>");
        while (types.next()) {
            buffer.append("<type name=\"");
            buffer.append(types.getString("TYPE_NAME"));
            buffer.append("\" dataType=\"");
            buffer.append(types.getString("DATA_TYPE"));
            buffer.append("\"/>");
        }
        buffer.append("</types>");
        out.println(buffer.toString());
    }

    private static void printError(HttpServletResponse response,
                                   String message) {
        try {
            PrintWriter out = response.getWriter();
            StringBuffer buffer = new StringBuffer();
            buffer.append("<html><body>");
            buffer.append(message);
            buffer.append("</body></html>");
            out.println(buffer);
        }
        catch(Exception ignore) {
        }
    }
}
```

```java
/**
 * Listing Available SQL Types Used by a Database. This method
 * retrieves the SQL data types supported by a database and driver.
 *
 * @param conn the Connection object
 * @return SQL Types as a ResultSet object.
 * @exception Failed to get the Available SQL Types Used by a Database.
 */
public static ResultSet getTypes(Connection conn)
    throws Exception {

    // Get database meta data
    DatabaseMetaData meta = conn.getMetaData();
    if (meta == null) {
        return null;
    }

    // Get type infornmation
    return meta.getTypeInfo();
    }
}
```

Invoking GetTypes for MySQL

Figure 9-11 shows how to run the solution for the MySQL database.

Figure 9-11. *Invoking GetTypes for MySQL (XML output)*

Invoking GetTypes for Oracle

Figure 9-12 shows how to run the solution for the Oracle database.

Figure 9-12. *Invoking GetTypes for Oracle (XML output)*

9.7. What Are the Table's Privileges?

A database table's *privileges* refers to finding a description of the access rights for each table available in a catalog or schema. DatabaseMetaData provides a method, getTablePrivileges(), to do just that. This method returns the result as a ResultSet where each row is a table privilege description. In web-based applications, returning the result as a ResultSet is not useful. It is better to return the result as an HTML/XML object so that the client can extract the required information and display it in a desired format. It would be wrong to assume that this privilege applies to all columns; while this may be true for some systems, it is not true for all.

getTablePrivileges() returns only privileges that match the schema and table name criteria. They are ordered by TABLE_SCHEM, TABLE_NAME, and PRIVILEGE. Each privilege description has the columns shown in Table 9-5.

Table 9-5. *Result Columns for Invoking getTablePrivileges()*

Column's Position	Name	Type	Description
1	TABLE_CAT	String	Table catalog (may be null)
2	TABLE_SCHEM	String	Table schema (may be null)
3	TABLE_NAME	String	Table name (as a String)
4	GRANTOR	String	Grantor of access (may be null)
5	GRANTEE	String	Grantee of access
6	PRIVILEGE	String	Name of access (SELECT, INSERT, UPDATE, REFRENCES, etc.)
7	IS_GRANTABLE	String	YES if grantee is permitted to grant to others; NO if not; null if unknown

The getTablePrivileges() method has the following signature:

```
public java.sql.ResultSet getTablePrivileges(String catalog,
                                             String schemaPattern,
                                             String tableNamePattern)
    throws java.sql.SQLException
```

where

- catalog is a catalog name; "" retrieves those without a catalog.

- schemaPattern is a schema name pattern; "" retrieves those without a schema.

- tableNamePattern is a table name pattern.

Next we'll look at a Java servlet, GetTablePrivileges, which has the following signature:

```
GetTablePrivileges?vendor=<db-vendor>&
                   catalog=<catalog-name>&
                   schema=<schema-name>&
                   table=<table-pattern>&
                   format=<xml/html>
```

The Solution

```
import java.sql.*;
import javax.servlet.*;
import javax.servlet.http.*;

import java.io.PrintWriter;
import java.io.IOException;
```

```java
import jcb.util.DatabaseUtil;
import jcb.db.VeryBasicConnectionManager;

public class GetTablePrivileges extends HttpServlet {

    public void doGet(HttpServletRequest request,
                      HttpServletResponse response)
        throws ServletException, IOException {
        ResultSet tablePrivileges = null;
        Connection conn = null;
        try {
            String dbVendor = request.getParameter("vendor").trim();
            String outputFormat = request.getParameter("format").trim();
            String table = request.getParameter("table").trim();
            conn = VeryBasicConnectionManager.getConnection(dbVendor);
            if (dbVendor.equals("mysql")) {
                //String catalog = request.getParameter("catalog").trim();
                tablePrivileges =
                    getTablePrivileges(conn,
                                       conn.getCatalog(), // catalog,
                                       null,              // schema Pattern,
                                       "%");       // table. Pattern
            }
            else if (dbVendor.equals("oracle")) {
                //String schema = request.getParameter("schema").trim();
                tablePrivileges =
                    getTablePrivileges(conn,
                                       conn.getCatalog(),  // catalog
                                       "%",                // schema Pattern,
                                       table+"%");         // table. Pattern
            }
            else {
                printError(response, "unknown db vendor");
                return;
            }

            if (outputFormat.equals("xml")) {
                printXML(response, tablePrivileges);
            }
            else {
                printHTML(response, tablePrivileges);
            }
        }
        catch(Exception e) {
            e.printStackTrace();
            printError(response, e.getMessage());
        }
```

```java
        finally {
            DatabaseUtil.close(tablePrivileges);
            DatabaseUtil.close(conn);
        }

    } // end doGet

    private static void printHTML(HttpServletResponse response,
                                  ResultSet tablePrivileges)
        throws Exception {
        response.setContentType("text/html");
        PrintWriter out = response.getWriter();
        StringBuilder buffer = new StringBuilder();
        buffer.append("<html><body><table border=1 cellspacing=0 cellpadding=0>");
        buffer.append("<TR><TH>Catalog</TH>");
        buffer.append("<TH>Schema</TH>");
        buffer.append("<TH>Table Name</TH>");
        buffer.append("<TH>Grantor</TH>");
        buffer.append("<TH>Grantee</TH>");
        buffer.append("<TH>Privilege</TH>");
        buffer.append("<TH>Is Grantable</TH></TR>");
        while (tablePrivileges.next()) {
            buffer.append("<TR><TD>");
            buffer.append(tablePrivileges.getString("TABLE_CAT"));
            buffer.append("</TD><TD>");
            buffer.append(tablePrivileges.getString("TABLE_SCHEM"));
            buffer.append("</TD><TD>");
            buffer.append(tablePrivileges.getString("TABLE_NAME"));
            buffer.append("</TD><TD>");
            buffer.append(tablePrivileges.getString("GRANTOR"));
            buffer.append("</TD><TD>");
            buffer.append(tablePrivileges.getString("GRANTEE"));
            buffer.append("</TD><TD>");
            buffer.append(tablePrivileges.getString("PRIVILEGE"));
            buffer.append("</TD><TD>");
            buffer.append(tablePrivileges.getString("IS_GRANTABLE"));
            buffer.append("</TD></TR>");
        }
        buffer.append("</table></body></html>");
        out.println(buffer.toString());
    }

    private static void printXML(HttpServletResponse response,
                                 ResultSet tablePrivileges)
        throws Exception {
        response.setContentType("text/xml");
        PrintWriter out = response.getWriter();
```

```java
        StringBuilder buffer = new StringBuilder();
        buffer.append("<?xml version=\"1.0\"?>");
        buffer.append("<table_privileges>");
        while (tablePrivileges.next()) {
            buffer.append("<table_privilege><catalog>");
            buffer.append(tablePrivileges.getString("TABLE_CAT"));
            buffer.append("</catalog><schema>");
            buffer.append(tablePrivileges.getString("TABLE_SCHEM"));
            buffer.append("</schema><tableName>");
            buffer.append(tablePrivileges.getString("TABLE_NAME"));
            buffer.append("</tableName><grantor>");
            buffer.append(tablePrivileges.getString("GRANTOR"));
            buffer.append("</grantor><grantee>");
            buffer.append(tablePrivileges.getString("GRANTEE"));
            buffer.append("</grantee><privilege>");
            buffer.append(tablePrivileges.getString("PRIVILEGE"));
            buffer.append("</privilege><is_grantable>");
            buffer.append(tablePrivileges.getString("IS_GRANTABLE"));
            buffer.append("</is_grantable></table_privilege>");
        }
        buffer.append("</table_privileges>");
        out.println(buffer.toString());
    }

    private static void printError(HttpServletResponse response,
                                   String message) {
        try {
            PrintWriter out = response.getWriter();
            StringBuffer buffer = new StringBuffer();
            buffer.append("<html><body>");
            buffer.append(message);
            buffer.append("</body></html>");
            out.println(buffer);
        }
        catch(Exception ignore) {
        }
    }


    /**
     * Get Table Privileges: retrieves a description of the access
     * rights for each table available in a catalog. Note that a
     * table privilege applies to one or more tablePrivileges in the table.
     * It would be wrong to assume that this privilege applies to
     * all tablePrivileges (this may be true for some systems but is not
     * true for all.)  The result is returned as a ResultSet object.
     *
```

```
 * In JDBC, Each privilege description has the following tablePrivileges:
 *
 * TABLE_CAT String => table catalog (may be null)
 * TABLE_SCHEM String => table schema (may be null)
 * TABLE_NAME String => table name
 * GRANTOR => grantor of access (may be null)
 * GRANTEE String => grantee of access
 * PRIVILEGE String => name of access (SELECT, INSERT,
 *     UPDATE, REFERENCES, ...)
 * IS_GRANTABLE String => "YES" if grantee is permitted to grant
 *      to others; "NO" if not; null if unknown
 *
 *
 * @param conn the Connection object
 * @param catalogPattern a catalog pattern.
 * @param schemaPattern a schema pattern.
 * @param tableNamePattern a table name pattern; must match
 *  the table name as it is stored in the database.
 * @return a ResultSet object
 * @exception Failed to get the Get Table Privileges.
 */
public static ResultSet getTablePrivileges(Connection conn,
                                      String catalog,
                                      String schemaPattern,
                                      String tableNamePattern)
    throws Exception {
      if ((tableNamePattern == null) ||
          (tableNamePattern.length() == 0)) {
          return null;
      }

      DatabaseMetaData meta = conn.getMetaData();
      if (meta == null) {
          return null;
      }

      // The '_' character represents any single character.
      // The '%' character represents any sequence of zero
      // or more characters.
      return meta.getTablePrivileges(catalog,
                                schemaPattern,
                                tableNamePattern);
  }
}
```

Invoking GetTablePrivileges for MySQL

Figure 9-13 shows how to run the solution for the MySQL database.

Figure 9-13. *Invoking GetTablePrivileges for MySQL (XML output)*

Invoking GetTablePrivileges for Oracle

Figure 9-14 shows how to run the solution for the Oracle database.

Figure 9-14. *Invoking GetTablePrivileges for Oracle (XML output)*

9.8. What Are the Column Privileges?

A database column's *privileges* refers to finding a description of the access rights for columns of a table available in a catalog or schema. DatabaseMetaData provides a method, getColumnPrivileges(), to do just that. This method returns the result as a ResultSet object where each row is a column privilege description. In web-based applications, returning the result as a ResultSet is not useful. It is better to return the result as an HTML/XML object so that the client can extract the required information and display it in a desired format. It would be wrong to assume that this privilege applies to all columns; while this may be true for some systems, it is not true for all.

getColumnPrivileges() returns only privileges that match the schema and table name criteria. They are ordered by COLUMN_NAME and PRIVILEGE. Each privilege description has the columns shown in Table 9-6.

Table 9-6. *Columns for Result of Invoking getColumnPrivileges()*

Column's Position	Type	Name	Description
1	TABLE_CAT	String	Table catalog (may be null)
2	TABLE_SCHEM	String	Table schema (may be null)
3	TABLE_NAME	String	Table name (as a String)
4	COLUMN_NAME	String	Column name (as a String)
5	GRANTOR	String	Grantor of access (may be null)
6	GRANTEE	String	Grantee of access
7	PRIVILEGE	String	Name of access (SELECT, INSERT, UPDATE, REFERENCES, etc.)
8	IS_GRANTABLE	String	YES if grantee is permitted to grant to others; NO if not; null if unknown

The getColumnPrivileges() method has the following signature:

```
public java.sql.ResultSet getTablePrivileges(String catalog,
                                             String schema,
                                             String table,
                                             String columnNamePattern)
    throws java.sql.SQLException
```

where

- catalog is a catalog name; "" retrieves those without a catalog.

- schema is a schema name; "" retrieves those without a schema.

- table is a table name pattern.

- columnNamePattern is a column name pattern.

Next let's look at a Java servlet, GetTablePrivileges, which has the following signature:

```
GetColumnPrivileges?vendor=<db-vendor>&
                    catalog=<catalog-name>&
                    schema=<schema-name>&
                    table=<table-name>
                    format=<xml/html>
```

The Solution

```
import java.sql.*;
import javax.servlet.*;
import javax.servlet.http.*;

import java.io.PrintWriter;
import java.io.IOException;
```

```java
import jcb.util.DatabaseUtil;
import jcb.db.VeryBasicConnectionManager;

public class GetColumnPrivileges extends HttpServlet {

    public void doGet(HttpServletRequest request,
                      HttpServletResponse response)
        throws ServletException, IOException {
        ResultSet columnPrivileges = null;
        Connection conn = null;
        try {
            String dbVendor = request.getParameter("vendor").trim();
            String outputFormat = request.getParameter("format").trim();
            String table = request.getParameter("table").trim();
            conn = VeryBasicConnectionManager.getConnection(dbVendor);
            if (dbVendor.equals("mysql")) {
                columnPrivileges =
                    getColumnPrivileges(conn,
                                        conn.getCatalog(), // catalog,
                                        null,              // schema
                                        table,             // table
                                        "%");              // all columns
            }
            else if (dbVendor.equals("oracle")) {
                String schema = request.getParameter("schema").trim();
                columnPrivileges =
                    getColumnPrivileges(conn,
                                        conn.getCatalog(), // catalog,
                                        schema,            // schema
                                        table,             // table
                                        "%");              // all columns
            }
            else {
                printError(response, "unknown db vendor");
                return;
            }

            if (outputFormat.equals("xml")) {
                printXML(response, columnPrivileges);
            }
            else {
                printHTML(response, columnPrivileges);
            }
        }
        catch(Exception e) {
            e.printStackTrace();
            printError(response, e.getMessage());
        }
```

```java
        finally {
            DatabaseUtil.close(columnPrivileges);
            DatabaseUtil.close(conn);
        }

    } // end doGet

    private static void printHTML(HttpServletResponse response,
                                    ResultSet columnPrivileges)
        throws Exception  {
        response.setContentType("text/html");
        PrintWriter out = response.getWriter();
        StringBuilder buffer = new StringBuilder();
        buffer.append("<html><body><table border=1 cellspacing=0 cellpadding=0>");
        buffer.append("<TR><TH>Catalog</TH>");
        buffer.append("<TH>Schema</TH>");
        buffer.append("<TH>Table Name</TH>");
        buffer.append("<TH>Column Name</TH>");
        buffer.append("<TH>Grantor</TH>");
        buffer.append("<TH>Grantee</TH>");
        buffer.append("<TH>Privilege</TH>");
        buffer.append("<TH>Is Grantable</TH></TR>");
        while (columnPrivileges.next()) {
            buffer.append("<TR><TD>");
            buffer.append(columnPrivileges.getString("TABLE_CAT"));
            buffer.append("</TD><TD>");
            buffer.append(columnPrivileges.getString("TABLE_SCHEM"));
            buffer.append("</TD><TD>");
            buffer.append(columnPrivileges.getString("TABLE_NAME"));
            buffer.append("</TD><TD>");
            buffer.append(columnPrivileges.getString("COLUMN_NAME"));
            buffer.append("</TD><TD>");
            buffer.append(columnPrivileges.getString("GRANTOR"));
            buffer.append("</TD><TD>");
            buffer.append(columnPrivileges.getString("GRANTEE"));
            buffer.append("</TD><TD>");
            buffer.append(columnPrivileges.getString("PRIVILEGE"));
            buffer.append("</TD><TD>");
            buffer.append(columnPrivileges.getString("IS_GRANTABLE"));
            buffer.append("</TD></TR>");
        }
        buffer.append("</table></body></html>");
        out.println(buffer.toString());
    }
```

```java
private static void printXML(HttpServletResponse response,
                            ResultSet columnPrivileges)
    throws Exception  {
    response.setContentType("text/xml");
    PrintWriter out = response.getWriter();
    StringBuilder buffer = new StringBuilder();
    buffer.append("<?xml version=\"1.0\"?>");
    buffer.append("<table_privileges>");
    while (columnPrivileges.next()) {
        buffer.append("<table_privilege><catalog>");
        buffer.append(columnPrivileges.getString("TABLE_CAT"));
        buffer.append("</catalog><schema>");
        buffer.append(columnPrivileges.getString("TABLE_SCHEM"));
        buffer.append("</schema><tableName>");
        buffer.append(columnPrivileges.getString("TABLE_NAME"));
        buffer.append("</tableName><columnName>");
        buffer.append(columnPrivileges.getString("COLUMN_NAME"));
        buffer.append("</columnName><grantor>");
        buffer.append(columnPrivileges.getString("GRANTOR"));
        buffer.append("</grantor><grantee>");
        buffer.append(columnPrivileges.getString("GRANTEE"));
        buffer.append("</grantee><privilege>");
        buffer.append(columnPrivileges.getString("PRIVILEGE"));
        buffer.append("</privilege><is_grantable>");
        buffer.append(columnPrivileges.getString("IS_GRANTABLE"));
        buffer.append("</is_grantable></table_privilege>");
    }
    buffer.append("</table_privileges>");
    out.println(buffer.toString());
}

private static void printError(HttpServletResponse response,
                              String message) {
    try {
        PrintWriter out = response.getWriter();
        StringBuffer buffer = new StringBuffer();
        buffer.append("<html><body>");
        buffer.append(message);
        buffer.append("</body></html>");
        out.println(buffer);
    }
    catch(Exception ignore) {
    }
}
```

```java
/**
 * Get Column Privileges: retrieves a description of the access
 * rights for each table available in a catalog. Note that a
 * table privilege applies to one or more columnPrivileges in the table.
 * It would be wrong to assume that this privilege applies to
 * all columnPrivileges (this may be true for some systems but is not
 * true for all.)  The result is returned as a ResultSet object.
 *
 * In JDBC, Each privilege description has the following columnPrivileges:
 *
 * TABLE_CAT String => table catalog (may be null)
 * TABLE_SCHEM String => table schema (may be null)
 * TABLE_NAME String => table name
 * COLUMN_NAME String => column name
 * GRANTOR => grantor of access (may be null)
 * GRANTEE String => grantee of access
 * PRIVILEGE String => name of access (SELECT, INSERT,
 *     UPDATE, REFERENCES, ...)
 * IS_GRANTABLE String => "YES" if grantee is permitted to grant
 *     to others; "NO" if not; null if unknown
 *
 *
 * @param conn the Connection object
 * @param catalog a catalog.
 * @param schema a schema.
 * @param table a table name
 * @param columnNamePattern column name pattern;
 * @return a ResultSet object
 * @exception Failed to get the Get Column Privileges.
 */
public static ResultSet getColumnPrivileges(Connection conn,
                                            String catalog,
                                            String schema,
                                            String table,
                                            String columnNamePattern)
    throws Exception {
    if ((table == null) ||
        (table.length() == 0)) {
        return null;
    }

    DatabaseMetaData meta = conn.getMetaData();
    if (meta == null) {
        return null;
    }
```

```
        // The '_' character represents any single character.
        // The '%' character represents any sequence of zero
        // or more characters.
        return meta.getColumnPrivileges(catalog,
                                        schema,
                                        table,
                                        columnNamePattern);
    }
}
```

Invoking GetColumnPrivileges for MySQL

Figure 9-15 shows how to run the solution for the MySQL database.

Figure 9-15. *Invoking GetColumnPrivileges for MySQL (XML output)*

Invoking GetColumnPrivileges for Oracle

Figure 9-16 shows how to run the solution for the Oracle database. As you can observe, Oracle driver does not implement the getColumnPrivileges() method.

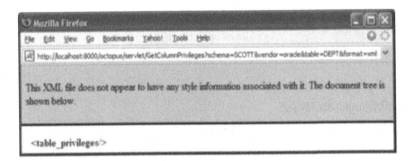

Figure 9-16. Invoking GetColumnPrivileges for Oracle (XML output)

9.9. What Are a Table's Optimal Set of Columns That Uniquely Identify a Row or Record?

To return a table's optimal set of columns that uniquely identify a row, you can use the DatabaseMetaData.getBestRowIdentifier() method. This method returns the result as a ResultSet object, which is not very useful to the web clients. I provide a Java servlet, GetBestRowIdentifier, which returns a table's optimal set of columns that uniquely identify a row:

```
public ResultSet getBestRowIdentifier(String catalog,
                                      String schema,
                                      String table,
                                      int scope,
                                      boolean nullable)

    throws SQLException
```

This retrieves a description of a table's optimal set of columns that uniquely identifies a row. They are ordered by SCOPE.

Each column description has the columns shown in Table 9-7.

Table 9-7. *ResultSet Columns for getBestRowIdentifier()*

Name	Type	Description
SCOPE	short	Actual scope of result: DatabaseMetaData.bestRowTemporary: Very temporary; valid while using row DatabaseMetaData.bestRowTransaction: Valid for remainder of current transaction DatabaseMetaData.bestRowSession: Valid for remainder of current session
COLUMN_NAME	String	Column name.

Name	Type	Description
DATA_TYPE	int	SQL data type from java.sql.Types.
TYPE_NAME	String	Data source–dependent type name; for a UDT the type name is fully qualified.
COLUMN_SIZE	int	Precision.
BUFFER_LENGTH	int	Not used.
DECIMAL_DIGITS	short	Scale.
PSEUDO_COLUMN	short	Specifies whether this a pseudocolumn like an Oracle ROWID: DatabaseMetaData.bestRowUnknown: May or may not be a pseudo-column DatabaseMetaData.bestRowNotPseudo: Is not a pseudocolumn DatabaseMetaData.bestRowPseudo: Is a pseudocolumn

The parameters are

- catalog: A catalog name; must match the catalog name as it is stored in the database. "" retrieves those without a catalog; null means that the catalog name should not be used to narrow the search.

- schema: A schema name; must match the schema name as it is stored in the database. "" retrieves those without a schema; null means that the schema name should not be used to narrow the search.

- table: A table name; must match the table name as it is stored in the database.

- scope: The scope of interest; use same values as SCOPE.

- nullable: Include columns that are nullable.

To be as complete as possible, I've included the table name in XML syntax. This can aid clients in distinguishing the best row identifiers as easily as possible.

```
<?xml version='1.0'>
<BestRowIdentifier>
    <RowIdentifier tableName="database-table-name">
        <scope>scope</scope>
        <columnName>column-name</columnName>
        <dataType>data-type</dataType>
        <typeName>type-name</typeName>
        <columnSize>size-of-column</columnSize>
        <decimalDigits>0</decimalDigits>
        <pseudoColumn>pseudo-column</pseudoColumn>
    </RowIdentifier>
    <RowIdentifier tableName="...">
    </RowIdentifier>
    ...
    <RowIdentifier tableName="...">
    </RowIdentifier>
</BestRowIdentifier>
```

The servlet signature is

```
GetBestRowIdentifier?vendor=<db-vendor>&
                      Schema=<schema name>&
                      table=<table-name>&
                      scope=<scope-of-the-result>&
                      nullable=<true/false-include columns that are nullable>&
                      format=<xml/html>
```

Some things to keep in mind about the GetBestRowIdentifier servlet are

- The MySQL database does not understand schema; you have to use catalog.

- The Oracle database does not understand catalog; you have to use schema.

- For other databases, you should check their JDBC documentation.

Oracle Database Setup

```
SQL> desc dept;
 Name                                      Null?    Type
 ----------------------------------------- -------- ---------------
 DEPTNO                                    NOT NULL NUMBER(2)
 DNAME                                              VARCHAR2(14)
 LOC                                               VARCHAR2(13)
```

MySQL Database Setup

```
mysql> use octopus;
Database changed
mysql> desc emps_table;
+--------------+-------------+------+-----+---------+-------+
| Field        | Type        | Null | Key | Default | Extra |
+--------------+-------------+------+-----+---------+-------+
| badge_number | varchar(5)  | NO   | PRI |         |       |
| name         | varchar(20) | NO   |     |         |       |
| email        | varchar(20) | NO   |     |         |       |
+--------------+-------------+------+-----+---------+-------+
3 rows in set (0.02 sec)
```

The Solution

```
import java.sql.*;
import javax.servlet.*;
import javax.servlet.http.*;

import java.io.PrintWriter;
import java.io.IOException;
```

```java
import jcb.util.DatabaseUtil;
import jcb.db.VeryBasicConnectionManager;

public class GetBestRowIdentifier  extends HttpServlet {

    public void doGet(HttpServletRequest request,
                      HttpServletResponse response)
        throws ServletException, IOException {
        ResultSet bestRowIdentifier = null;
        Connection conn = null;
        try {
            String dbVendor = request.getParameter("vendor").trim();
            String table = request.getParameter("table").trim();
            String outputFormat = request.getParameter("format").trim();
            String scope = request.getParameter("scope").trim();
            String nullable = request.getParameter("nullable").trim();
            conn = VeryBasicConnectionManager.getConnection(dbVendor);
            if (dbVendor.equals("mysql")) {
                bestRowIdentifier =
                    getBestRowIdentifier(conn,
                                         conn.getCatalog(), // catalog,
                                         "",                // schema
                                         table,             // table
                                         scope,             // scope
                                         nullable);
            }
            else if (dbVendor.equals("oracle")) {
                String schema = request.getParameter("schema").trim();
                bestRowIdentifier =
                    getBestRowIdentifier(conn,
                                         conn.getCatalog(), // catalog,
                                         schema,            // schema
                                         table,             // table
                                         scope,             // scope
                                         nullable);
            }
            else {
                printError(response, "unknown db vendor");
                return;
            }

            if (outputFormat.equals("xml")) {
                printXML(response, bestRowIdentifier);
            }
            else {
                printHTML(response, bestRowIdentifier);
            }
        }
```

```
        catch(Exception e) {
            e.printStackTrace();
            printError(response, e.getMessage());
        }
        finally {
            DatabaseUtil.close(bestRowIdentifier);
            DatabaseUtil.close(conn);
        }

    } // end doGet


    private static void printHTML(HttpServletResponse response,
                                  ResultSet bestRowIdentifier)
        throws Exception  {
        response.setContentType("text/html");
        PrintWriter out = response.getWriter();
        StringBuilder buffer = new StringBuilder();
        buffer.append("<html><body><table border=1 cellspacing=0 cellpadding=0>");
        buffer.append("<TR><TH>Scope</TH>");
        buffer.append("<TH>Column Name</TH>");
        buffer.append("<TH>Data Type</TH>");
        buffer.append("<TH>Type Name</TH>");
        buffer.append("<TH>Column Size</TH>");
        buffer.append("<TH>Decimal Digits</TH>");
        buffer.append("<TH>Pseudo Column</TR>");
        while (bestRowIdentifier.next()) {
            buffer.append("<TR><TD>");
            short scope = bestRowIdentifier.getShort("SCOPE");
            buffer.append(getScope(scope));
            buffer.append("</TD><TD>");
            buffer.append(bestRowIdentifier.getString("COLUMN_NAME"));
            buffer.append("</TD><TD>");
            buffer.append(bestRowIdentifier.getInt("DATA_TYPE"));
            buffer.append("</TD><TD>");
            buffer.append(bestRowIdentifier.getString("TYPE_NAME"));
            buffer.append("</TD><TD>");
            buffer.append(bestRowIdentifier.getInt("COLUMN_SIZE"));
            buffer.append("</TD><TD>");
            buffer.append(bestRowIdentifier.getShort("DECIMAL_DIGITS"));
            buffer.append("</TD><TD>");
            short pseudoColumn = bestRowIdentifier.getShort("PSEUDO_COLUMN");
            buffer.append(getPseudoColumn(pseudoColumn));
            buffer.append("</TD></TR>");
        }
        buffer.append("</table></body></html>");
        out.println(buffer.toString());
    }
```

```java
private static void printXML(HttpServletResponse response,
                            ResultSet bestRowIdentifier)
    throws Exception {
    response.setContentType("text/xml");
    PrintWriter out = response.getWriter();
    StringBuilder buffer = new StringBuilder();
    //buffer.append("<?xml version=\"1.0\" encoding=\"ISO-8859-1\"?>");
    buffer.append("<?xml version=\"1.0\"?>");
    buffer.append("<bestRowIdentifier>");
    while (bestRowIdentifier.next()) {
        buffer.append("<identifier><scope>");
        short scope = bestRowIdentifier.getShort("SCOPE");
        buffer.append(getScope(scope));
        buffer.append("</scope><columnName>");
        buffer.append(bestRowIdentifier.getString("COLUMN_NAME"));
        buffer.append("</columnName><dataType>");
        buffer.append(bestRowIdentifier.getInt("DATA_TYPE"));
        buffer.append("</dataType><typeName>");
        buffer.append(bestRowIdentifier.getString("TYPE_NAME"));
        buffer.append("</typeName><columnSize>");
        buffer.append(bestRowIdentifier.getInt("COLUMN_SIZE"));
        buffer.append("</columnSize><decimalDigits>");
        buffer.append(bestRowIdentifier.getShort("DECIMAL_DIGITS"));
        buffer.append("</decimalDigits><pseudoColumn>");
        short pseudoColumn = bestRowIdentifier.getShort("PSEUDO_COLUMN");
        buffer.append(getPseudoColumn(pseudoColumn));
        buffer.append("</pseudoColumn></identifier>");
    }
    buffer.append("</bestRowIdentifier>");
    out.println(buffer.toString());
}

private static void printError(HttpServletResponse response,
                              String message) {
    try {
        PrintWriter out = response.getWriter();
        StringBuffer buffer = new StringBuffer();
        buffer.append("<html><body>");
        buffer.append(message);
        buffer.append("</body></html>");
        out.println(buffer);
    }
    catch(Exception ignore) {
    }
}
```

```java
/**
 * Retrieves a description of the given table's BestRowIdentifier.
 * @param conn the Connection object
 * @param catalog a catalog.
 * @param schema a schema.
 * @param table name of a table in the database.
 * @param scope the scope of interest; use same values as SCOPE
 * @param nullable include bestRowIdentifier that are nullable.
 * @return the BestRowIdentifier as a ResultSet object
 * @exception Failed to get the table's bestRowIdentifier.
 */
public static ResultSet getBestRowIdentifier(Connection conn,
                                             String catalog,
                                             String schema,
                                             String table,
                                             String scope,
                                             String nullable)
    throws Exception {
    if ((table == null) || (table.length() == 0)) {
        return null;
    }

    DatabaseMetaData meta = conn.getMetaData();
    if (meta == null) {
        return null;
    }

    int theScope = DatabaseMetaData.bestRowSession;
    if (scope.equals("bestRowTemporary")) {
        theScope = DatabaseMetaData.bestRowTemporary;
    }
    else if (scope.equals("bestRowTransaction")) {
        theScope = DatabaseMetaData.bestRowTransaction;
    }

    boolean isNullable = false;
    if (nullable.equals("true")) {
        isNullable = true;
    }

    //
    // The Oracle database stores its table names as
    // Upper-Case; if you pass a table name in lowercase
    // characters, it will not work. MySQL database does
    // not care if table name is uppercase/lowercase.
```

```java
            //
            return meta.getBestRowIdentifier(catalog,
                                             schema,
                                             table.toUpperCase(),
                                             theScope,
                                             isNullable);
        }

        public static String getScope(short scope) {
            if (scope == DatabaseMetaData.bestRowSession) {
                return "bestRowSession";
            }
            else if (scope == DatabaseMetaData.bestRowTemporary) {
                return "bestRowTemporary";
            }
            else if (scope == DatabaseMetaData.bestRowTransaction) {
                return "bestRowTransaction";
            }
            else {
                return "scope is unknown";
            }
        }

        public static String getPseudoColumn(short pseudoColumn) {
            if (pseudoColumn == DatabaseMetaData.bestRowNotPseudo) {
                return "bestRowNotPseudo";
            }
            else if (pseudoColumn == DatabaseMetaData.bestRowPseudo) {
                return "bestRowPseudo";
            }
            else {
                return "bestRowUnknown";
            }
        }
    }
}
```

Invoking GetBestRowIdentifier for MySQL

Figure 9-17 shows how to run the solution for the MySQL database.

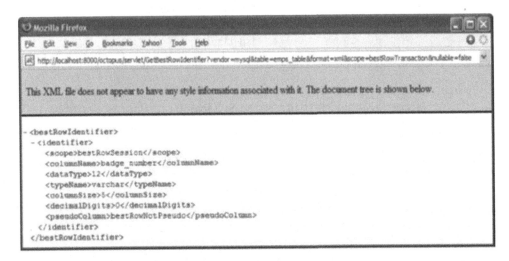

Figure 9-17. *Invoking GetBestRowIdentifier for MySQL (XML output)*

Invoking GetBestRowIdentifier for Oracle

Figure 9-18 shows how to run the solution for the Oracle database.

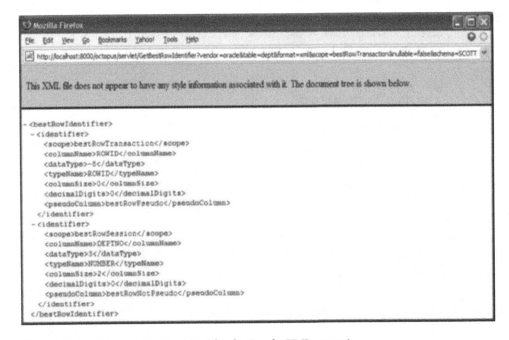

Figure 9-18. *Invoking GetBestRowIdentifier for Oracle (XML output)*

9.10. How Do You Get a RowSet's Metadata?

According to the JDBC Tutorial (`http://java.sun.com/developer/Books/JDBCTutorial/chapter5.html`):

> *A RowSet (javax.sql.RowSet) object contains a set of rows from a result set (ResultSet) or some other source of tabular data, like a file or spreadsheet. Because a RowSet object follows the JavaBeans model for properties and event notification, it is a JavaBeans component that can be combined with other components in an application. As is true with other Beans, application programmers will probably use a development tool to create a RowSet object and set its properties. Rowsets may have many different implementations to fill different needs. These implementations fall into two broad categories, rowsets that are connected and those that are disconnected. A disconnected rowset gets a connection to a data source in order to fill itself with data or to propagate changes in data back to the data source, but most of the time it does not have a connection open. While it is disconnected, it does not need a JDBC driver or the full JDBC API, so its footprint is very small. Thus a rowset is an ideal format for sending data over a network to a thin client.*

RowSetMetaData (defined in the `javax.sql` package) is an object that contains information about the columns in a RowSet object. This interface is an extension of the ResultSetMetaData interface with methods for setting the values in a RowSetMetaData object. When a RowSetReader object reads data into a RowSet object, it creates a RowSetMetaData object and initializes it using the methods in the RowSetMetaData interface. Then the reader passes the RowSetMetaData object to the rowset.

A RowSetMetaData object's format is not suitable for web-based applications. For this reason, I will provide a Java servlet to display that object in an XML object; a client may extract the desired information from that XML object. Disconnected RowSet objects (such as CachedRowSet and WebRowSet) provide an XML format for their data metadata, and I will take advantage of such methods. Note that one of the main reasons to use a CachedRowSet or WebRowSet object is to pass data between different components of an application. Because it is serializable, a CachedRowSet or WebRowSet object can be used, for example, to send the result of a query executed by an enterprise JavaBeans component running in a server environment over a network to a client running in a web browser.

What follows is a Java servlet, GetRowSetMetaData, which will display SQL queries metadata as an XML object. The signature of GetRowSetMetaData is

```
GetRowSetMetaData?vendor=<database-vendor>&query=<SQL-Query>
```

You may modify and update this servlet to pass additional dynamic parameters to your SQL queries.

MySQL Database Setup

```
mysql> use octopus;
Database changed
mysql> create table emps(
    -> id varchar(10),
    -> name varchar(20),
    -> resume TEXT,
    -> photo BLOB,
    -> primary key(id)
    -> );
Query OK, 0 rows affected (0.05 sec)
mysql> desc emps;
+--------+-------------+------+-----+---------+-------+
| Field  | Type        | Null | Key | Default | Extra |
+--------+-------------+------+-----+---------+-------+
| id     | varchar(10) |      | PRI |         |       |
| name   | varchar(20) | YES  |     | NULL    |       |
| resume | text        | YES  |     | NULL    |       |
| photo  | blob        | YES  |     | NULL    |       |
+--------+-------------+------+-----+---------+-------+
4 rows in set (0.00 sec)
```

Oracle Database Setup

```
$ sqlplus scott/tiger
SQL*Plus: Release 10.1.0.2.0 - Production on Fri Oct 7 14:39:09 2005
SQL> desc emp;
 Name                                      Null?    Type
 ----------------------------------------- -------- ----------------------

 EMPNO                                     NOT NULL NUMBER(4)
 ENAME                                              VARCHAR2(10)
 JOB                                                VARCHAR2(9)
 MGR                                                NUMBER(4)
 HIREDATE                                           DATE
 SAL                                                NUMBER(7,2)
 COMM                                               NUMBER(7,2)
 DEPTNO                                             NUMBER(2)
```

The Solution

```java
import java.sql.*;
import javax.sql.*;
import javax.servlet.*;
import javax.servlet.http.*;
```

```java
import javax.sql.rowset.WebRowSet;
import com.sun.rowset.WebRowSetImpl;

import java.io.StringWriter;
import java.io.PrintWriter;
import java.io.IOException;

import jcb.util.DatabaseUtil;
import jcb.db.VeryBasicConnectionManager;

public class GetRowSetMetaData extends HttpServlet {

    public void doGet(HttpServletRequest request,
                      HttpServletResponse response)
        throws ServletException, IOException {
        Connection conn = null;
        try {
            String dbVendor = request.getParameter("vendor").trim();
            String sqlQuery = request.getParameter("query").trim();
            conn = VeryBasicConnectionManager.getConnection(dbVendor);

            // create metadata
            String metadata = getMetaData(conn, sqlQuery);

            // write xml to client
            response.setContentType("text/xml");
            PrintWriter out = response.getWriter();
            out.println(metadata);
        }
        catch(Exception e) {
            printError(response, e.getMessage());
        }
        finally {
            DatabaseUtil.close(conn);
        }
    } // end doGet

    private static String getMetaData(Connection conn,
                                      String sqlQuery)
      throws Exception {
      StringWriter writer = null;
      try {
        WebRowSet webRS = new WebRowSetImpl();
        webRS.setCommand(sqlQuery);
        webRS.execute(conn);
```

```java
            // writer to hold and manipulate XML data.
            writer = new StringWriter();

            // generate the XML document
            webRS.writeXml(writer);

            // Convert the writer object data to a XML String.
            return writer.toString();
        }
        finally {
            // Close the Writer object.
            writer.close();
        }
    }

    private static void printError(HttpServletResponse response,
                                   String message) {
        try {
            PrintWriter out = response.getWriter();
            StringBuffer buffer = new StringBuffer();
            buffer.append("<html><body>");
            buffer.append(message);
            buffer.append("</body></html>");
            out.println(buffer);
        }
        catch(Exception ignore) {
        }
    }
}
```

Invoking GetRowSetMetaData for MySQL

Figure 9-19 shows how to run the solution for the MySQL database.

Figure 9-19. *Invoking GetRowSetMetaData for MySQL (XML output)*

Invoking GetRowSetMetaData for Oracle

Figure 9-20 shows how to run the solution for the Oracle database.

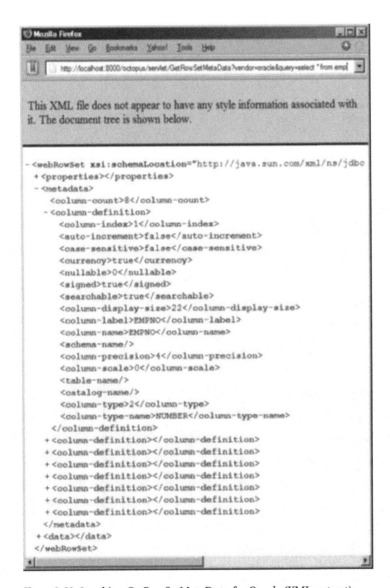

Figure 9-20. *Invoking GetRowSetMetaData for Oracle (XML output)*

CHAPTER 10

■■■

RDF and JDBC Metadata

If you find that you're spending almost all your time on theory, start turning some attention to practical things; it will improve your theories. If you find that you're spending almost all your time on practice, start turning some attention to theoretical things; it will improve your practice.

Donald E. Knuth

In this chapter, I explore the possibility of expressing JDBC metadata as an RDF application. As of this writing, there is no formal mapping of JDBC metadata into RDF.

10.1. What Is RDF?

The Resource Description Framework (RDF) is a W3C (http://www.w3.org) standard (http://www.w3schools.com/rdf/) for describing web resources, such as the title, author, creation date, modification date, content, content type, and copyright information of a Web page. RDF is written in XML, and its purpose is to describe metadata for web resources. RDF is metadata (data about data) and is used to describe information resources. Databases (data and metadata) are an integral part of web resources, and their contents and associated metadata are accessed by web pages and resources. Therefore, database *content* and database *metadata* can be expressed as an RDF notation (actual records and metadata can be expressed in RDF/XML).

According to Wikipedia (http://en.wikipedia.org/wiki/Resource_Description_Framework), the Resource Description Framework (RDF) is a family of specifications for a metadata model that is often implemented as an application of XML. The RDF family (http://www.w3.org/RDF/) of specifications is maintained by the World Wide Web Consortium (W3C). The RDF metadata model is based on the idea of making statements about resources in the form of a subject-predicate-object expression, called a *triple* in RDF terminology. The *subject* is the resource, the "thing" being described. The *predicate* is a trait or aspect of that resource, and often expresses a relationship between the subject and the object. The *object* is the object of the relationship or value of that trait. This mechanism for describing resources is a major component in what is proposed by the W3C's Semantic Web activity: an evolutionary stage of the World Wide Web in which automated software can store, exchange, and utilize metadata about the vast resources of the Web, in turn enabling users to deal with those resources with greater efficiency and certainty. RDF's simple data model and ability to model disparate, abstract concepts has also led to its increasing use in knowledge management applications unrelated to Semantic Web activity.

According to Eric Miller, author of "An Introduction to the Resource Description Framework" (`http://www.dlib.org/dlib/may98/miller/05miller.html`), RDF is an infrastructure that enables the encoding, exchange, and reuse of structured metadata. RDF is an application of XML that imposes needed structural constraints to provide unambiguous methods of expressing semantics. RDF additionally provides a means for publishing both human-readable and machine-processible vocabularies designed to encourage the reuse and extension of metadata semantics among disparate information communities. The structural constraints RDF imposes to support the consistent encoding and exchange of standardized metadata provide for the interchangeability of separate packages of metadata defined by different resource description communities.

10.2. Where Can You Get More Information on RDF?

For more information on RDF, refer to the following documents:

- Resource Description Framework (RDF): `http://www.w3.org/RDF/`

- RDF Primer: `http://www.w3.org/TR/rdf-primer/`

- Introduction to the RDF Model: `http://xulplanet.com/tutorials/mozsdk/rdfstart.php`

- What Is RDF?: `http://www.xml.com/pub/a/2001/01/24/rdf.html`

- The Dublin Core Metadata Initiative: `http://dublincore.org/`

10.3. What Is an Example of RDF?

Consider the following tabular data about authors (let's call this `author-list`):

Author	Title	Publisher	Year
Don Knuth	The TeXbook	Addison-Wesley	1984
Mahmoud Parsian	JDBC Recipes	APRESS	2005

This is a few lines of an RDF document:

```
<?xml version="1.0"?>
<rdf:RDF
    xmlns:rdf="http://www.w3.org/1999/02/22-rdf-syntax-ns#"
    xmlns:author="http://www.mybookshop.computers/author#">

    <rdf:Description
     rdf:about="http://www.mybookshop.computers/author/Knuth">
       <book:author>Don Knuth</book:author>
       <book:title>The TeXbook</book:title>
       <book:publisher>Addison-Wesley</book:publisher>
       <book:year>1984</book:year>
    </rdf:Description>
```

```
<rdf:Description
 rdf:about="http://www.mybookshop.computers/author/Parsian">
  <book:author>Mahmoud Parsian</book:author>
  <book:title>JDBC Recipes</book:title>
  <book:publisher>APRESS</book:publisher>
  <book:year>2005</book:year>
</rdf:Description>
  .
  .
  .
</rdf:RDF>
```

The first line of the RDF document is the XML declaration. The XML declaration is followed by the root element of RDF documents: `<rdf:RDF>`. The `xmlns:rdf` namespace specifies that elements with the `rdf` prefix are from the namespace `http://www.w3.org/1999/02/22-rdf-syntax-ns#`. The `xmlns:author` namespace specifies that elements with the `author` prefix are from the namespace `http://www.mybookshop.computers/author#`. The `<rdf:Description>` element contains the description of the resource identified by the `rdf:about` attribute. The elements `<book:author>`, `<book:title>`, `<book:publisher>`, and `<book:year>` are properties of the resource.

10.4. How Do You Access RDF?

RDF documents are expressed in XML. There are many ways to read, write, and manipulate XML files. You may use the Document Object Model (DOM) to represent an XML document, and you can also create XML documents from DOM (the XML DOM defines a standard way for accessing and manipulating XML documents; JDK 1.5 provides an API for reading, writing, and manipulating XML).

A *DOM* is a tree data structure, where each node contains one of the components from an XML document. You may use DOM functions to create or remove nodes, change their contents, and traverse the node hierarchy. Also, you can use Simple API for XML (SAX) to manipulate XML documents. SAX is an event-driven, serial-access mechanism for accessing XML documents.

The W3C (`http://www.w3.org/`) describes the query language called SPARQL for easy access to RDF stores. For details on SPARQL, refer to `http://www.w3.org/TR/rdf-sparql-query/`.

10.5. What Are the Applications of RDF?

- User interface data-binding used by Mozilla (Firefox) technology: `http://xulplanet.com/tutorials/mozsdk/rdfsources.php`

- RDF Site Summary, one of several "RSS languages" for publishing information about updates made to a web page; it is often used for disseminating news article summaries and sharing weblog content: `http://en.wikipedia.org/wiki/RDF_Site_Summary`

- FOAF (Friend of a Friend), designed to describe people, their interests, and interconnections: `http://en.wikipedia.org/wiki/FOAF_%28software%29`

- DOAC (Description of a Career), which supplements FOAF to allow the sharing of resume information: `http://en.wikipedia.org/wiki/Description_of_a_Career`

10.6. Can JDBC Metadata Be Expressed As RDF?

The simple answer is yes. JDBC's metadata can be expressed in XML and this is all RDF requires (of course, RDF's required format and regulations should be followed). Let's say that you want to express some metadata (such as names of database tables for a given Connection object) in RDF. I propose the following format for the names of database tables in RDF. Further assume that you have several databases and you want to express the name of tables for the octopus database, which has two tables: table1 (as a table) and table2 (as a view).

```xml
<?xml version="1.0"?>
<rdf:RDF
    xmlns:rdf="http://www.w3.org/1999/02/22-rdf-syntax-ns#"
    xmlns:dbtables="http://www.mycompany.com/db/octopus/table#">

    <rdf:Description
     rdf:about="http://www.mycompany.com/db/octopus/table/table1">
       <table:catalog>common</table:catalog>
       <table:schema>scott</table:schema>
       <table:name>table1</table:name>
       <table:type>TABLE</table:type>
       <table:remarks>description of table1</table:remarks>
       ...
    </rdf:Description>

    <rdf:Description
     rdf:about="http://www.mycompany.com/db/octopus/table/table2">
       <table:catalog>common</table:catalog>
       <table:schema>scott</table:schema>
       <table:name>table2</table:name>
       <table:type>VIEW</table:type>
       <table:remarks>description of table2</table:remarks>
       ...
    </rdf:Description>
    .
    .
    .
</rdf:RDF>
```

The first line of the RDF document is the XML declaration. The XML declaration is followed by the root element of RDF documents: <rdf:RDF>. The xmlns:rdf namespace specifies that elements with the rdf prefix are from the namespace http://www.w3.org/1999/02/22-rdf-syntax-ns#. The xmlns:dbtables namespace specifies that elements with the table prefix are from the namespace http://www.mycompany.com/db/octopus/table#. The <rdf:Description> element contains the description of the resource identified by the rdf:about attribute. The elements <table:catalog>, <table:schema>, <table:name>, <table:type>, and <table:remarks> are properties of the resource.

I just presented an example of JDBC metadata as an RDF/XML. There is no formal mapping from JDBC metadata to RDF yet.

10.7. How Do You Exploit RDF Data Models in Your Java Applications?

RDF is increasingly recognized as an excellent choice for representing and processing structured and semi-structured data. In his article (`http://www-128.ibm.com/developerworks/java/library/j-jena/?ca=dgr-jw766j-jena`), Philip McCarthy shows you how to use the Jena Semantic Web Toolkit to exploit RDF data models in your Java applications.

Index

You Need the Companion eBook

Your purchase of this book entitles you to its companion eBook for only $10.

We believe this Apress title will prove so indispensable that you'll want to carry it with you everywhere, which is why we are offering the companion eBook for $10 to customers who purchase this book now. Convenient and fully searchable, the eBook version of any content-rich, page-heavy Apress book makes a valuable addition to your programming library. You can easily find, copy, and apply code—and then perform examples by quickly toggling between instructions and the application. Even simultaneously tackling a donut, diet soda, and complex code becomes simplified with hands-free eBooks!

Once you purchase this book, getting the $10 companion eBook is simple:

❶ Visit **www.apress.com/promo/tendollars/**.

❷ Complete a basic registration form to receive a randomly generated question about this title.

❸ Answer the question correctly in 60 seconds and you will receive a promotional code to redeem for the $10 eBook.

2560 Ninth Street • Suite 219 • Berkeley, CA 94710

Offer valid through 9/06.

Printed in the United States
By Bookmasters